D0323372

WAR, PEACE, AND VICTORY

STRATEGY AND STATECRAFT FOR THE NEXT CENTURY

Colin S. Gray

SIMON AND SCHUSTER

New York   London   Toronto   Sydney   Tokyo   Singapore

Simon and Schuster
Simon & Schuster Building
Rockefeller Center
1230 Avenue of the Americas
New York, New York 10020

SIMON AND SCHUSTER and colophon are registered trademarks
of Simon & Schuster Inc.

Designed by Irving Perkins Associates
Manufactured in the United States of America

1 2 3 4 5 6 7 8 9 10

Library of Congress Cataloging in Publication Data

Gray, Colin S.
War, peace, and victory: strategy and statecraft
for the next century / Colin S. Gray.
p.   cm.
Includes bibliographical references.
1. United States—Military policy—1989– 2. Strategy. 3. World
politics—1945– 4. World politics. I. Title.
UA23.G785   1990   90-34592
355′.03—dc20   CIP

ISBN 0-671-60695-6

For Keith Payne—friend and colleague

Contents

Modern warfare resembles a spider's web: everything connects, longitudinally or laterally, to everything else; there are no "independent strategies," no watertight compartments, nor can there be.

—JOHN TERRAINE, *A Time for Courage:*
The Royal Air Force in the
European War, 1939–1945

All forms of strategic action are interrelated and are conducted on the basis of a unified plan, under the control of the Supreme High Command, to achieve the general aim of the war.

—GRAHAM HALL TURBIVILLE, ed., *The Voroshilov Lectures, Materials from the Soviet General Staff Academy:* Vol. 1, *Issues of Soviet Military Strategy.* Compiled by Ghulam D. Wardak

Introduction:
Five Themes

We need strategists.

—GENERAL JOHN R. GALVIN,
Supreme Allied Commander,
Europe[1]

We ought to be seeking tentative answers to fundamental questions, rather than definitive answers to trivial ones.

—JAMES H. BILLINGTON[2]

AS GENERAL Galvin says, we need strategists and strategy. The Cold War wanes—in the opinion of many people, it may even have died—but the challenge to strategy becomes more severe. When policy goals, which is to say political purposes, are increasingly uncertain (e.g., does the U.S.S.R. still need to be contained and deterred?), how can they best be supported by suitably designed armed forces? *Strategy,* the direction of power so that it serves policy purposes, is not in demand solely in times of acute national peril. Indeed, as the U.S.S.R., one of the greatest land powers that the world has ever seen, passes through a period of great instability, many of the issues treated in this book assume new and more difficult aspects. Before one waxes lyrical over the apparent Western victory in the Cold War, let alone over "the end of history,"[3] it would be well to consider the following thoughts of Henry Kissinger and Samuel P. Huntington, respectively:

> An empire assembled over a period of 400 years by force will not disintegrate passively. And the Western alliance is bound to be shaken by the very events it is celebrating.[4]

9

> Gorbachev may be able to discard communism but he cannot discard
> geography and the geopolitical imperatives that have shaped Russian
> and Soviet behavior for centuries.[5]

Francis Fukuyama's hypothesis about "the end of history" is not
at all persuasive in and of itself, but it is powerfully expressive of a
climate of opinion dominated by the view that the Cold War has been
won and a historical corner definitively turned. Few people rushed
to sign on as disciples of the Fukuyama hypothesis, but the importance
attached to it by the would-be leaders of fashion in policy ideas attests
to the shallowness of intellectual fashion.

The stakes in strategy can vary enormously from marginal national
political advantage, through the prevention of wars great and small,
to the outcomes of wars of all kinds. The title of this book includes,
indeed encourages, the thought that strategy is about winning in peace
as well as in war. If a polity can succeed well enough in peace, it will
not need to win in war. Thus far, notwithstanding many errors or
arguable errors over secondary matters, the United States has provided on balance an admirable record of winning in the nuclear age.
Consider U.S. "big game" achievements: a large number of willing
allies have been organized, led, and supported for more than forty
years in a global antihegemonic coalition; major war has been avoided
or deterred (if it needed deterring); principal foes have been, in one
case, transformed into a functional ally (the Chinese People's Republic), and in the other case (the U.S.S.R.) successfully contained
and outlasted in the broad-fronted competition for power and influence; and the United States has neither beggared itself economically
nor become a "garrison state" in a pejorative sense, as the price to
be paid for such success.

One can point to a failure in policy or strategy, or both, over
Vietnam; to tactical and operational incompetence over Grenada; to
bloated defense bureaucracies, civilian and military; to near-permanent grounds for questioning whether the defense posture is too
large or too small; and so on and so forth, as evidence of imperfect
performance. However, what really matters is that the United States
as a national security community has performed *well enough* when
and where it really mattered. On any reasonable accounting, U.S.
national security behavior since World War II has been a resounding
success.

When the peace is not challenged, deterrence can seem to be easily
achieved. Indeed, a society can come to believe that peace is its
birthright. The 1990s are not the first period in history wherein the

achievements of a generation of vigilance may be squandered. In 1025, the last year of the reign of Basil II (felicitously known as the Bulgar-Slayer), the Byzantine Empire was more secure than it had been for half a millennium. In the Balkans, the Bulgarians had been smashed definitively after a thirty-year war, while in the East the Saracen powers were obliged to accept virtually any terms that were favored in Constantinople. Yet, forty-six years later, the empire suffered a military defeat with such devastating consequences that it never truly recovered as a great power. What had happened in the years between the death of Basil II (1025) and the Battle of Manzikert (1071)? Above all else, the politician-bureaucrats and intellectuals in Constantinople forgot that the peace born of victory was both won very much by the sword, and could be protected only by the same. It is a familiar story. The eleventh-century Byzantine case happens to provide particularly dramatic support for the aphorism that "nothing fails like success."

Strategists and historians speak for their times. The bureaucrats of eleventh-century Byzantium were neither the first nor the last people irresponsibly to confuse a temporary condition of external peace with a permanent state. In our own century there have been long periods wherein fashionable opinion deemed war to be obsolete—not to say illegal (after the Kellogg-Briand Pact of Paris of 1928). Hence preparations for waging it had to be viewed at best as yesterday's solution to yesterday's problem.

Whether the leading national security problem of the day is defined as a Soviet threat to geostrategically exposed U.S. allies, the threat posed by Britain's Royal Navy to U.S. commerce and coastal cities, the threat of secession by the slave-holding states, or the threats by terrorist-zealots to U.S. citizens and property, solutions require the services of strategy. I have chosen to provide historical and hypothetical future examples of strategy in action very largely from the upper end of the violence spectrum. The choice of major war cases is intended to underscore the point that competence in strategy, or its absence, can be a society-threatening question.[6]

The proper relation of power to purpose, which is to say sound strategy, must serve a country well in any circumstances of external peril. There is absolutely no way of knowing today whether or not the Soviet Union will require very much, indeed if any, deterring in the 1990s. Similarly, no one today knows whether Mikhail Gorbachev's attempt at far-reaching reform will succeed or fail. More to the point, perhaps, no one today can possibly predict who the domestic beneficiaries will be of Gorbachev's legacy of success or failure (or some mix of both). It is for these reasons that this book is about the contribution of strategy to national success in a nuclear age, not about achieving success over a very particular Soviet Union, although it troubles me that the United States might choose to define the Soviet Union prematurely as a newfound friend rather than as a foe who is resting. American statesmen need to function well enough as grand strategists in the service of policy objectives that are always open for reconsideration. If that is the case, U.S. national security and the international order on which it depends and to which it contributes can adjust to whatever twists and turns the future course of Soviet history will reveal.

Strategy and strategic reasoning do not provide magic passwords for success. Furthermore, I am worried lest poverty in strategic think-ing should assist the United States in dispersing the heritage of se-curity with which the 1990s are opening. Poor strategy, like the wrong medicine, can kill. If policymakers seek the impossible—seize a world empire, build a "nation" in a multitribal postcolonial society, or construct a technical peace through arms control—then no choice of strategy can much help them. Similarly, if strategic ideas do not work tactically at the foxhole or deckplate level, assuredly they will fail. As Allan R. Millett advises:

> Theoretical coherence and logical consistency do not always provide happy results in the real work of military operations, for the character of the enemy's forces and the limitations of one's own units may con-found doctrine.[7]

However, if strategy is poor, victory is always much more expensive to attain than it should be, if indeed victory is possible at all. At the most basic level of all, this book is about winning in world politics. It is about how to succeed in peace and crisis by deterrence, and— if deterrence fails—about how to win wars for the purpose of securing the goals set as war aims. Strategic analysis never loses sight of the logical truth that means make sense only with respect to ends. Ends, or goals, are not all that matter, because the cost of reaching them can be so high that they are not worth securing. Nonetheless, it would be difficult to exaggerate the importance of winning in the great game of international politics.

Because security is an interdependent, shared condition, it is tempt-ing to assert that for a nuclear age in particular the first concern for policymakers should be not to lose, or victory-denial to enemies— rather than victory. This temptation should be resisted. Those who try to play to a draw tend to lack a margin of safety against unforeseen adversity, and as a consequence they lose. Victory, success, or important advantage—pick your preference—may, and often should, be defined in distinctly nonheroic ways. But it is critically important that the concept be kept alive and not delegitimized totally by the current spokespeople for security dilemmas, the joys of parity, and the blessings of "stability" (whatever that slippery idea may mean).

With reference to James Billington's good advice, quoted above, the most fundamental, yet thoroughly and necessarily pragmatic question for a strategist is "How do we win?" Of course strategic relationships need to be *managed* in times of peace, crisis, and war. But management is meaningless unless the managers know what constitutes success.

The United States has a permanent need to match its power and its purposes—whether that power be relatively waxing or waning and whether the purposes be heroic or modest or even mundane. This book should be viewed neither as one of the last books on the Cold War nor as one of the first books predicting a Cold War II. Neither characterization would hit the mark. The argument here, though steeped in history, is fundamentally as forward-looking as it is resolutely agnostic over the future course of East-West relations. All of the historical cases cited or outlined in this book—modern or ancient—are provided as examples for the illustration of more general argument on issues of strategy and statecraft (on how peace can break down, how technology can be more, or less, useful in war, on the importance of people as contrasted with machines, and so forth). This book is a contribution to the very thinly populated library shelves devoted to strategy. The fact that this work, and the historical examples employed, plainly reflect the life, times and cultural inheritance of its author does not render it any less general in purpose.

My attitudes and opinions on such questions as the prospects for benign systemic change in the Soviet Union and the utility of nuclear weapons for some limited purposes of deterrence necessarily shape this text. But the substance of my beliefs on the Soviet Union or on nuclear weapons is not really important. What matters is that people should learn to reason strategically. One reason why this book so often has to resort to historical examples to make a point is to avoid the barriers to effective communication created by substantive, yet really irrelevant, disagreements over contemporary matters. For example, the much-praised INF treaty of 1987 is, in my opinion, a crime (a felony, not a misdemeanor) against strategy (and prudent statecraft). However, heavy exemplary use here of the INF treaty would risk triggering the phenomenon of perception of guilt by association. To repeat, this is a book about strategy and its application for the success of statecraft in the future; it is not about refighting old struggles of U.S. national security policy or about analysis of the latest phase in Gorbachev's political adventures. No book (or even article) could possibly be updated so as to stay au courant with the events in the East in 1989–90. To repeat, although current cases in strategy naturally are presented in as up-to-date a form as possible, this book does not chase the policy problems of the day with solutions. For the broad purposes of this work on strategy, it really does not matter who is up or down in Moscow on the date of publication.

Five closely linked themes dominate this book: the unity of strategic phenomena; the influence of geography; the value of historical experience; the power of national culture to help shape expectations, beliefs, and behavior; and the consequences of technological change for statecraft and strategy.

First, it has been, and remains, my experience in the American community of students of strategy that the different pieces of the strategy mosaic are seldom addressed with sufficient, empathetic inclusiveness. The sub-communities which focus, for example, upon land warfare in Central Europe, war at sea, "strategic" nuclear warfare, war in space, and arms control—and the many unions within these extensive categories—tend to lack, indeed even tend to be relatively disinterested in, comprehension of the total activity of armed and potentially violent statecraft of which their piece of the action is only one part. Consequently, in this book particular attention is focused upon the neglected truth that everything pertaining to strategy relates, or at least might relate, to everything else.

Second, the meaning of the several dimensions of geography for political and strategic relationships continues to be underappreciated—both in the small, as in the problem of understanding the different tactical terms for combat which are very specific to particular physical environments (land, sea, air, space), and in the large, as in the intellectual and policy challenge of grasping the geopolitical and geostrategic realities which set the stage and help draft the plot for the game of nations. Geography is the most fundamental of the factors which condition national outlooks on security problems and strategy solutions. Geography, treated properly in political and strategic analysis, is not a rigidly determining factor. But it conditions the outlook of an insular people, just as it conditions the outlook of a continental community. The influence of geography truly is pervasive, notwithstanding the fact that that influence must vary in detail as technology changes. The apparently conflicting, but ultimately complementary, natures of land power and sea power (with air power and space power adjuncts), and their historical relationship in systems of statecraft and war, make up a geostrategic thread running through these pages.

The third theme is the use, abuse, and often simply the nonuse of historical experience in strategic theorizing and strategic planning. There is an important sense in which history is made up by historians who are interpreters, not mere chroniclers, of the past. As interpreters of human experience, historians necessarily speak from and to their age and culture. The ambitiously interpretative work of history, be it Edward Gibbon's *Decline and Fall of the Roman Empire* in the 1770s and 1780s,[8] Barbara Tuchman's *The Guns of August* in 1962,[9] Paul Kennedy's *The Rise and Fall of the Great Powers* in 1987,[10] or Francis Fukuyama's "The End of History?" in 1989, has an immediate impact upon public discourse because it speaks to concerns, and supports beliefs and attitudes, that already are extant. Those beliefs and attitudes may or may not be well founded. Moreover, the potential for mischief of a work of historical scholarship is singularly great if it attains fashionable status in a society which is not historically literate. The United States in the closing years of the twentieth century is a political culture characterized *(inter alia)* by a short attention span for difficult issues of international security; by a proclivity to seek pragmatic solutions to problems which may be conditions to be accommodated rather than puzzles to be solved; and by a very noticeable historical ignorance and general disinterest. The bold historical theory and the dramatic historical anecdote tend not to be interrogated knowledgeably by a historically educated intelligence in such a society. Nonetheless, there is much to recommend Alfred T. Mahan's observation that "historical instances, by their concrete force, are worth reams of dissertation." Is not "history . . . the experience of others, recorded for our use"?[11]

Fourth, American scholars and commentators at last have begun dimly to be aware of the influence of different national cultures upon choices for, and performance in, statecraft and strategy. Rooted in particular geographies, the national security communities of the modern world have each had more or less distinctive historical experiences. Those separate experiences express and help shape future adaptive behavior to security challenges. Such major players in the world politics of the twentieth century as, for example, Nazi Germany, the Soviet Union, and the United States have each advertised, and propagandized domestically, a distinctive sustaining myth which has spoken powerfully to the cultural attitudes and beliefs of German, Soviet, and American societies.

Policy motives are always mixed. Consequently, secular ambition can usually find a religious or ideological sanction—whether in the case of the land- and loot-hungry crusaders (heavily armed pilgrims) of the Middle Ages; the imperial urges of the Soviet inheritors of the Third Rome after 1917; Germany's bid for world military dominion which died on the Volga in the winter of 1942–43 (and hence never concluded even its Eurasian-continental phase); or the benign American economic and political hegemony in the West from the mid-1940s until the late 1960s. As Henry Kissinger has been wont to argue, American culture has been molded by the extended historical experience of hegemony; first in North America, and then in the world in the circumstances of the 1940s, 1950s, and 1960s. The hand of God tends to be seen by the beneficiaries of a very fortunate history to have guided the destiny of the community. Both American strategic thinkers and the foreigners who are most concerned about the course of American policy and strategy need to understand the cultural traits which continue to have an important influence upon American behavior.

Finally, this book explores the relationship between strategy and technology. The *bête noire* of this discussion is the sin of technicism—the proclivity of a materialist school of thinking about defense questions to reduce issues of means and ends to the promise in particular new military machines. Technicism shows itself in an unbalanced interest in the machine in a *man*-machine system (i.e., in the crossbow as contrasted with the crossbow and crossbowman). Relative technological competence is of course important. But technicism refers to the disorder when that which is only technical displaces, and effectively substitutes for, that which has to be considered tactically, operationally, and strategically in far more inclusive analysis. More often than not, a heavy focus upon the technologies of war does not ascend from contemplation of the tactical application of machines to consideration of their operational value, let alone to calculation of their putative strategic effect. Indeed, the mark of true technicism is the paying of a near-exclusive attention to how machines work and—perhaps—what they can do to an obligingly passive enemy, rather than to their tactical worth in battle.

The discussion in this book cannot help but be a commentary upon the quantity and quality of strategic thinking, planning, and behavior in the U.S. defense community of which I am a member. My starting point is the proposition that strategic thinking, planning, and behavior need to be far more inclusive, or holistic, than usually is the case. For example, the "strategic" offensive forces and possible "strategic" defensive options typically are not analyzed sufficiently together. Technical and effectively separate consideration of "strategic" offensive and defensive issues has a way of avoiding altogether the strategic dimension of its subject. If treated, that dimension would address the question of the strategic effect required of so-called strategic forces for the goals of national and coalition military strategy and grand strategy. Recent defense debate in the United States shows not only that it is unusual for strategic forces issues to be analyzed strategically, but that the strategic connections, or disconnections, between long-range nuclear-armed forces, land power, sea power, and even "space power" are honored more in the breach than in the observance.

Practical neglect of, or failure to understand, the five central themes of this book tends to have the consequence that instead of functioning as a theory of victory, strategy in action results in stalemate or defeat. It should be little more than common sense to affirm that strategy must accommodate, and indeed exploit, the interconnectedness of environmentally *(et al.)* or functionally specific behavior—the action of sea power and land power, and the overarching menace of long-range nuclear weapons, for example; is influenced pervasively by geography; should benefit from the education that historical scholarship can provide; often is culture-specific, and always is culture-influenced; and must never be captured by technological, as contrasted with political, visions of security and peace.

Nonetheless, states, and even many respected strategic thinkers, seem almost to glory in rejecting such common sense. For example, American readers need look no further than to their country's Vietnam experience to find the common sense in these five themes simply ignored. The Johnson administration did not wage the war as a unity, domestically and in Southeast Asia. Its theory of victory (such as it was) and chosen methods for the waging of the war were fundamentally at fault, given the geography of South Vietnam (the enemy was allowed geographically contiguous, cross-border sanctuaries, and had no fear of amphibious assault from the world's greatest maritime power). French *and* American historical experience in Vietnam was not taken seriously and allowed to influence policy-making as the U.S. role in the war expanded explosively in 1965. Furthermore, President Johnson and his principal advisers behaved as if they were as ignorant of American political culture as they certainly were of Vietnamese culture. Tactically, the U.S. armed forces waged their preferred forms of war, mechanical and logistically massive.

These critical remarks bear not at all upon the political and moral merits of U.S. intervention in Vietnam. Also, they do not really bear upon the military performance of American soldiers—which would seem to have been no better or worse than it had been in Korea or World War II. But as strategy, as a protracted exercise in the reciprocal adjustment of means and ends for the advancement of the political goals set by high policy, the American adventure in Vietnam was appalling. History has a way of punishing those societies that allow their policymakers to ignore the means-ends nexus that is the essence of strategy. There are no prizes for coming in second. Failure in deterrence means war; failure in war means defeat. Strategy, along with the five themes examined here that are central to its sound design and execution, is about winning and losing.

CHAPTER 1

Strategy

The essence of the strategic art is the tailoring of means to ends and ends to means.

—JEFFREY RECORD[1]

THE BRIDGE

If deterrence failed, how would the United States wage, and presumably try to win, a World War III against the U.S.S.R.? What should the strategy be? If strategy is thought of as the bridge between military means and political ends, what does it, or should it, look like for a major war? Public discussion of the possible control of military forces—as in arms control—and tactical evaluation of items of military technology—as with the Bradley armored fighting vehicle or the Aegis fleet air defense system—are topics as common as genuinely strategic debate is rare. Technology and tactics are raw materials for strategy, but strategy they are not.

The size, character, and deployment of the U.S. armed forces should express some clear theory of how, and for what ends, they would fight should deterrence fail. In the absence of strategic reasoning, the quantity, quality, and location of armed forces make no sense. Pending the exceedingly unlikely transformation of the Soviet Union into a gigantic Russian Switzerland, capable only of effecting a defensive defense, or the emergence of some new principal threat to U.S. security interests, defense planning against the Soviet empire will continue to be the first charge—for a while at least, a declining charge—laid upon the Department of Defense. So, to repeat, the overarching strategic question remains: how would the United States seek to win a war over the Soviet empire, should deterrence fail? The silence which tends to greet this almost indecently phrased ques-

19

tion can be deafening. Some readers may be astonished to learn that relatively very few defense professionals, inside or outside of government, have ever been asked and required to answer this nontrivial question.

Many people seek to escape this central question of strategy via convenient, and now reflexive, theoretical sleight-of-hand. They assert, in common with the official rhetoric of the U.S. government, that nuclear war cannot be won—having first assumed, not wholly unreasonably, that a Soviet-American conflict would have to be nuclear. Implicitly rejecting the idea that great wars can be rooted in great clashes of vital national or imperial interests, the notion persists that issues of strategy can be sidestepped via an arms-control process. Even many alleged strategic experts adhere to this notion, being paralyzed in their strategic faculties by a nuclear dread that is understandable but unhelpful.

If those in the United States who worry about the arms controllability of this or that military posture or weapon would expend upon questions of U.S. military strategy one-tenth of the effort that they typically waste in the futile pursuit of a legislated "technical peace" through arms control, the Republic would be in a safer condition.

Yet defense professionals know that they cannot slide out from under the question by counterattacking with the claim that the U.S. mission is to deter, not try to win, what could be a very great war indeed. That kind of evasive debate-stopper can work in front of audiences who either have no conception of strategy or who believe that a strategic worldview is part of the problem of, rather than part of the solution to, national security. But a strategically educated audience will not permit a speaker to hide behind the idea of deterrence. Deterrence is not an effect totally apart from actions, and the consequences of actions (victory, stalemate, defeat), anticipated by the enemy.

The following questions illustrate the generic concerns central to this book: Upon what idea, or ideas, of military success should the United States and its allies prepare to wage war upon the Soviet empire—albeit for the primary though not exclusive purpose of deterrence? What actions by the Soviet Union should the United States oppose—with what, where, and at what level of intensity and risk? Pragmatically, how should the geographically far-flung and maritime-oriented coalition of the West prepare to fight the geographically concentrated continental empire of the Soviet Union in this nuclear age? The currency common to all of the possible answers to these questions has to be *strategic effectiveness,* because U.S. (and NATO) defense planners require a theory of victory, a theory explaining how particular kinds and quantities of military action should generate the effect either of persuading Soviet leaders to cease and desist from their aggression or of physically denying them the ability to fight on.

Bearing in mind that war is not a game of solitaire, that the enemy— not to mention some of his, and some of our, allies—has an independent will, broadly there are three alternative theories of victory for Western arms in a World War III. Generically, these alternatives can be labeled the nuclear, the continental, and the maritime. As a caveat, it must be noted that these three broad alternatives are by no means exclusive. All theories of strategically effective action must have a persuasive nuclear element (if only to explain how the enemy is deterred from using *his* nuclear weapons), and all have to relate ultimately to the seat of policy purpose, which must be *on land*.

It is very unlikely that the United States could force a satisfactory war outcome through nuclear escalation, at least not until a real active defensive capability to preclude most nuclear damage to the U.S. homeland has been fielded. Nonetheless, the nuclear theory of policy success in war is U.S. strategy today, enshrined in NATO's mid-1960s concept of flexible response. The concept amounts in practice to the commitment to wage a necessarily short nuclear war rather than accept regional defeat in a nonnuclear struggle. If Soviet forces broke through in Central Europe, the United States might be willing (and ought to be assumed willing by prudent Soviet policymakers) to take any and every nuclear action to attempt to restore deterrence—at least so the façade of NATO's nuclear dependent strategy maintains. Former Under Secretary of Defense Fred C. Iklé has argued that following its formal adoption in 1967,

> [t]his Flexible Response strategy has since been reaffirmed at every NATO meeting as if it were the alliance's Holy Writ. The allies like to emphasize that Flexible Response is *the* NATO strategy and that it must never be questioned, notwithstanding the revolutionary changes in technology and the massive deterioration in the U.S.-Soviet nuclear balance that have occurred over the 22 years since the allies agreed to Flexible Response.[2]

In contrast, the continental theory of Western strategy holds that Pact forces probably can be halted (*à la* 1914) and functionally defeated by means of a great continental campaign. NATO-continentalists would accept battle on terms that the Soviet empire wage a one-front war at a time of Moscow's choosing. However, whereas the trouble with the nuclear theory of Western strategy is that it poses too many risks to its NATO initiators, the central problems with the 1914 school of continental attrition are that it poses too few risks to a Soviet aggressor and that it is likely to fail as a deterrent and as a concept of war.

If we look to history we also see failure. The much modified Schlieffen Plan failed in front of Paris and on the Marne in late August and the first week of September 1914. And while Germany's strategy for victory was thwarted before the war was six weeks old, it took the Allies four years to discover, and develop, the material means to apply a convincing theory of victory. So even if the growing number of optimists among NATO analysts were proven correct, and the Soviet Union could indeed be denied a swift continental victory—and perhaps any victory at all—the strategically intriguing question would remain: "How do we win?"

The maritime theory of Western strategy differs from the continental in that it is truly global and, if need be, long-term in its vision, although without discounting the prospects for initial success in NATO Europe. The heart of the strategic concept of the maritime theory is to pose to Soviet leaders a kind of war, in geographic scope and duration, that they will recognize they cannot win. The contemporary Soviet Union appears to be thoroughly persuaded that nuclear war would be counterproductive. Indeed, reasoning unduly narrowly, the respected British commentator upon Soviet military developments Christopher N. Donnelly has judged that in the Soviet view it is only nuclear use by NATO that really threatens fatal damage to the Soviet imperium.[3] Certainly it is difficult to imagine a truly desperate Soviet leadership—and no lesser character of deterrence problems should be assumed—being deterred from waging a war that they believed could be concluded with a short continental campaign.

The maritime theory of Western defense says: deter nuclear use by nuclear counterdeterrence; be prepared to fight hard for those continental holdings of the Western coalition that unfortunately are readily accessible to Soviet land power; but emphasize that the Soviet Union cannot necessarily win a war by winning a land campaign in the European region.

The short-order defeat of a Soviet invasion should suffice to provide the political context appropriate for a satisfactory negotiated ending to a war. However, the maritime theory is open-minded over the likelihood of early war termination. The theory envisages generating sufficient strategic effectiveness by means of the flexible global application of Western sea-based power (in support of continental allies and by way of the initiation of raids or fighting fronts at the discretion of the insular superpower) operating for many months, or even several years, so that Soviet leaders should be pessimistic over their ability to win in any time frame. Western seapower effectively should own the oceans, and the lion's share of the gross world product should be exploitable by the Western maritime coalition that enjoys flexibility in global transportation.

The Soviet empire is not going to be brought down by nuclear action; that would be far too dangerous. But neither is it likely that Moscow could be defeated definitively in a single great continental campaign (that has been tried several times in modern history). However, the bloated, politically illegitimate multinational empire of the Soviet czars certainly could be brought to self-ruin by the critical domestic troubles that a long and unsuccessful war surely would encourage.

Whatever one's views of the sense for statecraft in the nuclear dependent strategy which remains authoritative for the United States and NATO today, there is everything to be said in favor of bolstering the legitimacy of the question, "What is our end-to-end theory of war?" The superpowers could supersede all relevance of statecraft with a full-scale nuclear "exchange." But it does not follow that a theory of success in war is beyond drafting. Indeed, the very possibility of a combat outcome intolerable for all participants, and many nominal bystanders also, should energize the quest for a strategy that would not have military means obliterate the relevance of political ends.

An education in strategy should inoculate against undue fascination with means and processes as ends in themselves. The strategic thinker must ask "So what?" and "How?" when presented with the latest schemes for salvation by arms control or by the latest wonder weapon. The advocates for any new weapon or force structure should be able to explain why the tactical effect expected would advance particular operational goals. Similarly, the enthusiast for specific *operational* schemes (seize Sakhalin Island, raid the Kola peninsula, and so forth) should be able to explain how and why the operational success envisaged would bring the successful outcome of a war measurably nearer—or why the advertisement of such threatened actions would add significantly to deterrence.

For example, the great Athenian expedition to Sicily in 415 B.C., though widely condemned after its failure, was in fact a perfectly sound operation of war. What is more, it was almost certainly tactically feasible.[4] If successful, as it would have been with competent leadership, the Sicilian expedition might have denied Sparta and her allies access to critically needed grain supplies from the west. J. F. C. Fuller has speculated boldly that had Athens succeeded swiftly in Sicily,

> [t]his would have resulted in so complete a strangulation of Peloponnesian food supplies that, faced by the returned and triumphant [had Syracuse been taken promptly] Athenian army, Sparta and Corinth would have been unable to maintain sufficient men in the field to wage a successful war against Athens. Athens would, consequently, and in spite of her inferior man-power, have been able to impose her will on both without resorting to battle.[5]

History is strewn with examples of polities which functioned operationally but not strategically. Particularly stark examples include Germany in both world wars, the United States in Vietnam, and Israel after 1967. By way of an ancient example, Hannibal's operational artistry during his fourteen years (218–204 B.C.) of undefeated campaigning in Italy during the Second Punic War should have been the cutting edge of Carthaginian victory in the war as a whole. Hannibal knew how to defeat Rome in war, as contrasted with beating Romans in battle after battle. But Carthaginian war policy and strategy were not gripped effectively from the capital.

Choice of national security policy, grand strategy, and military strategy matters more than any other subject for the well-being and occasionally even literal survival of societies. Without national military security there can be no other kind of security. Societies can nevertheless exhaust themselves through imprudently large economic allocations for defense—as did Imperial Spain in the late sixteenth and early seventeenth centuries—or might assume so oppressive a garrison aspect that physical security is purchased at too high a price in civil liberties. Errors in national security policy, grand strategy, and military strategy have frequently wrought terminal damage upon states and empires. History offers many examples of polities that failed to respond adequately to security challenges (for example, the Western Roman Empire and the barbarians, Kievan Rus' and the Mongols, the Third French Republic and Nazi Germany). Strategy is a bridge connecting means with ends. That bridge must facilitate a two-way traffic. Policymakers should ask neither too much nor too little of their armed forces, while the forces should be developed and applied only for feasible purposes set by policy. In the real world, military power and policy objectives need mutually to be adjusted via a dynamic strategy as the means-ends relationship constantly evolves.

A PRACTICAL SUBJECT

Strategy is the pursuit of useful knowledge. It is a pragmatic subject that has a practical outcome for good or ill in the realm of the security of states, nations, and coalitions.

Issues of strategy tend to be exceedingly difficult, certainly much more difficult than either means or ends considered in isolation. And vast though the public market should be for genuinely strategic reasoning—explaining why things are done—poverty in strategic thought is the norm, not the exception, among public and private commentators on questions of national security.

Apparent laws of statecraft and strategy are really subjective probabilistic claims. Moreover, the probability at issue is not of a kind familiar to a statistician, since probability cannot be calculated for unique events. Recognition of indeterminacy necessarily pervades this analysis. The history of war and defense preparation is a history of struggle against uncertainty and ignorance. There is no more a science of war than there is, or can be, a science of peace. Every wise maxim and valuable principle in the domains of statecraft and strategy require qualification for specific application. More and more study begets an expanding list of unanswered and perhaps unanswerable questions.

Strategy, properly effected, entails a permanent dialogue among objectives, resources, and the methods for the suitable utilization of available resources in order to attain identified goals. Life is very much easier if one can forget the strategy bridge and either focus upon means (i.e., an arms-control process, strategic defenses, summit diplomacy, foreign economic assistance, and the like), or devote one's energies to favored ultimate goals (i.e., peace, understanding, democracy, freedom, security, and other culture-bound and ideologically charged concepts).

The neglect of strategy is not confined to one section of the political spectrum. Many people confuse the means of arms-control diplomacy with the goal of enhanced security. But the identical error is committed by others who confuse armaments per se with security. The merit of a particular arms-control treaty cannot be assessed intelligently outside the contexts provided by the strategic purposes served by competitive arms, both those to be constrained and those unconstrained. To be told that an agreement is verifiable and balanced in some simpleminded arithmetical sense may be important, but it does not even begin to answer the questions of a strategic kind which should be posed to officials who are seeking ratification of an arms-control treaty. Similarly, it is important, indeed essential, that, for example, candidate SDI deployments be explained with regard to their probable effectiveness against Soviet missiles. But to cite the expected tactical merit of new weaponry leaves open the strategic question of why it is important that some Soviet missiles should be at such risk.

Statecraft and strategy are practical arts which require decision-makers to make decisions, whether or not they are confident that they have an adequate vision of the truth of the matter at hand. Moreover, as a general though not universal rule, policymakers and military planners are much hampered by the inconvenient fact that they do not know exactly when an acute international crisis or war will occur. As two historians have noted in the context of a critique of pre–First World War British military preparations "None [of the succeeding Chiefs of the Imperial General Staff] marked 4 August 1914 on his calendar as *der Tag*, by which the Expeditionary Forces should reach the peak of perfection."[6] The superior practice of statecraft and strategy requires character (including moral courage), judgment, and no little luck. The mind of the statesman and strategist should be educated, but it cannot be schooled, let alone drilled, for assured success. Formally well-educated soldiers can lose battles and campaigns to scholastically ignorant but more determined, luckier, better armed, or simply much larger adversaries.

There may be a place for strategic theory which is abstract and innocent of historical context, but that place is not here. Strategy is always developed and applied by historical figures confronting very particular problems who are heirs to, and representatives of, more or less distinctive national traditions in approaches to statecraft broadly and military behavior more narrowly. Moreover, strategic theory, no less than strategic practice, is culture-bound. For example, the Anglo-American tradition in theorizing about sea power is informed, unsurprisingly, by the assumption that the audience for the theory is most interested in learning how superior sea power can influence the course and outcome of war. Most states have not enjoyed, and have never expected to enjoy, the benefits of mastery at sea. The classic texts in the Anglo-American tradition have little to say (save in the important sense of knowing the enemy) to a Frenchman, German, or Russian, who must grapple with the problem of how best to employ a second-class navy. Most typically, the strategic objective of the second-class navy of a continental power is the negative one of denying freedom of maritime passage to an enemy who depends upon sea lines of communication to prosecute a war—sea denial, as it is known today. The fact that France and Germany, in their turn, failed over the course of two and a half centuries so to harass Britain at sea that she would be unable or unwilling to continue a conflict may say less about the merit in a strategy of commerce raiding than about the strength and skill which France and Germany successively were able to devote to the purpose.

As a complementary example, the Western arms-control literature of the past three decades by and large has meaning, and hence merit, both to a characteristically Western tradition in diplomacy (derived primarily from the practices of the Italian city-states of the fifteenth century) and to a very American proclivity to redefine political problems as technical issues. Alas, the Soviet Union is the legatee of the Byzantine-imperial approach *(inter alia)* to diplomacy, and recognizes few topics in the field of competitive armament as being truly technical in character.

Strategic thinkers or theorists and strategists tend to be different people, the former developing—indeed often rediscovering—knowledge, the latter applying it. Those who aspire to competence in strategy would do well to ponder Adda B. Bozeman's judgment on the source of greatness of much of the jurisprudence evolved in the later Roman Republic: "The lasting reputation of the Roman jurists rests, briefly speaking, on the following record. They were conversant with the world of letters as well as with the world of politics, and so were able to find meaningful relationships between philosophical truths and empirical situations . . ."[7]

The policy scientist, unlike the physical scientist, cannot build theory by means of empirically testable hypotheses. Historians cannot agree on why the Roman Republic acquired its empire, why (or even when) the Roman Empire fell, whether British sea power or Russian land power was more significant a cause of Napoleon's demise, and whether or not Germany could have won either world war—to cite but a handful of illustrative cases. Similarly, defense philosophers do not agree on the practical merits of an arms-control process, on the mechanisms which drive the superpower arms competition, or on the probable dynamics and outcome of a war in which nuclear weapons are used. All of the topics of controversy just cited, those which refer to the past and those which look forward, have in common the discouraging fact that they are incapable of resolution beyond a reasonable doubt by further scholarship.

The propositions of abstract theory for statecraft and strategy can be useful aids to mental discipline, provided the ever-concrete character of the real subject is not forgotten. Soldiers should know that defense is the strongest form of waging war on land, while sailors should know that offense is the strongest form of waging war at sea. However, the practical relevance and detailed implications of such propositions-qua-principles can only be determined empirically, not deductively. One cannot proceed from such principles logically to identification of superior strategy and tactics for U.S. strategic nuclear or naval forces, for example. Napoleon waged a masterly offensive campaign in June 1815 (as he had so often before). Unfortunately for him, he confronted in Wellington a master of the defensive battle who was vastly experienced by five years in the Peninsula in countering the formulaic pattern of French tactics. His corps, which should march divided yet, when needed, fight united, were not concentrated in time before Waterloo (*Où est Grouchy?*). He made catastrophically inappropriate choices in his corps commanders, and he did not fight a truly combined-arms battle (the allied army was at liberty to deploy in line to repulse attack by infantry columns and then to redeploy in squares to repulse unsupported cavalry).

This book is concerned with the "wholeness" of statecraft and with the unity of security concerns and indeed of war itself. Just as military action makes no sense save with reference to the policy objectives it should serve, so defense policy writ large should not be discussed without recognition of the influence both of national political and strategic cultures and of geopolitical patterns in interstate relations. Public debate typically is as narrowly focused and context-free as official activities can be parochial. The improper disconnects most frequently encountered include those between or among offense and defense; deterrence and defense; conventional and nuclear weapons; the application of force (tactics) and the consequences (strategy); conflict on land, at sea, in the air, and in space; domestic society and foreign and defense policy preferences; different geographical regions (e.g., Atlantic and Pacific); defense preparation and arms control; military and other forms of power; and military power, war aims, and conditions of relative security.

WORDS OF POWER

Discussion cannot usefully proceed unless some ideas central to the story are identified, defined, and related to one another. Definitions are arbitrary and can be neither true nor false, merely more or less useful both for clear communication of what is intended and for delimitation of those activities which it is helpful to identify separately.

Policy is the purpose of governments and *policy-making* is the process by which high government officials determine what those purposes should be. President Roosevelt set policy for the (Western) Grand Alliance in January 1943 at Casablanca when he committed the Allied course to the goal of achieving "unconditional surrender."[8] With equal or greater doubts as to its wisdom, the British cabinet in the early summer of 1940 had set the policy course of continuation of the war—rejecting *a priori* any variant of a negotiated peace with Hitler's Germany. Both of these illustrative cases of major policy decisions were characterized by an absence of careful calculation of the relationship between means and ends. For a more recent example, on August 23, 1983, President Reagan declared that it was U.S. policy to explore the possibility of developing strategic defenses capable of "rendering these nuclear weapons [carried on strategic ballistic missiles] impotent and obsolete."[9]

Grand strategy, sometimes called *national security strategy,* is the art of employing all of the relevant assets of a country for the political purposes set by high policy.[10] It is U.S. policy today to keep power (latent force) divided and well balanced on the continent of Europe. The implementation of this antihegemonic policy is the domain of grand strategy. In order to secure the policy objective of keeping Europe, or today Eurasia, divided, Britain and later the United States have organized and subsidized, and to a degree directly supported militarily, continental alliances.

As another example, in periods of relative weakness the Byzantine Empire had a policy objective of surrounding itself with barbarian buffer states which could be culturally penetrated, bribed to fight one another, and impressed with the glittering trappings of empire. Byzantium sought to manage its "barbarian problem" with skillful diplomacy, indeed with a total system of grand strategy, so that no overwhelming concentration of hostile power would pose a problem incapable of being handled by the modest military strength of the empire. Thanks to its maritime control of the Dardanelles, and the impregnable land-facing fortifications of Constantinople, the empire had secure access to the assets of its heartland in Anatolia—whence, for an early example, in the mid–fifth century it could draw the wealth to bribe Attila's Huns to invade Western Europe rather than to ravage the Balkan territories of the Roman Empire in the East. Unfortunately, in periods of relative strength the efficient prosecution of the grand strategy of the Byzantine Empire was hindered by the persistence of the mandate, or burden, of Roman history and Christian duty to reconquer whatever territory was sufficiently weak to lend itself to reconquest (the theory of a universal Christian Roman Empire).[11] This meant that time and again such critically important buffer states as Bulgaria, Armenia, and Georgia were ruined militarily by Byzantine strategic opportunism.

A permanent problem for the architects and operators of grand strategy has been the difficulty in deciding how heavily to lean upon the military instrument of power and how far to pursue it. Where is the "culminating point of victory"? When is the clear-cut and apparently reliable solution of military conquest to be preferred to the cheaper, less reliable, but perhaps in the long run more prudent option of preponderant political influence? From the Byzantines in the Balkans and Eastern Anatolia in the tenth and eleventh centuries, to the contemporary Soviet Union, the role of military power in grand strategy persists in challenging the judgment of statesmen.

Grand strategy in support of national security policy functions in peace and in war and encompasses positive as well as negative sanctions. It is the solemn duty of the statesman to set the political framework for a conflict so that his generals have a reasonable chance of succeeding. But also it is the statesman's duty to reduce the basis for the demand for military power: to minimize the political incentives discerned by other countries to trigger crises or seek military solutions to pressing problems. Through its persistent policy of continental divide-and-influence for century after century, the British government reduced the scale of the deterrent and fighting burdens that were placed upon the Royal Navy. Continental alliance with the second strongest state or coalition ensured that the enemy of the day would not be at liberty to devote all of his resources to competing with Britain at sea. Similarly, a policy of prudent accommodation of political interests—up to a point, but only up to a point—helped to manage the scale and pace of military threats which might otherwise be mounted. A considerable reason for the endurance of the Pax Britannica of fact and legend after 1815 was that no great continental power was sufficiently motivated to challenge it.

On the one hand, the emergence of two true superstates has had the inevitable consequence that coalition and countercoalition diplomacy has been relatively less important since 1945 than it was in times past. On the other hand, the absolute destructive potential of nuclear armaments has reduced critically the political value of military power even, in fact perhaps particularly, for the superstates.

Through a process of détente or positive engagement more generally, perhaps the burdens of deterrence which lie upon Western armed forces and their political framework of multinational alliance could be reduced to a noteworthy degree. The attractions to Western democracies of the proposition that a much changed Soviet Union may require a great deal less deterring than heretofore are too obvious to warrant specific notice. It is very expensive to match Soviet forces in a militarily suitable fashion, so there is always a political market for the idea that those Soviet forces do not really mean us harm. In the later 1930s the British government did not so much misassess the pace of German rearmament as rather miscalculate the uses to which Hitler would put his "showcase" military forces.

Errors in grand strategy can be vastly more damaging than errors in military strategy, operational art, or tactics—just as errors in policy can be much more expensive than errors in grand strategy. Some compensation can be found in military competence for error in policy and grand strategy. But as the history of the two world wars demonstrates beyond a reasonable doubt, if a country (Imperial and then Nazi Germany) embarks upon a policy which its grand strategy cannot support with adequate means of all kinds, it is bound to fail. If a *preponderant* coalition cannot be assembled and successfully directed, then even extraordinary military skill will have the consequence simply of prolonging a struggle that cannot be won.

Impracticably ambitious policy goals or strategic objectives have a way of not being attained. Historians are prone to confuse wisdom with the revelations of hindsight. The Schlieffen Plan failed to conquer France in 1914, ergo it was impracticable—or was it? Similarly, Germany's *Barbarossa* plan failed to bring down Stalin's U.S.S.R. in a five-month campaign so, again, the task must have been beyond achievement—or was it? History is generous with earnest endeavors to attain what even the most authoritative of contemporary wisdom judges to be unattainable. Writing of the detailed war planning conducted in Germany in the 1880s, a historian has observed that "the General Staff was dominated by a spirit of pure professionalism, which led the officers on it to toy with ever new operational plans in an attempt to solve an insoluble problem."[12]

The plain lesson of the long "trailing edge" of the Franco-Prussian War in the winter and spring of 1870–71 was, or appeared to be, that a modern society could not be defeated via one or two "decisive" battles, after the fashion of the old days of cabinet or dynastic war. Nonetheless, although the protracted popular French resistance of 1870–71 was a harbinger of true "people's war"—as 1914–18 was to demonstrate—the Franco-German experience of 1940 was to show that even very careful assessment of what is and what is not possible by way of swift battlefield success cannot reliably be extrapolated from recent experience.

Neither superpower purposefully is positioning itself for *der Tag* for a decisive military resolution of its principal security problem, and by no means only because of the very likely self-defeating consequences even of a well-conducted war. Grand strategy does not provide Soviet or U.S. policymakers with a sufficiently plausible theory of definitive victory (even if one presumes, for the sake of argument, that a sufficient policy incentive to fight is present).

National or *coalition military strategy* is the art of employing all of the armed forces of a state or coalition for the political purposes expressed as high policy. Policymakers should set the stage politically so that their generals, if competent and lucky, can win wars. But those policymakers have to be alert to the possibilities both that military plans and operations by design may affront the political terms of conflict as intended by policy, and that through what Clausewitz called the "grammar" of war (which should be expanded to embrace the dynamics of crisis) the process of combat may far outstrip the bounds originally intended. If framed and conducted with little consideration of grand strategy or of political culture, military strategy can maximize the prospects for the failure of policy. Clausewitz wrote: "The first, the supreme, the most far-reaching act of judgment that the statesman and commander have to make is to establish by that test [of fit with policy purpose] the kind of war on which they are embarking; neither mistaking it for, nor trying to turn it into, something that is alien to its nature. This is the first of all strategic questions and the most comprehensive."[13]

It is not always obvious what kind of war is likely to ensue beyond the initial clash of arms (planned by one side). Furthermore, it is in the very nature of war that the suitability of objectives sought by military strategy in support of the aims of policy must be determined in contention with the independent will of the enemy. Imperial Japan was to learn from 1941 to 1945 that a national military strategy intended to secure limited geographical gains against enemies whose warmaking potential could not be defeated at source (preeminently in North America), and who were motivated to seek total victory, was doomed to failure. Though compounded by errors in national military strategy, by the plain absence of an Axis coalition strategy (grand or military), and by sins of overcomplexity in operational art, the truly fatal errors committed by Japan were political and sociological. A country might, *just,* succeed in waging a limited war which damaged American interests, but not—under any circumstances—if that war is initiated by means certain to be characterized in the United States as treacherous (or infamous), and by methods which cause prompt and quite heavy loss of American life *on American soil.*

Thus excellence in national or coalition military strategy, in the selection of objectives for military attainment (meshing with all military means at hand or to be developed), is a topic which lacks integrity in and of itself. Military strategy can serve a state or coalition only to the extent that the policy goals to which it is committed are sensible ones. Moreover, strategy can only be as good as the military instruments which it directs. If those instruments cannot secure the objectives of strategy, then the strategy needs to be changed, as well as the high policy which the military strategy serves (in the event that other arms of grand strategy—such as diplomacy, subversion, economic assistance, and the like—are unable to substitute for missing national military muscle).

Notwithstanding popular and official misuse of the adjective "strategic," it is an error to think of any weapon as being inherently strategic. Military strategy selects objectives for seizure or neutralization by armed force. Action by all elements of the armed forces, acting in whatever combination, has strategic consequences. If the most pressing war aim of the NATO Alliance would be to eject Soviet forces from NATO territory, what sense would there be in contrasting the influence of the menace posed by U.S. long-range (strategic?) nuclear-armed forces with the influence of U.S. and allied "tactical" forces in Europe? Ground forces, tactical air forces, naval forces, and long-range nuclear strike forces could all, in different ways, contribute strategic effect.

In the interest of avoiding apparent semantic perversity, this book refers to "strategic" forces (offensive and defensive) in line with common, if unwise, usage. Objection to "strategic" forces is not a trivial academic one. The words that we use shape the relationships we perceive. Appreciation of the need for, and relevance of, strategy for strategic forces is hampered by the fact that semantic abuse *a priori* has bequeathed a strategic quality to particular weapons. By definition it should follow that forces other than those nuclear-armed and of long range somehow are not strategic in the implications of their potential use. More than half a century of semantic imperialism by strategic air power cannot usefully be challenged. However, readers should appreciate that atavistic distinctions between the realms of strategy and tactics, no matter how inevitable for the present, can have unfortunate results.

In a final note about the semantics of strategy, there is the popular use of "strategic" to mean "independently decisive." According to this convention, long-range nuclear-armed forces are strategic because they can wage and conclude war quite independently of other forms of military power. Or U.S. naval-air power could be regarded as having had the potential for playing a truly strategic role in the defeat of an Imperial Japan which was dependent upon sea lines of communication for its functioning. Since the purposes of this book lean toward the clarification of that which is obscure, the promotion of consistency in language, and the advancement of ideas which—in the opinion of the author—encourage people to approach problems realistically, the notion that "strategic" is synonymous with "independently decisive" is rejected summarily.

Below the level of national military strategy, indeed serving as the bridge between strategy and tactics, is the activity known as *operational art*. Operational art is the direction of large groups of forces within a particular geographical theater of war. The responsibilities of a corps commander lie on the most modest rank of operational art, whereas command of several groups of armies (each comprising several corps with several divisions) marks the upper boundary. The campaign which NATO's Supreme Allied Commander, Europe (SACEur), would have to conduct should deterrence fail would be a case of operational art at a very high level. SACEur would have to wage his battles with regard to his theater campaign objectives, just as his military and civilian superiors—acting at the levels of policy, grand strategy, and national and coalition military strategy— would have to set objectives for, and release (or withhold) scarce resources to, his theater campaign in the light of the global course of the war.

Some of the copious recent writings by American military and civilian scholars on operational art claim that this level of warfare is the highest that is strictly military in character (strategy being understood to be suffused with political judgments). In practice, as the records of the U.S. Civil War and both the world wars demonstrate, the conduct of military campaigns can be heavily dominated by considerations of high policy. General William Tecumseh Sherman's great raid from Atlanta to the sea and then up through the Carolinas was conducted very much for the purpose of demonstrating to all Southerners that no place in the Confederacy was safe from the reach of Union military power. Generals Sir John French and Sir Douglas Haig launched offensive after offensive in France and Belgium from the fall of 1915 until the fall of 1917 for the purpose *(inter alia)* of encouraging Britain's French and Russian allies not to seek a separate peace. In World War II, to cite only one from among a myriad of potential examples, General Dwight Eisenhower's invasion of North Africa was at least as much political as military in motivation, and was conducted throughout with an attempted measure of political sensitivity which far transcended the narrow bounds of a strictly military operational art.

Tactics are the art of employing forces in the presence of the enemy. Tactics are about the handling of all kinds of forces, not about the effect of forces upon the course and outcome of campaigns of war. In the face of an intercontinental threat, one can talk of ICBM launch, or firing, tactics. In fact all elements of the armed forces are both *tactical* and *strategic instruments*. A tank battalion and an ICBM squadron are tactical instruments in their prospective or actual employment in combat; they are both strategic instruments with reference to the ultimate effects of their activities upon the securing of the political objectives for which a war is waged.

Classically, the domain of tactics was the battlefield, while the domain of strategy was the off-battlefield direction and preparation of forces and their supporting elements, including—preeminently— the selection of the time and place of battle. In short, strategy set the stage and related the engagements to be fought to the purposes of the war; tactics fought the forces on the field of battle (or at sea) in direct confrontation with the organized armed might of the enemy. Strategic air or missile power hence may be held to be strategic in that it menaces the enemy far beyond the zones of immediate military or naval confrontation on the ground or at sea. Whatever the highly dubious merits of a battlefield/off-battlefield distinction for the contemporary world (what exactly defines the scope of the battlefield?), the U.S. defense community is plagued with a cultural problem in thinking about deterrence and war in anything other than what reduces to engineering terms. Means and ends, application and consequence, typically are confused. If, as argued here without prejudice to particular theories or political preferences, Americans have a history of severe difficulty in relating military power or military force to the political purposes that power or force should serve, it is unwise to be casual about the distinction between tactics and strategy.

To a far greater degree than for statecraft and strategy, tactics can and must be taught. Soldiers have to be drilled in the correct solutions to confidently predictable tactical problems (problems of fire and movement with force components of known character and hence calculable effectiveness) according to the nature and performance of the weapons technologies of the day, the unique circumstances of the relevant geography, and the known tactical preferences of the enemy. Unlike strategy, tactics are specific to technology.

Nevertheless, the relationship between strategy and tactics is reciprocal and continuous. By and large the profession of arms does not, nor does it need to, train a person to think strategically. Judgments on how war should be broadly conducted, or on how much latent force (military power) a country should purchase in peacetime, are matters of high policy for which military expertise functions only in an advisory role. In World War II, for example, President Roosevelt repeatedly overruled the military advice he received from the Joint Chiefs of Staff, and generally historical judgment has been kind to the President's decisions. American fighting men were fortunate to be blessed with a Commander in Chief who, in the years of U.S. material weakness and tactical and operational amateurism, more often endorsed the war policy favored in London than in the topmost military echelon in Washington, D.C. One may recall with a shudder the joint memorandum from General George C. Marshall and Fleet Admiral Ernest J. King of July 1942 which insisted that the United States should abandon the principle of "Germany first" if Britain would not agree to a cross-channel invasion in that year.[14]

With reference to the political purpose of it all, strategy and tactics can only be as good as each other. Grand and sound strategic conceptions have a long and very expensive history of foundering on tactical incompetence (as well as on ill fortune—for example, Haig's protracted offensive of Third Ypres [1917] was washed out by a quantity of rainfall more than twice the average for Flanders in the months of July–October). Strategy always has a sharp end. In the First World War, 1915 could have been a year of great strategic opportunity for the Western allies. Unfortunately, they lacked the tactical skills and weight of munitions needed to exploit the fleeting opportunity which German preoccupation on the Eastern Front might have accorded them.

As was shown by the experiences of Philip II of Spain and Napoleon at sea, and of the Western allies through the major parts of both world wars on land, the absence of a military instrument capable of achieving a favorable tactical decision must prove fatal for the ambitions of strategy. However, the performance of the army of the Confederate States of America, of the German army in both world wars, and—arguably—of the U.S. armed forces in Vietnam may serve to illustrate the point that tactical, and even operational, superiority cannot substitiute for sound strategy and policy. The United States lacked a strategy for victory in Vietnam. Indeed for cultural reasons it is at least possible that the United States could not have devised, let alone carried through, the kind of war which such a strategy would have mandated. Quite properly and understandably the focus of the person in uniform at the sharp end of the spear is upon tactical effectiveness and personal risk control. But the paradoxical logic of war which holds that nothing (in the longer run) so fails as incomplete success alerts us to the point that tactical and operational excellence, if unguided by sound strategy, can promote an unbridled military opportunism.

It is by no means foolish to argue that valuable strategic opportunities must be built upon, in fact emerge from, tactical success. But this proposition can be reduced to a belief: if the armed forces are unequaled in combat prowess, problems of strategy essentially will take care of themselves. For a peacetime analogy, in 1981 there appeared to be a belief in circles close to the Reagan administration that questions of defense and arms-control policy should be treated for a while as practically subordinate to the need to build up military assets. In a speech in that period, Secretary of Defense Caspar Weinberger was scornful of the necessity for "some elaborate 'conceptual structure,' a full-fledged Reagan strategy."[15] In his first *Annual Report* the Secretary wrote as follows: "Even though it is essential that we reform our defense policy, one must not regard this reform as a substitute for an increased defense effort. The adoption of new ideas and thinking is sometimes presented as an alternative to sustained growth in the defense budget. It is not. Part of the needed reform in strategic thinking is precisely the new realization that we must devote more resources to defense."[16]

It is common sense, though not wholly true, to claim that defense policy and strategy are what the armed forces can do. There is an old saying: "Show me your programs and I will tell you your policy." Alternatively, it should be sound to argue that defense policy comprises capability, declarations, and action. But capability may be misassessed, by its owner as well as by its potential victim; declarations may be mainly political theater; and actions may not be a reliable guide to future intentions.

For a superpower with global responsibilities which—very unusual among the great powers of historical record—is committed heavily to the achievement of excellence in every geographical environment of war, it is probably impossible to identify a quantity of war-fighting capability which should suffice. If an administration enters office with the claim that it has a mandate urgently to correct the consequences of a "decade of neglect" of the nation's defenses, it is not surprising that its defense policy translates into a budgetary demand for "more." Similarly, an administration may enter office believing sensibly that the arms-control process is not a quest after truth wherein the two superpowers struggle with the problems of applying the revealed wisdom of stability theory to the real world of competitive weaponry, but rather a protracted arm-wrestling contest whose outcome is determined by relative military muscle and political character. In the latter case it becomes plain why war-fighting prowess (tactics) dictates what is possible for policy.

Policy and strategy are arts of the possible that should be guided by a clear sense of the desirable. It is precisely because countries cannot afford to purchase everything that might be desirable, and should not attempt everything that is possible, that strategy is so important.

How Do We Win?

Strongly complementary to the concepts of policy, strategy, operational art, and tactics are two ideas that are familiar in their essentials, are recognized ubiquitously to be important, but are rarely presented properly and coherently. Namely, any study of strategy, be it official and action-oriented, or scholarly and reflective, is likely to be fatally flawed if it neglects to recognize the importance of what may be called *theories of war* (or victory) and *doctrines of war*. Truly these are master concepts which have no close substitutes as tools for historical assessment, for the provision of advice on contemporary defense subjects, and for the provision of frameworks of comprehension for officials otherwise presented with a dangerously compartmented universe of concerns.

A *theory of war* explains how a particular war can be won. A theory of war is a special, restricted case of grand strategy. It does not explain why a war should be waged, nor does it specify what the war aims should be—those are the realms of policy. A theory of war explains how a particular country or coalition can be beaten at a tolerable cost. The objectives selected by strategy, and judged feasible at the level of tactics, should make sense according to the operative theory of war. This theory specifies methods of war-making appropriate to the particular character of the enemy of the day and to the weight of the political stakes of the conflict. The meaning of the theory of war, and of how theories have to be changed radically under the pressure of unexpected events, may best be clarified by historical examples.

In 1914 the British government intended that, as in the wars with Imperial Spain, and with Royalist, Republican, and finally Imperial France, allies in Europe would function as Britain's "continental sword." In the fall of 1914, the British theory of war envisaged that the allied French and particularly Russian armies would fight Germany (and Austria-Hungary) to a standstill during two or more years of campaigning. The British all-volunteer New Armies raised by Lord Kitchener—the minister of war and the dominant figure in war policy—were expected to peak in their strength in early 1917, by which time all of the great continental powers, enemies and allies alike, would be exhausted. In the words of historian David French:

> Kitchener raised the New Armies in 1914–15 to ensure that Britain would be the strongest military power at the peace conference. They were intended not only to win the war for the entente alliance but also to win the peace for Britain. . . . He [Kitchener] intended that the French and Russian armies would bear the brunt of wearing down the enemies' military manpower in 1915–16 so that the British army could administer the final blow in early 1917.[17]

As in the War of the First Coalition against Republican France (1792–98; Britain entered in 1793), London was prepared to subsidize continental allies; make a modest gesture of support on land, command at sea, and secure enemy colonies and overseas trading networks; and arrive at the peace conference as the organizer and paymaster of victory, economically probably strengthened by the conflict. This theory of profitable war did not work in the 1790s and was to fail no less conclusively in 1914–16. The same reason for failure applied in both periods; Britain's (allied) "continental sword" was blunted or broken unexpectedly early in the conflict. Beginning with the Battle of Loos in September 1915, continuing on a massive scale with the Battle of the Somme in 1916, and culminating with the Third Battle of Ypres in 1917, Britain was obliged to conduct vastly expensive, substantially "political" offensives of her own on the Western Front, for the purpose of relieving the pressure on failing continental allies. The relatively cheap eighteenth-century-style land war that the British government believed it was undertaking in August 1914 was superseded by the reality of Britain providing her own massive continental sword of fifty-nine divisions which—because of French exhaustion and Russian revolution (the product principally of war weariness)—at a price of nearly one million fatalities came to bear the brunt in defeating the German army.

Unlike the situation in 1914, the British Expeditionary Force (B.E.F.) of 1939 was committed firmly (if belatedly, winter 1938–39) to a continental campaign. This time, again unlike 1914, the British government did understand the French war plan. The British theory of war in 1939 and early 1940 expressed a partial repudiation of the operational theory which had sanctioned the unprecedented (for Britain) bloodletting in Flanders and on the Somme from 1914 to 1918. It is worth mentioning, for it is a point of enduring relevance concerning coalition warfare, that the French in 1939 were at least as determined to avoid the necessity of their bearing the principal part in a great land war of attrition as were the British. Overimpressed with the achievements of the economic blockade of the Central Powers from 1914 to 1918, and indeed with the efficacy of economic warfare in general, Britain in 1939–40 expected slowly to be able to strangle the German economy and wage an orderly peripheral war of position against Axis targets of opportunity. In the face of a military stalemate on the ground on the Western Front, and an ever-worsening economic condition at home, it was anticipated—or rather hoped—that the Third Reich would crumble politically from within.

As a theory of relatively cheap war this was, to be polite, feeble. In mid-1940 Britain had no plausible theory of victory pertaining to extant political and strategic conditions. However, British freedom of high-policy choice narrowed markedly in May–June 1940, when the German conquest of France and the Low Countries, and the forcible expulsion of the B.E.F. from Flanders—in addition to the seizure of Denmark and Norway in April—reduced the British theory of (victory in) war to "hanging on" until Hitler made a fatal error in grand strategy. But since peace with Hitler's Germany was politically inconceivable, Britain had to hold out until German errors catalyzed a second antihegemonic coalition. By the close of 1941, Britain had rendered itself unconquerable through wartime mobilization and, this time through Axis errors, had acquired in the U.S.S.R. and the United States Great Power allies capable of providing sufficient military, and particularly continental, muscle to win the war.

From 1916 to 1918 Britain had no practical choice other than to assume a larger and larger share of the burden of ground warfare if the Allies were not to accept a peace of defeat. But in 1943–44 Britain had to acquiesce to an ever-greater degree in American strategic preferences if the United States was to be held to the fundamental concept of "Germany first" in the conduct of global war.

If a theory of war, as a particular case of grand strategy, explains with variable plausibility how to win a particular war against a particular enemy at a particular time in history, a *doctrine of war* explains how to fight. Such doctrine, which a French general could not discern in the British army of 1914, "was the body of ideas that guided the parts of the system."[18] Whereas a theory of war, albeit speculatively, should pierce the veil concerning the anticipated political significance of an indicated general course of military events, a doctrine of war should specify how the different arms can fight effectively together. The theory of war of a maritime power may aspire to wage economic warfare at so damaging a level to a continental enemy that the enemy will be driven to overreach himself on land as he seeks to close trading access points (Imperial France in Iberia in 1808 and in Russia in 1812), or open new ones for himself, triggering thereby a winning counterhegemonic coalition (as in 1813–14). Theory of war utilizes the output of doctrine of war to craft the way to victory.

In the small, a doctrine of war instructs, for example, infantry, artillery, armor, combat engineers, and so forth, how to fight as a combined-arms team. In the large, a doctrine of war should say important things about synergistic relationships among environmentally specific military instruments. But geography and the matching technology produce different kinds of conflict in different environments. Thus the different technologies, tactics, and geographical conditions which direct the character of war on land, at sea, in the air, or in space produce distinctive mind-sets on the part of environmentally specialized military professionals. Consequently, soldiers, sailors, airmen, missileers, and—one day, no doubt—"spacemen" have had a long history of preparing for, and waging, distinctive wars which may not be at all well coordinated.

Although there is no controversy over the principle of the interdependence of land power, sea power, and air and long-range missile power, the fact remains that each kind of power is optimized for a preferred form of war guided by preferred and possibly distinctive strategic objectives. For example, in World War II the U.S. Army, Army Air Forces, and Navy had distinguishable preferences in strategy for the subjugation of Japan (as did the U.S. Army and Army Air Forces for the subjugation of Germany). Today there is noticeable distance between the dominant theory of war implicit in the U.S. Navy's maritime strategy and the ideas of the U.S. Army concerning its duties in a World War III.

Deficiencies in the realm of doctrine of war can be fatal for national security. Characteristically, at the higher level of interservice cooperation such deficiencies take the form of countries mishandling their traditionally nonpreferred military instrument. Notwithstanding a historical record of major achievement, Britain persistently failed to design, train, equip, and employ its army in a way so as to complement most effectively the excellence of its navy and the efforts of its continental allies. Imperial Athens under Pericles may have been guilty of the same fundamental error in the opening years of the Archidamian War—electing to stand unduly passive on land and overly relying on the pressure which its navy could bring to bear against Sparta and its allies. Arguably, Imperial Germany committed the same generic sin in not having a maritime strategy complementary to its Schlieffen Plan.

The contemporary U.S. national security debate demonstrates the pull of the trivial. People are more comfortable with *defense issues,* presumably because they are easier to grasp, than they are with the frameworks of assumptions which provide strategic meaning for those issues. For example, gatherings of experts come to life on the issue of how much deMIRVing the United States should pursue for its land- and sea-based missile forces under a START regime. But those same experts freeze mentally on the subject of the potential contribution of single- or two-warhead missiles to deterrence or to the likely course and outcome of a war. Like the drunkard who searches for his lost coin under the streetlight for no better reason than that the light is better there, people prefer to tackle the topics which lend themselves most easily to analytical treatment by the familiar techniques of the expert. This is not to criticize narrow defense analysis per se. Nevertheless such analysis all too often provides an apparently safe haven for people who decline to acknowledge that there should be an audit trail linking particular defense issues to national military strategy, grand strategy, and policy.

Of Tigers and Sharks: Geography, Culture, and Strategy

The crucial point is clear: simply because the two sides [the United States and the U.S.S.R. in World War II] did not use the same strategy does not vitiate the comparison. The key question is not how they used military power but what they achieved.

—JONATHAN R. ADELMAN[1]

National security policies reflect the culture of the society creating them. Each society's forms of war and politics express its unique culture.

—MICHAEL VLAHOS[2]

WHILE STRATEGY generally will be applied abroad, it is made at home. Choices for policy, grand strategy, military strategy, and tactics may well be exercised by individuals or groups suitably educated in a universal paradoxical logic of war, but they will be individuals or groups schooled in a particular society and selected by that society to perform their duties. Societies differ widely in their selection processes, in the substance of what they teach—purposefully as well as by general environmental enculturation—and in the character of problems, opportunities, and duties they lay upon the individuals and groups charged specifically with ensuring the external security of the community.

THE CULTURAL ROOTS OF STRATEGY

Perhaps because it is so pervasive, the influence of culture on state-craft, defense preparation, and the conduct of war tends to escape notice. In the words of the first and greatest of all military classics, Sun Tzu's *The Art of War:*

> *Therefore I say: Know the enemy and know yourself; in a hundred battles you will never be in peril.*
>
> *When you are ignorant of the enemy but know yourself, your chances of winning or losing are equal.*
>
> *If ignorant both of your enemy and of yourself, you are certain in every battle to be in peril.*[3]

However important, the knowledge of self and others is not information generally conveyed under the rubric of "intelligence," as we know it. Even political intelligence on intentions or policy choices is too narrow and temporally confined to capture our subject. Furthermore, one should recognize that information gleaned from possibly ambiguous data in the fields of political, strategic, and tactical intelligence is influenced heavily by prior assumptions concerning both the character of the political community that is the object of security interest and the preferred ways in which it conducts its security affairs in peace and war.

Adda Bozeman has observed: "In approaching this subject [diplomacy] one must remember that each society is moved by the circumstances of its existence to develop its own approach to foreign relations. This means that diplomacy, or for that matter every other social institution, is bound to incorporate the traditions and values peculiar to the civilization in which it is practiced."[4]

Nevertheless, preparations for war in hope of peace (with security—i.e., on acceptable terms), and war itself, are near-universal phenomena common to all accessible historical periods and all varieties of societies organized as security communities. The closer one approaches "the face of battle," as it has been called, the more dominating are the features common to all humanity.[5] British military historian Michael Howard has made the points that "after all allowances have been made for historical differences, wars still resemble each other more than they resemble any other human activity. All are fought, as Clausewitz insisted, in a special element of danger and fear and confusion. In all, large bodies of men are trying to impose their will on one another by violence."[6]

At the sharp, distinctly tactical, end of war, the human problems in functioning effectively are as ubiquitous over time and place as are the remedies—leadership, discipline, training, self-respect, pride, comradeship, and good equipment. However, this book is not about the commonality of men at war; rather is it about the ways in which different societies prepare for war, seek to avoid the necessity for war, and plan to conduct war should national policy or an external foe opt for trial by combat.

Culture is the key concept here. Culture refers to the socially transmitted habits of mind, traditions, and preferred methods of operations that are more or less specific to a particular geographically based security community. Culture may be qualified for more precise usage, as in strategic culture or political culture. In other books I have developed the concept of culture with specific application to the idea of there being national styles in nuclear strategy and to the influence of geopolitical factors.[7]

As with the concepts of theory of war and doctrine of war, the concepts developed here tend to emphasize the fundamental unity rather than the fissionable character of phenomena. In addition to argument for the relevance of culture, this discussion should arm readers with the complementary, indeed overlapping, concepts of *system of statecraft, system of war, system of strategy,* and *national style.* These concepts are advanced to help people to see what societies are about in their security policies; to understand where particular strategic objectives and ideas come from; and generally to maximize the probability that important connections between apparently separate streams of behavior will not pass unnoticed.

Strategic culture is the result of opportunities, of resources, of the skill with which those opportunities and resources have been managed, and of the lessons which a society decides its unfolding history should teach. To a considerable degree societies are prisoners of their past. Policymakers have been educated both formally and by life experiences in their particular society to expect certain relationships generally to hold true (for example, between the accumulation of

military power and respect abroad, between solemn contracts undertaken and subsequent behavior—though in the latter regard the
point has been well made that Americans tend to be law-respecting
rather than law-abiding).

While strategic culture educates the approach of a nation to its
defense problems and opportunities, its product is national style in
defense preparation and the conduct of war. Style can be an elusive
concept to explain in operational terms, but it is important. Properly
disciplined by recognition that national style evolves over time, the
concept alerts policymakers to the fact that there are, for example,
typically Russian "thoughtways"[8] and modes of behavior which are
deeply rooted and, as a consequence, are likely to persist far into the
future.[9] Because of the relatively unchanging geographical context
for each state's national security, national (or imperial) policy-
strategy systems are proven to work by events, and they become
almost habitual as central pillars for the guidance of policy, grand
strategy, strategy, and operations. Successful states and empires—
from imperial Athens to the superpowers today—have discovered
policy-strategy systems which, at the very least, ensured national
survival for a good long while.

Joseph Rothschild concludes an important essay on culture and
war with the following advice:

> Conservatively, we must learn to appreciate that the power of culture
> derives from its deep roots, to understand that in the military dimension
> it leads to patterns of thought, planning, and behavior that are per-
> ceived to be historically validated and hence are likely to change only
> slowly (if at all)—and then only in response to deeply unsettling new
> historical experiences, and not in response to mere technological
> "fixes" or cerebral lessons in "rational" opportunity-cost program-
> ming.[10]

He warns against the danger that in correcting the errors in the
assumption of a transcultural strategic rationality, one does not tilt
unduly "in the opposite direction, of becoming intellectually mes-
merized by culture and thus failing to appreciate that the patterns
and traits of many societies and of their military establishments are
probably quite rational for them, given their historical experiences
and demographic-geographic situations."[11] Much more controversial
is Rothschild's earlier citation of what he alleges is "the more general
truism that societies and states with vastly different cultural heritages
often tend to adopt similar military postures if they confront similar
strategic problems."[12] If one pays due attention to the qualifiers

"often" and "tend," the alleged "truism" has some merit. However, notwithstanding the military logic of the hedgehog which inspired the generically similar systems of war of contemporary China, Sweden, Switzerland, and Yugoslavia (the examples cited by Rothschild), the strategic histories and traditions of many states—and particularly of great powers—anchored as they have been to unique, if dynamic, geopolitical situations, have yielded identifiably distinctive strategic cultures.

Frequently, cultural-stylistic analysis is endorsed for its presumed value in interpreting behavior on "the other side of the hill," and as a vaccine against ethnocentrism. However, thinking of Sun Tzu, the greatest benefit to be gleaned from sensitivity to the phenomenon of national style almost certainly lies in the realm of self-knowledge. Secretary of Defense Weinberger's conditions for the U.S. use of force were formed not to express great truths about the utility of military power, but rather to root policy debate over the U.S. use of force firmly—perhaps too firmly—in American soil.[13] Yet the duties of the Western maritime superpower toward international order do not always mesh well with leading characteristics of U.S. society as expressed in preferred national style. Subsequent experience in the Persian Gulf, for example, showed that even when the Weinberger conditions were not obviously met, U.S. culture and preferred style of operating can and did yield to the very pressing demands for action or military presence that are placed on the U.S. superpower simply because it is a superpower.

As another example, it was not the British way to commit very large armies to continental campaigns. But under the pressure of events Britain did what she had to do in 1914–18. Traditional policy-strategy systems are, however, prone to wreak vengeance when their tenets are flouted. The cry of "never again," which in the 1920s and 1930s dominated popular British views of prolonged participation in continental warfare, has had some recent analogues in the American reactions to Vietnam and to the bitter Lebanon experience of the early 1980s.

Countries can and do behave out of cultural character, as these cases illustrate, but they are recognized—or claimed to be—aberrations from history-sanctified norms of sound national conduct. The relationship between domestic political support and military success in war is two-way in character. Although there is much to recommend the view that the United States should wage only those wars which are popular at home, it would be quite wrong to suggest that the level of popular support is not affected significantly by the visible course of combat. In other words, there is an important truth in the proposition that a popular war is a war which Americans believe that they are winning.

As an effectively insular democracy, it is the U.S. way to oscillate in the measure of security alarm that is felt. In American political culture, unlike Russian, war and peace are sharply distinguished—though since the "police action" in Korea and particularly since the decade-long Vietnamese imbroglio, they are not as sharply delineated as many members of the Congress would like. Notwithstanding the near-permanent insecurity of settlers on the shifting continental frontier for more than two centuries, it is no part of the American way in statecraft to believe and behave as if interstate relations fluctuate on a continuum from "real peace" to a Clausewitzian "absolute war." Pearl Harbor on December 7, 1941, certainly was a profound shock to the American sense of transoceanic security, but it cannot reasonably be judged to have had anything even remotely resembling the impact of the battle of Jena-Auerstadt (October 14, 1806) upon Prussia, where in a single day and two battles the country was lost. Similarly, although they were saved by geography, climate, their enemy's egregious errors, and the tenacity of their soldiers, the Russian/Soviet experiences of 1812 and 1941–42 have no close parallels in American annals. In short, American history teaches that war is episodic, is waged abroad, that progress is probable in human affairs—so one should not be fatalistic about the danger of war—and that there is not a constant, high level of menace in the external world. Instead, security problems arise, are overcome, and peace returns. Even for a superpower gridlocked in a political-military competition with the other superpower, American political culture does not provide sustenance for a steady estimation of threat, though it does fuel a seemingly endless quest for an absolute quality of national security.

Sharp discontinuities in political and strategic contexts can produce discontinuities in previously settled habits in defense preparation. However, new defense issues are perceived through the prism of culture and are addressed with a style which reflects a unique national experience. For example, there is an engineering spirit or ethos which pervades U.S. society and the U.S. government. On balance this spirit is a healthy one and in the context of alliance security it provides an important corrective to the more passive attitudes of other countries. But Americans imbued culturally with a determination not to tolerate unsolved problems can have severe difficulty distinguishing among problems which can be solved, problems which really are conditions and hence cannot be solved soon (if ever), and problems which allies—for their own locally persuasive reasons—would prefer were not assaulted at all.

Questions of statecraft and strategy cannot be treated competently either solely in their domestic setting or strictly with reference to some hypothesized universe peopled by Strategic Men bereft of the influences of a particular society. It is what may be called the Jominian (after the writings of the Baron Antoine-Henri de Jomini) fallacy to believe that there is what amounts to a science of strategy which can be taught and applied independent of local political context and shifting tactical forms.[14] The character of U.S. national military strategy and the scale of its military instruments for contingent (upon policy decision) use are at least as much a function of the nature of the United States as they are of threats perceived in the external world. (Threats comprise a composite perception of potential enemy capability and of his propensity or willingness to use that capability.)

Political and strategic culture is the product of a particular national historical experience which has been shaped by a more or less unique, though not necessarily unvarying, geographical context. For any kind of activity, belief, or preferred set of objectives to attain traditional status, on balance it has to have had positive consequences for the society in question (at least in the view of those charged with policy navigation for that society). The strategic culture of a particular security community—as with its preferred systems of statecraft and war—is not the random and erratic product of ever-changing national opinion leaders; it is not immutable in the face of cumulatively radical changes in the domestic and external circumstances of society; and it is not derivative in detail from some allegedly universal logic of statecraft and strategy. The most that such universal and ahistorical logic can tell us is that states will strive to improve their condition of external security, and that if they strive too hard they are very likely to achieve negative results. Plainly, the greater the capabilities of the state relative to other states, the greater the means for manipulation of the foreign world, and the greater the temptation to try such manipulation. However, no textbook aspiring to provide a general theory of statecraft and strategy can indicate whether a particular, historical state will—or, normatively, should—aspire to establish a territorial empire, a hegemonic empire, or to seek extensive influence by cultural-religious-political penetration, by economic connections, or by adroit multilateral diplomacy.

Geography in all its aspects—physical, political, economic, and social—specifies national location, neighbors (and hence most probable enemies), neighbors-but-one (and hence most probable allies), and national assets for employment by grand strategy. None of the above necessarily are fixed for all eternity. Thirteen former colonies can seize the basis for a continental empire, scientific-industrial and demographic changes will alter the relative power potentials among states, while changes in transportation and other technologies will affect the military and hence political meaning of spatial relationships. For example, steam power, the internal combustion engine, heavier-than-air flight, and rocket technology successively and synergistically have shifted people's calculations of the security that reposes in distance. The introduction of steam power into the French navy promoted waves of invasion scares in Britain in the 1840s and 1850s. Most recently, the development of intercontinental ballistic missiles has destroyed the traditional American experience and expectation of transoceanic invulnerability.

In due course most societies have confronted security challenges which they have been unable to meet, due to poor adaptiveness, inadequate resources, incompetent leadership, or simply bad luck. Recorded history demonstrates the rise and fall of many civilizations and individual states which either tried for too long to apply obsolescent formulae for statecraft and strategy, or which adapted unwisely and ultimately unsuccessfully. Paul Kennedy's celebrated study, *The Rise and Fall of the Great Powers,* is careful to avoid the kind of simple monocausal (in this case, economic) explanation of why great powers rise and fall which would invite a plausible charge of determinism. Nonetheless, his work still veers perilously close to arguing that there are limits to the economic hand which statesmen either are dealt or can deal themselves on the basis of which they bid and play for power. In practice there are always limits to what a state can achieve. However, the strategic theorist is probably more likely than is the historian to be impressed with what wise policy and strategy might achieve by way of expansion of the economic basis of state power. This is a matter of respective skill biases. Historical phenomena can appear in a very different light depending upon whether one argues, for example, that Imperial Spain (or France, or Britain) lacked economic (broadly understood) means on a scale suitable to support its foreign policy; or alternatively, if one argues that Imperial Spain lacked a good enough system of statecraft and strategy to secure the necessary economic means. In his generally empathetic treatment of the contemporary U.S. strategy (i.e., means-ends) dilemma, Kennedy may be vulnerable to the charge that he allows too little scope for national statesmen and strategists to make their own history.

Although it has been mentioned that the kinds of grand strategies and military strategies preferred by individual states have been those proved by historical experience to yield superior results (given the persisting strengths and weaknesses of the states in question), there should be no bias in attention for study in favor of success. In fact, there may well be more to learn from the experience of failure than from success. One may be dazzled by the achievements of Athenian, Roman, Byzantine, Venetian, Spanish, and British statecraft and strategy, but eventually the systems of imperial security developed and practiced by those states all failed more or less gracefully as the world changed. States tend to develop fairly well-settled habits and attitudes toward their security problems. If those habits and attitudes prove to be ill adapted to circumstances, or if the material and human resources available or obtainable no longer suffice, then the state may be retired forcibly from the society of polities (as happened to Imperial Rome in the fifth century, to Byzantium in the fifteenth, and to Poland in the late eighteenth), may be relegated to the minor league of powers (as happened to Venice, Spain, Portugal, and Sweden in the seventeenth and eighteenth centuries), or may be accorded a respectable middle rank in world politics, though one quite drastically more humble than before (as in the cases of Germany, France, and Britain in the mid-twentieth century).

Lest there be any misunderstanding, national stereotyping must strictly be eschewed. By definition, strategic culture is about social, not genetic phenomena. Italian soldiers generally fought very unenthusiastically for Mussolini's new Roman empire in East Africa and the Western Desert in 1940 and 1941, but their parents had fought heroically if to no operational avail in, for example, no fewer than twelve battles of the Isonzo between July 1915 and November 1917. Italians fought with unquestionable bravery, typically with (barely) adequate skill (until they confronted new German assault tactics at Caporetto in October–November 1917), over most forbidding terrain, in an uncertainly popular national cause—even though Austrians were the traditional enemy. Italian policy plainly was highly opportunistic in both world wars, but that fact is not uniquely Italian nor does it yield any important generalizations concerning the subsequent quality of Italian military performance. Furthermore, the highly variable qualities of Prussian-German and French military performance from the early seventeenth to the mid-twentieth centuries emphasize the fact that whatever one chooses to investigate in search of the basis of military excellence, some innate national character of a biological kind should not be a candidate.

The proposition that some peoples made better soldiers than did others was popular in the floodtide of popularity for Social Darwinism in the late nineteenth and early twentieth centuries. The European colonial powers were wont to confuse superiority of material culture with superiority of race. Even when the general staffs of Europe considered strategy and tactics for war in Europe, the idea that there was a natural style of warfare best suited to one's countrymen secured influential adherents. The French persuaded themselves that offensive tactics in support of an offensive strategy best suited the national character of their soldiery. After all, had not the great Napoleon won virtually all of his battles with his inspired direction of the enthusiasm of his often barely trained soldiers?

The racialist cult of the warrior, Japanese samurai or Germanic SS knight, inclined Japan and Germany to overrate the value of fighting spirit as a force multiplier, and for a while rationalized what might otherwise have been recognized widely as the commission of terrible mistakes in grand strategy. It should be noted that Nazi Germany and Imperial Japan, culturally set upon courses of expansion, had little practical choice other than to exalt the fighting power of their warriors. Neither country had the manpower, the defense-industrial base, and still less the security of access to critical strategic raw materials necessary for rational contemplation of a lengthy war of attrition against what would amount to the rest of the world.

Although the strategic cultures of Nazi Germany and Imperial Japan served to discount (and rationalized the absence of need for) mere mechanical mass, the continental/maritime distinction is important for an understanding of the strategic context that played so large a role in shaping the course of events which led to the forcible demise of those two exceptionally warlike states. Both Germany and Japan were continental-minded cultures, although Japan, a collection of islands, had a large and very professional navy. It was their disadvantage at sea, above all else geostrategically, that condemned both Germany and Japan to be on the wrong end of an ultimately fatal material disadvantage in deployable assets for the waging of war. Furthermore, German *Geopolitik,* very much following Halford Mackinder's analysis, recognized that the political future belonged to the superstates with a continent-wide base for the generation of military power. If Germany was to be in the first rank of states, it would have to seize the economic base that it required. Germany's short-range war machine of 1940–42—the critical years—could not do the job. In 1914–18 and again in 1939–45, Germany was defeated by what may be called the British system in statecraft and strategy—

by a theory of war to which German continental power could not find a sufficiently effective answer.

Somewhat similar in kind to the belief that particular peoples make better or worse soldiers, but far more popular today, is the comforting proposition that soldiers for democracy (Western-style, that is) will be superior in combat because they enjoy the benefits of superior political motivation. As an ethnocentric error rooted in an ideological bias, it would be difficult to surpass the following claim issued by the U.S. government:

> *The Strength of the Individual.* One of our greatest advantages in com-
> peting with the Soviet Union is the character of our people. Western
> societies, with their stress on the importance of the individual, stand
> in sharp contrast to the repressive nature of the Soviet state. The
> initiative, enterprise, and motivation of free people is a source of great
> strength when individuals are put to the supreme test of combat. While
> intangible, these qualities are an important asset, which the Soviets
> cannot match. Defense policy recognizes this by stressing unit integrity
> and leadership, while our training and tactics place great value on
> individual initiative, and aggressive exploitation of opportunities.[15]

Would that this were true; unfortunately it is not. It so happens that the model for what the official authors describe in the final sentence of the passage quoted was the *Auftragstaktik* of the German army as practiced superbly, if ultimately to futile effect (for reasons of policy and grand strategy), in the two world wars.[16] The authors of the quotation should be correct in their implied argument that an authoritarian Russian state which discourages initiative and enterprise is likely to be represented by armed forces afflicted with similar ills. However, German history demonstrates beyond doubt that a total-itarian, let alone merely repressive, state is fully capable of developing armed forces second to none in tactical and operational skills, and can be so inefficient in defense-industrial management that initiative and enterprise flourish to the point of chaos. In short, the strengths and weaknesses of the United States and the Soviet Union in the field of defense preparation and potential combat prowess are by and large the strengths and weaknesses of those particular security communi-ties. Popular democracies, as "free people[s]," American-style, are neither uniquely peace-loving nor uniquely effective in war. It has been said of both the British and the American peoples that they are warlike but unmilitary.

Thus, the idea, or conceit, that status as a citizen-soldier in a one-man, one-vote pluralistic democracy (i.e., where there is a genuine choice among parties) bears a distinct relationship to combat effectiveness is not merely silly; it is dangerously silly. The principle that the individual is very important *as an individual* and is the repository of rights is virtually unique to Western political cultures. History is not a morality tale. The Western Roman Empire did not fall because it was corrupt and Nazi Germany did not lose its great war because of an acute deficiency of domestic virtue. To the uncertain and probably highly variable degree to which a political element can be identified and intuitively weighted as a factor in troop morale and combat effectiveness, it will likely be found that identification with the state, and recognition of the legitimacy of its authority in war direction, is much more important than is the detail of the political nexus between soldier and state.

One of Bernard Brodie's most memorable thoughts was that "good strategy presumes good anthropology and sociology. Some of the greatest military blunders of all time have resulted from juvenile evaluations in this department."[17] The surprises that tend to matter most are not the technical (e.g., the ignorance of the RAF of the *Zero* fighter in 1941; the ignorance of the German army of the T-34 tank in the same year), or even the strategic (*Barbarossa*, Pearl Harbor), but rather the human-cultural. In short, the surprises that have been most damaging have tended to be those that bore upon the willingness of a nation to fight, and to fight on in face of real or apparent disaster. The all-time classic example of recorded history is the case of Carthage, which twice believed erroneously that it could wage a limited war of commercial advantage against Republican Rome. Unfortunately for Carthage, Rome was not just another like-minded political culture, prepared to accommodate on the basis of a lost battle or campaign. In common with the United States in the first half of the twentieth century in its attitudes toward the enemies of peace and freedom, Republican Rome in the third century B.C. sought total victory.[18] In the case of the Pacific war, the popular racial antipathy which multiplied in wartime (on both sides) rendered utterly vain the hopes of Japanese statesmen for a favorable peace settlement in which the United States would recognize most of Japan's conquests.

Racial and ideological disdain helped disincline Nazi Germany from making realistic assessments of the fighting power of the Red Army (there were other reasons, good and bad, encouraging disdain), just as the German General Staff prior to August 1914 could not bring itself to believe that Belgians would actually fight. "They were just Belgians. Why should they fight?"[19] Great Power hubris and unflattering racial-cultural stereotyping misled the Germans into discounting any noteworthy will to resist on the part of the Belgians.

Thus there is a sense in which strategic culture may contribute a trained incapacity to cope with new strategic challenges. Just as the Carthaginians had a strategic culture forged from the experience of limited commercial conflict, the Japanese similarly had been trained by a state history of successful limited conflict abroad. For a medieval example, Kievan Rus' had been miseducated by three centuries of tolerable experience with steppe raiders into the mistaken belief that the Mongols were but the latest example of a familiar strategic problem. Rome, the United States, and the Mongols, unfortunately for their antagonists, presented strategic challenges of a magnitude beyond the adaptiveness of, respectively, Carthaginian, Japanese, and Kievan-Russian culture.

SEA POWER AND LAND POWER

Strategic culture and traditions in statecraft are very much the product of constrained responses to objective geopolitical circumstances (subjectively viewed, naturally). It would be a gross exaggeration to argue that everything worth knowing about strategic culture and traditions in statecraft can be learned with reference to two ideal and simple models, the continental and the maritime. But there can be little doubt that the continental/maritime dichotomy is far and away the most powerful single theoretical tool for any attempt to understand how and why particular states, empires, and alliances have functioned as security communities.

The environmentally conditioned worldviews of the sailor and the soldier continue to challenge the coherence of national and coalition military strategy. On their mental world maps, soldiers tend, understandably, to see more or less extensive lakes surrounded by land (the dominant feature). In contrast, sailors tend to see islands, more or less extensive in scale, surrounded by water (the dominant feature). As Eric Larrabee has noted, "For the army, water is a forbidding barrier, for the navy, a broad and inviting highway, and these are habits of mind engendered from earliest training."[20]

Geopoliticians with a landward orientation have argued that the effective shrinkage in the size of the world (real travel and communication time and not mere distance) effected by modern technology has rendered the oceans more lakelike in this century. Although an

ICBM can span an ocean in half an hour, and a jet aircraft in less than half a day, the air and missile age has obliterated neither the strategic significance of distance nor the difference between continental and maritime environments.

In his classic work, *Military Strategy*, Rear Admiral J. C. Wylie wrote:

> Where the sailor or airman thinks in terms of an entire world, the soldier at work thinks in terms of theaters, in terms of campaigns, or in terms of battles. And the three concepts are not too markedly different from each other.
>
> Where the sailor and the airman are almost forced, by the nature of the sea and the air, to think in terms of a total world or, at the least, to look outside the physical limits of their immediate concerns, the soldier is almost hemmed in by his terrain.[21]

Because of the geographical constraints upon their agility, it is natural for soldiers to think in terms of campaign strategy for a theater, the operational level of war. Equally, it is natural for the thinking of sailors to encompass the level of national or coalition military strategy, embracing many actual and potential theaters for campaigning, because of the global maneuver character of maritime power. Sea power and land power tend to be able to accomplish different kinds of objectives; they wage different, if complementary, forms of war and, as a consequence, as often as not their practitioners have different perspectives on the conduct of war. This generalization can be extended to the features of national systems in statecraft and strategy most characteristic of maritime as contrasted with continental states.

Below the level of Luttwak's "universal logic that conditions all forms of war," one finds that there is very little literature worth reading on the historically enduring subject of how great land powers and great sea powers have maneuvered diplomatically to fashion a pleasing peace and have sought to come to grips to achieve a favorable decision in war. Carl von Clausewitz, for all his brilliance, did not—indeed did not even attempt to—transcend the geographical domain of his own life experience as a Prussian officer whose interests were confined to the land. Despite the fact that in many ways the most critical contest of Clausewitz's period was that between France and Britain, he has nothing to say about the strategic consequences of Napoleon's catastrophic failures to find a solution to his British problem. Britain, it should be recalled, was the one constant element in the anti-French coalitions over the course of more than two decades, was the paymaster of all of those coalitions, and was—at the least—a major cause of the fatal overreach *on land* to which Napoleon ultimately succumbed.

The principal maritime theorists still (variably) revered today, Alfred T. Mahan and Julian S. Corbett (though not in a class with Clausewitz as philosophers of war), generally were as unbalanced in their treatment of what one may call national military strategy as was Clausewitz. Without advancing any grandiose claims for universal application in all periods, it is my contention that the focusing of a spotlight upon the continental/maritime distinction can help clarify a great deal about strategy, statecraft, and war. With only the rarest of exceptions, and none of those in modern times, every country has a principal environmental orientation to its security concerns, either maritime or continental. The advent of air and missile technologies has not introduced a third environmental option for national military focus alternative to the land or the sea (there are no air-power or missile-power states!). In recent centuries no country simultaneously has enjoyed the benefits of a truly excellent fighting instrument on land and at sea (such excellence being defined as the ability to challenge the army or the fleet of any other single country in the world with a fair prospect of emerging victorious). For reasons of geopolitics, every country is obliged to specialize in its national defense preparation in quest of excellence *vis-à-vis* the kind of military threat most critical to its national security.

Great land powers have constructed powerful fleets and great sea powers have fielded powerful armies, but only in very occasional and isolated cases was there any substantial doubt as to whether the navy or the army was the more important element in the security of the state. (Byzantium is one of the very rare arguable cases.)[22] The performance of maritime powers at sea and of continental powers on land varies widely—even for one country from one war to the next—but a certain "cultural" stability in statecraft and in strategic style is conferred by the geographical focus of the country in question.

The terms of the political, economic, and military character of the Soviet-American antagonism are dominated by the geography—or, strictly, by the geopolitics—of the relationship. The geostrategic nature of the relationship of conflict is between a superstate which is a continental empire and a superstate which heads a maritime alliance. Even nuclear strategy is pervaded by geographical considerations, and by treatment of the cultural influences which flow from particular geographically conditioned traditions and largely subconscious habits of mind. At the level of general theory about conditions for peace and the nature of war in relation to policy, specific geography signifies scarcely at all. But, as practical arts, statecraft and strategy are about the security of particular tracts of territory, about systems of order for particular regions, and about the problems and opportunities provided by the location of the state players and their strategic relations each to the others.

For the most obvious of examples, the evolving national military strategy of the United States has been driven since the late 1940s by the perceived need to deter, and if need be defend against, a Soviet army that was deployed—and rapidly deployable on mobilization for reinforcement—forward in Central Europe. That Soviet army was geographically contiguous to the truncated region most important to the vital U.S. interest in preservation of the balance of power in Eurasia—Western Europe. The systems of statecraft and strategy practiced by the United States today are as traceable to the geographical terms of national security reference as were the systems of ancient Athens, Sparta, Macedonia, Carthage, and Rome; later of Byzantium, Venice, the Ottoman Turks, Portugal, and Spain; and in more modern times of France, Britain, and Russia/the Soviet Union.

THEORY AND HISTORY

A great deal of empirical work remains to be performed by historians, cultural anthropologists, and theorists of international politics and strategy, working, if not together, at least in communication in parallel, before there will be a body of sound scholarship in the novel field of *comparative* statecraft and strategy.

Navalist and antinavalist writings over the centuries have been prone to discuss sea power and land power as great abstractions, imbued with certain properties of a quasipermanent character. Furthermore, the relations of net strategic advantage between sea power and land power have been assessed with reference to general trends in technology, economic development, and political organization. For example, the British geographer Sir Halford Mackinder wrote in 1919: "We have defeated the danger [from German land power to British sea power] on this occasion [1914–1918], but the facts of geography remain, and offer ever-increasing strategical opportunities to land power as against sea power."[23]

It was Mackinder's thesis, first, in argument advanced initially in public in 1904, and then refined at intervals until his death in 1947, that sea power had enjoyed a historically very unusual period of ascendancy over land power in what he termed the "Columbian epoch" from 1500 to 1900 (approximately). Second, as suggested in the 1919 quotation above, that Columbian epoch allegedly was passing or already had passed, and the future appeared to belong to the great continental states. The basic reason lay in the field of relative advantage in transportation economics as between sea and land mobility. In sharp contrast, the bedrock of Alfred Thayer Mahan's theory of sea power lay in the plausible claim that "notwithstanding all the familiar and unfamiliar dangers of the sea, both travel and traffic by water have always been easier and cheaper than by land."[24]

The new technologies of the seagoing sailing ships and ancillary (but essential) navigation aids had opened the shorelines of the entire world—aside from the unnavigable polar regions—to penetration by the trading and fighting sail of the ocean-facing states of Western Europe. In technical terms, sailing ships had a truly global mobility that was not enjoyed by the coal- and oil-fueled ships of the second half of the nineteenth and the first half of the twentieth centuries. Only with nuclear power has the maritime instrument regained the autonomy at sea enjoyed by the sailing ship. For the first three centuries of Mackinder's Columbian epoch, by far the most serious practical limitation upon the commercial and strategic reach of the sailing ship was the health of the crew.

It was Mackinder's thesis that the Industrial Revolution—from which Britain had been the first to benefit—particularly in its ramifications in the area of land transportation, had effected a radical shift in the terms of advantage as between sea power and land power. In 1904 he wrote: "A generation ago steam and the Suez Canal appeared to have increased the mobility of sea-power relatively to land-power. Railways acted chiefly as feeders to ocean-going commerce. But trans-continental rail-ways are now transmuting the conditions of land-power, and nowhere can they have such effect as in the closed heart-land of Euro-Asia."[25]

Mackinder was predicting that the railroad (and later the internal combustion engine) would permit the effective economic and political unification of great landmasses. In Mackinder's worldview, the most important landmass was that very large portion of Eurasia, which he termed the Heartland, inaccessible from the readily navigable sea. The Heartland was defined and redefined in 1904, 1919, and finally in 1943. By that last date, Mackinder had come to equate the Heartland with the U.S.S.R. and with those contiguous areas which the Heartland power strategically could dominate and close to penetration from the sea (i.e., much of the Baltic and the Black Sea).[26]

A very good deal of the apprehension, even pessimism, which one can discern in Mackinder's writings is very specific to his British orientation. Mahan's U.S.-continental frame of personal reference for the world (notwithstanding his anglophilia and the focus on the Royal Navy in his histories) in important ways made for a sounder comprehension of trends in the balance of power than was expounded by Mackinder. But Mackinder's theoretical framework, organized around the enduring opposition between whichever power or coalition controlled, or threatened to control, the Eurasian continental Heartland and the ocean-facing states, was fundamentally correct. The persisting historical pattern of conflict between continental powers striving to achieve hegemony on land and coalitions organized by offshore sea powers for the purpose of thwarting those repeated bids for hegemony has been too steady to be dismissed as a passing phase or an accident of particular circumstances. Where Mackinder can mislead is in his exaggeration of the power of the Heartland states in coalition relative to the power of what the Dutch-American geopolitician Nicholas Spykman was to call the Eurasian Rimland,[27] and to the power of the extra-Eurasian world. Belatedly, Mackinder came to appreciate what the United States could mean for the protection of the human values that mattered to him the most. These seemingly abstruse points are critically important for current and future U.S./NATO decisions on defense strategy. The historical record of British, and later Anglo-American, sea-based power, in contest with aspiring continental-hegemonic land power, shows that much less has altered geostrategically in the twentieth century than many people have claimed.

First, critics of the offensively framed strategy preferred by the U.S. Navy in the 1980s argued with an air of revelation that the Soviet Union, a distinctively continental land power if ever there was one, could not be defeated by action on, or directly from, the sea (setting aside the option of sea-based nuclear bombardment). This is true, but it is a very long-standing truth: it is not a truth unique to this century, expressive of some cumulatively radical shift in the terms of engagement between sea power and land power. Even in the eighteenth century, when economic conditions rendered France, the greatest continental power of the period, distinctly vulnerable to (financial) pressure resulting from action at sea, there were strict limits to what sea power could accomplish strategically. In historical succession, the continental superstates of France, Germany, and the U.S.S.R. could be overthrown only as a consequence of ruinous defeat on land.

Second, the decline and generally fairly graceful fall of the world-wide British sea-based empire in the twentieth century points to the truth in Mackinder's 1904 (and after) prediction that weight in the balance of power increasingly will accrue to the larger, territorially contiguous states. Through improvements in internal (landward) communications, those states increasingly have been able to realize their economic potential. The British Empire vanished in a generation for two reasons, neither of which had anything to do with the strategic value of sea power *vis-à-vis* land power. First, Europe—including Britain itself—exported the concept of nationalism to its colonies, while the political cultures of the metropolitan societies ceased to deem colonialism a legitimate political form. Second, forced to wage two Europe-focused wars of national survival, Britain lacked the economic strength to continue to enforce imperial control.

Thus the important and interesting question for East-West strategic relations today, as also with regard to the antihegemonic coalitions which thwarted the France of Louis XIV and Napoleon I, and the Germany of Kaiser Wilhelm II and Adolf Hitler, is not foolishly to attempt to pick the "winner" as between sea power and land power (and air and missile power today) in the downfall of continental tyrants. Instead, the salient issue, and the real challenge to history-based but forward-looking strategic understanding, is the operational and strategic relationship between sea power and land power.

It is almost certainly true to claim that Hitler's Germany could not have been beaten by Anglo-American sea-based power without the massive assistance of Soviet land power. However, it is no less plausible to argue that Soviet land power alone could not have defeated Germany. The lack of historical novelty in the complementarity of Soviet and Anglo-American military power in coalition is quite striking. Alone, Britain could not possibly have brought down the continental empire of Napoleon, notwithstanding the excellence of the Royal Navy in that period—albeit an excellence somewhat dulled by complacency and war weariness in the later years, as American sailors demonstrated very painfully in the War of 1812. Yet the British political, financial, and military contribution was literally critical to the complex of factors which eventually brought about the destruction of that empire.

Certainly it is the case that global economic development and political modernization has meant a "closed world": there are no more open and politically ineffectively organized (if organized at all) frontier shorelines for sea power to penetrate at will. But the threat to the balance of power which Mackinder foresaw in the modernization of the Eurasian Heartland has been more than offset by the expansion of, indeed transfer to, the domestic base of Western sea power in the form of the United States. Furthermore, the political and economic modernization of the world which is beyond the easy reach of Heartland ground forces has diminished greatly the potential value of achievement even of a true hegemony over Eurasia. In addition, the modernization of the Rimland state of China is a growing strategic complication for any future Soviet leadership seriously interested in securing freedom from local continental distraction in order to challenge the U.S. superpower in its oceanic realm.

SOLDIERS AND SAILORS, OR FOXHOLES AND WIDE HORIZONS

The geophysical character of an environment has profound implications for the nature and military operational purposes of conflict, for the military means suitable for combat, for tactics, and—fundamentally—for the perspectives of combatants. Some of the differences between war at sea and war on land are so obvious that they have a way of functioning as a barrier to achievement of a deeper comprehension of the individuality of the two environments.

Strategically speaking, as observed already, more often than not navies and armies have represented two reasonably distinct "cultures," whose mutual comprehension has left much to be desired. When great powers go to war, they are not usually at liberty to go to war strictly at sea, on land, or in the air (or looking to the future, in space). Instead they are obliged to wage war as a whole. However, in peacetime the degree to which the landward and seaward (with their tactical air-power adjuncts) instruments of military power may be planning for quite different wars usually can be concealed, or even pass unnoticed.

J. H. Parry began his masterful study, *The Discovery of the Sea*, with a simple but strategically profound observation: "[A]ll the seas of the world are one."[28] With only minor exceptions there are no barriers of terrain or political frontiers to maritime transport. The horizon for the unaided senses of the sailor is the horizon provided by the curvature of the earth. The horizon for the soldier may be a hedgerow, or a wall, or a hill; it is vastly restricted compared with

that for the sailor. Not surprisingly, then, the open space for maneuver which is fundamental to war at sea can have a psychologically
debilitating effect upon soldiers when they are confronted with the
need to campaign in country which bears some resemblance to the
open sea (for example, the desert or the steppes of southern Russia).
Writing of "the foreignness of it all" in his *War on the Eastern Front,
1941–1945: The German Soldier in Russia,* James Lucas observed,
"The same thought occurred to many; that extending from the German front line and reaching to as far as Vladivostok there existed a
vast area of enemy territory wherein they, their regiments, indeed
the whole German Army, could vanish without a trace."[29]

The differences between war at sea and war on land can be exaggerated, but it is true to claim that armies most often have occupation (or possession) goals, while navies have use or denial-of-use
goals. In both cases the goals are instrumental, though they can be
more than that for armies. Armies seek to occupy enemy territory
in order to put pressure on the foe directly, either eventually to
accomplish his overthrow or to persuade him to accept a compromise
peace. Secure military possession, or repossession, of national or
allied territory is both instrumental for victory and an absolute value
in its own right. Unlike the ocean, the air, or space, effective ownership of territory has value in and of itself. German occupation of
nearly all of Belgium and of a part of northern France throughout
the First World War had the consequence of compelling the Western
Alliance to assume the offensive in that region, virtually regardless
of broader strategic considerations.

In contrast to the land, the sea is a medium for movement. It cannot
be occupied and fortified. Navies cannot "dig in" at sea, or seize and
hold ocean areas that have great intrinsic value. By definition, since
man lives on the land, the effect of sea power on the course and
outcome of a war can only be indirect. However, indirect does not
necessarily mean secondary or indecisive. For example, the intended
instrument of decision in war for continental Germany in 1917 and
again in late 1942 and early 1943 was the U-boat. This choice indicates
that the relative importance of a kind of military power is a function
of the particular vulnerability of the enemy of the day. Such importance is not a function of the technical (or any other) character of
the military instrument itself.

By virtue of the distinctive environments in which they function,
sailors and airmen have tended not to think in terms of the operational
level of war. Indeed, it is an open question whether operational art
has any real meaning for sea power and air power. Another open

question is whether the very concept of operational art, with its focus upon higher generalship in a particular theater of war, can make much sense for a period wherein modern transportation technologies have reduced markedly the practical autonomy of any such theater. However, the handling of very large bodies of soldiers by way of campaign direction is a vital skill, no matter what it is called. Edward Luttwak almost certainly is correct in his important argument that "if the operational level is to have any substance of its own, the action must also consist of more than the sum of tactical parts"[30] (though he then proceeds to an overly simple analysis of the subject of "style of war" on the spectrum of attrition-maneuver).

Heretical though it may sound in the face of the new orthodoxy, it is worth considering whether the concept of operational art is not perhaps verging upon constituting a continentalist fallacy or aberration in the art of war properly considered in its entirety. My doubts about the operational art of war for a democracy leading a worldwide coalition are similar in kind to some of my reservations about the arms-control process. Both the concept of an operational art of war and the pursuit of arms control, though innocent in themselves, encourage the carriers of American political culture to approach as separate fields of endeavor activities which should be treated as integral parts of larger wholes.

Readers of this book who are in the Anglo-American strategic tradition understandably are reared in the strategic perspective of a great sea power repeatedly confronting continental (European or Eurasian) hegemonic or territorial imperialism. Every strategic culture and tradition is inclined to erect what purport to be general theories on the basis of national historical experience and circumstances. Writing as an Englishman (actually a soldier), Charles E. Callwell was correct in his 1897 assertion: "The effect of sea-power upon land campaigns is in the main strategical. Its influence over the progress of military operations, however decisive this may be, is often only very indirect."[31]

For a great sea power waging war against a great land power, success at sea can have only enabling consequences. The land-power enemy may be brought down by the eventual consequences of his poor performance at sea, but that poor performance cannot itself produce defeat because he has nothing of a survival character at stake at sea. Contrasting argument applies to the sea power. Defeat at sea, the inability to move assets as needed on the oceans, would not have a "strategical"—in Callwell's sense of important but long-term and indirect—impact on a Britain or a Japan (or a United States vis-à-

vis its ability to fight beyond North and Central America). Instead, such defeat at sea would have more or less immediate and devastating consequences for the conduct and outcome of war. It should be recalled that Sparta eventually discovered how to defeat the Athenian system of war when, thanks in part to Persian gold, it secured the use of a fighting fleet adequate to wage an offensive against Athens' grain supply—her sea-lines of communication from the Black Sea through the maritime defile, or chokepoint, of the Dardanelles.

The inherent, direct, potential significance of sea power or of land power cannot be assessed according to their distinctive characters, but only with reference to who is using them and against whom. Although in modern history there is a very long pattern of antagonism between the greatest land power and the greatest sea power (with only the identities of the players changing), land power and sea power are strictly complementary forms and sources of strength. As a corollary, a sea power is prone to misuse its land power and a land power is prone to misuse its sea power.

In recent decades both the United States and the Soviet Union, in different spans of years, have believed that in the engines of intercontinental nuclear bombardment there was a way in which an end run could be effected around or over the traditional military long suit of the other. But by the 1980s, enthusiasm for nuclear-dependent theories of victory had worn exceedingly thin. Just as generals and admirals can have difficulty sufficiently appreciating each other's problems, so sea powers and land powers at the highest level of national policy can have difficulty appreciating the extent of damage that can be wrought by the successful exercise of the enemy's military instrument of excellence.

One should hesitate before generalizing across historical periods, but the evidence of success in modern times (which is to say, arbitrarily, after 1500), comprising some very different national casts of characters, suggests strongly that the wide horizon of the maritime worldview, *on balance,* makes for sounder decisions on the conduct of war as a whole than does the view "from the foxhole" of the more narrowly continentally minded. Lest there be any misunderstanding, this claim does not allege superiority of sea power per se over land power. The issue is not, indeed cannot be, that of soldier versus sailor, land power versus sea power. Rather, the issue is, and long has been, that of sea-based, encouraged, and organized land power versus land-based, encouraged, and organized sea (or more narrowly, naval) power.[32] Throughout modern times Britain and later the United States have been more able to generate a decisive quantity and quality of land power to bring down continental enemies than those continental enemies have been able to generate a decisive quantity and quality of sea power. It is no accident that this has been so—to employ a favorite Soviet turn of phrase.

Time and again in modern history, great continental states have been unable or unwilling to craft and execute effectively either grand or national military strategies, by way of contrast to their proficiency at the tactical and operational levels of war. But such are the differences between the occupied land and the empty sea that—thus far at least—preponderant land power is far more likely, in effect, to wreak its own destruction than is preponderant sea power. To date, the operational-level potency of the best army of the day (Spanish, French, German) repeatedly has proved incapable of offsetting the eventual negative operational-level consequences of conflict with an enemy whose center of strategic gravity is unreachably offshore. There is a half-millennium-long pattern of sea powers being able to make better grand and military-strategic use of their superiority at sea for the generation and regeneration of landward fighting strength, than land powers could turn to advantage on the continent into power of decision at and from the sea.

OCEAN AND CONTINENT IN GRAND STRATEGY

Bearing in mind the strategic fact that sea power and land power are natural complements and allies, not enemies, the history of the past several centuries reveals the grand strategy of a sea power (Britain, the United States) persistently to have the following key elements:

- organization and partial subsidization of continental allies in a maritime-continental coalition;
- a modest but noticeable continental commitment of soldiers on the ground, intended to fight alongside continental allies in the main theater of operations;
- maritime blockade/economic warfare to isolate continental enemies from overseas supply (an activity much enhanced in effectiveness when continental allies close landward frontiers to the enemy);
- a peripheral raiding strategy on the continental flanks of the enemy (reflecting the limited merit in B. H. Liddell Hart's advice: "[A]mphibious flexibility is the greatest strategic asset that a sea-based power possesses");[33]

• the isolation or conquest of the overseas assets of the land-power enemy.

Preponderance at sea—with, today, the backstop of a robust nuclear deterrent—means that the strategic center of gravity of a sea-power-led coalition (the coalitions against Louis XIV, Napoleon, Germany [twice], and the U.S.S.R.) cannot be reached, grasped, and conquered by the army of a continental enemy, *no matter how victorious he is on land.* Furthermore, superiority at sea, unlike superiority on land, tends to be general and tolerably complete. Even if there is no readily accessible continental ally to succor, maritime superiority positions the strategic frontier of the conflict on or close to the enemy's coastline. As the major wars of modern history all have illustrated, the power or coalition preponderant at sea has enjoyed, time and again, a critical advantage in strategic and operational flexibility.

In a lecture in 1958, Britain's foremost soldier, Field Marshal Sir Bernard Montgomery, delivered a mature professional judgment on the relationship between the land and the sea in war which merits quotation at some length.

> We must confine Russia to a land strategy. *From the days when we humans first began to use the seas, the great lesson of history is that the enemy who is confined to a land strategy is in the end defeated.* This has been true since the days of Carthage. In more recent times, there is the example of the French in the Napoleonic wars and the Germans in the Kaiser's war and Hitler's war. Another example can be found in the Russo-Japanese War in 1904. Japan had sea control; she fought Russia at the end of long communications with her own short; and won.
>
> The Second World War was, fundamentally, a struggle for the control of the major oceans and seas—the control of sea communications—and until we had won that struggle we could not proceed with our plans to win the war.
>
> Today, our strategy must be based on confining Russia to a land strategy, by retaining control of the seas in our hands and by preventing Russia interfering with our use of the air flank. Any other strategy is useless.[34]

The field marshal did not claim that sea powers eventually always succeed in wars against land powers. Rather he argued that powers "confined to a land strategy" eventually lose. If those powers happen to be critically dependent upon maritime communications, they will lose sooner rather than later.

The military constraints in particular circumstances can mislead statesmen into believing that fairly pure forms of the principal pillar of their country's preferred way in warfare can secure success even when exercised in isolation. Thus the leaders of great land powers repeatedly have succumbed to the temptation to believe that their army can defeat the grand strategy of a sea-power enemy. Similarly, the leaders of great sea powers have been known to endorse the fallacy that sea-based action alone can bring intolerable pressure to bear upon continental enemies. These parallel errors—when truly they are errors, and are not simply examples of politicians making a virtue of necessity—reflect a common phenomenon. Statesmen at war require a theory of victory; they cannot admit that they do not know how to win. Moreover, there are always projects which a superior army or navy can attempt in and from its own environment which, by more or less tenuous logic, just might set in train a sequence of events which would either bring the enemy down or induce him to accept satisfactory terms for peace.

It is not unduly cynical to observe that war can be regarded as a contest in which each side competes to set the stage most effectively for the other to commit fatal errors in policy or grand strategy. Such errors tend to have the consequence of posing problems of a severity beyond favorable resolution by excellence in military strategy or in operational art and tactics. For example, mistakes in statecraft at the highest level can have the effect of generating an enemy coalition of such strength that military victory is very close to impossible—this was the situation of France in 1813–14, and of Germany in 1918 and again in the period 1942–45.

The distinction between forced and unforced errors is familiar from the game of tennis, but it has relevance also for performance in war. Although modified by the operation of Clausewitz's notions of the diminishing power of the offensive and the culminating point of victory, as well as by the likely consequences of an enemy grown overconfident by success, there is a tendency for policymakers and generals who are under great pressure to commit uncharacteristic mistakes. For example, policymakers may be fundamentally disadvantaged at the grand-strategic level of conflict by an enemy who has a system of war which defies effective assault, or soldiers may be embarrassed at the operational level of war by an enemy who has seized and kept tight rein on the initiative. In those situations policymakers and soldiers may be attracted to panaceas to effect a radical improvement in their situation, all the while their practicable range of choice is being narrowed by an enemy who has confined them to a tardy response mode.

When frustrated by their inability to bring a conflict to an immediate satisfactory conclusion, a land power or a sea power typically will attempt what it can with the limited strategic reach of the preferred and available instrument of excellence. The continental power will consider how it can use its thus far victorious landward assets to defeat the strategy of the sea-power enemy, while the sea power will cast around for ways in which maritime supremacy can bring pressure to bear on the continental foe. 1801, 1806, and 1940 were all cases of the situation just outlined. In those years, as naval historian Geoffrey Marcus has written (of 1801), "The strategical stalemate between land power and sea power was complete. The French army could no more overcome the British navy than the British navy could overcome the French army."[35]

Given the obvious difficulty, not to say impracticality, of direct engagement for a definitive military decision between the battle fleet of a sea power and the principal field army of a land power (respectively the military "crown jewels" of sea power and land power, prior to the nuclear-missile age), what were the rival grand-strategic solutions to the engagement problem?

War on seaborne trade is a strategy of weakness chosen because a strategy of strength (aiming at the achievement of some facsimile of "command") is impracticable. If, as near universally has been the case, a continental power lacks the naval assets early in a conflict necessary for an assault upon the strategic center of gravity of a sea-power enemy, it can wage such maritime war as it is able (i.e., the *guerre de course,* or commerce raiding), while it seeks to set the continental stage for a stronger form of naval war or of strategy more broadly. This aspiration was stated very explicitly by Napoleon on December 6, 1806, when he wrote to his brother Louis, king of Holland, "*Je veux conquérir la mer par la puissance de terre* [I intend to conquer the sea by the power of the land]."[36]

In practice, Napoleon endeavored to bring financial ruin upon Britain through the imposition of a landward continental blockade against British commerce. Also, Napoleon sought to intimidate or bribe continental allies and other security dependents into contributing ships and sailors toward a great continental fleet for the smashing of British naval power. For reasons that, in detail, need not detain this discussion, not only did Napoleon fail to impose an effective continental blockade against Britain, but the effort to achieve a sufficiently impermeable system of economic pressure led him into catastrophic military overextension on land. The "Spanish ulcer" of 1808–14 and the Russian adventure of 1812 were both motivated nontrivially by the determination to close all of the continental littoral to British commerce.

In modern times, with only the rarest of arguable exceptions (1690, 1779), no great continental power has built, rented, or otherwise acquired a naval fighting instrument capable of challenging the British (later the U.S.) navy in a stand-up fleet battle with some reasonable prospect of success. At different times, French and then German leaders aspired eventually to enjoy the services of a first-class fighting (surface) fleet. But the exigencies of continental distraction always obliged those French and German leaders to seek shortcuts to success at sea via naval strategies appropriate to the weaker side. Specifically, the French, the Germans—and possibly, one day, the Soviets in their historical turn—have had to resort to a (dispersed) raiding strategy, assaulting the maritime communications of the sea-power enemy while endeavoring to avoid the concentrated strength of his naval forces.

Aside from the options for economic warfare, a hardy perennial feature in the grand-strategic calculations of continental statesmen has been the belief that once bereft of the armies of continental allies, the sea-power enemy will be unable to wage war on land and, indeed, will be so thoroughly deprived of a plausible theory of eventual victory that it must choose to come to terms. Peter Gretton has reminded anybody in need of reminding that "a maritime strategy assists and supports a continental strategy."[37] Sea powers such as Britain or the United States could not, indeed still cannot, have a continental strategy in the absence of continental allies. It follows, or should follow, that if a France, a Germany, or a Soviet Union can eliminate the actual or potential continental allies of Britain or the United States, there can be no theory of victory in war for the sea powers (save, implausibly, through nuclear coercion) because the center of strategic gravity of the continental enemy is on land. It has come to be orthodox to believe that Britain—admittedly with variable competence—used her sea power to sustain an antihegemonic policy vis-à-vis the continental balance of power. However, that orthodox view can be overstated and certainly can be accorded an authority that it does not merit.[38]

A sea power which enjoys, or can enforce at will, working control of maritime lines of communication can exploit the agility of its naval assets so as to raid, carefully and very selectively, the coasts of an enemy-dominated landmass. But those operations will have the character of raids for the purposes of local "ravage and destruction,"[39] or for the making of a political gesture—they cannot prudently aspire to "conquest and occupation" from a beachhead or an enclave from which a major land campaign could be launched. Britain could wage continuous war in the Iberian peninsula from 1809 to 1814 only because Napoleon was massively distracted in Central and Eastern Europe, and because Spanish guerrillas obliged the French greatly to weaken their field armies in order to secure their exceedingly vulnerable (landward) lines of communication. Similarly, the Anglo-American amphibious ventures against Hitler's *Festung Europa* from 1942 to 1944 were militarily feasible only because the German armed forces were very heavily preoccupied by the war on the Eastern Front.

As a grand strategy for hegemonic land power, the idea of partially disarming a sea-power enemy by defeating its continental allies is entirely sound *in principle*. When Hitler informed his military advisers on July 31, 1940, that he intended to invade the Soviet Union by no later than May 1941, and to defeat that country in a five-month campaign, certainly he was following his long-established personal agenda for expansion of the Reich. But, in addition, Hitler was advancing explicitly a theory of how Britain could be deprived of all reasonable hope of success in the war. The rapid defeat of Soviet land power was intended to remove British hopes for regeneration of an anti-German coalition with an active continental fighting front. General Franz Halder, chief of staff of the German army, made the following entry in his war diary for July 13, 1940: "The Fuehrer is greatly puzzled by Britain's persisting unwillingness to make peace. He sees the answer (as we do) in Britain's hope on Russia, and therefore counts on having to compel her by main force to agree to peace."[40] Also, the effective removal of the Soviet Union from the scales of the balance of power in Eurasia would render Japan so menacing in East Asia in U.S. perception that British hopes for American entry into the war in Europe would be dashed.

But this theory was to work only in principle. In a rare burst of wisdom, Field Marshal Wilhelm Keitel once observed that errors in strategy could be corrected only in the next war. He was in a position to know. Hitler's failure to invade Britain early in the summer of 1940 was an error that could not be corrected. Its consequence, the misdirection of the invasion of Russia in the summer and early fall of 1941, led directly to the ruin of the German army.[41] Two classes of difficulty are most pertinent here. First, one has to recognize what needs to be done (i.e., invade Britain very soon; go for Moscow, or the Ukraine, but not both in a single campaigning season). Second, one has to be as prepared as one can be for impediments "in the field" to accomplishment of the goals that have been set, however wise those goals may be. Strategy is a constant dialectic between means and ends. Goals are not sensible if they are beyond the range of feasibility, while tactical success is not guaranteed to translate into strategic victory.

It may be worth mentioning that in circumstances somewhat similar to the above, in 1802, Britain decided to sign a disadvantageous peace settlement with France. But in the summer of 1940, when British grand-strategic options again appeared to be distinctly unpromising, the character of the Nazi regime was such that London decided, in effect, to wait for something (i.e., the United States and just possibly the Soviet Union) to turn up. As late as the fall of 1940, it was hoped at the highest level in Berlin that a peace on favorable terms essentially could be dictated to a London which would choose simply to acquiesce in Germany's continental hegemony. Such a temporary settlement would have been after the fashion of the peace of Amiens of 1802–1803, in which a war-weary and isolated Britain recognized that it had no theory of success in war against a Napoleonic France everywhere victorious on land in Europe. The danger to Britain in 1802, narrowly averted in 1914, full-fledged in 1940, and possibly for the United States at some time in the future, was explained as follows by Halford Mackinder:

> What if the Great Continent, the whole World-Island [Europe, Asia, and Africa] or a large part of it, were at some future time to become a single and united base of sea-power? Would not the other insular bases be outbuilt as regards ships and outmanned as regards seamen? . . . must we not still reckon with the possibility that a large part of the Great Continent might some day be united under a single sway, and that an invincible sea-power might be based upon it?[42]

In principle, through conquest and intimidation the greatest land power of the day could use its army to acquire the production base and the ocean-facing geostrategic positions necessary for the development of really first-class sea power. However, no land-oriented state, empire, or coalition *in modern times* has been able to translate preeminence in land power into preeminence at sea. In ancient history, Republican Rome did exactly that; but the closed sea of the Mediterranean in the age of galley warfare geostrategically was very different from the open oceans today, notwithstanding the technological evolution that has reduced some of the significance of mere distance. A global scale of geography denies to Soviet legions the policy option noted by Mackinder as the preference of Rome: "land-power terminated a cycle of competition upon the water by depriving sea-power of its bases. . . . that command [over all the sea] was not afterwards maintained upon the sea, but upon the land by holding the coasts."[43]

The United States has been very well advised in organizing, subsidizing, and directly supporting an anticontinental-hegemonic coalition around the periphery of Eurasia—lest Mackinder's nightmare of a politically consolidated continent, reflecting centuries-long British fears, become a reality. However, the relevant contemporary trends look distinctly unpromising for Soviet prospects of freeing its hands of major Eurasian continental distractions, as a precondition for organizing and effecting a global maritime challenge to the United States. To secure its base in Eurasia, the Soviet Union requires a grand strategy which, by whatever mix of means, would deny continental access to the United States. Even if one can write plausible scenarios for Soviet *Blitzkrieg* success in a nonnuclear war in Europe, how could the Soviet Union, prudently and reliably, deny the United States continental access, or reentry, via the "back door" of mainland China? As China modernizes, albeit very fitfully, and Japan realizes at least a modest fraction of its defense potential, the problem of bicontinental perimeter defense for a probably endemically ailing Soviet defense economy assumes absurdly impractical dimensions. A U.S. system of statecraft and strategy driven by the policy objective of keeping power in Eurasia divided can count very reliably upon at least the informal cooperation of China and Japan—for the persuasive reason that they have to be even more opposed than is the United States to their incorporation in the currently ailing Soviet security system.

Frequently in modern times, a hegemonic land power has toyed more or less seriously with the idea of assaulting an insular sea-power enemy directly by invasion. However, as Julian Corbett explained in 1911 with unsurpassed clarity, invasion over an uncommanded sea is not a practical operation of war.[44] Moreover, invasion would not be necessary if the navy of the land power could wrest maritime command from the sea power. A sea power effectively defenseless at sea could not continue a war.

A grand-strategic option for land power eminently more feasible than the invasion of the sea power's home territory is the seizure of continental "hostages." An important function of Britain's continental allies in the wars with France after 1689 (from the perspective of London) was so to limit French hostage-taking on land in Europe that Britain would not be obliged to hand back to France and her allies all of the colonial conquests that the (British) Royal Navy managed to secure in the course of hostilities. Since the 1790s, however, no continental European power has possessed colonies or had other security wards at risk to wartime isolation and seizure by preponderant insular sea power of such value that their conquest could balance the gains achievable by land power in Europe. French, German, and in the future possibly Soviet conquests in Europe were, and remain, beyond capability of offset through British and American seizure of "sugar islands" and the like. However, the hostage problem could take the form of a Soviet Union successful on land throughout all or much of Western Europe inviting the United States to negotiate a peace treaty (if only to secure the release of captured Americans).

The great sea powers of history have all had in common a geostrategic insularity bequeathed by nature or by engineering artifice. Specifically, to each of them the sea could be a protective moat or a highway for foreign threat, depending upon the balance of naval strength. Maritime excellence can be developed and sustained only if there is an absence of intense competition for scarce resources with the army. As Mahan claimed, "History has conclusively demonstrated the inability of a state with even a single continental frontier to compete in naval development with one that is insular, although of smaller population and resources."[45]

Imperial Athens contrived its insularity by the construction of city fortifications and of the Long Walls to the port of Piraeus—thereby for a long time depriving its continentalist foes of an effective system of war (the Persians had twice devastated the city of Athens, experiences which the citizens were determined should not be repeated). The Byzantine Empire had a pivot or center of gravity in a superbly sited capital, Constantinople, which was protected by the most formidable system of fortification in medieval Europe. Venice was established on offshore islands (mudbanks, at least). The Dutch Republic was protected by major rivers and estuaries, by a network of fortress towns, and by very low lying land which could be flooded at will. Britain, of course, is an island, and the United States effectively is insular, albeit on a continental scale, courtesy of the military weakness of its landward neighbors.

In its grand strategy, a sea power competent in statecraft does not repose its security simply in the fact of a national geography which lends itself to maritime exploitation. The *final line* of national defense is provided by those military assets which directly protect the more or less insular homeland. However, the *first line* of defense for a well-governed sea power is a bevy of land-oriented allies, or—strictly—the diplomacy which forges and then helps sustain a mixed maritime-continental alliance. Those allies distract the hegemony-seeking enemy of the period from concentrating his potentially formidable resources upon construction of a truly first-class naval fighting instrument. Readers are advised that even though continental allies are generally important, and can be critically important, still that importance does lend itself to exaggeration when, Jomini-style, it is advanced uncritically as a universal principle governing the grand strategy of insular polities.

Whatever the flashy triumphs of continental operational art in success in battle and even in campaigns, in modern times the sea power has been able to outlast the land-power hegemon and to set the stage thereby for its self-destruction through imprudent overextension. British military historian C. R. M. F. Cruttwell penetrated to the heart of the matter when he wrote: "Still, generally speaking, it is true that British influence over continental wars has not been to determine their strategy in the narrow sense, but rather their general course and character. And this is so just because in naval as opposed to military strategy we have maintained our choice and control practically unfettered."[46]

As discussed, sea power is not about the military effect of fighting ships; rather, it is about the use of maritime lines of communication for the effective interconnection, organization, and purposeful application of the warmaking potential of many lands. Because of the unity of the oceans the coalition superior at sea is able, uniquely, to wage a global war. Notwithstanding the advances in transportation technologies registered in this century, Mackinder's World-Island of Eurasia-Africa remains very far from comprising a strategically easily unifiable landmass. Geostrategically, much of Eurasia-Africa continues to constitute a great "promontory" or salient (with a baseline in the relatively inaccessible Arctic), far more easy of access from the sea than controllable from the Heartland by the ailing Soviet continental empire.

Because the use of nuclear weapons is more likely to prove self-defeating than prospectively decisive in a classical military sense, and because both historical experience and common sense inform us that conflicts between great states and very powerful coalitions are extended in time and geography, this discussion should recognize the merit in a judgment proffered by Herbert Rosinski in 1944: "In global war, merchant shipping is the ultimate key to strategy."[47] Even so skilled a strategic theorist as Edward N. Luttwak appears to have difficulty grasping the complementary nature of sea power and land power.

> With Western air power now offset to a large degree by Soviet air defenses, and with naval power relevant only in the less critical theaters remote from Europe, the Middle East, and East Asia, *the ground-forces divisions are the basic currency of East-West strategy*. Because of the Soviet Union's energetic countering efforts, its advantage in ground forces no longer can be offset by Western strengths in other forms of military power, including nuclear.[48]

Because man lives only on the land and states are territorial creations, in any war against a continental power "ground forces divisions" must be the "basic currency" of strategy. Operationally and tactically, naval power cannot offset ground forces save at the margin. But strategically, such power can limit the consequences of adverse events on land and, more important, can—and repeatedly has—enabled a maritime combatant to protract a war in time, extend it in geography, and assemble a coalition able to field a superior landward fighting instrument.

Wars are deterred or waged by all of the armed services. In modern times the leading Western sea power of the day has won (or at worst fought to a draw) all of its major conflicts with the leading land power. Although that fact certainly attests persuasively to the enduring strategic influence of sea power upon the course and outcome of war, it does not attest to the unilateral influence of sea power. Whereas British sea power set the stage for the coalition endeavors which finally ruined Napoleonic France and Imperial and Nazi Germany on land, to turn to a future wherein prewar deterrence could fail, U.S. (and U.S.-allied) sea power alone could not bring down the Soviet continental empire. But, granted sufficient time, that sea power would knit together the war economies of several continents for the more or less agile and flexible global application of force. Sea power is about the transfer of the power of the production base on land at times and to places of strategic choice; naval warfare is about the security of that process of transfer.

At best, these familiar words of Francis Bacon should be regarded as a half-truth: "But this much is certain, that he that commands the sea is at great liberty, and may take as much or as little of the war as he will."

British, and later American, policy and strategy frequently have taken practical operational advantage of the truth in Bacon's claim. The effective insularity of the homeland of the sea power does allow for a flexibility in military plans and operations typically not accorded a continental state obliged to defend its territory against actual or imminent landward invasion. Nonetheless, British and American statesmen, with tolerable—though certainly not absolute—consistency, have recognized a force of geopolitical prudence which Bacon's words could incline one to miss. Specifically, disdain for, or unreliability in, continental commitments could have the result of the insular sea power being confronted by a continent-wide hegemony. The discussion in this chapter has yielded some empirically based propositions which help frame the analysis in the rest of the book.

First, objective facts of geopolitics generate habits and traditions in statecraft and strategy which, by longevity, come to assume cultural significance. Some of those objective facts purposefully may be created, as when Pericles built the Long Walls to the sea in 461–456 B.C., rendering Imperial Athens an island largely impervious to the (then) Spartan system of (land) warfare.

Second, even in an era of nuclear ordnance, ICBMs, and orbiting spacecraft, state geographies often still mandate a principally maritime or continental centerpiece to national military strategies. Consequently maritime or continental orientation imposes more or less severe challenges upon policymakers and military planners to achieve the necessary complementary competence in the other environment. This is the problem of the "tiger and the shark."

Third, whereas in ancient and medieval times, when Western "international" politics were focused upon lands more or less contiguous to the closed sea of the Mediterranean, great land powers tended eventually to triumph over great sea powers, the reverse has been true in recent centuries as politics and conflict have assumed more and more of a global character. The claim has been advanced that the unification of great landmasses by railroads, motor vehicles, and even by air power has awarded land power a competitive edge over sea-based or sea-dependent power. This argument was presented in the early 1900s and is still asserted today by those American defense theorists who argue that the Soviet-American conflict could be settled, perhaps definitively, by the outcome of a clash of arms in Central Europe. Such argument has been refuted by the historical experience of the two world wars of this century, and would seem to flow from a fundamental misunderstanding of the nature of sea power and of the systems of statecraft and strategy which its proper utilization requires and permits.

Finally, the military systems traditional to particular states are not simply the security expression of distinctive political cultures, more or less well modified to cope with shifting perceptions of external (and in many cases internal) threat. Political culture, while logically superior to strategic culture, itself has been created in no small part by the military experiences of the societies in question. Societies and their forms and habits in political organization and behavior reflect their historical experiences as particular national security communities. Societies and their state structures are, of course, the products of their history. Therefore, it could be almost as misleading to examine a society in any constricted period, let alone at one point in time, in quest of the domestic roots of strategic behavior as it would be to neglect altogether the differences of cultural reference which inform local policy-making. A Roman Republic where "almost every year the legions went out and did massive violence to someone,"[49] was functioning in the grip of a strategic culture, conditioned by geography, which expresses long-standing anxieties or ambitions.

CHAPTER 3

National Security Policy and Military Strategy

In the final analysis, it is not clear that the United States really has the option of renouncing its status as a great power, or that it would in fact exercise that option if it were available. The fantasy of retreating to the sidelines from which Americans could resume their old habits of judging the iniquities of states engaged in the political arena has its attractions, but in truth most Americans recognize it as an exercise in nostalgia. It is not the destiny of the United States to be a Belgium or a Paraguay. Having attained the stature of a great power, the United States has unavoidably acquired the responsibilities that accompany that stature.

—INIS L. CLAUDE, JR.[1]

TWO KINDS of expertise should complement each other in developing national security policy and in the making of decisions on strategy and weapons. The *historical approach* looks to the political-military record for inspiration, while the *materialist approach* focuses upon the performance (or promise of performance) of new weaponry. Both kinds of expertise are represented on all sides of defense debates; this is not a conservative-liberal distinction. Historical and materialist analysts have their respective potential strengths and weaknesses. The historical analyst is prone to look for, and hence to

79

find, more continuities among future, present, and past than perhaps really exist. Historical analysis can coexist with dangerous ignorance of technical progress and even with the attitude that technical developments do not much matter. In contrast, the materialist analyst typically sees the military world made over anew by the latest device or capability.

The contemporary debate over SDI provides a classic illustration of the two approaches, even cultures, in action. To simplify, both sides of the debate (those generically favorable toward strategic defense, and those generically unfavorable or highly skeptical) have developed fairly detailed technical arguments concerning *unbuilt* weapons and *undemonstrated* military-technical countermeasures, but to date neither has shown a firm grasp of the possible grand-strategic or military-strategic implications of new defenses. What passes for policy debate on the SDI tends to comprise the exchange of Jominian formulae allegedly expressing eternal verities about "stability" (itself a borrowing of dubious relevance or utility from the engineering sciences). While technical argument on the SDI is essential, its quality necessarily is hampered by the immaturity of the data base. As for the other side of the debate, in the absence of careful historical research the U.S. defense community is offered argument resting on unsound history. ICBMs are condemned often simplemindedly with reference to the offensive doctrines of 1914, while the SDI is vilified because the Maginot Line allegedly failed in 1940.

Michael Howard has observed, "It would be a mistake to try to establish too close a connection between the doctrine of the offensive current before 1914 and the terrible losses incurred during the First World War." He writes, "The worst losses were those due not to faulty doctrine but to inefficiency, inexperience, and the sheer organizational problems of combining fire and movement on the requisite scale."[2]

The history of the war was to show that a defensive stance did not necessarily result in the suffering of fewer casualties than the offense. In fact, German defensive doctrine, requiring prompt counterattack, came very close to ruining their army in the Somme battles of 1916. The Maginot Line may be criticized on two levels. At the level of fit with policy it was unhelpful because of its implication of disinterest in forward offensive action in support of allies in Central Europe; at the tactical level it drained scarce money which might better have been devoted to material modernization of the mobile forces. However, the Line did not fail in 1940 and it cannot be cited as demonstrating anything in particular about the wisdom of prepared defenses.

French tactical doctrine was at fault in 1940, as was the Anglo-French military plan of rapid forward movement (too) far into Belgium (and even Holland). The fact was that France did not make the proper use of the operational advantages which should have been conveyed by the Maginot Line.

MEANS AND ENDS

The fundamental indeterminacy of the future precludes the demonstration of provision of correct solutions to the means-ends problems of strategy. For a leading example, since there is no historical experience of bilateral nuclear war, it is particularly difficult to know what would happen in such a war, what tasks would be worth attempting, and how much force would be required in order to fulfill them. Academic theorists long have assumed that almost the only task worth performing by nuclear-armed forces is the deterrence of war, but there is agreement neither on how difficult or easy that task may be, nor on the closely related issue of how much force-in-reserve might be needed for intrawar deterrence and postwar security.

What the United States chooses to afford by way of a strategic force deterrent fluctuates with feelings of insecurity. The goals set for achievement by the strategic forces—the measure of an adequate deterrent—have shifted more in response to fashions in analytical judgment than with reference to policy needs or to actual military-technical possibilities. Short of manifest failure in action, one cannot demonstrate a disintegration of grand strategy, that is to say, an intolerably severe mismatch between means and ends. However, it is common for democracies to seek solace in economical theories of deterrence: for example, the substitution of political will for military muscle, or the assumption that the putative enemy will not require very much deterring. The costs of defense preparation are known and certain, while the benefits of such preparation, at the margin, are strictly speculative.

The difficulty of reconciling means and ends can be seen in the issue of intermediate-range nuclear forces (INF) in Europe. With some good reason, proponents of the "double-zero" arms-control (disarmament) option argued that this treaty would effect an asymmetrical draw-down in forces very favorable to NATO. The Soviet Union would be obliged to remove at least 1,568 warheads from its inventory, while NATO would remove only 420. Critics of the treaty were unimpressed by this favorable measure, arguing that the strategic mission of NATO's INF was not to contribute to the winning of a war in Europe, but rather—for deterrence—to add vital flexibility on the range of NATO responses in the event of attack. Strategic argument could be mustered quite reasonably on both sides of this issue, though in practice the case for the treaty was not presented in strategic terms.

The military balance should be important for deterrence, but if one is pessimistic over the ability of NATO to field and sustain all kinds of forces capable of resisting attack, then the absolute quality of particular military instruments as contrasted with their relative quantity assumes major and even overriding significance. The coalition strategy of NATO has an objective of deterrence keyed to the notion of controlled (nuclear) escalation. This NATO preference can provide a major source of tension with a more popular idea in the United States: that the best defense is the best deterrent. Europeans were almost entirely uninterested in the military value of the *Pershing* and ground-launched cruise missiles. In the dread event of a successful Soviet invasion it is difficult to imagine that any NATO-European government would have been at all interested in those missiles actually being launched. Consequently NATO's INF were a near-perfect expression of the truly immortal spirit of flexible response. They helped deter because they connected what otherwise might be perceived in Moscow as separable levels of conflict. No outcome to a war is prospectively attractive for the continental European members of NATO, and even the distinction between winning and losing might prove to be elusive. Logically, those countries place war-fighting effectiveness at a severe discount, preferring a strategy and forces which, after a decent show, should be expected to fail deadly in a slide to nuclear catastrophe. Soviet anticipation of such deadly failure on NATO's part ought to persuade them that they do not have a theater-conventional option for the waging of war.

Because defense policy is an activity conducted against an intelligent opponent with an independent will, one can never claim that "other things being equal, 'X' number of bombers, or warheads, or carrier battle groups, will suffice." Other things are never equal. The effect of U.S. military programs upon the calculations and will to compete (in particular ways) of the U.S.S.R. cannot be known in a thoroughly reliable fashion. The Soviet threat cannot be portrayed strictly graphically or numerically, because the most important variable is its political velocity. While the quality of Soviet political determination should be affected by their calculation of what ought to be militarily feasible, it is more likely to be affected by Moscow's sense of the political stakes at issue than by narrow military analysis.

In theory, there should be a constant dialectic between ends and means. However, in practice policy ends and settled strategic objectives can be frozen for long periods, even if the relevant balance among friendly and adversary means evolves very nonpermissively. Settled formulae can work or appear to work for decades or even centuries (in the case of British grand strategy and naval deployments to prevent invasion), but from time to time means and ends must be rebalanced or the country risks diplomatic impotence or military catastrophe, or both.

There is some danger that the U.S. political system, and particularly the dynamics of the budgetary process, compels an undue fascination with the details of means at the expense of consideration of their fit with policy ends and strategic objectives. In fact, skilled operators will function opportunistically and flexibly to stretch limited means (through prioritizing the sequential application of force, for example). Missile accuracy, ammunition stocks, and personnel retention rates are vastly more easy to understand and to assess than are the related qualitative issues. Are the missiles sufficiently accurate to perform their missions (and are those missions sufficiently important as to warrant large expenditure for the purpose of improving performance at the margin)? Is there sufficient ammunition for the war which might have to be waged? And does the personnel pool, active and reserve, present a tolerable fit with likely wartime need?

The interests of the state lie behind and instruct the ends in the means-ends equation of grand strategy. It is only a half-truth to assert, as do many textbooks on political science, that "states pursue their interests." Quite often, and indeed very often for a superpower whose capabilities have yielded global responsibilities, states are not clear exactly where their interests lie or just how intense particular interests really are. For example, in retrospect it is plain that the North Korean invasion of June 25, 1950, was a profoundly educational experience for the United States with reference to the quality of its interest in the Korean peninsula, as was the Soviet reoccupation of Hungary in October–November 1956 (for the other side of the coin of commitment). It is close to a universal law that states seek such control over their external environment as their power and general circumstances permit—only the mix of methods will vary. The scope and intensity of identified national interests tend to expand with national capabilities for influence and action.

Most typically, however, the U.S. problem lies not so much in locating its national interests as in deciding upon their intensity. As a tool for the guidance of policy design and execution, the concept of national interests can be important if applied in a sophisticated manner. The inherent worth of an interest may be far less significant than its value in a particular temporal context. Very strictly speaking, an isolationist-minded American could look at the outside world and find very little indeed that is "worth" his country risking a nuclear war to secure. However, in the face of similar self-regarding policy behavior by other security communities, policymakers are motivated by counsels of prudence to seek such influence over the external world as national capabilities and adroit diplomacy permit.

The revival of debate among intellectuals in the United States over basic options in foreign policy (a debate led by contributors to the journal suitably entitled *The National Interest*) has yet to kindle any major upheaval in the body politic more broadly. Without a firm architecture of principle and geopolitical assumptions, states (and democracies in particular) are prone to muddle pragmatically from international issue to issue, judging each case *seriatim* on its narrow merits. Given the possible connections between small events and great events, it is always tempting to seize available excuses for not taking a policy stand. If there is an absence of national consensus on the character of external threat, and on the implications of small issues for great issues, then assertions and counterassertions of quality of national interest simply are political rhetoric which lack authority for policy. Not only may the interests of the United States clash among themselves, but from time to time those interests will differ at least in intensity from the interests of its allies. Each American ally wants the U.S. security connection on its own locally preferred terms.

At the level at which national interest analysis can be most useful, interests are indeed stable over long periods of time. For example, it can be argued with the authority of historical experience as well as common sense that the greatest threat to the security of Americans lies in the realm of a potential imbalance of power in Eurasia. A United States suitably attentive to that danger is unlikely to commit gross errors in its national security policy. Nonetheless, critics of the contemporary framework of U.S. policy can argue that the dominating *means* in U.S. balance-of-power policy—the nuclear arsenal—has come to imperil the goals of policy. Moreover, allegedly, the architecture of regional security which the United States substantially has organized, subsidized, and directed after the classic manner of a maritime great power, while variably of benefit to U.S. security, also happens to comprise a wide range of "Balkan triggers" which could lead more or less precipitately to the nuclear-enforced demise of American society. The demise of the Soviet imperium may lead to a condition of insecurity wherein the "Balkan trigger" is more than just an archaic figure of speech.

Prominent among the criticisms to which policymakers and military planners are liable is the charge that priorities have not been set. The classic dilemma for the responsible official is the problem of how to allocate scarce resources among problems which differ markedly in their apparent urgency and inherent importance. In theory at least, an excess of potential demands upon limited assets is rendered tolerable by the determination of priorities, while demands for greater prioritization often reflect an unspoken criterion of assessed likelihood of occurrence. However, inherent importance and urgency or likelihood of crisis have a way of being inversely related.

The most appropriate criterion for deciding upon priorities is damage to the national security in the event of malperformance. The balance of world power could be shifted dramatically in the Soviet favor were Moscow able to neutralize the continental Eurasian dangers on either its Western or Eastern flanks—far fetched though such a prospect may seem at the present time. First priority for U.S. national security policy, however, is not the denial of Soviet hegemony in Europe or in Asia. Instead, it is maintenance of a sufficiency of strategic nuclear strength so as to deny the Soviet Union military utility in the use or threatened use of its strategic forces against the U.S. homeland. Similarly, it has to be first priority for the design of U.S. strategic forces that they must be unambiguously *mission-*survivable in the face of a potential "bolt out of the blue."[3] The occasions when the use of strategic forces assumes live significance in policy-making are, we may assume with high confidence, very rare. Furthermore, the occasions when a Soviet leader might be motivated to consider seriously launching a surprise strategic nuclear attack out of the blue are going to be rarer still. Nonetheless, the center of gravity or the pivot of U.S. national security has to be considerable confidence that the country is not at risk to a carefully prepared Soviet strategic-nuclear first strike.

The posture of U.S. strategic forces is the pivot upon which all U.S. military activity, worldwide, depends. There are severe practical limits to the extent of the deterrent or compellent writ of that posture, but the U.S. requirement for it to function as a counterdeterrent is so intense that the strategic forces must be classed as absolute first priority.[4] This priority is necessitated because the only direct, immediate, and potentially nonrecoverable threat to the U.S. homeland reposes in the strategic offensive forces of the U.S.S.R.

There are ample grounds for dispute over just how much, and what kind of, strategic nuclear strength can fulfill the first priority duty identified here. But there can be no dispute over the scale of the stakes. If the Soviet Union ever should achieve a state of imbalance in strategic forces which, in Soviet estimation, could translate into a decisive military advantage, it would appear to enjoy what is known as escalation dominance for a theory of victory in war. One must hasten to add that it is much more likely than not that any condition of escalation dominance revealed as truth by analysis would be treated with the contempt which practical people tend to bestow upon fragile theories.

By way of a historical parallel, for four centuries British statesmen understood that in the medium and long run intolerable threats would loom as a result of unbalanced continental power. Winston Churchill made the point with unparalleled eloquence, and only modest exaggeration, in a speech in March 1936:

> For four hunded years the foreign policy of England has been to oppose the strongest, most aggressive, most dominating Power on the Continent. . . . the policy of England takes no account of which nation it is that seeks the overlordship of Europe. The question is not whether it is Spain, or the French Monarchy, or the French Empire, or the German Empire, or the Hitler regime. It has nothing to do with rulers or nations, it is concerned solely with whoever is the strongest or the potentially dominating tyrant.[5]

Vital as it was to garner and help sustain continental allies for the purpose of balancing power in, rather than with, continental Europe, the pivot of British strategy was maintenance of battle-fleet command over coastal waters so as to preclude continental naval powers from striking at Britain at home. For long periods there were no decisive stand-up fights at sea between battle fleets. Nonetheless, British battle-fleet command was the pivot upon which all else depended. As with the U.S. strategic forces today, the battle fleet of the Royal Navy was the *sine qua non* of national security. However, there is an important difference between the prioritization in favor of strategic nuclear forces today and that expressed in the need for the British Royal Navy to command the Channel and the North Sea. Specifically, the course of a continental campaign related very directly indeed to the quality of the invasion threat directed at Britain. The armies available to Britain— both allied and national—distracted the enemy of the day from concentration upon the heart of his grand-strategic problem, the security of insular Britain and its sea-transported sources of wealth. By way of some, though not total, contrast, the quality of strategic nuclear threat to the United States is not controllable to any very important degree by the heavy distraction of Soviet military effort toward continental security problems. The inability of Soviet strategic forces to defeat their U.S. counterparts in decisive battle is rooted in technological, tactical, and operational infeasibility, not in a lack of resources to apply to the task. With strategic forces today, as with the land forces of 1914–1918, quantity is important but alone it is not the key to victory.

Sheer quantity—mere numbers—of strategic nuclear weapons will not deliver victory today, or tomorrow, just as the sheer quantity of allied forces does not explain why the German army was beaten in the First World War. Popular impressions to the contrary notwithstanding, the First World War on land was far from being the leading historical example of the blind application of national energies in a war of quantities. Military method evolved greatly, if belatedly, through four years of war, translating brute force into tactical (though not operational) effectiveness.[6] Thus the Western Allies won the First World War because their (hastily improvised—in the British and U.S. cases) armies were good enough, though certainly not superior, in tactical and operational method to exploit their basic and expanding advantages in the relevant quantities.

For reasons of their reach and destructive potential, the strategic forces of the superpowers enjoy parallel covering duties for all other military endeavors. Strategic geography mandates that the U.S.S.R. is obliged to accord first attention to the landward threats from West and East. In order to pursue *Weltpolitik* at tolerable prospective cost (i.e., while eschewing nuclear adventure), the Soviet Union first must neutralize the menace on its continental frontiers. Soviet statesmen have sought clients in Central America and Africa for the sake of the reputation of the Soviet state at home and abroad and as distracting irritants to the United States. But Soviet power effectively is landlocked, or landlockable, by the Western Alliance between North America and much of peripheral Eurasia.

Whereas the necessary precondition for an expansive global policy for the Soviet Union is the absence of proximate menace on land, so the precondition for a forward U.S. containment policy in Eurasia is a working control of the relevant sea lines of communication and the absence of major military problems in the Americas. U.S. security designs around the Rimland of Eurasia could be undone if the Soviet Union could either obtain a decisive advantage in strategic nuclear power or close (or at least vigorously dispute use of) the oceans to U.S. power projection and Western trade. U.S. strategic counter-deterrence and working command of the seas can limit the damage that Soviet land power could inflict upon U.S. interests, but cannot thwart it directly. Readers are reminded that these paragraphs are about the means-ends relationship that is the core of strategy; they are not crafted as predictions of active U.S.-Soviet problems in the years immediately ahead. Nonetheless, one can hardly state too plainly that the U.S.S.R., or a successor polity, is *always* going to be a very large military power potentially menacing to its neighbors.

Writing about General Nivelle, who promised early in 1917 to win the war on the Western Front in twenty-four hours, historian Correlli Barnett observed: "In despair men turn to quacks who promise them their dreams."[7] The public U.S. and European debate over security policy is well populated, if not with "quacks," at least with people convinced that they have *the* solution to the nation's security prob-lems. The European Left proffers détente as defense. The Left and Left-Center in the United States trust the notion that arms control can and should be the master framework for security policy, while the Right tends to equate weapons with security. On all sides there are voices advancing different policy instruments as, allegedly, the keys to the nation's safety. Unfortunately, the U.S.' Soviet problem is more of a condition than a problem, and U.S. policy toward Mos-cow tends to be a collection of several parts rather than a vehicle moved by a single directing brain and purpose.

Diplomacy is only an instrument of foreign policy, but frequently it is confused with foreign policy. Foreign policy defines objectives in external affairs, while diplomacy is but one method, with a dis-tinctive ethos in the West, for their accomplishment. The traditional rules, even the general spirit, of Western-style diplomacy are not wholly appropriate for informing the U.S. approach to dealings with states whose political cultures are sharply at variance with the legatees of the Renaissance and the Enlightenment which comprise the leading polities of the West. As Richard Pipes has observed, the U.S. State Department can give the appearance of being a giant law firm, seeking reasonable deals on behalf of its client.[8] Soviet diplomacy, on the other hand, while observing many of the outward forms of standard (Western) international practice, has been very much an instrument of political struggle resting upon a worldview which did not recognize that other states have legitimate interests warranting respect.

The dominant Western view of the arms-control process is that it is a special, uniquely important, case of diplomacy. Unfortunately, Western governments approach arms control, as they tend to approach East-West political issues more generally, in the spirit of reasonable people who expect other (Soviet) reasonable people to be fundamentally interested in the mutual adjustment of interests for the good of international order. Of course, deals can be struck with the Soviet Union. However, Moscow does not share a common frame of conceptual or policy reference with the United States. The U.S.S.R. has been an imperial state eminently realistic in its calculation of the respect and influence it is due, but revolutionary in its commitment both to alter the contemporary distribution of power in its favor and to encourage the reordering of security arrangements for the Eurasian Rimland so as to promote an imbalance of power. Mikhail Gorbachev plays the game of nations with a style novel to the U.S.S.R., but not necessarily with downstream objectives in mind that affront the traditional goals of Russian and Soviet statecraft.

Because the United States ultimately failed to employ military power in a way that was strategically effective in Southeast Asia (though a North Vietnamese victory was postponed for ten years), many parochial American theorists argued that military power no longer enjoyed high value as a currency in international politics. This view was nonsense, as Hanoi proceeded to demonstrate. However, a debate has sputtered on since the mid-1970s over the utility of military power to the United States. This debate was refocused in the 1980s by the "military reform caucus" on the issue of the competence of the U.S. armed forces. On the one hand there is a running argument over the occasions on which the United States ought to fight; on the other hand there is a dispute over just how well the U.S. armed forces have performed in combat from Vietnam through Grenada (October 1983), through the raid on Libya (April 1986), to the intervention in Panama (December 1989), and over how well they can perform.

The U.S. debate over the utility of military power has been organized, in part, by the proposition that such power comes in (arguably) usable and unusable categories. Nuclear weapons, and particularly strategic nuclear weapons, make up the latter—unusable—category. This might be a tolerable division were there excellent grounds for confidence that nuclear weapons will never be called upon by policy and strategy in trouble to perform in action. Also, this crude but popular distinction might be useful were the United States and its allies to have designed and provided nonnuclear forces on such a scale and of such quality that only exceedingly modest tasks were allotted to nuclear forces. These conditions have not been met. It is almost trivially easy to criticize nuclear-dependent strategies, indeed to lambaste nuclear weapons as not properly being weapons at all. However, critics have severe difficulty outlining sensible and practicable alternatives to nuclear dependence for NATO or to the so-called war-fighting theme in U.S. strategy for central war.[9]

Knowledge is power only if a country is willing and able to act on the basis of reliable information. One cannot usefully will ambitious ends for policy without also willing the necessary means. For praise-worthy reasons of political culture, Americans are, at the very least, uncomfortable with the kinds of state behavior for which individuals would go to prison were they to undertake it on their own behalf. But a wise commentator has observed that "successful foreign policy is the domain of the head, not of the heart. Its focus is on the future, not the past. And in the long run, the morality of our choices will be judged by their consequences."[10] British Foreign Secretary Lord Castlereagh made much the same point when he spoke before the House of Commons about the purpose of the Congress of Vienna: "The Congress was not assembled for the discussion of moral prin-ciples, but for great practical purposes—to establish effectual pro-visions for the general security."[11]

Competent statecraft has to approach its subject as a unity. It is the job of grand strategy to select and apply the several instruments of policy as may be most appropriate—ensuring that none of them individually are required to bear more of a burden than they can carry. Undue focus upon the instruments of policy, at the expense of strategic assessment of whether the preferred means wielded in isolation are capable of achieving the desired ends, leads all too often in a democracy to what amounts to the choice of soft options; a selective and even ideological commitment to benign methods (i.e., arms-control diplomacy, diplomatic process more generally, eco-nomic cooperation, and the like).

A HOLISTIC VISION

The title of this section expresses the fact that there is a basic unity at the sharp end to defense preparation and military performance, no matter how disconnected may be the several streams of relevant national performance or the analysis conducted in peacetime of dif-ferent aspects of the total defense mosaic. Carl H. Builder affirms,

"In its broadest terms, analysis is an examination of something by its parts and the relationships of those parts to one another."[12] The relationships of those parts not only to one another but to some notion of the whole often escape attention.

All ideas and methods of analysis in the field of national security are not created equal. Readers should be alert to approaches to the subject which should be rated superior or inferior (Clausewitzian or Jominian), broadly complementary (historical and materialist), inescapable but requiring self-awareness (reflecting national style), and thoroughly undesirable (disaggregated for isolated expert, or perhaps merely specialist, treatment). Regardless of where one stands on issues of policy and military strategy, it is instructive to interrogate substantive positions in the light of the methods treated briefly here.

Clausewitz and Jomini. The argument can be overdrawn, but two quite distinctive views of war, and hence of approaches to defense preparation, can be identified with Clausewitz and Jomini. The distinction is of immense practical significance because although the reputation of the former has never stood higher, it is the spirit and method of the latter which typically dominates the actual conduct of the national security business of the United States. It is popular to affirm that "we are all Clausewitzians now," but such a self-flattering ascription does not withstand very close scrutiny.

For Clausewitz, war was a realm of chance, of uncertainty, of behavior in a resistant medium. He developed the concept of "friction," which "is the only concept that more or less corresponds to the factors that distinguish real war from war on paper."[13] In contrast, Jomini sought to identify and develop the timeless principles that can and should serve as guides to military success. Jomini believed that he had captured the essence of the Napoleonic style of war, and that that essence could be reduced to some simplified, quasiscientific formulae for the education of professional soldiers—which is not to say that Jomini conceived of war as a science; he did not.

The teaching of the principles of war stems from Jomini. He emphasized the conduct of operations on "interior lines," the turning movement (looking to annihilation of the enemy), and the value of falling successively upon different parts of the enemy's forces with locally overwhelming strength. The key to success in Jomini's universe of war was the "bringing [of] superior forces to bear on a point where the enemy is both weaker and liable to crippling damage."[14] More often than not, the "decisive point" to be assaulted would be a flank on the enemy's lines of communication. It should be noted that Jomini was sensitive to the criticism that his advice was of little use unless he also taught how to recognize the points that would be decisive.

The reductionism in Jomini's treatment of strategy was borrowed quite consciously by Alfred T. Mahan, who endeavored to uncover eternal truths bearing upon success in war at sea in much the same way as Jomini had sought the permanent truths of strategy (really of operations) in war on land (particularly as revealed in the campaigns of Napoleon). Mahan wrote, "From time to time the superstructure of tactics has to be altered or wholly torn down; but the old foundations of strategy so far remain, as though laid upon a rock."[15]

In fact, Clausewitz and Jomini did not differ dramatically in their detailed treatment of the mechanics of Napoleonic strategy and battlecraft. Their difference was more at the level of the approach to war as a whole. There is little wise appreciation of statecraft in Jomini's voluminous writings. He was in quest of those secrets of success in war most relevant to the military commander. His principles for strategy are not seriously diluted either by consideration of political and social context or by recognition that changes in weapons (and other) technology, by influencing the scope of the tactically feasible, may have important consequences for strategy. For instance, the Napoleonic method in operational art could not work on a flankless Western Front in World War I, where grandiose operational, let alone strategic, objectives repeatedly were frustrated by tactical incapacities. Similarly, concentration of strategic air-power effort against the believed "decisive points" of the Third Reich at home was, at least until the summer of 1944, rendered abortive by the quantitative and qualitative limitations of the tactical instrument, as well as by very poor target, and more general economic, intelligence. However, the operational art shown in the right hook effected by General George Patton's Third Army out of Normandy in 1944, or the amphibious left hook by General Douglas MacArthur against Inchon in 1950, were both classic cases of operational maneuver in the Jominian style.

Jomini plainly recognized the political variety of conflicts (see his Chapter 1, "The Relation of Diplomacy to War"), but he affirmed consistently that "[w]ar is always to be conducted according to the great principles of the art."[16] From firsthand experience he understood how the wars in Spain and in Russia assumed a national and popular political character, just as he appreciated the dangers of "Double Wars, and the Danger of Undertaking Two Wars at Once"[17] (an appreciation whose significance could hardly be exaggerated for continental statesmen and generals).[18]

It is a valid generalization to claim that the U.S. military establishment, and defense community more broadly, has been firmly in the Jominian tradition for well over a hundred years. Examples abound of the placing of undue confidence in the scientific method—allegedly capable of providing certain knowledge—from the Civil War to the contemporary arguments about ICBM survivability, "nuclear winter," strategic defense, and arms control. Indeed, the treatment of the elusive concept of stability by liberal and conservative defense commentators and theorists is virtually a testament to the continuing influence of Jomini.

Yet the United States must seek to deter and prepare for war in the face of many uncertainties. What Clausewitz teaches (*inter alia*) is that the military planner himself should not be fooled by the apparent precision of his logistical and operational analyses. For example, no Clausewitzian soldier would treat with respect an analysis which purported to show nuclear war casualties to three or four decimal places—but a Jominian soldier just might. Whatever credulity pertains to aspirations for achievement of a true "science of war" in the United States[19] pales by comparison with the authority of similar aspirations in the Soviet Union. Notwithstanding V. I. Lenin's praise of Clausewitz's treatment of the relationship between war and policy, the Soviet military profession gives the appearance of obsession with a distinctively Jominian search for scientifically correct solutions to calculable military problems.

While much about warfare can and should be calculated, the fatal error lies in believing that there are elementary and universal formulae for success. The principles of war are certainly not wrong, but their value lies almost wholly in an intelligent application that cannot be taught reliably in a classroom, if indeed it can be taught at all. Wholesale violation of the principles of war, as by the United States in Vietnam, was as obvious at the time as it is in retrospect. An unusually perceptive participant-observer of U.S. strategic malpractice in Vietnam, General Bruce Palmer, has argued persuasively: "In Vietnam, we violated both principles [of *the objective* and of *the offensive*]. We lacked a clear objective and an attainable strategy of a decisive nature, and we relinquished the advantages of the strategic offensive to Hanoi. The best of initiatives, resources, exemplary conduct, and fighting spirit cannot make up for these deficiencies."

General Palmer proceeded to argue: "Our flawed strategy precluded the concentration of force, the principle of *mass,* in a decisive way. Likewise, the deployment of U.S. forces in numerous areas all

over Vietnam tended to create an open-ended commitment and prevented the effective application of the principles of *economy of force*
and *maneuver.*"[20]

Anticipation of Clausewitz's friction, or uncertainty, can serve as
an excuse for slipshod thinking and careless military preparation. To
say that war is a very uncertain enterprise is not to say that careful
planning cannot reduce some of the uncertainty. It may be that war
plans invariably fail fully to meet the needs of real-world conditions,
but it does not follow that planning is a useless exercise. Indeed, it
is not unknown for war plans to succeed beyond the expectations of
their authors (witness 1940 and 1967). Too often, both officials and
theorists forget that friction is not only an inevitable condition of
war; it can also be an offensive instrument of great potency.[21] Surprise
attack, for example, is a leading answer to the problem of friction
and uncertainty in military operations. To seize, hold, and exercise
the initiative is to oblige the enemy to respond as best he can to
unexpected events—in effect, to deprive the enemy of his independent will. An enemy behaving desperately in a reactive mode is likely
to suffer uncommonly from the irritants which cumulatively inhibit
effective military action.

Historical and Materialist Schools. Even when a theorist of the historical school is advancing arguments which depend critically upon
the technical performance of new weapons, as, for example, was the
case of B. H. Liddell Hart with reference to air power and tanks in
the 1920s and early 1930s, he is prone to be unduly casual over the
prospects for near-term technical achievement. Some of the advocacy
in the 1980s of a strategic "defensive transition" and of a radical
overhaul of NATO's military posture for the defense of the Central
Front in Europe, while strong on historical referents, was less than
thoroughly persuasive in the realm of near-term tactical (i.e, technological) feasibility, even though Soviet military experts were very
impressed. To be fair, there are materialist-minded critics of both
the radical recasting of NATO's posture and of strategic defense who
are profoundly ignorant of the useful strategic achievements of defensive tactics and systems in history. The thirty-mile-long lines of
Torres Vedras which the Duke of Wellington constructed in 1810
between the Tagus and the sea were impregnable to a logistically
disadvantaged, land-bound French army. The so-called Hindenburg
Line (Siegfried Zone) constructed in 1916–17, and even Hitler's
"Westwall" (reached by the Allies in October 1944), can be cited as
examples of defensive systems which amply rewarded their builders.

It is rarely very useful to think of weapons as either defensive or offensive, since even the most passive products of military engineering may be employed for strategically offensive purposes (e.g., fortification on one frontier to "lock the back door" while an offensive is prosecuted elsewhere), and most military equipment can be used for both tactical offense and defense.

Materialist analysis can manifest itself as a fixation upon what weapons can do, to the neglect of the question of whether the capability at issue is needed. Furthermore, materialists tend neither to be alert to the concept of friction as revealed by the historical experience of war nor to see war as a whole. Materialist analysis focuses upon the technical, tactical, and—rarely—the operational level of war, but never, at least not competently, on national military or grand strategy. The world of the defense materialist is the world of politically meaningless nuclear exchanges or of clashes of armor on NATO's Central Front. His subject matter is important, indeed it comprises critical elements among the building blocks for strategy, but it is not war that he is analyzing. Consequently it is not the phenomenon of narrow materialist analysis which is disturbing—after all, operations analysis has to be conducted. What is disturbing is the extent to which the nuclear-exchangers and the latter-day Heinz Guderians fail to recognize that they have confused tactics or operations with strategy: even more disturbing is the frequency with which official and public audiences share this confusion.

For reasons of political and strategic culture, the U.S. defense establishment is far richer in materialist than in expert historical analysis. This claim is attested to by the prevailing relative poverty of debate on questions of strategy. However, it would not be true to argue that the U.S. defense community has always been much stronger in preparing the application of force than it has in relating such application to strategic objectives or to the goals of high policy. Recent studies of U.S. military effectiveness in the two world wars demonstrate persuasively that, notwithstanding their many tactical and operational deficiencies, the strategic utility of the U.S. resort to force was high on both occasions. However, the simplicity of the U.S. policy objectives of 1917–18 and 1941–45 and the measure of (repeated) allied material superiority were not unduly taxing on strategic performance.

Aggregation and Disaggregation. States deter or go to war *writ large;* they do not deter or go to war on land, at sea, in the air, or in space. Unfortunately, in good part for apparently sensible and entirely practical reasons, few people in or out of uniform are motivated or required to think about war as a whole and about the connections among its various geographical and functional parts. By and large, Western political culture and indeed scientific and philosophical methods of inquiry encourage us to disaggregate subjects for detailed separate treatment. One becomes increasingly expert by knowing more and more about less and less. Military history reveals the prevalence and recurrence of critical disconnections: between policy purpose and strategic goals; between strategic design and logistical feasibility; between strategic ambitions and tactical practicability; and even between tactics and technology. Nevertheless politicians functioning as policymakers in international politics are obliged to think of war as a whole, as a unity. Even so, most of the analysis used by the U.S. defense community pertains to one, at most two (and more often only to sub-components of just one) geographical or functional dimensions of warfare, because the various sub-communities of experts in the U.S. defense establishment have a way of equating their areas of military interest with war as a whole. In the case of the strategic forces sub-community this equation is not unreasonable, though it is still wrong. That analysis and the debates that it feeds are essential, but if it is presented bereft of a context of national military strategy, the analysis will lack meaning and indeed can mislead seriously. Should there be neglect of national military strategy, and perhaps neglect of that subject in relation to grand strategy, how can the government decide how large a navy is required, or how much ammunition the army may need? National military strategy must express a theory of war and must be made to work by a doctrine of war for effectiveness in combat by combined or complementary arms, even though the future is by definition uncertain. Furthermore, tactical excellence is always desirable, though it is not always necessary. But even a competent doctrine of war for prowess in combat by combined arms cannot compensate for serious abdication in the fields of statecraft and strategy.

Incompetence at any level of analysis of defense subjects can be fatal for the integrity of national security endeavors. However, the character of problems and the nature of possible solutions differ from level to level, while countries vary in the weight of the burden of security generation that they place upon the several levels. Consequently one needs to be aware of the distinctive functions of high policy, grand strategy, coalition and national military strategy, operational art, and tactics.

Most directly because of reasons traceable to the influence of geography, British and American (though not in Vietnam) national security performance has tended to lean more heavily upon top-down grand-strategic excellence than upon the opportunistic skills of troops and commanders at the tactical and operational levels of war. As one would expect of a continental power, the reverse has been true of Germany. The Germans learned, indeed overlearned, from the trauma of October 1806 that national survival can be at stake in a single battle or campaign. Married to their protracted experience in the eighteenth, and particularly the seventeenth, century as the battleground of Europe (second only to the Low Countries), and to their recognition of the awesome problems of a two (plus)-front war, the Germans of the late nineteenth and early twentieth century understandably, if still unwisely, confused battlecraft with excellence in the conduct of war.

Amidst the great logistical truths about global coalition warfare, and in the face of the geopolitical policy logic which organizes bids for, and responses to, hegemony, it is easy to forget that individuals count. Two examples at very different levels of responsibility will illustrate this point. First, a German leader other than Adolf Hitler might well have decided on May 21, 1940—when the issue first was raised as a serious and pressing question—both that Dunkirk should be taken without delay (which could have been accomplished very easily at that time), and that an invasion of Britain should be improvised promptly upon the capture of virtually all of the B.E.F. in Belgium. Of course, it can be objected that a Germany led by anyone other than Hitler would not have been at war in May 1940, or that the odds would have been high that any German leader at war would have been encultured with much the same continentalist mind-set which so limited Hitler's performance as a statesman and strategist.

Second, it was a matter of critical moment for the course of the First World War that the allied military commander at Gallipoli was the scholarly, highly professional, but unduly passive and hence ineffective Sir Ian Hamilton. His deficiencies as a leader—which, in part, reflected prewar staff dogma concerning noninterference with the man in tactical command "on the spot" (i.e., corps and division commanders on shore)—meant that errors committed at lower levels of command were not corrected, and there was no compensation in drive from the top for the poverty of the troops in experience, logistics, and tactical intelligence. Tactical opportunities ashore were missed because Hamilton failed to take a grip upon the pace with which his troops were moving. Operational objectives could not be secured because of the tactical failures—which translated into a very expensive, not to say highly embarrassing, failure.[22]

Civilian defense analysts and strategic theorists are particularly prone to neglect the human element in their subject. The reasons for this frequent neglect are largely attributable to the rarity of tactical analysis by civilians (plainly they are not licensed experts on prospective combat), and to the dominance of the materialist approach. The authority of generalizations about geopolitical relationships or military strategy is not undermined fatally by recognition of human variables. There is a policy logic flowing from geopolitics just as there is a policy logic which should govern choice in strategy. However, the sharp end of statecraft and strategy is occupied by critically important individuals and groups of individuals who can vary dramatically in their competence, their courage, and their motivation. As Clausewitz had excellent reason to recognize, "genius"—the outstanding ability which lurks waiting to be bidden forth in most people—is both possible and significant. But in the narrow meaning of genius, states cannot afford to devise policy-strategy systems which can function well only when people of extraordinary talent are in command of the ship. The "genius" needs to be in the system of statecraft and strategy, not necessarily in the people operating it at any particular time of dire need.[23] That said, it can matter enormously who is at the political or military-operational helm.

Among the more significant of Clausewitz's analytical distinctions was the contrast that he drew between the policy "logic" and the "grammar" of war. This distinction is exceedingly important because it should remind people who may need reminding that whatever policymakers may intend, war is a blunt instrument with its own dynamic functioning and may not lend itself readily to real-time calibration by political authority. When policymakers decide to go to war truly it may be said that they risk choosing "to ride the tiger."

U.S. POLICY AND STRATEGY

Though a continental-size country which is not a natural sea power, the United States has assumed most of the duties for international security previously performed by small (if, by the early eighteenth century, relatively very wealthy), insular Britain. In the British tradition, the United States has discovered potentially fatal levels of threat to its national security in the prospect of domination of Eurasia by a single power or coalition.

Domestic American distaste for a polluting outside world is a permanent threat to the effectiveness of the United States in the politics of international security. A country with extraordinary strength in the material sinews of security politics, the United States nevertheless has had persisting difficulties reconciling the standards of decency that its society requires of public officials with the more brutal necessities of international life. In practice the "City on a Hill" has pursued the goals typical of a great power, but has done so from an arena of moralistic domestic scrutiny and debate that has been a mixed blessing. The openness of American politics is not fully compatible with the secrecy and deniability which universally are standard in the more sensitive areas of interstate security traffic. *Raison d'état* has an authority in the domestic politics even of the European democratic members of NATO which it cannot claim in the United States. However, pending reconstruction of a genuine local balance of power in Eurasia, the United States is essential as a player for the balancing of Soviet power.

There are periodic shifts in rhetorical fashion concerning the description applied to basic U.S. national security policy. However, from 1946 to the present day the intended reality has been a forward containment of Soviet power and influence. Thus far, aside from some handfuls of intellectuals on the Left and the Right, containment has not seriously been challenged as the leitmotiv for U.S. policy and grand strategy. Alternatives, even prospectively viable alternatives, do exist to a forward multilateral containment. But the U.S. government has learned through hard-won experience that the kind of zero-based review of possibilities which is attractive to scholars (and which indeed is a part of their duty to society) typically is not practical for endorsement by officials. However, the contemporary upheaval in East-Central Europe and in the U.S.S.R. itself all but mandates that, for once, the U.S. government needs to return to the basics of policy and grand strategy and reconsider its foreign policy objectives and the balance among the means and methods to be applied.

Save in the (eventually certain) event of the gradual emergence of a truly major third force, a third superpower, it is unlikely that there could be a general political settlement between the United States and the U.S.S.R. of an enduring, as contrasted with tactical, kind. Apart from residual ideological problems with such a settlement—and notwithstanding Gorbachev's "new thinking"—the Soviet Union is so situated geopolitically that the dynamics of a necessarily insecure territorial empire will continue to drive it to seek to expand the domain of its influence. Thus the "issue" between the current superpowers is not really territorially specific; rather it is about relative standing in the balance of power and the implications of that standing for the structure of security in Eurasia.

Containment per se has not been very controversial in U.S. national security politics, but as much cannot be said with reference to means and methods. For example, does a containment policy require that more than 300,000 U.S. military personnel be retained on garrison duty in Western Europe? Or, phrased in the political vernacular, should 249 million Americans be obliged to generate the lion's share of security for 381 million Europeans *vis-à-vis* 288 million Soviets? Is it essential that the territorial integrity and political independence of allies around the periphery of Eurasia continue to be underwritten by a not-implausible powder trail to nuclear holocaust (through extended nuclear deterrence)? How active should the United States be in encouraging, or even threatening, allies for the purpose of expediting the day when NATO's defense arrangements would be thoroughly Europeanized? More to the point, perhaps, as the Soviet extraterritorial empire in East-Central Europe visibly disintegrates, what should be the residual roles for the United States in the security of Europe and Asia? The Bush administration has spoken of moving "beyond containment," but what might that mean? The policy and grand-strategic challenge is not only to chart and protect a course "beyond containment." In addition, Washington has to be alert to the possibility that the current time of troubles for the U.S.S.R. could be arrested abruptly by new leaders. Those leaders might be determined not to cooperate with the West in the further dismantlement of the Soviet imperium.

Soviet foreign policy is so obviously at the tactical service of a domestic system in dire straits that it is all too easy to forget to inquire as to the probable future goals of the Soviet Union. Americans can enjoy on prime-time news the sight of their grand-strategic success over the evil empire. But they should remember that times of troubles do pass, that the Soviet Union is not the artificial product of some peace conference (*à la* Yugoslavia on a major scale), and that all of recorded history attests to the geopolitical unlikelihood of the two greatest states of an era establishing a security relationship of lasting entente. These observations do not contradict the logic of the images of change and instability that are currently on display in Eastern Europe; they do suggest that the Soviet Union/Imperial Russia is not at the end of its fourth quarter in the great game of international security politics.

The policy context for strategy-making and for the tactical application of military power is determined by the very structure of the international distribution of power. The security problems of the United States quite literally have been dominated by the prudential, overarching policy objective of restricting the potential growth of Soviet influence. Looking to the medium term, perhaps twenty years hence and beyond, it is entirely possible, indeed it is probable, that the emergence of super- or near-superstates in East Asia, functionally allied with non-Soviet-controlled Europe, will diminish very markedly the power-balancing role required of the United States. To those people whose frame of historical reference is almost entirely contemporary, this may seem to be an aberrant, if not atavistic thought. However, throughout most of its history the United States did not need to play an active role in the Europe-centered balance-of-power system for its security to be safeguarded. The fundamental terms of security have not altered—only the identity of the key players. To claim that U.S. security requires a balance of power in Europe and Asia is not to say anything in particular about the U.S. role in the maintenance of that balance.

Small countries have the same qualitative range of interests as does a superpower. But a small country knows that it can do little to influence its external security. Ambition grows with capability for action. The Dutch, for example, probably would feel more comfortable were Dutch values and practices to be on the ascendant in all continents. But, save through suitable support for multilateral associations, the Dutch know that their ability to encourage the emergence and spread of a compatible, supportive world is close to nonexistent. By way of contrast, a superpower is ever-tempted to render operational some of its ideological or milieu interests. Axiomatically expressed, states do what they can, and the more that they think they can do the more they are likely to attempt. For a super- or great power, the identification of interests tends to carry with it some sense of official obligation to take action to advance those interests.

The national military strategy of the United States, in common with that of all countries, is both beneficiary and prisoner of what amount to permanent geographical circumstances. (Strategic geography can, of course, be changed by success or failure in war.) With the exception of general nuclear conflict, the United States can wage war abroad only as transoceanic expeditionary warfare. This means that the United States requires enormous logistical reach in its forces, and—given the oceanic moats and the realities of comparative transportation economics—that it must secure a tolerable degree of control of sea lines of communication if it is to sustain combat.

Inescapably, though *inter alia*, strategy is logistics. To help balance Soviet power (the principal burden placed by U.S. policy on its supportive military instruments), the U.S. armed forces must be able to wage coalition warfare. Those forces must have guaranteed and preferably long-prepared access to (some parts of) the Rimland of Eurasia. It should be recalled that Britain's first geostrategic function *vis-à-vis* U.S. national security policy in World War II was its provision of access to Europe to U.S. military power. Active British belligerency alone could not be fatal to Germany, but that belligerency enabled the war to be won by providing the geopolitical framework for the eventual assembly and application of antihegemonic power of a variety and on a scale that the Axis countries could not possibly match. All the while that Britain remained in the war, Germany was denied an impermeable defense perimeter in the west and the south.

There is a limit to which the United States is at liberty to select a preferred national military strategy. Nominally, at least, an intelligent and very well armed Soviet enemy has options for imposing an unwanted character of war upon the United States. American officials and extragovernmental theorists may speculate about the desirability of purchasing a very robust conventional emphasis in national and alliance military posture, but war is (at least) a two-sided enterprise. Moreover, the character of war that the United States might prefer to wage certainly could be impacted very negatively should allies in Europe and Asia be moved to seek individual salvation via a separate peace, rather than to fight on as cogs in the wheel of a U.S.-oriented global theory of success in war.

In order to ensure that in resolving or alleviating some defense problems other problems are not magnified as a consequence, the outputs of the various sub-communities within the U.S. national security structure need to be considered together. Ideally, perhaps, as some military reformers advocate, the U.S. military establishment would educate a small but vital fraction of its officers in the mysteries of warfare in environments other than that of most concern to their service. However, in practice such cross-training is unlikely to prove practicable on more than a very modest basis. Historical experience suggests that air-, land-, and sea- (and perhaps space-) mindedness very rarely has been evenly spread within a single national strategic culture. The United States is a historically rather curious hybrid in its strategic culture and national military style. It is obliged by geography to be first-class in its maritime security provision, else it could not fight on the ground beyond North America. But as a power of continental proportions with at least a recent experience of abundance in material and human assets for the conduct of war, and with scant tradition of (or need for) subtlety in the measured application of force, its national military strategy—in World War II as today— reflects an uneasy compromise between the continentalist and the global-maritime.

Since the United States has in its column of allies and functional allies prosperous and well-populated countries around the Rimland of Eurasia, it can be argued that the economic principle of comparative national advantage should be applied to defense burden-sharing. The fact of the loss-of-strength gradient expresses the logistical reality that effective power diminishes with distance. It should follow, in principle at least, that it is not very sensible for the United States to plan on waging what would amount to expeditionary ground warfare when there are regional allies fully capable of providing locally the needed quantity of heavy units for land combat. The Nixon Doctrine of August 1969 proposed that key regional allies should provide most of the manpower for their own defense, with the United States providing a nuclear shield and focusing its defense efforts increasingly upon air power and sea power. Rigorously interpreted, this idea is not at present politically acceptable within the Alliance; but looking to the future it is a concept that has a great deal to recommend it on grounds of strategic effectiveness. It may be mandated by public opinion in the United States, and is a (not *the*) predictable end-state to the arms-control process in Europe. Cynically, perhaps, one might expect the years immediately ahead to see more of an intra-NATO struggle over burden-shedding than burden-sharing. Such is Gorbachev's "peace dividend."

For reason of established NATO ideas on "what deters," as well as for reason of political confidence among allies, the United States chooses wisely to emphasize the commonality of its security interests with those of its European allies. However, the U.S. Navy's 1980s-style maritime strategy, although designed to be coalition-supportive in a short war, had some implications quite different from those which flow from the current state of NATO preparation for ground-air conflict on the Central Front in Europe. By its very nature, sea power is most effective in a long, rather than a short, war, and it can be a supremely war-widening instrument. U.S. national military strategy at present gives the appearance of hovering between the standard assumption of a short intensive conflict very likely to see nuclear escalation in a matter of days, and the option (Soviet strategy willing!) of extending a conflict in time and space in avoidance of nuclear initiatives. Official U.S. concern in the 1980s over the state of planning for defense-industrial mobilization and over the decline in the U.S. mercantile marine attested further to newfound interest in the possibility of protracted war.

There is no argument that NATO-Europe must be the first U.S. geostrategic priority after North America itself. But what is the relationship between the defense of the NATO area and forward operations in Southwest or Northeast Asia? Geopolitically, it would be plainly desirable for Soviet military power to have to worry about at least two fronts (unlike their situation in 1941–45), but how much scarce naval and air power could the United States and NATO afford to allocate to extra-European problems and opportunities? The U.S. Navy has talked of operating sequentially in its offensive operations, but that could only be attractive if the Soviet Union were unable to respond effectively sequentially. Overall, what is the value for deterrence and defense in Europe of a posture that menaces the Soviet Union in Northeast Asia?

Some materialist-minded officials and politicians have urged an expeditious transition to a defense-heavy, if not defense-dominant, strategic-forces posture. But it should never be forgotten that new defensive weapons, in common with all weapons, are only instruments for the expression of strategy and the support of high policy. Notably near absent from the debate over strategic defense has been careful treatment of the all-important question "What are U.S. strategic forces (offensive and defensive) *for?*" For some purposes strategic defense may complement or substitute for strategic offense. However, a defense-very-dominant strategic posture would have implications for extended deterrence different from an offense-dominant posture. The former is focused tactically upon the mission of keeping enemy missiles away from one's society, while the latter is designed to hold the enemy at risk at home. The practical differences for policy and strategy between the two may be slight if fear of retaliation precludes the exercise of nuclear initiatives by an offense-dominant posture. But a defense-dominant U.S. posture might incline Soviet leaders to believe they could limit their liability in a regional conflict.

Policy, expressing calculations of national interest, sets goals for fulfillment by U.S. strategy in peace and war. The kinds of "competitive strategies" that the Department of Defense sought to identify and encourage in the 1980s were well and good, but it would be helpful for long-range planning, as well as for greater public understanding, if more attention were paid to the broad questions bearing upon the relationship of net advantage it would be prudent to seek over the long term, and upon the ways in which the generic competitive advantages of the West could best be exploited.

There is danger that attention paid to competitive strategies may be focused at too low a level of application to identify truly major and lasting net benefits, notwithstanding the encouraging signs of strategic vision which can be discerned. The fact that the idea of competitive strategies is regarded widely as a wise policy innovation, and that the Office of the Secretary of Defense solemnly could orchestrate an explicit venture on strategy writ large, suggest strongly that these enterprises, which should be second nature to the defense establishment, in practice have the status of fashions and are bound to be transient. Furthermore, "competitive strategies" are at severe risk of capture by an engineering spirit unschooled in the caveats of neo-Clausewitzian recognition of the paradoxical logic of conflict. New national security strategies, no matter how sincerely they are drafted and promulgated, must be at risk to the unsteady politics of the defense budgetary process, to hostility from entrenched interests, and prospectively to lack of endorsement by succeeding waves of political appointees. Historical analysis is always under threat of being overwhelmed by the materialist impulse in the U.S. defense community. The Department of Defense may have crossed an important threshold in geostrategic reasoning—though one doubts it—when it listed the following items among its "Highlights of four proposed initiatives [in competitive strategy]": "*Countering Soviet Global and Multitheater Operations:* . . . to exploit Soviet aversions to a multi-theater, protracted conflict, the task force [on competitive strategies] recommended developing an offensive warfighting capability for conducting large-scale joint and combined conventional offensive military campaigns."[24]

Whatever the political, operational, or tactical feasibility of this idea, it has the signal merit of comprising, or at least pointing toward, genuinely strategic reasoning. Its subject is the likely strategic effect of particular military campaigns upon the course and outcome of a war. One need hardly add that the tactical and logistical feasibility of global conventional operations would be critical for the quality of this competitive initiative as strategy. Furthermore, there may be a very wide gulf separating recognition of the competitive value in the conduct of multitheater conventional warfare from its full assimilation in a true theory of deterrence or of war. It is a relatively easy matter to identify multifront, nonnuclear conflict as a class of war which should discomfort the Soviet Union mightily. The more challenging task is to proceed to specify how the conduct of such conflict ought to enable the United States to secure its war aims at a tolerable cost.

Absent near-term revival of objective evidence pointing to sharp renewal of the Soviet threat, *the* strategy challenge for the U.S. defense community in the 1990s is how to adjust intelligently—i.e., strategically—to the onset of budgetary hard times. The official U.S. strategic planner faces the dilemma that—on the one hand—because political peace visibly is breaking out between East and West, his military means are certain to shrink to a cumulatively very substantial degree. On the other hand, the very events that undermine the political rationale for Western defense preparation also generate an instability that is unprecedented in the postwar period.

The American strategist confronts a daunting set of challenges. *What* military means does he require to secure *which* ends? Contemporary political events in East-Central Europe will leave a large and probably permanent mark on the structure of European security, but their implications for U.S. policy, let alone strategy, thus far, are not at all self-evident. The strategist has to adjust means and ends so that political uncertainty is very unlikely to promote some military tragedy. The Western Alliance is in the early stages of appreciating that the apparent success of very long standing policy and grand strategy can pose difficulties with which governments are intellectually ill-equipped to deal. There is a need for strategists.

The Fog of War, Friction, and Plans

. . . no plan of operation can extend with any prospect of certainty, beyond the first clash with the hostile main force. Only a layman can pretend to trace throughout the course of a campaign the prosecution of a rigid plan, arranged before-hand in all its details and adhered to to the last. All successive acts of war are therefore not pre-meditated executions but spontaneous acts guided by military tact.

—Field Marshal Helmuth von Moltke ("The Elder")[1]

My dispositions are made, my orders delivered. There is nothing for me to do but wait, so I must occupy myself usefully.

—Lt. General Sir Aylmer Hunter-Weston, Commander of VIII Corps, Gallipoli, 1915[2]

Everything in strategy is very simple, but that does not mean that everything is very easy.

—Carl von Clausewitz[3]

IT SHOULD not be supposed that friction, like Murphy's Law, points entirely to acts of God or to wholly random mischance. Furthermore, friction may be inseparable from war, but that fact does not render war wholly a realm of chance. Good and ample equipment, high morale, rigorous training, imaginative planning, historical education, combat experience, and sensitivity to potential problems are fairly reliable antidotes to the uncertainties of war.

Friction also includes tactical relationships that literally cannot be known ahead of time, but which certainly are not in the domain of random glitches. For example, when Soviet defense planners have to calculate how well their strategic forces might perform in execution of a first strike, they are very substantially in the realm of theory, and not only of engineering theory at that. They can calculate, based on educated guesswork, how many U.S. ICBMs should be destroyed. But, dare they assume that the U.S. National Command Authorities (NCA) would not receive strategic warning, or even if only tactical warning were provided that those NCA would decide to insist upon their ICBM force riding out the attack? If the United States should elect to shoot back very promptly on confirmation of attack, it would mean that the Soviet Union would be receiving fire within the first hour of the war. What would that imply for the orderly and purposeful conduct of long-preplanned operations? The wise defense planner endeavors to provide conditions wherein friction should be maximized for the enemy. Friction continues to be accorded much too little attention in defense analysis and, on the evidence of the Iranian rescue mission, Beirut, Grenada, and naval operations in the Persian Gulf, in military planning also. If observed intelligently, the overly denigrated, apparent simplicities of the principles of war provide practical counsel for the reduction of risk to the operation of friction.

Everything about war is difficult—certainly more difficult than study and planning activities would indicate to be the case. Clausewitz is not entirely persuasive when he claims that strategy is simple, though he merits unqualified respect for the argument that strategy is not easy. Clausewitz asserted correctly that nothing other than the experience of war properly can prepare people and organizations for war.[4] There is simply no other human activity which closely resembles war. His was not a foolish counsel of perfection, though in the absence of recent combat experience military establishments must plan and prepare as best they are able. The important point is that one must recognize as best one can that "war on paper," surrogate or mock battle, is not "real war."[5] Since the industrial revolutions of the nineteenth century, long periods of peace necessarily have resulted in military establishments being, to a greater or lesser degree, irreducibly ignorant about (hypothetical) contemporary war on a large scale. Anybody's confident prediction that a World War III would proceed on a particular course should be treated with deep skepticism. There are no true experts, only specialists, on nuclear war: no one has been there. Knowledge of weapon design and even of nuclear weapon effects (in many instances the knowledge is extrapolative and theoretical—scaled up from very limited test data) is not the same as knowledge of the interaction in combat of two independent wills, either using nuclear weapons or fighting under the shadow of possible or probable nuclear use.

Nevertheless, without the authority of experience there is no alternative but to seek guidance from careful study. But one must beware of the "scholar's fallacy," the temptation to believe that study must produce understanding, or that understanding is synonymous with effective action. As noted, the problem with nuclear-related military phenomena is that even if deep understanding can be secured by study, a government has no way of recognizing the truth in the absence of external tests of validity (i.e., of war itself). Gresham's Law rules scarcely opposed today. Variants of the law hold that the trivial drives out the important and that information tends to exclude knowledge.

Washington, D.C., is the city of a thousand "briefings." In the absence of reliable knowledge of the character of modern war, policymakers, analysts, and commentators seek refuge in the comfort of information. Oblivious to the perpetration of the pathetic fallacy, data on "the threat" is disseminated and almost casually confused with understanding of Soviet strategy. While recognition of the value of the discipline of experience and responsibility can lead one to be disdainful of "armchair strategy," it should be remembered that none of the senior U.S. and Soviet military commanders of today have any relevant experience of high command in war. This is not a criticism; it is simply a fact. All of military history tells us that effective wartime commanders cannot reliably be identified in peacetime. War is different from all other conditions.

THROUGH A GLASS VERY DARKLY

The difficulties [in war] accumulate and end by producing a kind of friction that is inconceivable unless one has experienced war.

Action in war is like movement in a resistant element.

Friction . . . is the force that makes the apparently easy so difficult.[6]

In the friction-free world of military theory, aircraft do not bomb the wrong targets, everyone who should receive orders does receive orders, equipment failure rates are only at the level of statistically expected norms, and the enemy does not attempt something utterly unexpected. In the real world of combat practice, communications are tenuous, key individuals break down under stress, tired people make very serious mistakes, and the weather throws the best laid plans off schedule (or may invalidate them altogether).

Too much can be made of friction, since—after all—the elements that produce it work to impede efficient performance *on both sides*. Nonetheless, Clausewitz was eminently justified in according friction the prominence that he did because it points to a layering of putative reality that theorists, uniformed and civilian, are wont to neglect in their schemes. It should not be forgotten that in a critically important sense military planning inherently is an exercise in speculative theory. A planner speculates, albeit in fairly concrete detail, that a certain allocation of assets applied in particular places will have a particular intended effect. Set against the independent will of the enemy, a military plan of operation amounts to an educated guess, even a gamble, that the enemy's will can be overcome or evaded.

Poor, out-of-date, and wrong information is a general condition of war rather than a pathological circumstance attending particular levels of technological competence or uniquely inappropriate command arrangements. The closest analogy to war is probably the large-scale, siege-type (by way of contrast to Alpine style) assault in mountain climbing. Mountaineering has most of the elements which make for friction in war (danger, extreme exertion, poor communications among physically separated team members, a weather "wild card"), with the critical exception of an intelligent enemy designing strategies and tactics to maximize friction.

The friction in war which impairs military performance is both the partial product and partial consequence of imperfect information. Defense establishments long trained in the relatively friction-free environment of peace always are surprised by the prevalence and thickness of the fog of war. What this means is that neither armed forces nor their civilian masters should design war plans which can work only if there is a near-perfect cooperative agility in command at all levels. War is a blunt instrument. The dynamics of combat may not permit the purposeful fine-tuning in real time which some ambitious theorists of the "diplomacy of violence" might encourage policymakers to believe feasible.

Recognition of the problem of the fog of war, and of the lost opportunities to which it can lead, has fostered some different kinds of intended solutions. On the one hand, there is a continuing technological push for the perfect real-time information system. Western defense literature is studded with references to a future "automated battlefield," fully "wired," as it were, for the benefit of high commanders. Computer terminals for use by tactical units would enable friendly commanders to know the location and condition of their own forces on a continuous basis, while electronic, visual, and infrared sensors on the ground, in the air, and (particularly) in space would provide near-real-time data on hostile forces. On the other hand, the fog of war can be not so much dispersed as sidestepped by the traditional means of superior doctrine, superior training, and a decentralized command style. If one potentially has an excellent fighting instrument at the tactical level, the most effective answer to the fog of war is to give that fighting instrument, organically, the assets that it needs to accomplish its tactical tasks; to provide battalion, brigade, and divisional commanders with mission-oriented orders (that are very light indeed on the subject of exact method), while preselecting those missions very carefully for their contribution to the objectives of theater operations.

Technology can indeed help disperse the fog of war, but theorists, particularly those with a materialist bias, are wont to forget that new solutions spawn new problems. In principle, improved communications and (two-way) reporting systems are neutral in their implications for command style. But in practice improved communications tempt superior commanders to usurp command functions that most properly belong at lower levels. Also, such communications can encourage timidity and buck-passing by tactical commanders fearful of responsibility. Finally, recalling the axiom that there is no free lunch in warfare, new communications technologies create new dependencies, while they certainly will engender new vulnerabilities. The technical marvel of radio permitted fairly—though only fairly—reliable real-time communication between tactical units and headquarters staffs in World War II for the first time in large-scale warfare, but at the price for Germany of literally catastrophic vulnerability. Britain's Colossus computer was able to decode (via Ultra) many of the radio transmissions of signals coded on the Enigma machines. Because of changes in technology, tactical lessons for the future cannot readily be drawn from the past. However, there is probably some value in recognizing the workarounds for an effective command style which were invented or refined by Napoleon, by the army staffs and fleet commanders in the First World War, and by all levels of command in the novel circumstances for military communications created by tactical radio in the Second World War.

Considerable vagueness endures concerning the value of military history for the professional education of the armed forces. Suffice it to say that military history is *the* laboratory of experience. It can never, or only very rarely, reveal identical situations for the extraction of detailed lessons, but it can and should alert military people to the questions that they need to pose. Similarly, history can signal to receptive minds the range of generic combat possibilities which may confront them. Overall, although the pace of change in weaponry can induce a tendency to discount the salience of history, it is well to remember that war in all periods, as a lethal contest of wills, does have a central constant, *man* and his nature.

Unlike the military establishments of the great powers in the late nineteenth century, or indeed unlike the Soviet military establishment today, the contemporary defense community of the United States gives the plausible appearance of being almost totally uninterested in what may be learned from history about the theory of war, or even in history-founded ideas about the conduct of war. A problem is that policymakers and military planners are always in more or less urgent need of immediately useful knowledge, while the ranks of professional historians are singularly ill-populated with scholars able, or willing, to risk their reputations in the unhistorical task of looking for general wisdom amidst the historically rooted particulars that are their professional stock-in-trade.

While few people would question the proposition that an education in history could (or should, or might?) improve public policy and even military performance, where are the bridges from scholarship to the world of action, and what can they say that has integrity as scholarship yet is useful to the nonspecialist reader? All too often, historians are content simply to affirm the self-flattering, if nonspecific, significance for policy of their specialty, while leaving the translation problem to others. It may not be an exaggeration to claim the existence of a historical scholar's paradox. The paradox is that on the one hand only the historical scholar is properly qualified to provide historical education for policymakers and professional soldiers. But on the other hand, the very qualities which tend to characterize the historical scholar serve virtually to disable him as a purveyor of knowledge in a form a policymaker or soldier is likely to find useful.

It is sensible to eschew search for a history-based "science of war." But the alternative to such a science is not, alas, the adoption of a Clausewitzian vision of conflict, educated by historical study to accommodate recognition of the variety of circumstance and hence opportunity. Instead, authority attaches to an ahistorical "science of war," more often than not environmentally exclusive in character, and bounded by a focus on tactical effect rather than strategic consequences.

In Clausewitz's writings, an *educated* intuition, determination, and courage cannot merely offset many of the uncertainties of war; in addition, they can turn uncertainty to advantage. Because chance and uncertainty tend to play heavily in war, there is scope for creativity in leadership. On the value of military theory to a leader, Clausewitz said, "It is meant to educate the mind of the future commander, or more accurately, to guide him in his self-education, not to accompany him to the battlefield."[7]

In its most distilled, reductionist form, military theory has been presented to professional soldiers for more than a hundred years in the guise of the principles of war. Variations are legion in the lists of these principles, but a representative presentation must include the following: purpose (or aim, or objective, or direction); initiative (or offensive); concentration (or mass); economy of force; maneuver (or mobility, or movement); unity of command; cooperation (or co-ordination); security; surprise; and simplicity. Some modern writers have vilified the principles, but—always provided they are not simply rote-learned for inflexible application—the enduring wisdom that they compress and express is ignored at the peril of military endeavor. They apply to warfare in all environments, unlike much of military theory at lower levels of generality, and disdain for their implications tends to produce disaster. A leading example of neglect of proper application of the principles was Japanese strategy and operational art in the Pacific war. The Japanese Imperial Navy dissipated its briefly held material advantages by dispersing its offensive effort in great raids into the Indian Ocean and the Coral Sea. In the battle of annihilation which it planned off Midway, it even contrived to be materially inferior at the decisive point.[8]

Needless to say, perhaps, it is not always self-evident just what concentration of force should mean in a particular context. Indeed the experience of the RAF and USAAF's (very loosely) Combined Bomber Offensive (CBO) after early 1943 illustrates how changing circumstances and disputed theories of war can render a strategy debate a *dialogue des sourds*. The British and U.S. governments, by 1943 at least, viewed strategic bombing as complementary to the invasion of continental Europe. In contrast, RAF Bomber Command and the USAAF's Eighth Air Force believed that they could win the war on their own. Hence, in this latter view, the bombing of U-boat pens on the Bay of Biscay and an interdiction campaign against the French railroads necessarily were classified as a dispersion of scarce effort.

At a high level of guidance, system can be introduced into strategy to enforce concentration upon the most important goals. But, time and again, system in strategy has proven to be inadequate in the face of prior and irretrievable errors in high policy (e.g., preparation only for a short war, as in the German and Japanese cases in World War II), as well as in the face of enemies whose military performance is materially so well backed that standard tenets of sound strategic practice scarcely apply. The Anglo-American conduct of World War II, with Germany massively distracted in the East, came to approximate this case. The Allies, and the United States virtually alone in the Pacific war, committed egregious strategic errors—but so did the enemy (as always), and the Allies were sufficiently well-endowed materially that even errors could be turned to advantage (as in the strategic mismanagement of the Pacific war, with the lack of unity of command).

Game theoretical constructs are of very limited utility as education for uncertainty. But there is some value in the minimax principle, in recognition of the worst that the enemy might do and identification of the best strategy to limit damage in such an event. Training and the doctrine on which it is based must help provide the self-confidence that is necessary for effective action in the uniquely stressful context of war.

Similarly, courage can be institutionalized to a degree by discipline and by the determination in mutual aid which is fostered by the cohesion of small groups in combat. Creativity in execution of mission-oriented orders by tactical units well schooled in suitable drills, when directed by a higher command that is firm of appropriate purpose, is the path that should produce superior combat effectiveness—always provided that the human "sharp end" of tactics is willing to fight to the death. With reference to the institutionalization of courageous behavior, it is interesting to note that a major study of the reasons for the tactical effectiveness of the British Royal Navy in the classic age of "fighting sail" isolated the superior staunchness of gun crews in serving their pieces in prolonged engagements, and the superior determination to fight *typically* demonstrated by British, in contrast to French, officers. When equipment, nautical skills, and orders of battle were approximately equal, the tactical edge to overcome the uncertainties of combat was conferred by a conception of duty flogged into the lower deck, and internalized by officers, which accepted all the hazards of battle unto death in obedience to revered standards of expected behavior.

It should be noted that just as the fog of war and the uncertainties of conflict cannot be cleared or resolved at a stroke by the shining light of Historical Truth, neither can they be dispersed by magical application of Strategy. The disease of a talismanic "strategism" has spread noticeably in recent years.[9] Consider the following words uttered by Representative Ike Skelton:

> The American fighting man—not to mention the millions of Vietnamese who now live under communist rule—was let down by a lack of strategic thinking on the part of military and civilian leaders alike [true enough: CSG]. . . . Well-meaning people who devoted untold hours of hard work at the White House, the Pentagon, the State Department and, yes, in Congress too, simply did not piece together the right strategy at the beginning of the war to ensure victory.[10]

Representative Skelton evidently believes that the uncertainties of war can be overcome reliably by the piecing together of "the right strategy" which will "*ensure* victory." However, there may not be a right strategy for victory in all circumstances; even if there is, it may not be compatible with U.S. political culture; and even if the right strategy can be identified and explained and applied in terms that are sufficiently American, it may fail at the sharp end in tactical application. Victory in war can never truly be assured, by strategy or anything else. Skelton's voice was the voice of Jomini.

Why did the United States wage the wrong war in Vietnam? This is not to prejudge the critical issue of whether or not there was a right war that U.S. political culture would have sanctioned for very long. The central, indeed overriding, error in U.S. policy (from which many, though certainly not all, subsequent mistakes in strategy, operations, and tactics flowed) in Vietnam was of the same character as the Japanese error in 1941. Washington, as had Tokyo, fundamentally misread the nature of the war upon which it was choosing to embark, and hence—inevitably—it designed a theory of victory for that war which could not succeed. In common with the Japanese, or even with the Carthaginians in their struggle with Rome, the United States believed mistakenly that its enemy could be brought to a favorable negotiated settlement as a result of suffering incremental military (and other) pain. Some of the critics of U.S. military performance in Vietnam, recognizing that the United States did not find and apply the right strategy, have overstepped the mark by implying that strategy—like tactics—is a craft which can be taught, learned, and applied by those skilled in its ways. Unlike an infantry company with regard to tactics, a country cannot be drilled into right thinking on strategy. U.S. culture, among other factors, stood between Washington and victory in Vietnam. It was grimly ironic that in 1968–70 the war against the Vietcong was indeed won, but this victory was lost because it was achieved too late and was overmatched strategically by the persisting U.S. failure to wage war effectively against North Vietnam.

THE SEARCH FOR CONFIDENCE

War planning, in its modern sense of the preparation and continuous updating of contingency plans in time of peace, was created by the general staffs founded in the nineteenth century by the continental European powers in order to cope with the novel complexities of industrial-age warfare. Among many functions, war planning may be thought of as a quest for confidence in the face of uncertainty. A quest for confidence through detailed war planning can assume pathological proportions and find expression in the belief that victory truly can be organized and orchestrated reliably in advance. Substantial misreading of the conduct and misconduct of the Austro-Prussian and Franco-Prussian wars encouraged that fallacy. However, those wars—particularly the Franco-Prussian—did demonstrate that competent staff work in mobilization planning could be a decisive factor when the enemy lacked that advantage. But even excellent staff work may be wasted if the missions assigned the armed forces are beyond their strength or are substantially irrelevant, or worse, to the purposes of the war as a whole.

Good staff work, like good military strategy (which effects a close fit between means and ends), is always important; indeed they both tend to be necessary conditions for success. But neither activity, no matter how well conducted, assuredly will be a sufficient condition for victory. The Pearl Harbor attack of December 7, 1941, was a military masterpiece in operational conception and in most aspects of tactical execution—though there should have been a follow-up strike to attack the oil-storage depots—but was a grand-strategic and policy catastrophe. Furthermore, brilliant execution of the wrong strategy almost invariably is an error that cannot be retrieved. The invasion of North Korea in the fall of 1950 was sufficiently thorough in the depth of its penetration—to the Yalu River in the west and to the Chosin Reservoir in the east—so as to render extrication under unexpected Chinese assault exceedingly difficult. Great but incomplete success (U.N. forces deep in North Korea, the German army on the Volga) has a way of punishing the partial victor both for his having exceeded the culminating point of limited victory and for his failure to reach the culminating point of thorough success.

Neither material damage nor casualties are inflicted simply for their own sakes. The punishment of a military machine or of a society is undertaken and executed for a purpose. Rarely, as in World War II, is the objective the definitive overthrow of the enemy's military power and political system. More commonly the policy object in war is to persuade an enemy that the costs of further combat outweigh the probable gains and that therefore it should settle for a negotiated outcome at least minimally tolerable for all principal belligerents. In theory at least, the extent and intensity of armed conflict should reflect the extent and intensity of the political interests in contention. But in practice statesmen are not always adept at forecasting the kind of war which they will unleash. The problem lies both with the dynamics of combat—the process of conflict may subsume and transcend original political intentions—and with the fact, so uncomfortable for theories of unilateral action, that war is an interactive phenomenon.

It might be an educational experience for U.S. defense planners today to visit the assumptions and expectations which were expressed in the war plans of all major belligerents in 1914 and 1939–41. The purpose would not be to seek possible parallels in detail for today, but rather to widen awareness of just how wrong careful defense professionals can be, and to provide some general pointers to the basis for sound predictions (who guessed correctly in 1914 and 1939– and why?). There is no small danger that the Western Alliance, in common with all the belligerents in 1914 and with the Axis powers in 1939–41, might find in the event of actual conflict that it had prepared for the wrong war. The nuclear fact, and the dominance of that fact in the peacetime calculations of NATO, probably enhances rather than reduces the possibility of surprise on a quite heroic scale.

The Combined Bomber Offensive of World War II and the belated, if periodically very successful, German defense against it provide a particularly rich haul of material on the subjects of strategic and tactical surprise. Those surprises pertain to Hitler, who did not expect the CBO to be waged at all, or if waged, not to be waged effectively; to the allied "bomber generals" who believed that they could preclude the need for an invasion of Europe (for all save mopping up and occupation duties); and to the stronger critics of strategic bombing who concluded mistakenly that the CBO was a strategic failure.

Morale and its close concomitant, "fighting spirit," also can be a source of confidence for a military establishment which eschews very detailed planning. For example, the French army launched its conscript masses at the German frontier in August 1914 on the basis of only a notional "plan" (Plan XVII) of attack. French generals reposed their confidence in the *élan vital* or *furia Francesa* which it was believed had produced the victories of the First Republic and of the first Napoleon. Fighting spirit is not necessarily synonymous with military prowess, but enthusiasm, particularly if multiplied by a great numerical advantage, may substitute for skill (as the U.S. Army demonstrated in its important contribution to the allied victory in 1918).

It is a quirk of human nature, or perhaps a conceit of all polities, to endorse the syllogism that virtuous causes are victorious; our cause is virtuous; therefore we must be victorious. However, cynicism aside, there is some arguable merit in the proposition that armies which are seriously infected with the bacillus of doubt about the justness of their cause lose fighting power as a consequence. A necessary caveat is the obvious point that war supremely is the realm of the morally and politically relative. Whatever the true relevance for combat effectiveness of foxhole-level belief in the justness of a conflict, there are no important modern exceptions known to this author of the rule that governments work energetically to legitimize particular wars in the minds of their citizen soldiers. Professional soldiers (and certainly true mercenaries) are presumed to be willing to fight hard for reasons of professional pride, comradeship, the "honor of the regiment," careers, and the like. But civilians wrenched from their homes to put their lives on the line are presumed to require some extraordinary measure of motivation. To be confident that the "soldiers" in a mass army of citizens-in-uniform are prepared, on a high average, to acquiesce (if not be enthusiastic) in the situations of absurdly high risk in which they may find themselves, demonization of the enemy typically has been believed to be expedient (though rarely effective or credible to the fighting men).

Above the universals of human behavior and motivation at the sharpest tactical end of war, every combatant country has demonstrated the distinctiveness of its political culture in the specific character of the propaganda which it has addressed to its own troops. The point of importance here is that politicians, unlike some theorists of strategy (particularly if they are civilian), generally understand that people matter most. The manifold uncertainties of war cannot usefully be resolved, or insured against, by sound strategy, appropriate tactics, and an abundance of good equipment if the human instrument of decision is not motivated to fight and, if need be, to die. Arguably, a deficiency of such motivation may ultimately have proved fatal for the political cause of the Confederate States of America, for example—too few Southerners were prepared to pay the price of independence[11]—and it could have proved fatal for Britain and the United States in World War II, had not geostrategic and material conditions been so favorably aligned for them. With some exceptions, the Anglo-American-Canadian armies in 1944–45 could proceed cautiously to inevitable victory, without a requirement for extraordinary sacrifice.[12] Even today, so many years after the event, many scholars are uncomfortable with the well-attested fact that Nazi ideology had a strongly positive influence upon the fighting power of German soldiers.

Historically, certainly in recent times, those countries which have placed very heavy reliance upon the military prowess of an elite warrior caste have been undone by the related facts of attrition and the duration of war. The harboring of great confidence in the combat skills of an elite is appropriate if a country can be really confident that war will be short. Unfortunately for the warrior-elite school of thought on military excellence, in a long war combat accomplishment tends to even out among belligerents, as the cadre of superbly trained professionals falls in battle and cannot be replaced under the exigencies of war. Experience reveals that a focus upon the prowess of the individual warrior tends to be accompanied by some disdain for mere technological excellence (men over machines, and so forth).

Both Germany and Japan exalted the military prowess of carefully trained modern "knights" (particularly in their air forces). Both nations had theories of (short) war which were not so much guided by a prudent statecraft as promoted by a very imprudent statecraft which refused to consider unwelcome possibilities. Ignoring the uncertainties of war, Berlin and Tokyo chose to believe that the military aristocracies of machine-age warfare could, through quality of inspired performance, preclude the necessity for the waging of mass warfare on the rejected model of 1914–18. Some of the leading Western theorists of armored and aerial warfare encouraged this fallacy. In the case of the Third Reich, it is accurate to say that a war of attrition was waged with armed forces trained and equipped (very imperfectly) for a war of "relational-maneuver."[13] If the enemy has the means to indulge a brute-force economic view of war, as the Germans and Japanese discovered in the Western (and Eastern) Allies, then the odds in combat simply are loaded too heavily against the declining ranks of once-superior warriors.

It is probably true to argue that a national preference for quality over quantity of combat power inclines a country's leaders to gamble on swift success while the elite military instrument remains relatively sharp and bright. On at least three critical occasions in the twentieth century to date, such gambles have effected the ruin of a nation's prospects in war: specifically, for Germany in 1918 and 1941, and for Japan in 1941–42. However, it has to be recognized that culture and geopolitics restricted very severely the range of choice for Germany and Japan in those fatal periods.

War begun in confident expectation of swift victory can explode into a global conflict for which the war-initiating country is not equipped and for which it has no theory of victory. Furthermore, a country or coalition confined to continental campaigning, almost no matter how brilliantly conducted, finds itself at a growing, and eventually fatal, disadvantage if the center of gravity of the enemy coalition is offshore. For confidence in victory, indeed for a competent theory of war, there have to be strategic designs and a suitable tactical fighting instrument capable of breaking the enemy on its primary terms of geostrategic reference. As Donald Kagan has written of Sparta and Athens:

> To win, each had to acquire the capacity to fight and succeed on the other's favorite domain. The Athenian defeat in Sicily [the great expedition to Syracuse, 415–413 B.C.] gave the Spartans the opportunity to succeed by making an alliance with Persia. After many failures, they won the war by defeating the Athenian fleet. There was no other way to win. To win a true victory rather than a Periclean stand-off, the Athenians would have had to find a way to defeat the Spartans on land.[14]

In common with surprise, fighting spirit, and military skill, in principle there is a great deal to be said in favor of superior technology and secret weapons (or of familiar weapons employed in surprising ways). The problem is one of balance. Genuine sub-optimization on any of the elements just mentioned can come with a heavy price tag. For example, emphasis upon achievement of a technological edge tends to be paid for in the coin of short production runs of new equipment. Short production runs entail the forgoing of the economies of scale that accrue from large-scale acquisition of well-tested weapons: moreover, those well-tested weapons probably would have been good enough.

The errors in high policy which align politically too few friendly elements against too large an enemy coalition naturally reinforce the drive to seek salvation in quality rather than in mass (since, plainly, mass is a systemic advantage enjoyed by the materially better endowed enemy). Indeed those high-policy errors have a way of generating desperate tactical and operational conditions. The lengthening of adverse quantitative ratios on the battlefield inexorably promotes a quest after qualitative equalizers (e.g., the supertank which can do the job of ten, or twenty, or thirty lesser supertanks, and the like). This search for equipment equalizers, while sensible in principle, in practice disperses scarce scientific-industrial assets, leads to the production of handfuls of technically unreliable prototype "superweapons," and generally accelerates unfavorable terms in the combat equation. (As Karl Marx observed, quantity becomes quality, or has a quality all its own.)

A familiar anticipatory response to the uncertainties of war is heavy investment in control networks of all kinds in the realm of command. Again in principle, the quest for reliable information and greater certainty in the mechanics of command is beyond reproach. However, the practice of the search for confidence through the sure feasibility of command and control easily can degenerate into an end in and of itself. That which is possible by way of reporting has a way of being demanded, whether or not such reporting is militarily useful where it matters.

Enemy perceptions of political determination generally are more important for deterrence than is military muscle per se. Unfortunately for economical theories of stable deterrence, however, a putative enemy's perception cannot reliably be manipulated at will. Furthermore, one cannot advance political determination as a certain formula for policy success, since human and bureaucratic factors may well operate to vitiate the effectiveness of the formula in practice. Perceptions of determination are the product of reputations earned. An ounce of political courage may well be worth a pound of military muscle, but an enemy is more likely to grant credit for courage if it judges courage to have a substantial material basis, as well as an undeniable history.

Moreover, deterrence, although logically superior to defense (it is far preferable to deter war than to wage it, albeit to an eventual successful outcome), cannot be accorded an absolute first priority.

There can be no certainty that deterrence will work forever. Should deterrence fail, prowess in actual defense would assume an immediate importance with which peacetime theorists of stability have great difficulty empathizing. For example, multitiered strategic defenses (*après* the total vision of the SDI) capable of reducing dramatically the extent to which the United States is at nuclear risk—say, from thousands of warheads, as today, perhaps to tens of warheads—should translate into the practical difference between a history-arresting cataclysm and an unprecedentedly painful catastrophe.[15]

Three points stand out from this analysis. First, one must beware of the popular fallacy which attributes a hoped-for effect to the intended cause. In other words, one should not refer to "the nuclear deterrent." Whether or not nuclear weapons deter is a matter to be resolved only in the minds of Soviet leaders and the processes of Soviet government. Second, although the uncertainties of deterrence in the future cannot reliably be removed by investment in military muscle, there is a connection between the development of military power and the likelihood that an enemy will choose to be deterred. Third, whether or not that enemy is deterred, relative military prowess is inherently important, always remembering that prior to trial by combat there can be no truly reliable guesstimating as to the military (combat) balance. One cannot be certain, really certain that is, that the U.S. strategic forces' triad maintained today, and planned for tomorrow, could bear all of the deterrence traffic that might be asked of it. There is just no way in which the vagaries of human nature and of decision-making under stress can be sidestepped entirely through the provision of military power. Even if the United States had purchased the services of a strategic arsenal twice as large and twice as diverse as is the case, there could be a Soviet leader who either was quite literally beyond deterrence, or who was persuadable by clever briefers that a command decapitation first strike for a cheap victory was feasible.

The above unlikely possibilities do not mean that improvements at the margin in military strength are not worth having. What those possibilities do mean is that absolute safety from aggression cannot be secured through defense budgetary largesse. If it is an error to place too much confidence in military strength, it is a yet greater error to believe that the (so-called) arms-control process can foster a more predictable and much safer future. Arms control figures prominently in the public relations of international security, but there is no historical evidence to suggest that arms-control agreements can encourage a predictability in rival military accomplishments helpful for the prevention of war. The reasons are not hard to locate: authoritarian powers cheat; advances in military technology (or in civilian technology with military applicability) cannot be proscribed; and arms control in general addresses (incompetently, for systemic reasons) only the symptoms, and not the causes, of international insecurity. By far the most ubiquitous and damaging deficiency in defense preparation is the disinclination, or even inability, to conduct "Red Team" analyses honestly and competently. Orthodox alleged certainties abound as a consequence of this deficiency, and they can work so as to overstate or understate the likely adequacy of national and allied defense efforts.

More attention needs to be paid to the twin factors of chance and uncertainty, and how they influence the choices that planners make and the advice that politicians receive and accept. Every country has careerist defense specialists, in and out of uniform, eager to tell policymakers what they want to hear. The case for 132 stealthy B-2 bombers in good part comes down to the prudence in making it that much more difficult for some military briefer in Moscow to persuade political leaders that victory is possible—in a political context wherein those leaders may be desperate to hear a plausible theory of victory.

Fighting power for optimum deterrent effect and, if need be, effectiveness in combat cannot reliably be engineered. Nations and their armed forces do not collapse when they have suffered some magic fraction of damage, just as the combat potential of a military unit cannot be calculated precisely. When morale is sufficiently high, units can perform quite extraordinary feats.[16]

Yet the engineering approach to war is imbued with the ethos which believes that victory can be planned with the precision, the material certainty, with which a bridge or a dam can be constructed or destroyed. A classic example of the engineering approach was the confident calculation by the USAAF War Plan Divisions that the nine selected major German target systems could be destroyed by *precisely* 66,045 sorties, while the parallel Japanese target systems would require 51,480 sorties.[17] This example points up the problem of strategy to which Clausewitz referred. Specifically: "Combat is conducted with physical weapons, and although the intellect does play a part, material factors will dominate. But when one comes to the *effect* of the engagement, when material successes turn into motives for further action, the intellect alone is decisive. In brief, *tactics* will present far fewer difficulties to the theorist than will strategy."[18] In other words, the strategist is concerned with the consequences of engagements, battles, or even of whole campaigns, for further terms of engagement in and the course and outcome of a war.

Modern U.S. defense history is sadly replete with examples of an inappropriate engineering approach to war. Some of the logistical influence upon allied strategy for the invasion of France and upon the plans for subsequent exploitation out of the beachhead is a plain example. Moreover, the contemporary defense debate is pervaded with the engineering mentality. The application of firepower against targets is equated with general strategic results, just as the armed forces, even weapons, are confused with their hoped-for effect in deterrence.

When it is not simply foolish (not to say morally insensitive), much of the quantification that accompanies presentations on strategic nuclear warfare, and particularly on strategic stability, tends to illustrate a very truncated view of warfare. SIOP-RISOP "exchanges" on the truly grand scale do not warrant description as war at all.[19] But what is of strategic interest is how the disciplined, purposive pursuit of a counterforce campaign should advance the likelihood of achievement of U.S. policy goals. Theoretical draw-down curves for sundry figures of merit, though worthy of receipt with much skepticism (like the 66,045 sorties), have to provide important data for the subsequent assessment of the strategic meaning of operations for the course and outcome of a war. At the present time, counterforce exchange modeling tends to persist in lacking necessary strategic and political overlays. In short, given the admittedly arguable outcome of a missile duel, what happens next and what does it mean? Often the listener is left with the conviction that the briefer has awarded a victory on points to one side or the other and that somehow, mysteriously, the United States or the U.S.S.R. therefore wins.

The supremely technical character of strategic-missile warfare lends itself uniquely to analytical capture by the engineering spirit. As a nation of problem-solving engineers—to venture only a slight exaggeration—Americans are particularly vulnerable to low-level analyses of military action masquerading, albeit innocently, as strategic analysis. Ironically, the disorderly process of defense policy- (and budget-) making in a democracy provides some protection against the damage that the engineering approach to defense could wreak via a much less politically trammeled executive branch of government. Americans know and listen to expert-specialists, particularly technical expert-specialists. To be expert on defense matters in the United States carries the implication that one has deduced, or could deduce, the correct solutions to problems. (What else can "expert" connote?) This definition of expertness necessarily carries the assumption that problems have solutions. Advice, to sound expert in American culture, needs to be exact rather than vague. If outcomes cannot be calculated, make the numbers up!

In contrast to (tactical) operations analysis, systems analysis inherently is "soft" because of the arguable parameters of the subjects at issue. That which is militarily most efficient on some criteria important for the peacetime maintenance of forces may not be militarily most effective for the deterrence of putative enemies, the sustenance of political determination on the part of allies, or in the actual conduct of war. For example, in the absence of an active enemy it is economically and administratively efficient to centralize command arrangements and logistical provision. But in the face of an enemy looking for military vulnerabilities, concentrated assets carry the promise of functioning as targets quite extraordinarily rewarding to assault with modest force. Further, it is common knowledge and entirely noncontroversial to claim that long familiarity among men in small units is the glue of cohesion under the stress of combat. But, notwithstanding this fact, the U.S. Army, for excellent reasons of peacetime readiness (on some nominal figure of merit), persists with the personnel policy of individual rather than unit replacement. It is difficult to resist the conclusion that the army is not coming to grips with the likely scale and character of its combat problems. In World War II, Korea, and Vietnam, the individual replacement system, though harmful to effectiveness at the sharp end of war, was more than neutralized in the damage that it caused by the generally favorable context of the fighting. But, in a World War III the U.S Army may find itself by analogy in the familiar German tactical and operational bind, of attempting to do too much with too little, where its own combat effectiveness on the ground may literally be critical to the strategic outcome.

Stridency and arrogance in contemporary public debate might usefully be diminished were all schools of thought to recognize the implications of the fact that a World War III today is only hypothetical: it is strictly a closed book with respect to *reliable knowledge* of the most likely circumstances of its outbreak, its course, and its outcome. Public discussion of leading defense questions—on the SDI, on NATO defense, on the utility of offensively cast naval operations, on satellite survivability, and the like—substantially is undisciplined by the modesty in prediction and prescription which a careful reading of military history should encourage. The historical record, even that accessible through living participants, is littered with failed theories of war, incompetent doctrines of war, deficient tactical nostrums, and hastily improvised adjustments in near real time to unexpected circumstances.

THE ART OF THE POSSIBLE

There is something to be said for the view that strategy is not the job of the soldier. So important and pervasive in their implications are the political objectives for which war is waged that the selection of campaign objectives with reference to the course of a war as a whole is more properly a political than a military function. But this is only a half-truth at best. Politicians are at least as prone to neglect critical issues of military practicality in their grand designs as generals are to neglect the political purposes for which battles and campaigns are waged at all. Not infrequently, in practice, one finds politicians playing inexpertly at being soldiers and soldiers playing inexpertly at being politicians. Field Marshal Sir Archibald Wavell once noted that the mark of the amateur in military affairs is a concentration upon strategy, while a mark of the professional is a concentration upon logistics, or, more broadly, upon what he termed the "mechanism of war."[20]

Judgment on operational feasibility, *le sens du practicable,* is the realm of the military professional. It is the duty of the military professional to seek to create and adapt means and methods for the accomplishment of objectives identified as necessary or desirable by policy. But it is no less a part of that duty to educate policymakers to the bounds of the militarily feasible within the material and political constraints set from on high, before a march of adverse military events effects such education for them.

Vietnam was a plain case of reciprocal failure: of failure by policymakers to set political goals which were achievable by the military means and methods available and usable; and of failure by the military establishment to explain honestly what could and could not be done with the military instrument that the U.S. body politic was prepared to countenance in action in the region. The point is not that the Joint Chiefs of Staff (JCS) neglected to tell President Lyndon Johnson how the war could best be waged (in fact that is not true), but rather that they acquiesced in a theory of war which they either knew, or should have known, could not bring success. American strategy in Vietnam surrendered the initiative to the enemy. It would seem to have been the case that although the JCS recognized very clearly how restricting was the policy guidance for the war, still they could not bring themselves to believe that the United States could fail in its mission.

For a much clearer example, recent scholarship on German military planning for the invasion of Russia in 1941 reveals unequivocally that the professionals on the General Staff were at least as much to blame for the means-ends, strategic and operational catastrophe that was to be the *Barbarossa* plan as was Adolf Hitler. "Drunk with victory" in the summer of 1940 following the unexpectedly cheap success against a much overrated France, the German generals did nothing to discourage the Fuehrer from pursuing his intention of resolving Germany's continental problems in a definitive fashion in 1941.[21] The German army's invasion of Russia in 1941, as with Napoleon's, was a logistical impossibility—at least with the operational style and fluctuation in choice of objectives of the invasion—given the near total absence of tracked supply vehicles capable of moving through the mud which dominates the Russian fall.

In Clausewitz's day it was still just about feasible for political authority and supreme *operational* military command to be combined in the same person: witness Napoleon, and earlier Frederick the Great, as warlord. The best one can say of "warlordism" in the twentieth century is that its record of accomplishment is a distinctly checkered one, with the column of negative examples being led by Erich Ludendorff and Adolf Hitler. As heads of state, Frederick the Great and Napoleon understood their military instrument in ways unapproachable by a contemporary U.S. or Soviet political leader. Indeed, for reasons of rapidity of technological change against the backcloth of a long peace, it is probably true to claim that few if any military professionals in the superpowers have a secure and reliable level of understanding of the military potential for decision of the military instruments which they command. That is not a criticism; it is just an unavoidable fact of life in peacetime.

The perspectives, as with the expertise, of the policymaker are different from those of the military professional and can be in a condition of some tension with them. The politician today typically has taken very much to heart Georges Clemenceau's aphorism that "war is too important to be left to the generals." Tension can arise when politicians want their military instrument to be used in ways which affront military common sense and prospective efficiency in action. Political responsiveness can mean military vulnerability. For excellent reasons, politicians do not want themselves to be the functional prisoners of military drills in time of crisis or war. Politicians like to send political messages by military means. This is particularly true in an era when military action alone is unlikely to be able to deliver a tolerable victory, since a superpower enemy cannot reliably be disarmed by timely preventive or preemptive action. As a consequence too little force may be applied too late against an enemy who adheres to a more classical style of warfare. In short, military incrementalism may express well the policy logic of a war from the perspective of one side's politicians; but it can fare very badly in the face of an enemy who believes that the grammar of war requires timely application of the time-hallowed principles of concentration and economy of force.

For reasons of their training and responsibilities, politicians are inclined to approach the use of armed force in two ways, neither of which prepares them well for enduring problems in the conduct of war. On the one hand, they are inclined to view the military instrument almost entirely as a manipulable tool for signaling in a context of crisis management. Crisis management is not to be despised, though it can be greatly overblown as an applicable skill-set or technique. As arms competition in the modern world is a partial substitute for war, so military posturing in time of crisis can be a surrogate of display with tests of nerve and will in lieu of combat. However, statecraft for the waging of acute crisis is distinct from, though obviously related to, strategy for the conduct of war. For example, crisis management which fails to arrest a slide to war may leave military assets grossly maldeployed for trial by combat (carrier task forces in the eastern Mediterranean, to cite but one case). On the other hand, politicians are wont to treat war as a "black box," mysterious in its inner wiring, yet which can be trusted to solve a problem unyielding to the nonlethal instruments of grand strategy on terms tolerably compatible with society's peacetime ordering of its values. Admittedly, *nuclear* war of course is known well in advance to be vastly impolitic and inexpedient a course of action, but this has served, if anything, to exacerbate rather than ease some key tensions between policymaker and military professional.

Although nothing fully can substitute for (survivable) experience of war in promoting military effectiveness, the pace of adaptation to the novel exigencies of combat is related to the quality and quantity of peacetime defense establishments. Hence, the domestic political effectiveness of the armed services in peacetime is a variable critical for crisis and early wartime performance. But the authority with which military professionals can argue their budgetary case tends to diminish with the passage of time from past victories. The disappearance from the scene of those authentic military heroes whose personal credentials lend legitimacy to arguments which rest ultimately upon appeals to the wisdom in professional military judgment weakens the authority of that judgment in debates over resource allocation for defense. In the last quarter of the twentieth century, the long peace and absence of recent victories of real note even in the conflicts which have interrupted that peace have rendered the U.S. defense debate thoroughly bereft of distinguished military figures who can act as "policemen" for strategic common sense. If nuclear dread sensibly must pervade most defense questions which bear upon East-West relations, what is the scope for professional military advice? Is a military person, *qua* a military person, more expert on nuclear war, let alone on matters of (nuclear) deterrence, than a civilian? The answer plainly is no.

The war planner is not a seeker after philosophical truth, after the right way to accomplish a mission in some absolute sense. Instead, he is obliged to plan how to fight today's forces as effectively as possible in attempted fulfillment of strategic tasks specified by higher authority. Some of the public debate that purports to be about strategy really is about truth in strategy (which may or may not have practical implications). For example, the average university audience does not respond warmly to having its attention drawn to the positive, or even simply the inevitable, roles of nuclear weapons in national security affairs. Nonetheless, such an audience, if coaxed empathetically, generally will recognize that the weapons cannot be abolished, that there has to be some plan for their contingent employment, and that *all* strategies are war-fighting strategies. Furthermore, such an audience tends to respond quite well to reasoned presentation of the inalienable dilemmas and duties of the responsible official. In short, one can invent a better world wherein there is no need for strategy to govern nuclear weapons, and one may choose to be agnostic as to its prospects for eventual realization. But, currently, nuclear weapons have well-established functions in a security system which has kept the peace between the superpowers for more than forty years.

That which is possible in strategy is a function of many interacting elements, prominent among which are time, space, and political determination. Properly crafted, U.S. grand strategy might carry the credible promise (for deterrence) of being able to ensure that time would be available in war for the mobilization potential of the West to become a materially overwhelming reality, or nightmare, for Soviet defense planners. In the likely absence of a decisive strategic nuclear advantage that a U.S. President would be willing to employ for compellent duties, the Western Alliance would require that U.S. nuclear forces deter Soviet nuclear use, and that the seas be commanded for the tolerably free movement of men and material in bulk. Although strategy is the art of the possible, that should translate into the art of the tactically and operationally possible, guided as to priorities for the allocation of scarce men and material by a theory of war informed by policy choice. Ahead of a real trial "in the field," one cannot demonstrate beyond all doubt that this or that operational objective is capable of seizure at a reasonable cost: indeed, given the vast complexity of modern warfare there is ample fuel for extravagant hopes, just as there is for deep pessimism. Military history shows time and again that particular military instruments have accomplished that which expert analysis had deemed impracticable (the introduction of the convoy system in 1917, the wholesale unraveling of the Anglo-French military position in May 1940). On other occasions that which was predicted to be eminently feasible turned out to be wholly impracticable (the defeat of the French army in six weeks in 1914, the seizure of Caen on D-Day and subsequent rapid exploitation into open country, the conduct in 1943 and 1944 of daylight bombing at high altitude without long-range fighter escort).

In part, though only in part, because of nuclear weapons, *grande guerre* is not what once it was—an instrument useful as the court of last appeal for decision. Among the pervasive problems for the war planner today is the need to identify strategic objectives attainable by military means and methods suitable for the securing of a better than Pyrrhic, radioactive victory. If strategy as a subject for study is a search for knowledge useful to those who must practice the art of the possible (and, in a democracy, those who comment on that practice), what is possible in a nuclear context? On both the left and the right of the political spectrum in Western countries there are radical urges to pursue a disarmament path which would take a meat ax to strategic paradox. A very bold and certainly well-intentioned interest in complete nuclear disarmament united President Reagan at the Reykjavik Summit of 1986 with Jonathan Schell and his scheme for "The Abolition."[22] The strategic paradox referred to here is the fact that the nuclear weapons which render *grande guerre* so difficult an enterprise to plan in reasonable hope of securing advantage are the very weapons which have underwritten the long peace since 1945.

There should be a permanent dialogue among policy, strategy, and the tactical means which implement the great designs of state. Hitler's vague dreams of a thousand-year Reich, married to vastly insufficient grand-strategic assets, is but an extreme example of a very familiar phenomenon—a mismatch between means and ends. Had Hitler been the bold warlord that he pretended to be, almost certainly he could have taken Britain out of the war in 1940 and thereby given himself a reasonable prospect of establishing at least a multidecade Reich. The U.S.S.R. might have been defeated by a Germany undistracted in the West, though the Wehrmacht's casual approach to logistics inclines one to be doubtful. Because it lacked geostrategic access, the United States could not have intervened in the war in Europe even had it wished to do so.

Historically speaking, policy imagination has failed the military instrument at least as often as vice versa. In the winter of 1940–41, Germany almost certainly could have coerced Spain into acquiescing in the passage of Axis forces and could have closed the western, and eventually probably the whole, Mediterranean to British power and influence.[23] The results may or may not have been decisive, but they would have helped Germany's bid to establish a defensible perimeter in the west and south. Similarly, had Japan seized Ceylon early in 1942, instead of merely conducting a raid, the geostrategic prospects for Germany—and prospectively, *ab extensio,* for Japan also—could have brightened dramatically. More recently, the inviolability of North Vietnamese and Laotian territory against seizure and occupation was a huge mistake in U.S. policy, because it freed Hanoi from the need to detain a large fraction of its army for home defense. Mindlessly faithful to the foolish Law of Recent Precedent, the U.S. government in the 1960s was determined not to repeat the error committed in the fall of 1950 with the invasion of communist territory on the border of China.

There is something to be said for the traditional German view that strategy is the product of tactical opportunism and feasibility as demonstrated by flexibly exercised forces. However, there is even more to be said against the German view (and German practice), with the evidence of German strategic malpractice in two world wars as persuasive witnesses for the prosecution. Real-time agility, or the ability to improvise in the face of ever-changing circumstances, plainly is a military virtue. But the corresponding vice of this virtue is that pragmatism may utterly overcome and substitute for principle in strategic direction. In that situation the armed forces attempt to accomplish whatever appears fleetingly to be possible, or whatever the shifting fashion in opinion among policymakers deems attractive. Some methods in the conduct of war may be pragmatically convenient but nonetheless strategically very inadvisable. For example, theorists and planners for air and missile power, as well as for sea power, have to remember that although there can be exceptions (Japan in 1945), the surest way to effect the political changes sought by the use of force is to have well-armed friendly elements on the local scene. In the words of J. C. Wylie, "The ultimate determinant in war is the man on the scene with a gun."[24] A clinching policy and strategic argument against the proposition that Germany should be bombed into defeat by the RAF and the USAAF, even had that been tactically feasible, was that such a Western military method would have guaranteed that the Red Army would inherit the continental rubble.

All organizations benefit from planning, though the process of planning usually is more valuable than are the details in the plans that are produced. Through planning, goals are set and the means and methods identified necessary for achievement of the goals. However, goals may have to be reset as circumstances evolve. Defense planning in peacetime can be considerably more durable in authority than planning in wartime, but the oscillatory style between surge and coast in the level of the U.S. defense effort renders truly long-range planning a vastly uncertain enterprise. Furthermore, if one must invent guidelines to goals for a period ten to twenty years hence, sweeping educated guesses have to be made about the possible maturing of new technologies. In truth one never really plans for the long term. What one does is identify desirable trends and, hopefully, understand better the legacy value of today's decisions for decisions on capability that might be taken and sought many years in the future. Both strategic and technological concepts should help educate the long-range planner. He must have some preferences concerning what U.S. strategic offensive forces, for example, ought to be able to accomplish ten to twenty years hence, as well as more than a notional acquaintance with what should be technologically feasible.

Planning can become talismanic in function, and particular plans historically have come to assume a life and even an authority all their own. From time to time planners may need to be reminded that a plan is a living design in the service of policy. There have been occasions when planning staffs have conspired to protect *The Plan* from potential mishandling on the part of politicians or of soldiers willing to be unduly responsive to the anxieties or transient wishes of fearful politicians.

Force planning, the bedrock of operational planning, is notoriously difficult to conduct in peacetime in a manner readily defensible in the face of skepticism. As a general rule the professional military planner will not know long in advance when war will come. Moreover, the policymakers for a superpower with global interests may not be able to provide policy guidance of a very useful kind for the military planner, at least outside the dominant scenario which long has centered on the defense of Western Europe. If a country's force planners surge too early in the procurement of new equipment, they will find themselves in the event of war in the condition of the Italian and German air forces in World War II—condemned to wage war with increasingly obsolescent equipment (with the exception of the jet-propelled Me 262, of course).[25] Alternatively, if war comes sooner than expected the armed forces may be embarrassed for a while with a gross shortage of up-to-date equipment and in the midst of a wrenching reorganization (the situation of the Soviet Union in 1941).

With the exception of their strategic nuclear forces, the superpowers today do not maintain fully war-ready military postures in time of peace. It is a trivially obvious point to observe that the United States, for example, has foreign security commitments considerably in excess of its actual military power. Force planning in peacetime for wartime must reflect a theory of war and identify the critical paths to acquire the means necessary to realize some approximation of that theory in practice. As operational designs for war cannot confidently be planned in detail long in advance, so neither can force levels and support services of all kinds reliably be specified. However, a general idea of how the war will be waged, and how the enemy is to be beaten—while recognizing the monumental uncertainties of the enterprise—or perhaps how much beating the enemy may require if he is to come to acceptable terms, has to frame the detailed guidance to the military planner. For example, a war plan worthy of the name for NATO should be drafted in recognition that two theories of victory are wholly impracticable. First, although the Soviet Union assuredly could be beaten through the agency of a wholesale nuclear assault, Soviet nuclear retaliation could not reliably be suppressed to a level compatible with a reasonable definition of Western success. Second, as Clausewitz recognized, "Russia is not a country that can be formally conquered—that is to say occupied. . . . Only internal weakness, only the workings of disunity can bring a country of that kind to ruin."[26]

Clausewitz argued that "the 1812 campaign failed because the Russian government kept its nerve and the people remained loyal and steadfast. The campaign could not succeed." It follows that in sketching notionally the favorable end-game to an East-West conflict, military planners need to consider how they can maximize the prospects of some facsimile of 1917 being reenacted (or at least, for deterrent effect, being reenacted in the fearful imagination of Soviet leaders).

Poor planning at any level is to be deplored, but historical experience suggests that the higher, and hence more encompassing, the level of planning error, the more damaging the consequences are wont to be. Incompetence in grand strategy may coexist with the competent conduct of military operations in wars where the armed forces cannot deliver victory by military means. Incompetence in military strategy overall, married to the competent conduct of some theater operations, can produce impressive successes in the wrong places at the price of terrible opportunity costs. It is important to recognize that the possibility of error on the grand and nationally irrecoverable (in the war in question, at least) scale which lurks in the choices of policy and the design of grand strategy is not a telling argument against grand strategy per se. Rather, it is a pressing argument for competence in grand strategy. This seemingly commonplace point is in urgent need of registration because Edward N. Luttwak—ironically enough the man probably most responsible for reintroducing the concept of grand strategy to the U.S. defense community—has suggested, perhaps mischievously, in his most mature work on strategy that schemes of grand strategy may be unduly risk-prone. In what appears to be an unconscious parody of the paradoxical logic of conflict which he has gone to book length to reveal, Luttwak advises, "It is not easy to devise properly strategic solutions that are also superior to mere pragmatic improvisation [it may not be easy, but Britain showed that it could be done, over the course of several centuries, while France and Germany demonstrated repeatedly the consequences of "pragmatic improvisation":CSG]."

He erects a straw-man target: "We now know that the frequent appeals heard in public life for a 'coherent' or consistent national strategy are not merely vacuous but actually misleading. They suggest that the policies of each department should be tightly coordinated into a national policy that is logical in common-sense terms, whereas in strategy only policies that are seemingly contradictory can circumvent the self-defeating effect of the paradoxical logic."

Luttwak's "Parthian shot" on the subject is to advise that "huge uncertainties of fact must be involved in devising any substantive scheme of grand strategy. . . . The successful application of a normative grand strategy should greatly reduce the prevalence of small errors of disharmony, but only at the risk of focusing energies to perpetuate much larger errors."[27]

He teeters on the brink of throwing the baby out with the bath-water. Without quite saying so, Luttwak suggests very strongly that because the government of a democracy is not to be trusted to design a grand strategy which properly accommodates the implications of the paradoxical logic of conflict, it may be better off not attempting to design a grand strategy at all. Stripped of high-sounding phrases, this amounts to praise for the practice of "muddling through" (sup-posedly, though generally incorrectly at the level of grand strategy, a British specialty), or perhaps for just plain muddling. Luttwak's near-axiomatic argument in the passages quoted can be opposed by the rival axiom that virtually any plan of action, consistently pursued, is preferable to a multiplicity of plans. One should recall the following Napoleonic dictum: "Better one bad general than two good ones." Lest anyone be tempted to take Luttwak overly seriously in his stric-tures against grand strategy, it should be recorded that in writings subsequent to *Strategy* we are advised that "caution must restrain our anticipation of an alternative grand strategy [to containment], so as not to erode the security ensured by the grand strategy we already have."[28] Prudent, if rather prosaic.

There is no question that planning is essential. Armed forces must be developed and trained for particular kinds of combat, againt par-ticular enemies, over particular terrain. Moreover, military plans will have a great impact upon the evolution of tactical doctrine, training, and the procurement of equipment. It is true to claim that poor planning can lose a war, but that good planning cannot guarantee success. Common-sense understanding of what constitutes good plan-ning has to recognize that there are limits to what can be planned for, or against. The ability to adjust plans to circumstances, provided it does not degenerate into mere opportunism, can be at least as important as the quality of the plans with which a war is begun.

There is no practicable, all-purpose education which must produce superior defense planners. Plainly, the education (including real-life, hands-on experience) desirable must vary with the level of military activity in question. Anglo-American experience in the conduct of multinational, multiservice, and multitheater (global) war from 1941 to 1945 suggests that most important among the keys to successful planning are: each level of government performing its own tasks (i.e., politicians must not shunt off political decisions to theater com-manders); coordination by committees of expert-specialists (rather than the reposing of undue authority in individuals who are required unreasonably to be masters of several military disciplines); and the organization of timely communication flows from the field to the staff (and vice versa). Of course superior planning in wartime must entail pragmatic improvisation, even on a quite heroic scale. But policy purpose and strategic objectives should not be improvised, and the constraints of geography and available assets over time may not be permissive of effective improvisation. Both of the world wars of this century demonstrated clearly that grand strategy can be planned to a useful, indeed decisive, degree. The enemy can be "set up" to make potentially fatal errors, and the ground can be prepared to take permanent advantage of those errors. (Needless to add, perhaps, a well-led enemy may decline to commit the worst errors that he has been set up to commit.) Furthermore, a superior quality in force planning, perhaps involving the taking of early major decisions on defense mobilization, is eminently possible. Under policy guidance, military planning is a matter of guessing as to the burden of strategic demand for deterrent effect that may be required, or as to the character of war that may have to be waged.

The more precise a prediction, the more likely it is to be precisely wrong. Defense establishments are in need of accurate predictions which are sufficiently precise to be useful. This is not as difficult an endeavor as can appear to be the case at first glance, provided common sense prevails. In public debate common sense can be an early victim—for example, specialist witnesses pro and con a particular defense program confidently will predict which military problems the Soviet Union will or will not be able to solve by a particular period. With their near-term focus, journalists are heavily prone to the encouragement of unwise detailed speculation by specialists promoted as experts. Many defense experts are susceptible to the thought that admission of ignorance, even on topics where there is no basis for prediction, somehow diminishes their expert standing. It is rare indeed to find an expert interviewed by the media who will both admit honestly that he does not know whether, for example, the Soviet Union can develop and deploy suitable technical countermeasures to a particular SDI design by a specified date, and who will adhere doggedly to that profession of ignorance under inquisitional pressure. Nonetheless, one person's opinion, say on the long-term future of the Soviet ICBM program, is not as good or bad as any other person's. Important defense decisions have a history and a context. Knowledge of Soviet strategic culture and style, of the relevant history, and of the more enduring features in the context should enable one to score higher in guesswork than would the person who is looking at a particular issue more or less wholly "on its individual merits," or pragmatically. A modern classic in illustration of this point is the contrast between the track records in prediction of those in the late 1960s who approached the superpower arms-control process in the context of both the nature of the Soviet system and the enduring dynamics of superpower rivalry, and those who approached arms control as a largely technical problem concerned to help solve allegedly mutual problems of stability. The former, sadly, were vindicated by the subsequent history of SALT, while the latter misunderstood the nature of their subject.

More generally, it is unsurprising to note how few of the liberal American commentators on Soviet matters either have recognized, or are honest enough to admit, that the current Soviet crisis provides abundant evidence of the systematic errors in their views. The same people who solemnly assured us that the Krasnoyarsk radar was not a treaty violation are still parading themselves as arms-control and Soviet experts (in the aftermath of formal Soviet admission of treaty violation!). American liberal opinion chooses to forget that the gentler, kinder U.S.S.R. that may be the U.S.S.R. of the 1990s, would or will be the product in noteworthy part of the conservative U.S. statecraft of the eight Reagan years. Gorbachev's goal is a more competitive Soviet Union, not a democratic-socialist Russia. To the degree to which Moscow practices a kinder politics at home and abroad, that will be official recognition of necessity. As noted, the fact of a reforming U.S.S.R. is not proof positive of the merit in long-standing American liberal worldviews; quite the contrary. Gorbachev's U.S.S.R. is a relatively smiling giant at present because, reasoning strategically, it has no practicable alternative in the near term.

Of recent years, the U.S. defense establishment, although recognizing that one cannot know what has yet to happen, may have come to be unduly impressed with the insights that might be gleaned from gaming. Gaming can be useful as a partial simulation of reality for the purpose of education. But gaming can become dangerous if it leads participants to forget that they have tested ideas and forces only in American-designed games in simulation of reality. Nonetheless, as Michael Vlahos has demonstrated in a superb case study of the war gaming conducted at the U.S. Naval War College between the wars, such gaming can—and in this case by and large did—function truly as "an enforcer of strategic realism."[29] The superior performance of the U.S. Navy in the war in the Pacific has to be attributed in part to the prior experience gained in the conduct of directly relevant, rigorous games over the course of the preceding twenty years.

Historical study informs us that great events have great causes, but that the precipitating details can be small indeed and utterly beyond prediction. The defense planner should benefit from studying a few of the better "alternative histories" that have been written to see if, for example, it is plausible to believe that the Western Roman Empire had to fall in the fifth century, that the American Revolution had to occur, that the South had to lose the Civil War, that the First World War had to occur (and had to be a long war of exhaustion), and that the Third Reich had to lose (or lose by the mid-1940s). The historian is confined to reinterpretation, but the policymaker and the defense planner have alternative futures among which they must choose, albeit very substantially in ignorance.

It is natural to think and to predict in what amounts to an incremental manner. But cumulative change can assume massive proportions over, say, a twenty-year-long span, always assuming that no radical discontinuities occur. Twenty years from now, U.S. ICBMs designed in the early 1970s should still be in the active inventory. But what will be the full strategic context of the early twenty-first century? Proceeding in the opposite temporal direction, one should seek to recall the circumstances of the early 1970s and assess their political and strategic distance from today. Twenty-two years ago an assertive and self-confident United States had more than half a million military personnel deployed in Vietnam defending "the process of modernization," as the hubristic social science jargon of that bygone age would have it. U.S. grand strategy aspired to engineer "nation building" in Vietnam, even though its operators were almost willfully blind to the constraints which the political culture of the American nation would impose upon freedom of action abroad.

CHAPTER 5

Technology and the Art of War

Who could stop us? Not the bloody Turks! . . . We have good fighters ready to tackle it [Gallipoli], and an enemy who has never shown himself as good a fighter as the white man.

—LT. COLONEL A. SKEEN, en route to Gallipoli, 1915[1]

There are no magic ways to victory against powerful enemies.

—CORRELLI BARNETT[2]

IN HIS classic study, *Armament and History,* British military theorist J. F. C. Fuller wrote imaginatively of the phenomenon of the "dominant weapon." Such a weapon enjoys a reach or range superior to other weapons and becomes the instrument around which military organization is built, in regard to which doctrine and tactics primarily are molded, and in whose shadow other capabilities assume ancillary status.[3] Candidate examples from twentieth-century military history must include: for sea warfare, the battleship of 1900–41, the aircraft carrier, and later the nuclear submarine (all *capital* ships); for land warfare, arguably the infantry or heavy artillery, followed by the tank; while for the air and later the missile age, the long-range heavy bomber and then the ICBM.

In practice, the dominant-weapon thesis has served more often as a very misleading half-truth than as a means to direct defense communities sensibly toward comprehending better the leading edge of contemporary military prowess. Time after time allegedly dominant weapons have been found to require the complementary assistance of other arms. In World War I, infantry and artillery had to work together to take and hold ground, while the naval line-of-battle could be hazarded only when screened massively by destroyer flotillas against torpedo attacks. In World War II and subsequently, it was demonstrated that against determined opposition, tank forces were an instrument of exploitation, not of "break-in." Similarly, aircraft carriers, if they were not to devote all of their energies negatively to self-defense, required antiaircraft gunfire cover by other ships; while the heavy bomber, contrary to USAAF doctrine (as late as 1943), could attack Germany with tolerable losses only if it attacked at night or if it was escorted all the way to the target by long-range fighters. Of recent decades, there is an important sense in which the long-range and nuclear-armed ballistic missile has assumed a dominant role, but that dominance is more logical than prospectively operationally useful in action. There is no doubt that the ICBM and the SLBM truly could be war-winning, or "decisive," weapons. But the inability of ICBMs and SLBMs to disarm the enemy of like forces means that the dominance at issue here more likely would be a dominance for potential bilateral catastrophe than a dominance exploitable as leverage for success in the conduct of crisis or war.

To affirm the superior importance of "moral" over material, and particularly technological, factors in war is neither to deny the significance of advances in weaponry nor to be blind to the problems occasionally generated by a true technical shortfall. However, to hazard a very bold claim, there has not been a great war in history decided plainly by a technological superiority in weaponry. The closest to arguable exceptions to that claim would be the advantages granted by the composite bow of the Hun horse archers in the fifth century,[4] the "Greek fire" employed by the Byzantine navy in the seventh century and subsequently,[5] and the atomic bomb in 1945. It has been the general rule that in great wars between polities of comparable, if culturally distinctive, modernity, the parties have employed a total mix of weapons which were good enough, with suitable doctrine, training, mass, and appropriate strategic context, so that weapons technology did not function as the critical element making for victory or defeat. After all, wars are not fought by weapons; they are waged by tactical units of armed men variously equipped, trained, commanded, and motivated to generate a combat outcome overall.

Technological advantage tends to be fleeting, lends itself to tactical or operational offset, and generally is swamped in its potential for decision by the sheer complexity of modern combat. In recent centuries, at least, no major country or coalition has lost a great war because its soldiers or sailors were too poorly armed. This judgment applies to the Napoleonic Wars, to the American Civil War (where battlefield salvage was common practice for the army left in command on the field at the conclusion of a fight), to the Russo-Japanese War, and to the two world wars. It has been the experience of the twentieth century to date, notwithstanding the increasingly technological character of *grande guerre* (as of arms competition in peacetime), that true technical shortfalls have either been shared by all combatants, as with the initially grave deficiencies in artillery means *and methods* for the siege warfare of 1914–18, or have lent themselves to rapid technical fixes or tactical workarounds, as with the antiarmor problems discovered by the Germans in the Western Desert and on the Eastern Front.[6]

It is the appropriate use of weapons in combination which critically helps to win or lose wars. The effectiveness of weapons in combat is a matter for tactics, operational art, and military strategy. With great states and coalitions competing for superior military effectiveness in and among four geographical environments—on land, at sea, in the air, and in space—it is exceedingly unlikely that one, or even several, individual weapon technologies or complete weapon systems would have the potential to be a true war-winner.[7] And that prudential judgment holds regardless of all that has been said above about possible tactical and operational compensation.

TECHNOLOGY AND WAR

In the same way that war is a great deal more than operational art, though skill in operational art is essential for success, so defense is a great deal more than economics, though economic strength is essential for national security.

Historically speaking, the rise and fall of the economic fortunes of a state invariably have had major and direct implications for its military strength. Skillful diplomacy (as with the Byzantines, the Venetians, or the contemporary British), or unusual battlefield competence (as with Frederick II of Prussia, or indeed with the Great German General Staff in the two world wars), may obscure for a while a fragility in the economic base of national power. But unless that diplomatic or military skill can expand the economic base of state power, political-military decline is the inexorable product of relative economic weakness. The economic weakness in question here is not so much the weakness of one great power relative to that of any other individual great power, but rather weakness as a coalition leader, financier, or manufacturer *vis-à-vis* the warmaking strength of a hostile coalition. For example, by late 1915, and certainly through 1916, it was quite apparent in London that the time-hallowed British role as banker of antihegemonic coalitions was about to end. American industry and credit literally became essential to the allied war effort. Twenty years later, Hitler's determination to secure continental *Lebensraum* rapidly was not only an atavistic quest after Aryan glory. In addition, Hitler's quest was a quite logical response to the terrible German domestic experience with the allied economic blockade in the Great War;[8] it was a bid to seize a continental hegemony capable, economically, of waging and winning a protracted coalition war. The great Russian adventure launched by Hitler in 1941 was a gamble intended to secure in one campaigning season the continental means to thwart British (or American) grand strategy.

The quantity and quality of military power which can be generated from a certain economic base are heavily dependent upon the effectiveness of political organization for military mobilization. The plainest illustration of this point in modern times was provided by the French Revolution. The Revolution liberated, indeed propelled, an explosive expansion of energy which the French nation could devote to its newly national goals—including liberation and foreign conquest.

In World War II the German economy underperformed, while the British economy, if anything, overperformed, as a result of the respectively very unsuccessful and successful political mobilization and bureaucratic organization of the forces of economic production for the purposes of the war. The leaders of the two countries were acutely aware of their respective national experiences with total war in the last years of the First World War. The British government had learned that mobilization for total war eventually produces victory for the economically stronger coalition in a protracted war. Hitler agreed with this argument, which was why he was determined to avoid the necessity of conducting a protracted war of attrition against an economically superior enemy coalition.

There was grand-strategic method in Hitler's policy madness. He understood very well indeed why Germany had lost in 1918. He believed that Ludendorff's endeavor to organize Germany for total war both sowed the seeds of the revolution of 1918 and had been foredoomed to failure because Germany and her allies lacked the economic strength to succeed in such a form of war. The great gamble of the invasion of Russia—which, wrongly, was not regarded as much of a gamble by military professionals in Germany (and Britain and the United States) in early 1941—had it succeeded, might have resulted in a Third Reich so continentally secure that it would have been unconquerable by sea-based power. Hitler's strategy was demonstrated by events to have been unsound because his continental means were insufficient to gain his proximate continental ends. However, it is well to remember that it was the German military system which failed in Russia in 1941, and not only Hitler's direction of policy and strategy. That relaxed approach to logistical details which produced the supply impossibilities which doomed the amended German war plan of 1914 in turn played no less fatal a role in the summer and fall of 1941.

Economic strength is not a matter of mere quantities. For example, the size of Canada is a source of economic weakness rather than strength, given its very small population and high latitudes. Similarly, the size and rate of increase of the population of many of the countries of Latin America and Africa, relative to the material resources to be worked and in the context of educational infrastructures typically of a rudimentary character, is a source of crippling and prospectively permanent weakness. For the purposes of this discussion, the elements of economic strength of most interest are those which bear upon the ability of countries to develop, borrow and adapt, and generally exploit high technology for the purposes of competing effectively in, or close to, the first rank of states in modern weaponry. This is not to despise quantity or mere size. Provided it can be adequately worked and controlled, more territory is preferable to less territory, while a large population—provided it is skilled—certainly is preferable to a small population.

It has long been recognized that national security for a great power can be compromised by a war economy unduly dependent upon overseas supply of raw materials, of critical manufactured components, or of finished products. As a consequence of the Industrial Revolution the value of economic autarky has been raised enormously. Prior to the creation and equipment of the mass armies of the industrial age, supply blockades, though not commercial blockades designed to wreak financial ruin, tended to be strategically irrelevant. Preindustrial, dynastic Europe did not maintain, or plan to provide in time of war, military machines critically dependent upon foreign supply of raw materials or manufactures. The strategic context wherein the allied economic blockade of the Central Powers could be a very

powerful weapon was the product of the industrialization and na-
tionalization of war in the century between 1815 and 1914.[9] The long
duration of the great coalition war of 1914–18, set against a backcloth
of unprecedented population growth and newly intensive agricultural
methods, functioned synergistically to create novel vulnerabilities.

There is a tension between innovation and procurement, between
the quest for technical excellence and the pressure to acquire weapons, which, if handled unwisely, can lead to serious military disadvantage. Since a better product can be produced tomorrow, it is
always tempting to wait for that product tomorrow rather than to
purchase the inferior product available today. If a country's defense
community knew for certain when it must cope with acute crisis or
war, it would know when to cease aspiring for future capability and,
instead, when to settle for feasible procurement of weapons of demonstrated competence. To the degree, then, to which acute crises and
wars purposively can be preplanned, rather than erupting as apparently capricious acts of God or accidents of history, it is possible to
argue that decisions on the timing of procurement of major new
weapons systems can influence foreign proclivities to adventure.

In at least three important cases in the twentieth century, rearmament and military-related programs intended to deter in fact
have helped significantly to prod fearful countries into war in the
near term. First, in the period 1912–14, Imperial Germany noticed
with understandable alarm that Russia's "Great Program" of armament—and associated strategic railroad construction—would produce by 1917 a peacetime army totaling 2,245,000 men, double the
size of the army of 1911. Moreover, with their Plan No. 21 (scheduled
for application in 1917), the Russians intended to be able to complete
their mobilization in only eighteen days—just three days more than
the Germans required to set their Schlieffen Plan in motion. As
Norman Stone has observed, writing of German alarm over this prospective fact: "Russians would be in Berlin before Germans were in
Paris."[10] The Russian "Great Program" was intended to deter war,
but in fact because it carried the plausible promise of falsifying the
assumptions upon which German military strategy was based, it contributed to German incentives to wage war as soon as was diplomatically practicable.

Second, Adolf Hitler's belief that time was not on his side in relative
war-waging capability led him on November 5, 1937, to advise his
principal lieutenants, in the words of an observer: "If the Fuehrer
was still living, it was his unalterable resolve to solve Germany's
problem of space at the latest by 1943–45 [case one]. The necessity

for action before 1943–45 would arise in cases 2 and 3. [Case two entailed civil strife in France which would yield Germany a free hand; case three entailed French embroilment in war with a third party, again thereby yielding Germany a free hand.]"

Hitler argued: "After this date [1943–45] only a change for the worse, from our point of view, could be expected. The equipment of the army, navy, and *Luftwaffe*, as well as the formation of the officer corps, was nearly completed. Equipment and armament were modern; in further delay there lay the danger of their obsolescence."[11]

Japan in 1941 is the third, and by far the clearest, case of a country going to war sooner rather than later, because of official pessimism over a predicted very adverse military balance in the "out years." U.S. naval rearmament, particularly as licensed by the Two-Ocean Naval Expansion Act of June 1940, meant that the Imperial Japanese Navy was facing the calculable certainty of increasingly serious material inferiority in the Western Pacific by late 1943. The total trade embargo against Japan declared by the Western powers on July 26, 1941—which amounted to economic warfare—compelled Japan (then culturally incapable of seriously considering a fundamental policy shift away from continental expansion in China) to plan to instigate war as soon as possible.[12] In each of the three cases just cited, defense economic reasoning, admittedly in narrowly bounded political-cultural contexts, would seem to have helped noticeably to propel countries to fight sooner rather than later, in fear lest their prospects for success, even just for self-defense, should diminish markedly over time.

Although the three cases illustrate the general argument that a medium-term strategic pessimism can fuel the urge to wage preventive war, it should be understood that most probably none of the three wars in question were avoidable. Russian military policy prior to August 1914, the first stirrings of British and French rearmament policies in the mid-1930s, and U.S. (and British) naval rearmament and foreign economic policies in 1940–41 all contributed fuel to the slides to war. But such were the perceptions of geostrategic beleaguerment in Imperial and Nazi Germany and Imperial Japan that all three decisions for war were beyond deterrence. The details of outbreak certainly could have differed, but it would be a profound error to see the eruptions of war in 1914, 1939, and 1941 as, in any really important sense, failures in Russian, British, or American policy, respectively.

It may be worth noting that it was not only the Western Allies who failed to deter in 1939 and 1940. The Molotov-Ribbentrop Pact of

August 23, 1939, was intended by Hitler to deter Britain and France from declaring war on Germany on the occasion of the imminent invasion of Poland. The pact deprived the Western Allies of a prospective Eastern Front and threatened the strategic integrity of a key element in the British way of war—the maritime economic blockade. Similarly, through the agency of the Tripartite Pact of September 27, 1940 (among Germany, Italy, and Japan), Hitler hoped to deter the United States from its domestically controversial policy of assisting the British war effort, let alone from contemplating seriously direct entry into the war in Europe. Hitler needed to overcome the damage wrought in German-Japanese relations by the Molotov-Ribbentrop Pact, and to bind Japan to the Axis so that the United States would face a massive prospective—and hoped-for actual—distraction from the Atlantic to the Pacific area. But British society in 1939 and the United States in 1940–41 were both beyond deterrence.

The U.S. government remains understandably uncertain about the place for defense-industrial mobilization in the calculus of deterrence, let alone as a subject possibly of critical significance for the successful conduct of war. Economic strength takes years to translate into military strength. Since the U.S. government does not have a defense mobilization policy for industry of much more than rhetorical status, U.S. mobilization style has to be a matter for speculation. In contrast, it is Soviet mobilization style to marry very large numbers of reservists to unit equipment sets (though neither the reservists nor their equipment would be militarily reliable first-line material), and to shift gears in a defense-industrial economy which already, by Western standards, is semimobilized for war. Viewed in concert, U.S. arms-control policy, the SDI, and the navy's maritime strategy carry the implication of a greater U.S. need to plan for protracted nonnuclear war. In principle, unquestionably, the economies of the Western Alliance could bury the Soviet Union under the weight of superior, late-model military hardware. But the gap in time between mobilization potential and performance in procurement and manpower training is awesome indeed.

It is very noticeable that Clausewitz had nothing to say about the relationship between technological innovation and war. This was understandable, if hardly prescient, because the art of war on land registered no major technological changes through the eighteenth century to the date of his death in 1831. The flintlock musket replaced the matchlock in the 1690s, while the socket bayonet was adopted in the same period, displacing the pike. Very considerable improvements were introduced in field artillery by way of standardization and weight reduction for mobility, but—notwithstanding the devastating employment by Napoleon (an artilleryman) of massed field guns— Clausewitz was not moved to single out weapons technology as a variable of great tactical and strategic significance. It is probably important, both in order to be fair to Clausewitz and to signal what may be a general truth, that none of the "great captains" revered suitably by Clausewitz (that is to say, Napoleon, Frederick the Great, Marlborough, Turenne, and Condé) were remarkable as technological innovators. The secrets of success, if such they may be called, of Napoleon, Wellington, Frederick, and Marlborough lay in their exceptionally able use of a given military instrument. In Napoleon's pioneering case, the military instrument was enormously augmented in its size and fighting power by the spirit of nationalism.

The idea of radical change in the logistical, tactical, operational, and hence strategic conditions of warfare, as a result of *rapid* technological change, was the product of the Industrial Revolution. From the second quarter of the nineteenth century to the present day, invention has been all but routinized. Moreover, the pace of technological change has increased and with it the speed with which armed forces have had to absorb the military meaning of new technologies. Lengthy though the process of gestation for new or radically improved weapons can be in peacetime, that process has tended to outpace the ability both of military organizations and governments to understand how much or how little they can prudently ask of their military instruments. The United States and Britain, not being warrior societies, have tended to exalt the military effectiveness of machines at some cost of underrating the importance of the military skills and virtues of people. The Germans and the Japanese committed the reverse error, with terminal adverse consequences for their security.

There is what may be called a culture of innovation which can transcend a healthy interest in the improvement of military equipment, and becomes instead a worship of novelty and a quest after new technical capabilities as an end in itself. This is not to criticize the process of innovation; neither is it to deny that desirable tactical capabilities, possibly of potentially profound operational and even strategic significance, may emerge as practicable possibilities whether or not the government of the day asked for them in advance. Suffice it to say that new or improved technologies do not necessarily perform better than older technologies in the man-machine systems known as weapons—tactically in combat, or in their operational and strategic effects. As examples, the character of the world wars of the twentieth century was less attributable to the technological circumstances of their conduct than to the fact that they were great coalition wars. The key difference between the swift and decisive wars waged by Prussia against Austria (1866) and France (1870–71) and the protracted attritional struggles of 1914–18 and 1939–45 was not so much the technologies of war as the total strength of the opposing sides. Operations may be synonymous with strategy in a continental war when a single enemy power is diplomatically isolated. But geostrategically isolated examples of operational virtuosity can deliver only campaign success in a war where the center of gravity of an enemy coalition cannot be reached by marching feet.

Nevertheless, technological innovation is embraced in pursuit of enhanced military effectiveness. And, as noted, the research and development community, and many of those who debate publicly the products of that community, are wont to forget that machines do not wage war. Instead, war is waged by man-machine systems in large numbers and of different kinds. As a result of focus upon individual units of a class of weaponry, as well as upon a class of weaponry in isolation, probable operational realities can vanish from view. People worry about the vulnerability of an ICBM or of a force of ICBMs in silos, without realizing that the vulnerability to which they refer is a static engineering judgment utterly divorced from the predictable operational difficulties of a Soviet attack planner. Similarly, people refer to an age of truly global surveillance which must see peril for mobile ICBMs and for surface ships. Often neglected are the nontrivial issues of how a weapon is to be placed on a target once a target is located (and presumably tracked), and how space and aerial-surveillance platforms could be maintained in a combat environment.

Historical experience suggests forcefully that the military merits of particular technological innovations can be tested reliably only through experience in war. Furthermore, the history of civilian and military technology does not reveal a pattern of great foresight on the part of officials or of self-styled seers from the scientific world. With a few exceptions which serve really to prove the rule, the history of military technology and of war itself shows that what can be done will at least be attempted by the desperate or the simply hopeful. In that regard, Bernard Brodie opened the concluding section of an essay on technology and war with the following observations:

> We have seen that, *in the long run*, technology has transformed war pretty much in its own fashion. The bumbling ideas of men about the

utilities of new weaponry have often caused painful and costly mal-adjustments, and have even determined at times which side would enjoy the victory [this would seem to be an excessive claim]; but the mistakes that have been made in the past in these matters seem rarely to have affected the technological conditions in which men found themselves, just as they seem not to have affected the technological conditions in which we find ourselves today. The main reason for this is that the conservatism of the military, about which we hear so much, seems always to have been confined to their adaptation to new weaponry rather than to their acceptance of it.[13]

The idea of progress, and particularly of progress through applied science and engineering, is central to American culture. Indeed the idea of progress may be traced both philosophically to those men of the European Enlightenment, the Founding Fathers, and to the exigencies of the frontier. The promise of American life is a vision of individual betterment, and for many if not most people that betterment is more material than spiritual. Practical endorsement of the proposition that there are always material solutions to life's problems is an American national trait, notwithstanding the religiosity of much public political rhetoric.

Probably it is fair to say that American engineering has a more distinguished history of steady accomplishment than has American diplomacy. With some qualification, it is noteworthy that in both world wars the Anglo-American defense communities tended strongly to look for material solutions to battlefield difficulties; whereas the German defense community stressed a connected mix of warrior virtue (spiritual strength), political-ideological motivation, and superior military method. Bluntly stated, it was the Anglo-American way to wage a rich person's war, and the German way (of necessity) to wage a poor person's war. Evidence apparently to the contrary should not be allowed to mislead. For example, as Tim Travers has argued in great detail,[14] the British army did persist—for cultural reasons pertaining to the Edwardian social values of the military profession—with a human-centered view of war through too many campaigns in 1914–18. Also, an endeavor to apply a technocratic approach to war was characteristic of Germany from late 1916 until the end of the conflict. Nonetheless, although the British looked for character and the offensive spirit in their troops, they came to seek operational decision through a tactical superiority in artillery, close-support aircraft, and tanks. The German midwar technocratic revolution, though expressed materially in concrete pillboxes and in radically augmented organic (automatic) firepower for assault troops, sought battlefield success via a superior doctrine of war (at the level of tactics).

The relationship between policy guidance and technological change is both complex and highly variable from case to case. National military strategy, and behind that, policy, often is insufficiently coherent to provide unambiguous guidance. Moreover, policy has a way of changing, at least at the level of important nuance, so rapidly that an orderly weapons acquisition process is the exception rather than the rule. Policy can be an amalgam of domestic-looking arguments that bear upon the *real* conflict in peacetime: over appropriations; over yearnings for arms-control success; and over the struggle to achieve some prudential modernization of forces (possibly of uncertain and unprioritized strategic function). The current state of policy on the future of U.S. strategic offensive forces in the context of a postulated, but distinctly hypothetical, "defensive transition" bids fair to warrant classic status in the library of cases of imprecise policy guidance. Specifically, the U.S. government has not demonstrated a persuasive policy grasp of the relationship between the demand for strategic defensive and strategic offensive forces. Successful technological innovation in the former is presumed to reduce greatly the need for the latter. But policy has not argued, indeed does not rest to date on the argument, that offensive and defensive capabilities are identical in their strategic effects. If new strategic defenses have implications divergent from strategic offensive forces, what would policy endorsement of such defenses imply for the future of offensive forces?

Efforts to curb or tame technology through arms-control designs, well meaning though they have often been, must be judged to stand as monuments to human vanity and to a quite unwarranted faith in the policy wisdom of the moment. Arms control variously is touted or opposed for reasons good and bad. In the context of this chapter, several points need to be registered on the utility of an alleged arms-control process. First, specialized though it often is, military technology is related very firmly to technological development in general. Unless one believes that technological advance across-the-board can be arrested, there is no realistic prospect for halting the onward march of military technology. Second, in practice there is little to recommend the central conceit of modern arms-control theory which holds that some weapons inherently are "destabilizing" and therefore "bad," while some other weapons are "stabilizing" and therefore "good." This sophomoric notion should have been killed for all time by the negotiating experience of the 1930s on the subject of the distinction between "offensive" and "defensive" weapons. The policy purposes of states, or the orientation of strategies—but not individual weapons—may be offensive or defensive.

Third, the seemingly common-sense, though erroneous, idea persists that military technologies in the form of arms-race moves somehow cause wars. It is certainly the case both that military technological innovation feeds threat analysis abroad, and that such analysis is likely to fuel prudential desires to provide some suitable offsets. But it does not follow that an arms-control process will dampen political incentives to compete in armaments, though it may redirect them (often in ways unanticipated, at least by one party). Neither does it follow that the modest redirection of a military competition necessarily must serve the cause of international peace and security. It is paradoxical that the proponents of new technologies for military modernization frequently are accused of advocating what amount to technological panaceas for the resolution of problems which really are political. The paradox lies in the demonstrated fact that this charge often is leveled by people who, presumably unwittingly, are offering political panaceas for military-technological challenges. Arms-control engineering, in the absence of some reasonable measure of mutual accommodation of national interests, cannot help but be just another vehicle for struggle. The public debate in the United States over, for example, antisatellite (ASAT) weapons is permeated with what amounts to the assertion from one side of the argument that a political peace is available in competition with the false god of a military-technological peace.

In short, it is neither arms nor the process of technological innovation in a process of competitive armament which stands between humankind and perpetual peace. Indeed, given the master function of politics, arms-control agreements can provide positive reinforcement for a process of accommodation-bound political engagement, but by their very nature they are probably more likely to do harm than good to the prospects for international security.[15] The goals of arms control, and in particular the objective of reducing the risks of war occurring, are best served by a sound national defense strategy and program. Not only can national defense endeavor forward the goals of arms-control policy, but also that endeavor itself functions as arms control.

All of history shows that superior military method applied by dedicated warriors is more important than technological advantage— *other factors being tolerably equal.* Of course, heroism and tactical skill in preindustrial warfare could avail naught against a machine-age army. It was the enormous technological gulf between the European powers and the tribal societies of Africa (in particular) in the late nineteenth century which rendered empire-building so feasible a mission (". . . we have got the maxim gun, and they have not"). For an earlier example, it was the technological and combat superiority of the caravel and carrack, armed to conduct standoff artillery duels at sea in line-ahead battle formation, which enabled Portugal to sweep the Indian Ocean of Arab naval power in the first quarter of the sixteenth century and found a new maritime trading empire.[16] There are circumstances wherein high technology or sheer mass of material can encourage such dependence upon machines that tactical skills atrophy or are never developed to a high level. Properly regarded, which is to say with a view to the effectiveness of combined arms in battle conditions—or the prospect thereof, for deterrence—technology is a vital servant of the soldier. In theory there are workarounds for most, though certainly not for all, technological deficiencies, but in practice those workarounds can require the presence of compensation in quantity, in skill in military method, or in enthusiasm, which may not be available.

There is some merit in the claim that military organizations have a way of needing more time to adjust to the meaning of new weapons than they do to develop and procure those weapons. Notwithstanding the propagandizing activities of a few visionaries, there is always an organizational inclination to accommodate new weapon technologies within the structure of existing, time-tested, and preferably battle-experienced doctrine and forces. New weapons tend to be oversold, at least with respect to the likely performance of their first- or second-generation products. Furthermore, the prophets for new "wonder weapons" have an impressive history of inattention to countermeasures.

The wonder-weapon syndrome has a very long history. Without meaning to denigrate the military significance of particular examples of technological change, exaggerated expectations for the military effectiveness of radically new weapons flow from: the triumph of desire over the lessons of experience—the conviction that that which is necessary must be feasible (consider Nazi Germany's wonder weapons of 1944–45—particularly the V-1 and V-2 rockets and the Type XXI U-boat); the tendency for states in desperation to rush into combat with unreliable prototypes rather than waiting for a critical mass of better-tested items; the perennial hope for the finding of a relatively cheap key to victory (for the utter demoralization, if not actual overthrow, of an enemy); and an unwillingness by the converted to consider realistically the competitive technologies, tactics, or operational options which may be available to a reasonably competent enemy.

To succeed in their functions, armed services need a strategic concept which both defines their mission and which the community at large acknowledges to be important and hence worthy of expensive support in peacetime.[17] In all of their aspects, military organizations tend to define their purpose and sustain their ethos with reference to preferred missions which are expressed actually and symbolically by particular weapon systems. Significance for the nation, budgets, careers, service self-esteem and so forth are tied to the roles of particular weapons which define the essence of particular military organizations.

There is a generally well-founded tradition of limited liability in warfare for offshore states which have a history of waging war abroad and through the exercise of capital-intensive rather than manpower-intensive combat forces.[18] The offshore democracies of the West, unused in very modern times to the experience of great land wars (with one exception, Britain's experience on the Western Front in the First World War), have been susceptible to the siren song of clean and possibly decisive technological warfare. It is a matter of record that the Combined Bomber Offensive which laid waste much of urban Germany was the practical end result of a rather romantic notion that bombardment from the air offered a clean path to victory, obviating the necessity for bloody attrition in ground conflict. The strategic policy debate in the United States continues to attract contributions by people who believe that new technologies (navigation aids for "zero-CEP," tailored-effect nuclear weapons, and nonnuclear warheads for strategic delivery vehicles) can limit very greatly the damage that might need to be inflicted in war. Some of the more recent writings of Albert Wohlstetter offer a perfect illustration of an abiding American aspiration for relatively clean military action.[19]

The generalizations offered above require clarification for their national applicability. From the age of "fighting sail" to the present day, the capital ship has been the most complex machine of its period. As a natural sea power,[20] the British way in warfare necessarily has been dependent upon the effectiveness of its capital ships and hence has been high-technological in character. But, high technology in the form of superior naval strength confronting—actually besieging—continental land power can be a prescription for a strategy of indecisive encirclement in a long war. The high-technology form of war in which Britain traditionally excelled, war at sea, was not capable, in and of itself, of achieving decision against natural land power. In its strategic culture, although Britain has been habituated to look to high technology as the *sine qua non* of national survival, it has no tradition of expecting victory to be achieved either rapidly or by unilateral British effort.[21] Further, basic though technology has to be to combat effectiveness at sea, particularly in the long era when maritime architecture essentially was static, the Royal Navy was never in any doubt that its fighting edge stemmed from superior seamanship and determination in combat.

Exploitation of the internal combustion engine was central to the image of modernity which Nazi Germany sought to project for domestic and foreign consumption. However, the high-technology, mechanized aspects of the Blitzkrieg, though critical to the fear which Hitler sought to generate in his victims, were not permitted by the Wehrmacht to transcend either basic combat skills in combined arms or ingenuity in operational art. This was just as well, given that the mechanization of the German war machine was more show than deep substance (a fact revealed all too painfully by the progressive demotorization of the German army as the war in the East proceeded). High technology had personal appeal to Adolf Hitler, it had deterrent value, and properly orchestrated in action it suited admirably *for a while* Germany's plan of progressive expansion via bite-sized Blitzkrieg assaults limited sharply in time and in necessary geographical reach.

The American affection for reliance upon technology in war has been altogether different in kind from the showy liking for engines displayed by Nazi Germany. In common with Britain, though for somewhat different reasons, by Great Power standards the United States has been very sensitive to (American) casualties. But because of its unique political culture, the product and expression of a continental-size popular democracy, the United States has been signally unfriendly to the strategic option of war protraction. As a country in the twentieth century of a potential magnitude in mobilizable military power quite above Britain's league, confident in the amount of war that it can wage, and impatient of delay in the face of an identified evil, the United States has favored adoption of the direct approach (typical of a continental power) to the forcible resolution of strategic problems. However, that continentalist direct approach is to be prosecuted with machinery, America's realm of comparative advantage, substituting wherever possible—prudently or not—for American bodies.

Hope springs eternal for the invention of an absolute weapon. Mild variants of this phenomenon appear regularly in criticisms of the weapon modernization projects of the day. Standards of perfection, with reference to shifting challenges by the invented "threat of the week," are applied to ICBM programs and to SDI deployment designs. Contrasting maladies scar sensible debate. On the one hand there is the belief that the nuclear weapon is the absolute weapon, and that all talk of modernization and product improvements amounts analogically to the extravagant illumination of a medieval manuscript. On the other hand, official congressional and public scrutiny of new weapon developments is so untidy and undisciplined an exercise that major projects can be subject to fatal criticism if they are not, like Caesar's wife, beyond suspicion of poor performance (under some highly unrealistic conditions).

The elements that produce skill in the conduct of war are as easy to list and interconnect logically as they are difficult to blend harmoniously in the real world of action.[22] Well it may be said that some aspects of the art of war can be learned but not taught, at least not pedagogically. Although tactical success in battle has value for the course of a war only through its contribution to campaign success, and campaign success has value only with reference to the securing of strategic objectives and policy goals, the character and scope of policy and strategy always should be governed by knowledge of logistical, and hence tactical, feasibility. Thus question marks in the mind of a commander about the quality of his fighting material (machines and men) and the tactical and operational skills of some of his subordinates inevitably restrain the range of tactical options, perhaps to a point where great tactical success is improbable of achievement (this was Sir John Jellicoe's dilemma at Jutland).[23] While technology *must* drive tactics, it can also drive strategy. Great or not-so-great strategic conceptions effectively are irrelevant, or dangerous, if the tactical instrument lacks the reach or the combat effectiveness to achieve the necessary objectives (occupy territory, catch, hold and defeat the enemy's army, and so forth). Armed forces which lack a long logistical reach are not suitable for pursuit of the policy objective of overthrowing an enemy who can employ a very extensive or hostile geography (and climate) in his defense. For a very obvious example, Nazi Germany sought to subdue an isolated Britain, even though it had no dedicated amphibious assets or experience, and had only a medium bomber force and a very short legged fighter inventory.

Studies of the relationship between technology and war, or of war and society (for a genre very popular in this debellicized era), unwittingly can slight the significance of individual ability and prevailing doctrinal belief on the part of commanders. For instance, Napoleon showed how a national army, because of the political strengths of a radically transformed French society, could be an instrument of rapid decision, contrary to the circumstances and experience of the previous century and a half.

As another example, it is the conventional wisdom to explain the duration of the American Civil War with reference to alleged revolutions in military and civilian technology, to the popularity of the rival causes, and to the sheer geographical extent of theaters of operation. But, as a recent study has argued, the geographical scope of the war was not significantly different from the continent-wide campaigning of Napoleon, and the armament of the belligerents had more in common with that familiar in 1815 than with that of 1914.[24] Because the spade was as useful as the rifle in 1914, it is all too easy to assume uncritically that the prodigious spadework of 1861–65 similarly was mandated by the range, accuracy, and quantity of infantry fire. But it is at least arguable that the American Civil War lasted for four years not because advances in military technology (e.g., widespread introduction of the rifled breech-loading musket) rendered tactical decision unusually difficult to achieve and operational decision in exploitation of tactical success remarkably elusive, but rather because neither side was led by men sufficiently determined, or able, to achieve operational-level success. If it is true that the Civil War was the last Napoleonic, rather than the first modern (looking to 1914–18), war, then military leadership and doctrine may explain more than can prevailing military-technological conditions. As Paddy Griffith notes, "The fact remains that by 1864 the great majority of armies and commanders, gray as well as blue, had wholeheartedly embraced the ideology of the engineers."[25]

The skills of the statesman, the strategist, the operational artist (theater commander), the tactician, and the logistician-administrator are all complementary, but they are distinctive and rarely are combined in equal measure in single individuals. A single individual does not have to perform simultaneously at all of these levels of activity. But lack of grasp of tactical possibilities, for example, or of logistical feasibility will doom the schemes of statesman and strategist alike. Such is the scale and complexity of modern warfare that—since genius cannot be routinized—in the nineteenth century professional general staffs came to provide all kinds of expertise, *save* that of the strategist and the grand strategist or statesman.

Following what Jomini appeared to teach, what amounted to a general staff culture evolved in Europe in the final decades of the nineteenth century, dedicated to the development of "warcraft" as a science. Approaching war as a science, highly professional staff-trained officers were encouraged to think of armed conflict as an activity apart from statecraft. Even in Britain, a country long accustomed to intrusive civilian control of military matters in time of war—as the experience of Marlborough and Wellington attested very plainly—the years 1914–18 witnessed politicians voluntarily taking a backseat (though criticizing from their backseats) while the military professionals plied their trade.[26] For example, in 1917–18 British Prime Minister David Lloyd George fundamentally disbelieved in the basic military strategy to which the British army was committed—the search for a military decision on the Western Front in France and Belgium. But Lloyd George lacked the political strength, or moral courage, to dismiss Douglas Haig, the commander of the British Expeditionary Force (though he did secure the removal of Haig's ally, William Robertson, the Chief of the Imperial General Staff); he lacked a plausible alternative theory of how the war was to be won; and he was constrained by the realities of coalition warfare. The Gallipoli venture of 1915 was both triggered by a Russian appeal for Western assistance, and was foredoomed politically by the fact that as early as November 12, 1914, Russia had been promised what amounted to a free hand with Constantinople after victory was won. That inter-allied agreement foreclosed upon a Turkish defection from its alliance with Germany. The Allies could not cut a deal with a new Turkish government if they were unable to guarantee that postwar Constantinople would remain Turkish.

If strategy is invented pragmatically as evolving opportunities arise, it is unlikely to drive tactics or operations effectively. Navies, long-range air forces, and high-quality armies cannot be created overnight, nor can they be transformed swiftly in the scope of their practical reach. Substantially unhindered German operational success in continental Western Europe from April through June 1940 opened up true strategic, as contrasted with merely operational, opportunities for success in the war. But the Wehrmacht lacked the means to exploit those opportunities. Similarly, the Wehrmacht, for all its incomplete tactical triumphs in the western U.S.S.R. in June and July 1941, could not roll tactical success even into genuine operational success in the theater, let alone into strategic victory in the war as a whole. Strategy can drive tactics if the political leadership and the potential enemy grant the time, and if the time that is granted is used wisely to fashion tactical military instruments of a character suitable to the waging of war against the center of gravity of the identified enemy.

Wars of movement for the achievement of rapid decision are not practicable if one lacks both a military instrument capable of rapid exploitation, a *corps de chasse,* and a military instrument which can be commanded reliably in near-enough real time (in the absence of a doctrinal consensus which minimizes the need for higher direction). These particular deficiencies, set against the material and human abundance for deployment by the great powers and the fact that it was a struggle between coalitions, go a long way toward explaining the static warfare on the Western Front from 1914 to 1918. In the words of the old saying, that which is tactically impossible cannot be strategically sound, or "strategy ignores tactics at its peril."[27] Although technology can solve some tactical military problems, war is a two-person game and the tactical dialectic between offense and defense, like the political dialectic of conflict, is continuous. Contrary to the expectations of the less restrained of the prewar prophets of armored warfare, the course of World War II demonstrated that tank-led forces could achieve great things only against either a very incompetent enemy, or against an enemy already drained of much of his strength by combat attrition.

To reiterate: technological choice can govern tactical feasibility which ultimately must influence strategy and the viability of foreign policy. Ideally, technological choice for the tactical instrument is exercised under the guidance of strategy properly informed by policy. For a contemporary case, there is no way of predicting reliably today just how competent Soviet ballistic missile defense (BMD) deployments might prove to be early in the next century against U.S. long-range ballistic missiles. However, there is a powerful policy and strategy imperative behind the U.S. drive to modernize its ICBMs and SLBMs. The inalienable uncertainties of conventional (and battlefield-nuclear) regional defenses mean that for deterrence to work it is only prudent for the United States to maintain the credible ability to punish Soviet assets of many kinds by long-range bombardment. The hazards of conventional conflict and the very structure of U.S. foreign policy require that nuclear deterrence be extended over distant countries and far-off U.S. garrisons and expeditionary forces. In time, technological changes favoring defense over offense might render extended deterrence by the strategic missile forces technically less and less credible, though political credibility is another matter. The point is that the U.S. defense community long will continue to have to respond to the strong policy, and hence strategy, push which flows from the geopolitical structure of a global Western Alliance. So long as the United States remains wedded to the concept of a geostrategically forward, multilateral containment of Soviet power, so long must great offensive reach be required of its armed forces.

OPERATIONAL ART

Allegedly, operational art is the highest purely military level of war and pertains to the planning and conduct of campaigns. In other words, operational art is the ability needed to employ battles for the purposes of campaign success, while the higher orchestration of campaigns is the domain of strategy and transcends purely military expertise.

Until the 1980s, military doctrine in the United States and Britain did not recognize an operational level of war.[28] An abiding reason why British and American soldiers have neglected (if that is a fair term) the operational level of war is that neither country, save briefly if critically in time of war, has a tradition of maintaining a mass army requiring an operational level of command (army and army group). The idea of handling an army or an army group in continental warfare was alien to an important stream of opinion on "the British way in warfare," while the American military tradition bequeathed by the nineteenth to the twentieth century had no practical place for the operational level of war. Furthermore, the need to perform on an operational scale of land-power effort generally has not been anticipated in advance in peacetime. Through the nineteenth century until 1917, the practical experience of the U.S. Army—with the vastly atypical experiences of the War of 1812, war with Mexico, the Civil War, and the war with Spain freely admitted—was that of frontier police duty. Similarly, though again with some exceptions, the British army from Waterloo (1815) to Mons (1914), and again from 1919 to 1939, was more of an imperial police force than an army in a continental European sense.

Military traditions necessarily flow from the dominant experiences of the societies in question. Regimental soldiering in the American Southwest, or on the far-flung frontiers of the British Empire, was not a particularly good school for the development of the operational artistry required for the conduct of European mass warfare. Skills do not develop in a vacuum, as the course and duration of the Civil War were to demonstrate. Neither Britain nor the United States entered the First World War (or the Second World War) with soldiers trained, let alone experienced, in the handling of tens of divisions.

There is a plausible basis to claims for the relevance of operational art for the United States today, both in the historically demonstrable costs of lack of skill at that level of conflict and in terms of contemporary U.S. military engagement in the defense of NATO-Europe. The operational scale of U.S. involvement in a future land war in Europe is predetermined by the scale of its peacetime commitments to NATO. However, recognition of the obvious potential importance of operational art for campaign direction in a conflict in Europe needs to be balanced by appreciation of the possible frustration of purely military skills by the political facts of coalition warfare. For it is doubtful if even operational art for a national army can be usefully approached strictly as a military craft. Common sense and historical experience inform us that theater commanders for a coalition endeavor rarely, if ever, are at liberty to plan or conduct their campaigns as strictly technical, military enterprises.

There is a distinct possibility that some of the contemporary fascination with operational art on the part of the U.S. Army reflects simply the enthusiasm for novelty. But, more seriously, this fascination probably flows also from the mistaken conviction that in operational art there is a craft which, properly applied, might enable the soldiers of NATO to perform effectively without potentially fatal interference by particularist national political considerations. It may not be wholly unjust to observe that doctrinal acceptance of the operational level of war may, in reality, function as a panacea for a U.S. Army which was frustrated by politics (i.e., by constraints upon strategy that were fatal for the prospects of victory), and which suspects strongly that strategy for a war in Europe may be directed and misdirected heavily by extramilitary considerations. Contrary to first appearances, perhaps, this rather negative line of thought is not intended as criticism of the U.S. Army or of the civilian theorists who have been emphasizing the importance of operational art.[29] The point in need of emphasis is that the constraints which policy places upon the application of force are not to be evaded by the rediscovery of the operational level of war.

If armies should look to operational artistry in generalship (the original classical Greek meaning of strategy) to save them from some deficiencies in tactical performance, and perhaps also to compensate for flabbiness in coalition military strategy writ large, they may need to be reminded that operational art traditionally is a realm of Soviet competence, as one should expect of a generally successful great continental power. Moreover, until 1989–90 it was the Warsaw Pact, not NATO, that enjoyed unity of multinational command. In principle, operational art is so important that it seems churlish, even reactionary perhaps, to be skeptical of its promise for NATO as a level of competitive engagement. But it is difficult to be optimistic over the promise of operational artistry for theater campaigning, when the national corps theoretically subject to SACEur's generalship may in practice be motivated and even commanded by distinctively national considerations. One need hardly make the point that Soviet leaders are fully aware of the fact that their enemy in the West comprises a *coalition*. Eliot Cohen reminds anybody in need of reminding that "[I]n no war has an alliance of *independent* states gone to war in lockstep."[30] In the absence of alliance cohesion of a quite remarkable kind in time of crisis and war, excellence in the operational art of war is more likely than not to be close to a practical irrelevance.

There is a Janus-like quality to recognition and development of operational art in the United States. On the one hand, the concept focuses attention upon what, arguably, is a valid and important level of military activity. On the other hand, some soldiers and military reformers with a Teutonophilic regard for the historically demonstrated—though frequently exaggerated—German accomplishments in operational art may well be encouraged to repeat the traditional American strategic cultural sin of failing properly to integrate political purpose and military action. The simple dichotomy between strategy and tactics, for all its faults, at least has the paramount virtue of asserting the interface between policy-chosen strategic goals and battlefield activity. Operational art, in less than outstanding hands, may serve to obscure that interface.

With the best of intentions, some of the better-known members of what loosely is known as the U.S. military reform movement have encouraged the idea that there is a style of warfare characterized by maneuver and a contrasting style characterized by attrition. Needless to say, perhaps, the latter is vilified as the preference of little minds and incompetent military forces. In order to avoid the risk of unintentionally misstating the arguments of particular military theorists, a risk that is nontrivial given the ambiguity of key elements in their theorizing, this discussion is framed in a positive way, and not explicitly as a critique.

The purpose of maneuver is in need of clarification. The "maneuver warfare" of the late seventeenth and the eighteenth centuries which

Clausewitz so despised was a form of conflict imposed by severe logistical constraints, reflected dynastic (rather than popular national) interests, and was compatible with an ethos of battle avoidance and limited political ambitions. The purpose of the maneuver warfare of the eighteenth century typically was to secure an advantage of position without the crude necessity for, or gamble of, a bloody passage of arms. Battles in the eighteenth century were exceedingly costly in casualties among the very highly trained, and hence expensive, soldiers of the period. If the issues at stake were not of a life-or-death character for the state-participants, why press matters beyond calculation of net advantage to actual trial by battle? It was standard and honorable practice, for example, for a besieged garrison to surrender once the besiegers had effected a "practicable breach" in the fortifications. Siegecraft *après* Vauban was a science.[31] Since both besieger and besieged could calculate—*ceteris paribus*—almost to the hour when a fortified place should fall to assault, the besiegers saw no need to accept the heavy casualties of actually carrying the breach (and the damage to discipline as the rough and licentious soldiery effected an enjoyable "sack"). The besieged, understandably, were not motivated to suffer the horrors of a sack, since contemporary standards of duty and honor required only that resistance be maintained until a practicable breach was battered.

By way of the sharpest contrast with the wars of maneuver conducted by the sensibly battle-shy generals of the *anciens régimes,* the maneuver warfare favored by the cognoscenti in the United States today is an operational and tactical form or style intended to effect great outcomes. Indeed, as reformist writings make all too clear, the model of maneuver warfare that they favor is not the intricate quadrille of very limited objective conflict which was swept away by French energy (and Napoleonic genius) in the wars of the French Revolution and Empire, but rather the *Kesselschlacht* doctrine of the later Prussian-German army. *Kesselschlacht* translates best as a battle or campaign of encirclement and annihilation. Marlborough's surprise march to the Danube in 1704 (which led to Blenheim), Napoleon's surprise march to Ulm in 1805 (his masterpiece), the encirclement of the principal French field armies at Sedan and Metz in 1870, the Schlieffen Plan of 1914, the Manstein Plan of 1940, the Soviet destruction of the Germans' Army Group Center in 1944, MacArthur's amphibious left hook at Inchon in 1950—these, at the operational level of war, are the campaign models of bold conception which have most inspired the contemporary adherents of maneuver in war.

The maneuver warfare which has had the most inspirational effect really has been the agility and flexibility displayed by the German and the Israeli armies both in the offense and the defense. Operational/campaign grand designs which seek to damage or rupture the cohesion of the enemy tend to require maneuvers to threaten his lines of communication. Such threats can be developed either via turning movements on his flanks (a threat to both flanks opens the possibility of effecting an encirclement and creation of a *Kessel* [cauldron]), or via an initially narrow but deep penetration of his front. There is no question, in principle at least, that the mind of the enemy commander, the confidence of his soldiers, and even the physical integrity of his command and control system are objectives of attack more likely to produce great decisions if unhinged or even just shaken, than are broad-fronted territorial aims. Frontal attacks engage the enemy where he is strongest and, even if successful, push him back on his lines of communication. This, in a phrase, is "attritional warfare," or in Luttwak's aptly pejorative description, "war waged by industrial methods."[32]

The problems with so-called maneuver warfare do not pertain to its desirability, but rather to the limited scope for its application. Several caveats of different kinds merit attention. First, skill in operational and tactical maneuver is not a wholly reliable equalizer *vis-à-vis* an enemy who can enlist terrain (and weather) on his side, and who has great material advantages. The German army was beaten in Russia in 1941 by the sheer geographical depth of the theater of operations, by the fall mud, by severe winter weather, and by its own human and material deficiencies in the face of an enemy unexpectedly willing to fight hard—as well as by the indecisiveness of its campaign direction (the invasion was far from a triumph of German operational art). In the Ardennes in December 1944, the German army was beaten by allied tactical air power, by a shortage of practicable roads, and by severe deficiencies of fuel. Second, incomplete success in bold operational and tactical maneuver tends to create vulnerable salients which are exceedingly expensive to hold. The great "bulges" created by incomplete German operational success in the spring of 1918, in the summer of 1942 (Stalingrad and the Caucasus), and in December 1944 all served to hasten the ruin of the German army. Third, for reasons of physical, political, or human-altered geography, the enemy may not have flanks which can be turned by agile maneuver. Witness the pain of the Italian campaign of World War II and the inability of the Allies to break out of their Normandy beachhead for more than six weeks in June–July 1944. Fourth, the indirect approach to the conduct of war is feasible for the side which enjoys maritime command, but hard fighting usually has to be done by somebody. The allied seaborne descents upon Sicily, Italy, and France in 1943–44 were feasible only because the Wehrmacht had been blunted and was still detained massively on the Eastern Front.

Military reformers have to be alert to the danger that in their abomination of attrition warfare they do not find themselves over-attracted to a magic formula, which may be more incantation than actual formula, for relatively cheap military success. Modern military history shows that first-class enemies are unlikely to be maneuvered into defeat, save in the context of the prior and contemporary attrition of their fighting strength; their armies simply are too large and too skilled in the art of war. Maritime-oriented coalitions cannot be maneuvered into defeat because even if they lose an opening campaign on land, their center of strategic gravity is untouched. Moreover, the dynamics of sea-power and land-power competition inexorably, *eventually*, should shift the initiative in maneuver to the maritime coalition.

However, Napoleon and Hitler both exploited the fact that, for a while, nominally first-class enemies, particularly when functioning as a coalition, were in fact less than first-class for reasons of obsolete doctrine, poor plans, deficient motivation, or incompetent leadership. NATO certainly is first-class, or very close, in the quantity and quality of the tactical military instruments provided by its members. But bold Soviet maneuvers—military *perestroika* permitting—could so unnerve and physically unhinge the Alliance that swift campaign success would ensue.

NATO's great equalizer to the problems in concerted military effectiveness which might frustrate its ambition to hold a Soviet invasion in Germany most probably lies in the realm of grand strategy rather than operational artistry on the ground. Neither "emerging technologies" (advanced conventional munitions, or ACM) nor superior operational artistry offers reliable paths to rendering continental NATO-Europe impregnable.

Theorists focused upon land power have been wont to assume that war is war, regardless of environment. At the level of high policy such an assumption is valid. But war at sea, in the air, and prospectively in space is inherently attrition warfare with maneuver forces (much less so for space forces deployed in necessarily predictable orbits). Battles or campaigns of annihilation can be, and have been, waged at sea and in the air, but annihilation has been achieved unit by unit in detail *by attrition*. The details vary among geographical environments, but as a general rule it is not helpful to compare and contrast maneuver with attrition, any more than it is helpful to compare and contrast offense with defense or deterrence with defense (or denial). Competent theories of war are inclusive, not exclusive. Maneuver (on land) is most likely to succeed when the enemy is fixed, held, and attrited elsewhere. Defense in maritime, aerial, and space warfare is vastly facilitated if offensive action has effected prior massive attrition of the enemy's power to strike. Deterrence at any level and in any kind of warfare should be maximized if the enemy is convinced that militarily he will not succeed.

It is near axiomatic that the central nervous system of a military instrument—be it a Napoleonic-era army deployed in line and column, or a strategic forces' triad today—is more fragile than are the sharp-end fighting elements themselves. Maneuver in war requires decentralization of command, or at least training and equipment for that end, in the anticipated event of disruption of command from the top down. Since the campaign-level, operational value of military action may be a great deal less than the sum of tactical successes, agility in war has the potential to be self-defeating. Uniformity of doctrine, the proper use of general staff officers (to provide the perspective, and remind of the intentions, of the commander-in-chief), tactical drills to combat the adverse consequences of the fog of war, and provision of redundant technical equipment for communication, are all means by which attempts have been made to render compatible the necessity for local creativity on the battlefield with adequate adherence to high-level purposes. The tensions between military agility and centralized command and control generically are little different with reference to strategic nuclear warfare than they were for the battle fleets of the age of fighting sail (for whom were written fighting instructions demanding linear formation for combat, as the only reliable means by which an admiral could exercise tactical command).[33]

An important point which frequently passes underappreciated is that style in warfare tends in good part to express the scope of strategic ambitions of the state or coalition. There is much to be said in favor of the proposition that the amount and character of combat that may be required really is in the hands of the enemy to determine. For example, NATO might well be very content indeed simply to conduct a successful forward defense of Germany and expel invading forces. But it would be within the Soviet ability to decline to accept an unfavorable decision in Central Europe. Moscow could bid either for theater-wide victory via a maritime-air assault on the northern and western oceanic flanks of NATO, or for definitive victory over the enemy coalition as a whole through a direct strategic nuclear assault upon North America. States and coalitions with very limited and distinctly defensive ambitions for their military prowess are most unlikely in peacetime to design, train, and equip for a maneuver character in warfare suitable, if successful in action, for the prospective overthrow of the enemy's forces. Proposals in the 1980s for a radically more aggressive operational-level doctrine for NATO in Central Europe ran aground on the political objection that such doctrine was incompatible with the policy goals of the Alliance. Moreover, there is the eminently practical point that a NATO outgunned, outmanned, and possibly engaged in a desperately confused scrambling series of encounter battles would be unlikely to have the disposable military assets, suitably flexible logistics, or the requisite quality of command cohesion needed to execute timely and decisive flank marches and counterattacks in best Jominian style.

The holistic thread running through the argument here, the conviction that everything relates inclusively to everything else, has been a notable player in this first chapter on technology and the art of war. There are grounds for skepticism over the scope of the promise in the proposition that "[t]echnology is a means of overcoming strategical and tactical handicaps and inequalities."[34] Technology is critical for possibilities in tactical effectiveness, but tactical skill—forged through doctrinal excellence—is no less critical for the operational and strategic value of technology. Michael Handel rightly affirms in an outstanding and innovative analysis that the considerably understudied subject of technological surprise might be a war-winner,[35] but in practice great wars between great states or coalitions have yet to be won unambiguously as a consequence of such surprise. The protracted "surprise" of Ultra in World War II may be as close to a plausible, monocausal technological explanation for a great victory as one can find. However, vastly important though Ultra undoubtedly was, is it true to claim that it made the difference between victory and defeat? Such a question is about as intelligent as asking whether sea power, air power, or the land-power and air-power attrition suffered on the Eastern Front *really* brought Nazi Germany down. Thus posed, the issue is an absurdity.

The literature of military history and contemporary defense analysis is studded with the indiscriminate employment of the adjective "decisive." The bacillus of reductionism is widespread. The fact of the matter is that great states and powerful coalitions in the twentieth century can rarely be undone by the outcome of a single battle, and have never yet been ruined by the allegedly decisive employment, alone, of a particular weapon. When one comes across an author who boldly describes a battle or campaign as decisive, one should ask just what it was that was decided (more often than not one is not told). Furthermore, one should be alert to authors who describe battle after battle as being allegedly decisive. If the adjective "decisive" is to retain any meaning, one cannot allow more than one campaign, battle, event, year, particular military instrument, or whatever pertaining to a war to be decisive. This seemingly pedantic point about the need for caution in the employment of the adjective "decisive" is advanced here because the U.S. defense community is not the beneficiary of a mature and sophisticated theory of war as a whole. Prophets with simple messages pertaining to the supposedly decisive significance of this or that theater (what used to be the Central Front, the Norwegian Sea/Northern Flank, the Soviet Far Eastern provinces, or of this or that strategy, tactic, weapon, or even device [e.g., reactive armor on Soviet tanks]) may capture audiences who have not been protected by inclusive strategic theory or by military-historical knowledge against reductionist fallacies.

CHAPTER 6

Technology and the Experience of War

Strange as it may seem, no modern war to date has been decided by the unexpected appearance of a new weapon or by superior technology alone.

—MICHAEL HANDEL[1]

We can wreck Berlin from end to end if the USAAF will come in on it. It will cost between us 400–500 aircraft. It will cost Germany the war.

—AIR CHIEF MARSHAL SIR ARTHUR "BOMBER" HARRIS, letter to Prime Minister Winston Churchill, November 3, 1943[2]

EXCELLENT WEAPONS in the hands of incompetent operators (e.g., the French and Spanish ships at Trafalgar),[3] in the service of faulty doctrine (e.g., Germany's Me 262 jet fighters employed in bombing roles),[4] or simply deployed too little and too late in a war already decided by errors in grand strategy (e.g., the Panzer Mk V *Panther*)[5] cannot snatch victory from otherwise impending defeat. Adequate technology is a necessary, but not a sufficient, condition for stability in deterrence and success in war.

The critical realms of German weakness in World War II, for example, were above all else in grand strategy, in a lack of mass, and progressively in operational art as the former corporal hailed by his sycophantic staff as the "Greatest Captain of All Time" assumed direct responsibility for the detailed control of military operations.[6] High technology per se was not a German weakness—quite the reverse. The German problem lay in the absence of effective central management of innovation and procurement. But Germany did not lose the war because it performed generally abominably in what has come to be called the weapons-acquisition process. Germany lost because its policy produced a materially overwhelming array of enemies against it. Better weapons, delivered earlier and hence eventually in larger numbers, certainly would have helped its numerically much overmatched soldiery. However, it is improbable that a tactically sharper military instrument could have fully offset the consequences of folly in policy at the highest level. Needless to say, perhaps, one can postulate hypothetically a Germany so different in its operational communication technologies and practices (no Enigma vulnerability), so coherent in its management of innovation and procurement, and so wisely armed in depth that in fact one would have postulated policies incompatible with features endemic to the somewhat feudal and administratively ramshackle Third Reich.

In retrospective prescription, as in prescription for the contemporary scene, one must be alert to the danger of recommending reforms intolerable to the political and strategic culture in question. "It was no accident" that Hitler's Germany mismanaged the defense-industrial basis for its war effort, just as it is no accident that strategy is underexplored territory in the contemporary United States.[7] "What if . . ." speculation needs to be disciplined when applied historically, just as it does when posed for the future. Particular political systems and cultures are not totally at liberty to select the wisest of grand strategies, or to adopt the most efficient methods in preparation of their policy instruments. For example, the competing jurisdictions, or rival baronies, of the Nazi state were not solely the casual products of incompetence. Rather they were created consciously for the purposes of curbing the emergence of candidate "crown princes" and of creating rivalries which would drive a need for policy decision at the very top. Nazi Germany, like the Soviet Union today, certainly could have been administered vastly more efficiently than it was. But such a "Nazi" Germany, or future "Soviet" Russia, simply would not be Nazi Germany (or Soviet Russia).

TECHNOLOGY, FIGHTING POWER, AND MILITARY EFFECTIVENESS

It is a general rule that there are no second prizes awarded to the "runners-up" in war. A state which loses a war can expect an "F" for failure, and not a sympathetic "C" for effort. The title of this section of the discussion draws attention to the crucial distinction between fighting power and military effectiveness. The latter is a strategic conception, while the former is not. Fighting power, however it is measured and whatever one believes it to be produced by, can be expressed either in absolute or in relative terms, but it is not a tool for the explanation of how well armed forces function as instruments of national or coalition grand strategy. Unit for unit, one may decide with good reason that the German army was the "A Team" in ground combat in both world wars. However, superior German fighting power plainly did not translate into victory in war. It should be recalled that strategy is a matter of means *and ends*. When misapplied according to a faulty theory of war, or when generated in too little quantity, (always selective) excellence in fighting power will not save a state or coalition from defeat.

As Clausewitz understood very well, having observed the ruin of his country at Jena-Auerstadt in October 1806, warfare is not simply a craft or a technique. The fighting power of a state's armed forces is very much an expression of the organization and ethos of the state in question and of the principal characteristics of its society. Americans, Germans, and Russians prepare for and wage war in reasonably distinctive American, German, and Russian ways. The effectiveness of national ways in defense preparation and warfare can and must be assayed through the discipline of the outcomes to competition and combat. National strategic cultures actually are tested against one another; war is not a realm wherein the merits of cultural relativism can be permitted much inherent value. It is well to bear in mind the cautionary words of Joseph Rothschild: "I am tempted to . . . suggest that war, being such a fiercely and fatally competitive activity, imposes a certain logic of imitation on those who engage in it or seriously prepare to engage in it. Thus, *toutes proportions gardées,* armed forces and their weapons tend to resemble each other at least as much as (and probably more than) they tend to express the ethnonational cultures or national characters of their societies."[8]

States unable to mobilize much of the political energy of their societies for the prosecution of war will fail in combat, and particularly in protracted combat, against states which can mobilize their societies more thoroughly. New weapons technologies per se could not save NATO in Europe from being overrun. What would be needed would be courageous political leaders and citizens prepared to fight and die in large numbers for the defense of their homelands. As Napoleon said, *"À la guerre, les trois quarts sont des affaires morales."*[9]

Military technique is important, as is a plentiful supply of state-of-the-art (or nearly so) equipment. Certainly a pronounced technological disadvantage in weaponry places a burden upon military method and morale which may be too heavy to bear. However, to deter and if need be to defend successfully against a very determined enemy, it is not enough simply to be skilled in the craft of war. The enemy must believe that he faces a foe possessed of the civic virtues essential for the determined prosecution of war. In addition, if it is to have external integrity, the craft of war must be employed in pursuit of essential, publicly understandable, and achievable strategic objectives that are critical for widely approved goals of high policy. In and of itself the long-standing cultural affection which American society feels for technology is not a source of weakness for national security. After all, it is sensible to substitute machines for men (i.e., casualties) where feasible; it is advantageous to place superior weapons in the hands of American fighting men; and—as a general rule—it is always prudent to go with, rather than go against, the cultural traits of one's society. The kinds of military method in which the German and, perhaps ironically, the Israeli armed forces have excelled cannot reliably be replicated by the armed forces of a distinctively (geostrategically shaped) American society. The path to military proficiency does not lie through the aping of alien strategic cultures, but rather through the exploitation of the comparative advantages of one's own, while paying attention to the need to provide compensation for whatever one's comparative disadvantages happen to be.

Military excellence in the absolute sense of superior fighting power, rather than the relative sense of military effectiveness, is no guarantee of victory in war. Excellence may be dissipated in battles and campaigns which, however successful, fail to achieve a death grip upon the enemy's will or capacity to fight. Furthermore, if military excellence is attained by a relatively small armed force, the effect of combat losses will be disproportionately devastating. For example, on any accounting the (all-) regular divisions of the original British Expeditionary Force (B.E.F.) of August 1914, even allowing for their large complement of reservists, were among the finest infantry and cavalry in the world at that time. However, by the close of the First Battle of Ypres (October 30–November 24), the B.E.F. with its mere six original divisions and 110,000 men had suffered in excess of 86,000 casualties from its original complement.[10] The British army never really recovered from this devastation of its professional ranks. The development of tactical doctrine, not a strong point even with the small regular army of 1914, suffered critically from a persisting lack of experienced professionals to direct the training of the new mass army. For another example, the combat arms of the U.S. Army— particularly the infantry, of course—in World War II suffered in their tactical and operational effectiveness because the worldwide army force structure of eighty-nine divisions really was too small to allow proper training and casualty replacement policies. The very high casualty rates among junior officers and senior NCOs became a self-perpetuating phenomenon, as combat units were committed to what amounted to "the duration."

Provided the opportunity costs of development and acquisition are not too high, and provided too high a price in numbers forgone is not paid, better weapons are always desirable. But, other things being tolerably equal, people matter most—to repeat a chorus line of this text. Superiority in military method tends to be more important either than a technological edge in weaponry or a *modest* advantage in numbers of soldiers. While numerical superiority at the "decisive" point is usually critical,[11] tactical advantage lies in the superior use made of weapons or arms in flexible combinations. The superiority of the most competent military instruments of historical record did not rest primarily, if at all, upon technological advantages. Historically outstanding were the Roman army (prior to its barbarization in the final quarter of the fourth century A.D.),[12] the Spanish infantry of the sixteenth and early seventeenth centuries, the army of France from 1800 until its ruin in 1812, the British Royal Navy of the late 1790s and the early 1800s, the German army of 1914–18 and 1939–45, and possibly the USAAF of 1944–45. The USAAF, which certainly enjoyed a progressive numerical and selective technical advantage over its German and Japanese enemies, came to benefit from an ever greater favorable margin in the combat skills of its personnel and the operational skills with which it was wielded in support of the war as a whole.

The weaponry of the Roman army and the German army, viewed overall, was no more than adequate at best. In the decades when it was unbeatable in fleet battles, and was rarely bested in single-ship engagements, the British Royal Navy fought weapon systems (sailing ships) which almost invariably were marginally technically inferior to those constructed by France and Spain (and the United States). This is not to say that inferior weapons do not matter. When important classes of weapons are inferior—as with British and American tanks, and German towed field artillery in World War II—compensation has to be provided. In the Anglo-American case just cited, that compensation was found in quantity of armored fighting vehicles and in the quantity and skill with which artillery and tactical air power were applied. In the German case, the weakness in dedicated field artillery was worked around by the use of antiaircraft guns in some specialized artillery roles, the proliferation of mortars, the invention, mass production and very courageous use of *personal* antitank weapons (the Panzerfaust and the satchel charge [a hero weapon if ever there was one]), and the agile use of self-propelled artillery (assault guns) and tanks.

Just as the effectiveness of a society in war is not totally a function of the narrowly military skills of its soldiers, sailors, and airmen, so the fighting power and the effectiveness of a military instrument are not mindlessly to be equated with its firepower (important though that output factor must always be). The destruction of people and property in war always should be subordinate to, and instrumental for, success in the field. In its turn, success in the field must be instrumental for campaign advantage and ultimately for victory in war as a whole. The proper combination of fire and movement is the tactical essence of war. Armies, navies, and air forces contribute to the national security in peacetime and crisis-time far more by their reputations for effectiveness than by any really certain knowledge of their current and near-term future efficacy in combat. Traditions of victory or defeat can be critical for the psychological enfeeblement of an enemy. Naturally, self-confidence can be misplaced. Nonetheless, it is true as a generalization to argue that military excellence tends to be forged over generations and cannot reliably be produced instantly simply by training and material acquisition.

On the subject of morale and combat prowess and the psychological enfeeblement of an enemy, one needs to balance Luttwak's neo-Clausewitzian arguments about the paradoxical logic of war (the "culminating point of victory" and the like)[13] with recognition of the value of confidence. It is true that confidence breeds overconfidence, and that thus far in recorded history every bid for great empire has overextended itself. On the maritime side, the Athenians and the British, for example, both overreached their strength in the hubris of imperium, while the phenomenon of continentalist overextension is seemingly a perennial feature of the grand-strategic competition of recent times between maritime and land-oriented states and coalitions. Nonetheless, while granting the confidence-overconfidence point its substantial due, the fact remains that initial success in war fosters expectations of further success and of further failure on the part of the enemy. With Olympian historical detachment one may note that, ultimately, "nothing fails like success,"[14] but the loss of the first battle or campaign in a war can have a prolonged effect upon the morale of those involved. Griffith has observed uncontentiously that Union troops in the East never fully recovered from the psychological blow of ignominious—if actually rather close-run—defeat at First Manassas in 1861. Johnny Reb was promoted to super-soldier both in his own eyes and in the eyes of his enemy. More recently, the British army acquired a respect for the German army in May 1940 which, though merited in good part, still was excessive and distinctly dysfunctional for later campaigns. This low self-esteem on the British side was reinforced massively by their rough handling by Erwin Rommel in Libya in 1941. It is the last battle which matters most, but an unhealthy overrespect for the enemy has the power to depress the will to fight and thereby to protract war.

THE FIRST WORLD WAR

Probably no war in history has been so misunderstood, or has remained so controversial, in its strategic and tactical dimensions as has the Great War of 1914–18. It is still fashionable to believe that the war was a protracted exercise in futility, that the art of war was missing in action for four years, and that—with very few exceptions—the generals on both sides were extraordinarily incompetent. But, in fact, many of the more popular beliefs about the Great War cannot withstand close scrutiny.

First, the offensive doctrines of 1914 were either a foreign policy necessity for the succor of exposed allies, or a strategic necessity imposed by the military logic of a two- (plus) front conflict. Furthermore, there were apparently good military reasons (which happened to be wrong) for believing that the tactical offensive could work to achieve operational success. Second, although no country produced a Marlborough, a Napoleon, or a Lee, the proposition that the B.E.F. (for example) comprised "lions led by donkeys" is not generally persuasive. The generals in all the participating countries were confronted with problems which probably were beyond the ability of military "genius" to solve. Those problems could not be solved, save crudely by attrition, by the various systems and doctrines of war of the powers in that particular period. Third, far from the art of war taking a vacation for four years, there was in fact substantial technological and tactical innovation in attempts to break the stalemate. Nor was operational ingenuity and strategic grand design lacking; the problem was that the tactical instrument could not succeed well enough at its own level of conflict.

Fourth, appalling though the casualties were, they were not uniquely high by any means. Phrases like "the slaughter on the Western Front" are considerably misleading at best. Casualty rates in war, *any war,* are a function of scale of national involvement and duration of direct and heavy military engagement. The Great War produced unprecedented (and unrepeated in World War II) casualties for Britain—908,371 dead and 2,090,212 wounded (British Empire; the United Kingdom total dead was 775,000)—because Britain waged continental war continuously for more than four years. Moreover, in 1917 and 1918, Britain, of necessity, assumed principal responsibility for defeating the German army in the field. Comparison with the British casualties of World War II—397,762 dead and 475,000 wounded—says nothing about the relative quality of generalship in the two wars, nor about the impact of technological progress upon casualty rates.[15] Anyone attracted by the idea that the high policy, generalship, tactical leadership, or weapons technology (check one or several!) of the Great War was uniquely lethal should be required to explain the fact that in the Great War Germany suffered 1,808,546 military dead and 4,247,143 wounded, while in the Second World War the figures have been estimated respectively at 2,850,000 and 7,250,000. Also, the technologies of long-range aerial bombardment meant that civilians were at military risk in a new way (Germany suffered approximately 500,000 civilian dead from military action, largely bombing).

Fifth, mythology to the contrary again notwithstanding, the tactical offense was not by any means invariably more expensive in casualties than was the tactical defense. Extraordinarily heavy casualties were suffered from time to time, as they have been in all wars, by faulty doctrine, half- or mistrained soldiers, inadequate battlefield leadership, and by deficiencies in suitable matériel. (The British army, for example, was almost totally unequipped for trench warfare in 1914: grenades, mortars, steel helmets, barbed wire, and effective entrenching tools were all lacking). Too many of the generals in 1914–18 were products of the staff culture already mentioned, but their ranks contained avid devotees of the "science of war"—albeit, perhaps, an unduly dated "science of war"—who were nothing if not professional about their trade. Norman F. Dixon proclaims: "Only the most blinkered could deny that the First World War exemplified every aspect of high-level military incompetence. For sheer lack of imaginative leadership, inept decisions, ignoring of military intelligence, underestimation of the enemy, delusional optimism and monumental wastage of human resources it has surely never had its equal."[16]

Although Dixon's robustly worded claims defy testing, they do suffer from an inherent implausibility. One must ask whether it is likely that generalship in such different military systems as the German, French, Russian, and British would be so uniformly abysmal simultaneously. If British generals were indeed as incompetent as alleged, how does one explain the incontestable fact that it was the British army which played the major role in the defeat of the German army in 1918? Moreover, the British army, for all its deficiencies of method, did not lose its great campaigns on the Somme in 1916 and in Flanders in 1917. Could it be that there was no clever way to win the war on the ground by inspired operational art? This is not to deny the weaknesses of Haig's style of command, to ignore an unsureness in operational grip, or to excuse plain tactical incompetence; but it is to suggest that the historian-critics of the commanders in the Great War have yet to specify available paths to victory which plausibly should have produced a radically better military outcome than in fact was obtained.

The central problem in 1914–18 was not, as too often is alleged, with the incompetence of the military systems engaged, but rather with the character of the policy goals which governments obliged their generals and admirals to serve. The belligerents suffered as heavily as they did because they sought total victory in a great war between very mighty coalitions. It may be sensible, with the wisdom of hindsight, to argue that it was a mistake to seek the military overthrow of the enemy in 1914–18. But it is a fact that that was the operative, proximate objective, while it has yet to be shown that a much less ambitious goal was either feasible or strategically prudent.[17] In their different ways both sides learned through expensive experience how best to wage war, given the constraints and advantages of their several national styles in the technical context of the period, and the expansive war aims which everywhere were increasingly popular.

Statecraft and generalship were handcuffed by two critical technical deficiencies in their attempts to achieve swift military decision from 1914 to 1918. First, the absence of man-portable radios meant that the mass armies which wealthy, railroad-united countries could sustain in the field could not reliably be commanded tactically in any meaningful sense once they were committed to the attack. The problems of coordinating the fire of *the* killer weapon of the war, the artillery, with the unpredictable rates of advance of different infantry units (which could not communicate their real-time location and need for support), and of committing reserves at the right times in the right places, were never fully satisfactorily resolved. Second, although every army on the Western Front could and did achieve break-ins to the enemy's trench lines or, by 1917, to his fortified zones, no army on the Western Front enjoyed a quality of tactical mobility in (or logistical mobility through) the zone of combat such that operational-level success could be secured. In other words, armies could break in but not break through. The Allies in particular, at great logistical cost, maintained substantial cavalry forces in reserve behind the infantry forces committed to an offensive. This was not, or not only, because the officers and gentlemen of the period were attached atavistically to the horse. Rather it was because the cavalry, for all its vulnerability in the face of modern weapons, quite literally was the only mobile arm available at that time capable in principle, though not in practice, of operational exploitation.

If there was a dominant weapon in the First World War it was the artillery. Once the armies began to dig in, which occurred as early as September 14, 1914, it soon became apparent that the character of the war was not that which had been anticipated and for which the artillery parks and ammunition supply had been prepared. The light, quick-firing field artillery most suitable for mobile open warfare was not very appropriate for a war which developed into a protracted siege. Through trial and a great deal of error both sides came to perfect their artillery arms, technically, in quantity, and in tactical employment as an integral instrument of combined arms for set-piece operations.

The Germans discovered that bombardments lasting many days both forfeited the advantages of surprise and rendered subsequent tactical movement exceedingly slow and difficult. With this knowledge, and confronting the certainty of eventual defeat in a war of attrition, the Germans were bold in tactical innovation in the use of artillery for the rapid paralysis and isolation of (often overly strongly held) enemy frontline positions. On the Eastern Front in September 1917, and on the Western Front in the spring of 1918, Georg "Breakthrough" Bruchmüller demonstrated what a whirlwind bombardment could accomplish when employed to facilitate an infantry attack by infiltration tactics. The Germans also developed a new kind of assault infantry (borrowing directly from the ideas of Captain André Laffargue of the French army) armed with a novel variety of unprecedentedly lethal weapons (light machine guns and flamethrowers, for example), thereby minimizing the need for an artillery support which must become tenuous as an offensive gains ground. Furthermore, the German introduction of chlorine gas in 1915 and of mustard gas in 1917 were semiplausible candidates for major technological surprises which barely, possibly, might have forced a restoration of mobile warfare in the West.

While the Germans responded to stalemate by tactical innovation in methods first of defense, in the winter of 1916–17, and then of offense, in fall 1917 and spring 1918, the Western Allies, characteristically, sought leverage through technological innovation in the form of the tank. In contrast to the operational and strategic vision of some theorist-practitioners (particularly in the interwar period), the tank of First World War vintage was only a formidable weapon for close support of the infantry—no less, but, alas, no more. For example, it is true that the surprise attack launched at Amiens on August 8, 1918—the "black day of the German army," as a psychologically broken Erich Ludendorff termed it—was spearheaded critically by a concentrated force of 415 tanks. However, only 145 of those tanks remained operational as "runners" on August 9. For all its utility in a combined-arms setting, the bloody record of the allied achievement in the final "Hundred Days" campaign demonstrated that the tank certainly was no wonder weapon. It was technically unreliable, very vulnerable to shell fire (which it attracted), extremely slow, and available only in small numbers on a regular basis.

In embryo at least, air power evolved radically in the course of four years. It moved from marginal utility for reconnaissance, both to a variably important adjunct to almost every operation of land and sea warfare, and to the threshold of being able to conduct an independent campaign designed to put direct pressure upon the enemy's society at home. Rather like the tank, the airplane in the Great War provided potent fuel for new strategic visions, but it had not *demonstrated* that it was, or even could be, an independently operating war winner.

The war witnessed an abundance of courage, growing professional competence by staffs, no little tactical skill at the sharp end, and—as always in war—a great quickening in the rate of military-technical invention, tests of new equipment in the field by trial and error, and procurement of military goods of all kinds on a vast scale. But, overall, neither side could develop a tactical striking power capable of achieving swift operational success. Under the technological conditions of the time, in the context of a land war in the West without flanks, the job simply could not be done. On the Western Front the net advantage in reinforcement and resupply for the defender was simply too great.

Decisive flank marches to turn the enemy's position could not be executed in the West after late October 1914 because the rival positions were fortified and effectively continuous from the coast of Flanders to the Swiss frontier. The great turning movement of the "right wheel" of the much modified Schlieffen Plan in August and very early September 1914 wheeled at the same pace at which Napoleon's (and Turenne's, and Caesar's!) armies had moved—the pace of exceedingly weary marching infantry, many of whom were reservists and not exactly in peak physical condition. More to the operational point, the Germans were marching to attempt a gigantic *Kesselschlacht* against an enemy who was falling back on his lines of communication, who could move troops laterally by railroad, and who had a massive fortress in Paris upon which a new line of resistance could be anchored and from which troops could sally forth (since the German First Army, contrary to plan, decided to wheel in front of the French capital). In their third and final great offensive in the West (Verdun, 1916, was the second), beginning on March 21, 1918, the Germans demonstrated again that even a tactically superior army could not exploit stunning initial success with sufficient speed so as to negate the superior mobility of the defense.[18]

Nevertheless, on balance, it was innovation in military method, rather than new technology per se, which came closest to achieving operational-level results. For example, the use of the submarine in an antimercantile shipping role, instead of as an arm of the battle fleet, had real potential to achieve decisive strategic results, properly so-called. It should be noted that the most effective solution to the submarine commerce raider was not technological in character; rather it was tactical, in the organization of a convoy system which created a largely empty sea for the technically rudimentary submarines of the period. By way of a further example, the most dramatic breakthrough achieved on the Western Front in four years—the German rout of the British Fifth Army in March 1918, which transpired to be no more than a very deep break-in—was secured not by the agency of a dramatic new weapon, but rather by effective employment of relatively new artillery and infantry assault tactics.

It is an interesting paradox to note that whereas on land prewar strategic expectations were borne out (initially, in the war of movement) but tactical judgments were found to be thoroughly flawed, at sea prewar strategic expectations were wholly confounded, but tactical judgments were discovered to be quite substantially reliable. Indeed, it was the soundness of the prewar tactical judgments, confirmed by early wartime experience, which produced the stalemate in the North Sea between two battle fleets whose commanders could not agree on conditions for engagement.

The grand-strategic functions of Germany's High Seas Fleet remain a realm for scholarly speculation. The fleet was an expression of Imperial Germany's ambition to be recognized as a world power and of her envy of Britain's maritime empire; it was judged to increase Germany's alliance, or nonbelligerent, value to a Britain preponderantly anxious about Franco-Russian ambitions (in the 1890s, the early 1900s, and even into the Great War); and it was probably intended, one distant day, to be of such a size that it would rival the tactical effectiveness of the Royal Navy. Berlin would seem to have hoped that somehow, miraculously, London would not notice the growth of the German fleet to a condition of new parity. Whatever mix of, and weight among, motives one prefers in explanation of Grand Admiral Alfred von Tirpitz's "risk fleet," there can be little doubt that Germany's bid for sea power (*pro tem* of the second class) was a grand-strategic error of war-losing proportions.[19] The High Seas Fleet was too weak to challenge the Royal Navy's Grand Fleet for command of the North Sea, but was sufficiently strong as to oblige Britain geostrategically *de facto* to join the anti-German alliance.

It was paradoxical that both the German and the British navies in 1914 had doctrines of maritime command via decisive battle, but that neither was able to execute those doctrines under the tactical conditions then prevailing. The High Seas Fleet would not seek battle on the open sea, because that would have been tantamount to a death ride to destruction. Ergo, the German fleet was obliged to resort to stratagems designed to entice the Royal Navy into ambush, where detached elements of the Grand Fleet might be destroyed in detail. In principle the Grand Fleet sought decisive battle; indeed professionally and politically as the legatee to the offensive tradition of Hawke, St. Vincent, and Nelson *(inter alia),* it could do no other. But, in practice, and arguably in the Nelsonian mold, it would not seek battle under just any conditions. Specifically, the Royal Navy's Grand Fleet would not seek battle in the fortified killing zone inside the Heligoland Bight where the High Seas Fleet probably would have accepted the challenge.[20] Almost beyond belief is the fact that in 1914 both the British and the German navies quite solemnly believed that the enemy would accept battle under the most disadvantageous of circumstances. The British expected the High Seas Fleet to offer itself up for the Trafalgar treatment in the middle of the North Sea. For their part the Germans persuaded themselves that the Grand Fleet, emulating the close blockading practices of the Royal Navy in the (mine-free, submarine-free, torpedo-destroyer-free, and long-range-coastal-artillery-absent) days of fighting sail, would offer itself off the Jade estuary for catastrophic attrition. Neither navy, prewar, had asked itself the critical question: what if the enemy declines to fight on acceptable terms?

Unfortunately for Germany, the inapplicability of the prewar battle doctrine of its navy was fatal for the strategic utility of its High Seas Fleet. For Britain, the refusal of the High Seas Fleet to present itself in manly fashion for destruction was a surprise, even an annoyance, but strategically was distinctly tolerable. After all, a German "fleet in being," while requiring much (distant) watching, was not contesting actively that British command at sea which assured the freedom of maritime passage essential to the functioning of the allied war effort. Admiral Jellicoe was fortunate in that his Grand Fleet, of uncertain technical and tactical merit, did not have to be placed at hazard in a desperate enterprise for it to fulfill its strategic function of keeping the oceans of the world effectively a British lake. By guarding the "breakwater" to Europe that was the British Isles, the Royal Navy could win its war with tactical inactivity. For the German High Seas Fleet, in contrast, inactivity meant strategic irrelevance.

Ever alert to the perils of perfect panoramic hindsight, one must never forget that in August 1914 the British and German governments, unlike us today, did not know that the war would endure for more than four years. The German strategic purpose was to win the war *on land*—in the West and probably in the East also—before Christmas of that year. Allied working control of the world's oceans was to prove fundamental as the enabling agent for the prosecution of a long and increasingly total war. But in German calculation in 1914 (notwithstanding the somewhat mindless battle doctrine of their fleet), the grand-strategic value of the High Seas Fleet was not its faint promise to knock Britain out of the war, because Britain was not deemed to be an important factor in a short war. Rather the High Seas Fleet, intact and undamaged, would weigh most usefully upon British minds when they came to consider their policy options following Germany's expected victory in the war on land. Only if Britain had continental allies still fighting could the Royal Navy function strategically to bring Germany down—or so the faulty argument went. In traditional continentalist fashion, Germany's leaders had misread the political and strategic history of modern Europe. They should have learned from the Napoleonic Wars that war with Britain meant both open-ended war and war with the resources of the extra-European world protected by British maritime mastery for British exploitation. Today, Soviet strategic planners sensibly self-deterred from endorsement of any quest for decision by nuclear means should be encouraged to ponder what history has to teach concerning the fate of continental empires which engage in hostilities with a maritime superstate.

As noted, the challenge of stalemate on land and at sea in the Great War was met with responses which were technological, tactical, and (very rarely) operational and strategic. Human and material deficiencies denied success to the one allied strategic response to the stalemate in the West—the provision of a new axis of assault upon the Central Powers at Gallipoli. The generals of 1914–18 were not foolish men careless of the lives of their soldiers. Many of them were students and practitioners of a science of war which provided no pat formulae for swift victory in conditions which very few experts had predicted. Paul Kennedy has observed that

> the military staffs planning for the *next* war drew conclusions from the *last* one, and thought it perfectly natural to do so. [But which was the *last* one? The Russo-Japanese War of 1904–1905, the Franco-Prussian War, the American Civil War?: CSG]. So it was. Yet it also contained some very large flaws. After all, what guarantee was there that history would repeat itself? How could one assume that the weapons which won the last war would not be obsolete by the next? In what way could the study of recent history help the planners to discover what was being secretly developed and prepared by potential enemies for the future?[21]

On the last point raised by Kennedy, the First World War, as noted in this discussion, saw few true technological innovations which just might have held the key to an operational success of strategic significance. No less tank-minded a commentator than J. F. C. Fuller had this to say about the conclusion of the war in 1918:

> The nearly universal reason alleged for the German defeat was the employment of tanks in masses by the Allied Powers. But although the tank played a leading part in the German *débâcle,* had there not been deeper reasons, in all probability the results of the battle would

have been not much greater than those after the battle of Cambrai [November 20–December 3, 1917].

> Of the many causes of the German collapse, first and foremost stood the blockade.[22]

Unlike his more journalistic contemporary, Liddell Hart, Fuller was no advocate of maritime-peripheralist alleged alternatives to the pursuit of victory on the Western Front—alternatives which he disparaged collectively as a "strategy of evasion."[23] Thus it is interesting to contrast Fuller's judgment on the value of the (very substantially maritime) blockade, with the following claim advanced by John Mearsheimer: "Insular powers like the United States can do little with independent naval forces to hurt a land power like the Soviet Union. This point was demonstrated in both world wars, *when Britain's Navy had little effect on Germany's ability to wage war. To the extent that there was an impact, it involved the much over-rated naval blockade of World War I."*[24]

Mearsheimer's error is a common one and it speaks to a purpose of this book. When a scholar as careful as Mearsheimer can fail to understand how dominant sea power enables a maritime-continental coalition to wage war in all its aspects more effectively than can a continentally confined coalition, the need for the holistic study of strategy has to be pressing. The Mearsheimers of ancient Athens were impatient of the Periclean strategy of landward defense and maritime offense, with a somewhat similar, limited understanding of how the proper use of sea power can frustrate the strategic purposes of an enemy on land.[25]

The First World War is of more than historical interest. The contemporary defense debate in the United States has arguments deployed against offensive strategies and tactics keyed to a doubtful reading of the alleged crisis instability of the rival military mobilization/deployment machines of 1914; has people condemning the offensive cast to the U.S. Navy's maritime strategy with reference to the prudent strategic defensive posture of the Royal Navy in the Great War;[26] has found inspiration for changes in (army) tactical and operational doctrine in the tactics of the agile German Stosstrupps of 1917 and 1918; and, somewhat strangely, perhaps, has come to focus upon the four-year-long deadlock on the Western Front as a condition it would be desirable for NATO to be able to impose upon a Soviet aggressor.[27]

THE SECOND WORLD WAR

The believed imminence and certainly the actuality of war provides the motivation to accelerate the pace of military-technological change. Consequently, the harnessing of technological ingenuity to industrial effort for war purposes was important in World War II as never before. However, it was not the case that the Axis powers "decisively" were outmatched in their competitive technological performance. Germany did not lose World War II because her technologists and defense industries failed to provide good enough weapons in sufficient quantity. The element of truth in such a judgment is wholly overborne by the critical errors in statecraft and grand strategy committed by Axis leaders on behalf of the semimodern political systems which they misdirected. Without exception, the Axis powers prepared for the wrong war. They prepared for a short war requiring only showcase defense-industrial mobilization, and then proceeded to commit strategic errors of such a magnitude that victory could not be seized from the wreckage of fundamentally unsound policy.

In principle, if very rarely in practice, the malign consequences of thoroughly unsound policy can be averted through brilliance in strategy or even through inspired performance at the operational level of war. Also, many an incompetent or uninspired general has made his reputation through the courage or skill of his soldiers, or the insubordination of his juniors. Probably the all-time classic example of this phenomenon was Horatio Nelson's decision to break away from his admiral's line of battle off Cape St. Vincent on February 14, 1797, for the purpose of preventing the escape of the bulk of the Spanish fleet. Nelson again demonstrated his proclivity for insubordination when he disobeyed his fleet commander on April 2, 1801, and pressed home the attack at Copenhagen.[28]

World War II, a conflict lasting five and a half years for two of the principals, illustrated some old truths. For example: skill in the art of war tends to equalize over time; initially the more competent combatant trains his enemy by highly educational negative experience;[29] weight of assets mobilizable for a struggle assumes more and more significance as that struggle is protracted in time; errors in grand strategy ultimately prove fatal, notwithstanding operational successes in the near term; and a maritime-oriented coalition is better able to sustain a long war and solve its strategic problems than is its continental enemy.

The warrior cultures of the leading Axis powers began the war with showcase forces on average better imbued with military virtues than were the forces of their enemies (West and East). For reasons of fundamental character of political systems and the reputation and authority of military professionals—with the Fuehrer, admittedly, a highly relevant "wild card"—the Axis powers did not mobilize their scientific and defense-industrial potential as productively as did Britain, the United States, and the U.S.S.R. However, save with reference to a true military-technological revolution, as with the employment of atomic fission for a militarily practicable weapon, the impact of technology on the Second World War was really more a matter of quantity than quality. Measured by casualty ratios, the German ground forces turned in a superior combat performance over all enemies in all circumstances (offense or defense). But the Wehrmacht was sustained by a defense-industrial system designed and mobilized until 1942 only for a short war, while its three Great Power adversaries of West and East had all mobilized in depth for a protracted and total conflict.

Viewed as a whole and with the arguable exception of the atomic bomb, the Second World War did not see a truly dominant weapon. The Blitzkrieg campaigns of 1939 and 1940 did not really demonstrate the operational arrival of tank or even of combined-arms mechanized armies as a new and reliable instrument of swift decision on land. Instead, those campaigns illustrated the old truth that (selectively) modern forces, utilizing a superior military method in a restricted geographical area, are likely to win considerable victories. It should be noted that *Blitzkrieg*, so-called (after the initial event), was not a technique of war utilizable in all circumstances. The German army was to win no great land battle, let alone campaign, after October 1941 on the road to Moscow. Geographical distance (and hence recovery time for the side falling back), climate, and increasingly competent and well-armed enemies (trained in the field by the Germans) showed just how fragile was the technique or craft which had delivered campaign victories in 1939, 1940, and the spring of 1941. The French army—the Armée de l'Air is another matter—was by no means, on average, as poor a performer as the campaign verdict of May–June 1940 could lead one to believe. But unlike the Russians in 1941 and 1942, the French lacked the space and the numbers to trade territory and casualties for time to recover and in which they could absorb and apply the lessons so painfully learned.

Air power, in any or all of its elements, did not win World War II. But the war could not have been won without the quality of superiority in the air enjoyed in the West and the East by the spring of 1944. Without air superiority over Normandy the D-Day landings would have been infeasible. That superiority was achieved at murderous cost by the resumed Combined Bomber Offensive of early 1944. (The U.S. Eighth Air Force actually was defeated, on any reasonable accounting, in the fall of 1943—as RAF Bomber Command was to be defeated over Berlin early in 1944—and had to suspend daytime operations in October pending the availability in large numbers of long-range escort fighters.)[30] At the policy level the strategic bombing offensive had its wartime genesis in 1940–41. At that time a Britain standing alone and prospectively permanently excluded from the continent aspired at least semiseriously to wreak fatal damage by bombing alone, leaving only "mopping up" duties for a ground-forces invasion (which might not even be necessary). Whether or not the CBO could have won the war more or less alone must remain a matter for speculation. Both the British and the U.S. governments underestimated the time required to generate a strategic bomber force sufficiently powerful to be a plausible candidate to function as a war-winner. By the time the strategic bomber forces achieved maturity in quantity and quality, which is to say by the spring and summer of 1944, the long-hatched plans to win the war in the more conventional manner of landward conquest were far advanced for application in action.

The expanding scope and scale of the land fighting by U.S. and British military power generated insistent demands both for the diversion of strategic bomber assets to interdiction tasks and for the creation of a large air instrument dedicated to close support of the ground forces. Moreover, the crisis of the Battle of the Atlantic in late 1942 and early 1943 had fueled requirements for the diversion of strategic air assets for maritime patrol purposes (and for attacks on the Biscay U-boat bases). If the Battle of the Atlantic had not been won in the late spring of 1943 the invasion of Europe would have been impossible. Similarly, if the Luftwaffe had not been destroyed in the spring of 1944 in the daytime campaign for freedom of passage through the air space of the Reich, the invasion would have been infeasible. It transpired that the CBO registered its greatest contribution to the combined-arms coalition victory of World War II not through the damage wrought on the ground by the strategic bombing of Germany, but rather by serving as a lightning rod attracting Luftwaffe assets to a quantity of air combat which they could not sustain. The all-important air superiority over the Channel and Normandy actually was won over Germany via the agency of a massive scale of aerial combat occasioned by the German need to oppose the CBO. Although the CBO has attracted enormous retrospective criticism on ethical grounds and on the basis of generally overstated claims of military ineffectiveness, by far the strongest critique of the offensive lies in the realm of opportunity costs. The strategic bombing campaign(s) waged by RAF Bomber Command and by the USAAF absorbed a high proportion of the best and the brightest from the manpower pool, laid the heaviest of burdens upon industry, and diverted resources from other air-power missions.

Air power, strategic and tactical, simply cannot be isolated from other forms of military power for a comparative assessment of its contribution to the winning of the war. It is as true as it may appear trite to argue, first, that Germany, as a great land power, had to be beaten on the ground. Second, it is highly improbable that Germany could have been beaten on the ground without the simultaneous Russian pressure from the east and Anglo-American pressure from the south and west. Third, although in an operational sense the Anglo-American conduct of the war required a secure working command of the Atlantic sea-lines of communication, that command could be exploited for the projection of armies ashore only if the Luftwaffe first was thoroughly defeated.

It is also true to claim that air power, particularly (though not exclusively) sea-based air power, was critically important for success in antisubmarine warfare (ASW). Equipped with the new centimetric air-to-surface vessel radar, ASV III (H_2S, or "home, sweet, home," for the overland version), maritime patrol aircraft by March 1943 could detect U-boats on the surface and hence compel them either to face a very high risk of destruction or to submerge, thereby cutting drastically their convoy engagement speed.[31] However, the undoubted great value of air power in ASW has to be viewed in a combined-arms context. Air power alone did not win the second Battle of the Atlantic. Also critically important were the evolution of new escort tactics; the Ultra intelligence advantage of the Allies (particularly the breaking in December 1942 of the Shark code for the operational direction of the wolfpacks); competence in radio direction finding; the combat loss of the elite of U-boat commanders; and the sheer quantity of U.S. ship construction. The Allies were very fortunate in that, for all the tactical flair and operational skill with which Germany's U-boats were employed, those boats were denied attainment of their strategic potential for reasons of fatal errors in high policy, mistaken decisions on technical development, and sheer stupidity over communications security. It was ironic that

Germany ultimately won the technical struggle between ASW and submarines, but her instrument of *technical* triumph, the Type XXI U-boat, became operational too late to have any operational or strategic significance (to be specific, the Type XXI went operational on April 30, 1945).

At the level of high policy, Hitler's ambitions proximately were continental in focus. The Blitzkrieg style of aggrandizement, and the military force structure and priorities pertaining to it, were intended to preclude emergence of the multifront protracted conflict which had worn Germany down to defeat in 1914–18. Well might Hitler exclaim "What now!" when Britain declared war on September 3, 1939.[32] Hitler did not want to fight the British Empire—at least not until he had resolved his continental security problems. He recognized that war against a great maritime power could be very difficult to win, and he did not direct Germany's naval and air rearmament with a view to constructing fighting forces most suitable for contesting British control at sea *in the near term.* Hitler had told his admirals in 1938, "For my political aims I shall not need the fleet before 1946!"[33] Trusting in the Fuehrer's statecraft, the Kriegsmarine devised its preferred "Z-plan fleet" (Z for *Ziel,* or target) program, which was inaugurated on January 29, 1939. The "Z-plan" envisaged creation of a balanced surface fleet that promised to pose a very serious menace to British naval supremacy by the mid- to late 1940s. Unfortunately for Grand Admiral Erich Raeder, who had dreams of fulfilling Tirpitz's frustrated ambitions, war came far too soon for the German navy and certainly far too soon for his balanced Z-plan fleet. Germany's naval building program was admirably supportive of German high policy. The problem was that the high policy—of peace in the near term with Britain—itself was unsound. Hitler's brief endorsement of the ambitious balanced "Z-plan" fleet design (impracticable though that design was in terms of material and personnel requirements) indicated that he did not intend to remain satisfied with continental imperium. But unlike Imperial Germany, the Third Reich had its priorities firm *and correct:* first Eurasia, then—and only then—the world.

At the end of 1941, though the fact became generally apparent only by late 1942, Germany had only one fragile theory of success for the war—the effective closing by the U-boats of the Atlantic sea lines of communication of the Western enemy. By 1942–43, landpower Germany again turned in desperation to its submarines as its only currently available instrument of potential decision against the Western Allies. It was a course reminiscent of the German policy decision of early 1917 to wage (for the third time) unrestricted U-boat warfare. Hitler had failed to neutralize Britain by statecraft in 1939; the victories of the German army in 1939, 1940, and 1941 similarly failed to provide a fatal level of discouragement to the British commitment to fight on; the Luftwaffe, through faulty campaign direction as well as for reason of its inappropriate force structure, failed over Britain in August–September 1940; and in the spring of 1941 the heavy units of the German surface fleet showed that they could not survive in the North Atlantic to wreak terminal damage upon the convoy routes, at least not when they were commanded as poorly as generally was the case. The Allies enforced critical competitive advantages because of the vulnerability of the operational communications of the U-boats to and from headquarters on land (though one should bear in mind that each side could read the other's naval and convoy codes for much of the war); because of Admiral Karl Dönitz's technological conservatism; and because of the general excellence of Britain's intelligence gathering, analysis and deception activities (quite aside from Ultra).[34]

The German U-boat force was deployed too little, too late, in key periods with critical communications insecurities, and just sufficiently too backward in technology and tactics to bear the burden which the Reich unexpectedly came to place upon it in 1942–43. New U-boat construction through 1940 was barely at a level sufficient to replace combat losses. Germany had begun the war with only twenty-one oceangoing U-boats at sea (with defective torpedoes). Deployment in the North Atlantic peaked in May 1943 at a level of 128, by which time the operational context had (just) turned radically to the U-boat's disadvantage. Nonetheless, the official historians of British intelligence in World War II record how close the U-boat came to winning the war for Germany: "It was only by the narrowest of margins that, despite the suspension of raids by the German surface fleet and the decline in the contributions of the GAF [German Air Force] to the Battle of the Atlantic, the U-boat campaign failed to be decisive during 1941."[35]

Retrospectively, it is child's play to demonstrate how Nazi Germany (or the Confederate States of America, pick your preferred example) had to lose the war. However, Germany came close to winning the Battle of the Atlantic not only in 1941, as just quoted, but also in the first three weeks of March 1943. Whether or not the North Atlantic sea bridge could have been repaired, once truly sundered, must remain a matter for speculation, though it seems probable that that could have been achieved. However, the dependence of the allied cause upon "luck and the amazing stupidity—amounting almost to pigheadedness—of the German intelligence as regards the unbreakability of their cyphers,"[36] and the fact that even with that blessed stupidity the Atlantic convoy battles were being lost as late as March 1943, should promote some healthy doubt over whether Germany's defeat was quite as inevitable as grand-strategic logic maintains. "Cajus Bekker" (a pseudonym) was correct when he wrote that "Germany's defeat at sea was the one which irretrievably lost her the war."[37] While there is no way to be certain, it is improbable that the Soviet Union could have defeated a Germany capable of fashioning a one-front war for itself.

Second-guessing Hitler's higher misconduct of the war is as popular a pastime as it can be overdone. The Fuehrer's grand-strategic judgment plainly was faulty in its handling of Germany's British problem, but it can be easy to miss the strategic integrity of Hitler's policy aims and military programs. Throughout the 1930s it was Hitler's grand-policy aim to reach a historic compromise with Britain. The agreement he sought would entail German recognition (*pro tem* at least!) of British sea-based and sea-supported interests beyond Europe, in return for Britain permitting Germany a free hand on the European continent. Hitler had absorbed the negative lesson of Imperial Germany's grand-strategically frivolous pursuit of naval greatness. Tirpitz's "risk fleet" guaranteed British hostility toward Germany. Hitler was determined not to repeat that error. Hence, the relatively low priority assigned naval rearmament in the 1930s, the Anglo-German Naval Agreement of 1935, and even the low rate of U-boat building in 1939 and 1940 all make strategic (means-ends) sense once one takes suitably seriously the proposition that Hitler was determined not to wage war, let alone protracted maritime war, with a maritime coalition led by Britain.

The war at sea in the Pacific did not so much see the advent of new weapons technologies as the revision and refinement of tactical methods for the conduct of operations of vast geographical scope, and the application of such quantities of state-of-the-art matériel that prior operational assumptions were rendered invalid. To illustrate the last point, it was a standard assumption of 1941 that carrier aviation could not compete prudently with land-based aviation; one may recall the related, much older, axiom that ships should not engage fortresses (very stable nonflammable gun platforms, generally housing larger-caliber ordnance). But relative quantities, and even relative quality of fighting prowess, can invalidate time-hallowed tactical principles. Whatever might have been sound and unsound in theory, the U.S. Navy could and did assemble in an agile fashion a weight of sea-based air power which literally overwhelmed the isolated and increasingly ill-trained and obsolescent land-based air power of the Japanese Empire.

The aircraft carrier was a twenty-year-old weapon system at the beginning of the Pacific war, but those were twenty years of theory of combat and war-game knowledge. The first carrier-to-carrier battle in history, the Coral Sea of May 7–8, 1942, saw two adversaries groping in the dark. More by luck than judgment, the U.S. Navy— rather like the Royal Navy in 1916 at Jutland—lost the battle on some tactical counts, but won the battle in two strategic senses. The planned Japanese assault upon Port Moresby in New Guinea was aborted en route and, most important, two Japanese fleet carriers were sufficiently damaged to be rendered *hors de combat* for the climactic encounter at Midway on June 4–5.

The will to fight and the readiness to die on the part of the warriors of Germany and Japan in general were not matched by British or American military personnel. Furthermore, the military method of the Germans at the tactical and (sometimes) operational levels of war outshone that of all of their adversaries. But the combat loss by attrition of the cream of their forces, the weight of their material disadvantages, and the incompetence of their high command had the consequence that superior fighting power, unit for unit, translated not into victory but rather into a maximally destructive protracted war that could not be won. Through errors in high policy and grand strategy, Germany had set the stage for her probable defeat as early as the close of 1941, even though the Allies were years away from achieving victory. The U-boat was not defeated until the late spring of 1943 and the Luftwaffe was not beaten until the late spring of 1944 (as, respectively, allied shipping and bomber losses attest). The wars at sea and in the air, necessarily, were capital-intensive and highly technological in character. However, war against a great continental empire cannot be won at sea and neither—in the prenuclear era— could it be won conclusively in and from the air. The allied victories at sea and in the air *enabled* the Russian and Western-allied armies to win the final battles on the ground.

PLANNING FOR TECHNOLOGICAL CHANGE

It is only common sense to assume technological change, to plan to exploit ripening technological plums, and to plan to offset predictable technological trends which could have a strongly negative net effect upon long-preferred national military capabilities. For example, military technologies threatening to the survivability of surface ships are particularly troubling to a United States which must exercise, rather than simply deny, command at sea. For another example, military technologies threatening to tank forces are uniquely prospectively damaging to a Soviet Union whose traditional military instrument of excellence has been its army, and which derives great respect, if not leverage, from the perception in the West (and at home in the East) that that army could seize ground rapidly. However, it is one thing to identify trends; it is quite another to be able to say anything about those trends with a level of precision useful for defense planners. Moreover, one must never forget that technology, no matter how general the knowledge of the science which it expresses in application, is the product of politically particular industrial systems. In addition, even at the so-called strategic level of operations, one must appreciate that technology is not synonymous with strategy and that it does not encompass the total phenomenon of war.

With respect to the strategic, as for all other, forces, planning has to be holistic. Neither a single "leg" of the triad, nor a single weapons system within that "leg," should be assessed as if the total burden of deterrence falls upon that "leg" or weapons system alone. Trends in policy, and the strategic demand for a particular weight and quality of military performance by different kinds of forces, are interdependent. Trends in technological relations of net advantage (e.g., guns and missiles against armor, submarines against ASW technologies) may be of long or short duration. One can be certain that even if an important trend cannot be offset directly by technological development, tactical steps may be taken which might negate or reduce its significance for yielding advantage. Combined-arms thinking and planning can both reduce the threat posed by exploitation of particular new technologies and enhance the military value of new technologies. A combined-arms perspective is as relevant today as ever it was for a Napoleon or a Marlborough.

Everyone favors planning for competitive advantage; indeed such planning points to the conflictual nature of strategy and war. But the relationships among the various levels on which competition occurs are insufficiently understood. While recognizing that the tactically impossible may be the strategically irrelevant (though some tactical failures are compatible with strategic success), still it is a general truth that the higher the level of competitive action or inaction, the more significant it can be. Countries with a comparable quality of military prowess win wars if their grand strategy can assemble and hold to-gether a materially overwhelming coalition; if their generals do not make too many very serious mistakes; and if they can identify in advance, or very early, wherein lies the center of gravity of the en-emy's power, and take action against that center. The recent fasci-nation in the United States with competitive strategies needs to be organized in such a way that proper guidance for the quest after technological advantage (for tactical superiority) can be provided with reference to the kind of war it would be in the U.S. interest to seek to impose.[38]

The quest for technological advantage should be guided by, al-though in its time it may well influence, a theory of success in war which should translate into a theory of success in deterrence. There can be nothing sacrosanct about such theories. As the histories of the two world wars illustrate, theories of war must alter to match the problems and opportunities created by shifting conditions of conflict. Strategic defense would not be pursued as a competitive "knight's move" to devalue Soviet missile forces with reference simply to some morally uplifting idea that nuclear disarmament (physical or func-tional) *ipso facto* is desirable. Instead, strategic defense technologies would be pursued in order to help demote the Soviet political standing in the world which is believed to derive from perceptions of Soviet offensive missile power; to have a strongly net positive effect upon Western military prowess of all kinds; more specifically, if possible, to yield to the United States a greater freedom of action over the employment of its strategic offensive forces; and, at the very least, to hold the ring square against Soviet nuclear escalation. These com-plementary purposes would look to a medium-term future wherein the vastly superior economic assets of the Western Alliance ought to be mobilizable for the conduct of global nonnuclear conflict.

The important point here is not the merit or otherwise in strategic defensive deployments, nor is it the (questionable) political viability of Western defense mobilization for global nonnuclear war. Rather the point is that the SDI, and arguments for its further control by formal Soviet-American agreement, should not be debated as a pol-icy, military-strategic, or tactical-technological matter, outside of some explicit framework of grand strategy and overarching theory of war and deterrence. There is an engineering bias in the U.S. defense community which is cultural in nature, and there is an astrategic bias in NATO toward that which is politically viable in peacetime with reference to Alliance cohesion. It follows that great skill in prediction is not required for one to anticipate that the United States is likely to fall short in strategic vision and reasoning, rather than in technological options for weapon or weapon-support application.

The study of history cannot provide a guide to the future, but it can educate the judgment. As Otto von Bismarck observed, it is preferable to learn from the mistakes of others rather than from one's own errors. Certainly history offers an abundant treasury of cases of military establishments: in general attempting to comprehend and manage technological change; being attracted to self-serving doctrines;[39] being insufficiently alert to the synergistic effects of a number of streams of technological change—or missing the forest for reason of preoccupation with individual trees; selecting the wrong recent cases from which to draw positive inspiration, or selecting the right cases but drawing inappropriate conclusions; and of having too little, too much, or simply the wrong things asked of them.

The minimal case for the disciplined study of history is that there is no stopping the undisciplined abuse of history for purposes of the illustration and advancement of contemporary argument. Careful historical study will not drive out careless or willfully false history, but at least it can diminish the influence in policy debates of assertions which otherwise could pass unchallenged. For example, and without passing implicit judgments on current issues, of recent years the U.S. defense debate has been marred by such errors in historical illustration of argument as: incorrect, at least incomplete, characterization of British maritime strategy; gross misunderstanding of how, and to what extent, Western sea power *enabled* superior grand strategy to defeat a landlocked Germany twice in this century; faulty interpretation of the value of interwar naval arms control; incorrect appreciation of the merit in fixed defenses in World War II; and a dangerously incomplete assessment of German military prowess from the 1860s to the *Götterdämmerung* of 1945. Arguments pro and con particular new classes of weapons technology, or even particular new weapons, are laced casually with erudite-sounding references—for example, to the "trench warfare of 1914–18," when actually trench warfare properly can be identified only with 1915–16. Or, still more popular, one can find references to the wisdom of Britain's distant blockade of Germany's High Seas Fleet by people who are woefully ignorant of the important particulars as well as the strategic context of 1914–18.[40]

One cannot predict or plan with certainty the legacy value for future policy of today's investment decisions in research and development (R and D). But, there is some considerable merit in the proposition that a destination is more likely to be reached if it has been identified in advance. There must be two-way flows of data and ideas between all the contiguous levels of national security activity, from R and D and procurement, through tactics, operational art, military strategy, grand strategy, and policy. In its broadest sense, the terms of engagement between East and West are set for the United States by the choices exercised at the level of grand strategy (policy having determined that there shall be security engagement). At each descending level the terms of prospective military engagement are structured critically by the choices made above. It follows that to the extent technological change can be planned, that planning must have integrity with reference to the tasks set for the U.S. armed forces by grand strategy charged by policy.

From defense issue to defense issue and year after year—given the typically incremental, *seriatim* character of U.S. public policy-making on individual weapons systems—salesmen, prophets of hope, and seemingly professional detractors regularly advance their well-rehearsed messages. A weapons-system focus for national security debate means not only that questions of strategy are slighted, but also that individual systems are wrenched out of their proper military contexts for unduly narrow examination. Sometimes it seems as if every perspective except that of strategy plays a critical role in the politics of technological change. Whatever the origins of a modernization program, the outcome can be determined not by rational debate, but rather by a political free-for-all with no rules of precedent, logic, or evidence. Players in this anarchic game include salesmen (in the financial sense), proponents who are convinced that the weapon at issue will be "decisively" important for national security, detractors who are no less convinced that the weapon at issue could make the difference on the downside between peace and war, and guardians of the public purse who understand costs but not arguments about effectiveness.

Short-changed though the U.S. taxpayer tends to be on strategic rationales for his defense contribution, the problem may be not so much the poverty of genuinely strategic argument, but rather the difficulty in educating opinion leaders to recognize, respect, and judge among strategic arguments when they hear them. A free-market view of the defense debate would hold that a sustained and insistent demand for careful strategic argumentation should trigger a healthy supply. Indeed, it is testimony to the enduring strengths of the United States that it competes as effectively as it does, despite a political culture which seems to resist education in strategy and is incapable of rewarding steadiness of purpose. On the contrary, steadiness of purpose and consistency in policy expression can attract punishment in a political culture which overvalues novelty and is impatient for visible marks of achievement. A recent case very much in point was the decline in political effectiveness of then–Secretary of Defense Caspar Weinberger. A noteworthy part of Weinberger's growing problem of credibility (a key "word of power" in Washington politics) was that he justified his budgetary requests, year after year, with reference to an essentially unchanging perception of external threat. In American politics it can be fatal to political effectiveness to sound like a broken record. Whether or not the perception expressed is fully honest and objectively plausible can be almost beside the point. Arguments, like media personalities, can suffer from overexposure.

Countries manage and mismanage technological change with styles distinctive to their domestic politics. Naturally, the Soviet and the U.S. styles in weapons acquisition reflect their political cultures. For example, the SDI shows American political culture as it bears upon national security both at its best and at its worst. On the one hand, it carries some considerable promise of being a glorious example of what U.S. applied science can achieve when it is fueled by enthusiastic support from the highest level, amply mirrored in popular endorsement. On the other hand, its political, military, and budgetary ramifications prospectively are so profound and pervasive that they raise complex strategy questions of precisely the kind that the U.S. body politic does not handle well.

The orderly management of innovation for the modernization of strategic offensive forces is threatened by doctrinal indeterminacy. The ever-unsettled strategic debate over whether military effectiveness is the key to a sound deterrent, or whether it is a potent menace to stability in times of crisis as well as constituting highly inflammable fuel for the engine of arms competition, surfaces with tedious regularity. Since questions such as this appear to be beyond resolution by the U.S. political system in peacetime, and may not be accorded the lead time in war conditions to be resolved, the outcome tends to be a process of innovation exploited belatedly in procurement by quarter and half measures. When military doctrine is very uncertain, virtually any scale of weapons acquisition is analytically as defensible as any other.

In theory, other factors being approximately even, weapons technology could function as the trump or decider in war.[41] To grant the minimum, in practice technological competence almost always is important in war. But for reason of the effective universality of scientific knowledge—through parallel discovery and various modes of borrowing—modern political entities in regular cultural contact are unlikely to move much out of phase in relative technological accomplishment. It is virtually a necessary truth that great powers in political communication with one another must devise effective enough systems of war, though probably within culturally distinctive guiding systems of statecraft and grand strategy, or they will be relegated from great-power status more or less forcibly. As the distribution of economic power evolves over time, so the newly disadvantaged countries must adjust their operational theories of state security. Countries unable from their own economic assets to sustain a technologically first-class military establishment may find compensation from abroad in technology transfer from, and military support by, the technologically more advanced forces of a great-power ally. Britain, and more recently (since approximately 1916) the United States, have been the arsenals as well as the bankers of antihegemonic coalitions.

Superior weapons help enable good soldiers to turn in superior combat performance. Superior weapons can help subaverage soldiers overperform. But better weapons technology offers no reliable compensation for lack of motivation to fight, or to fight on in desperate circumstances. Moreover, superior weapons will not contribute usefully to victory unless they are acquired and properly used in critical mass, with suitable tactics for sound operational purposes, and in support of competent national or coalition military strategy. It is worth noting that one of the conclusions to Martin van Creveld's pioneering study, *Technology and War,* is to the effect that "the idea that war is primarily a question of technology and so ought to be waged by technicians, that it should employ technologically-derived methods, and must seek victory by acquiring and maintaining technological superiority—that idea has been shown to be neither self-evident, nor necessarily correct, nor even very old."[42]

If one focuses narrowly upon the engines of mass destruction which comprise the nuclear arsenals of the contemporary world, much of the discussion in this and the previous chapter may appear to be heroically irrelevant. In a world of nuclear-armed second-strike forces, what room can there be for statecraft in war as contrasted with statecraft sensibly determined to prevent war, for strategy, for operational art, or even for tactics? What use in war could a Marlborough, Napoleon, or Wellington have made of a strategic nuclear arsenal which could destroy but could not defend (save through deterrence)? Framed thus, questions of strategy, operational art, and tactics, and even of *grande guerre* itself, approach absurdity. The shadow of the possibility of an epoch-ending nuclear exchange must and does influence all levels of superpower competition. But the general and transcultural distaste for self-destruction, married to an authoritatively undiminished commitment to conflictual interstate relations, yields a continuing relevance to the themes discussed here. Strategy, theories of war, and doctrines of war are prudential necessities of state in the nuclear era, as they were previously.

CHAPTER 7

The Soviet Union and the Strategy of Continental Empire

In any explanation of Soviet military power and its application, geopolitics may come up trumps.

—JAMES SHERR[1]

THE SOVIET Union is heir to the great continental empire of the Czars. Great continental empires become and remain great continental empires by the conquest and, where feasible, the colonization of contiguous territory. From the time of the removal of the Tatar yoke—as exercised by the Khanate of the Golden Horde—generally, if technically inaccurately, dated from 1480 with Ivan III's famous "Stand on the Ugra River," until nearly the end of the 1980s, outward territorial or hegemonic pressure was more or less steadily characteristic of the Russian way of empire. On the very rare occasions when Moscow stepped back voluntarily from areas previously territorially controlled, it was only on favorable terms. For example, the Austrian state treaty of 1955 had the effect of creating a very weak politically independent Austria whose neutrality added vitally to the strategic isolation of NATO's southern flank. The relatively generous settlement permitted Finland after World War II was important for the encouragement of neutral sentiment in Scandinavia, and has been followed by a tacit form of hegemonic *contrôle*. The Soviet evacuation

199

of Manchuria, the former Japanese puppet state of Manchukuo, was a special case in that it was the industrial heartland of a new Soviet ally after 1949, Mao's People's Republic of China. As a general rule, continental empires do not surrender territory or authority save in conditions of extreme duress (as was the new Bolshevik Republic at Brest-Litovsk in 1918 and Gorbachev's U.S.S.R. of 1989–90). The nonsurrender of territory is regarded as a matter of principle in imperial statecraft. To concede a province here or there could call into question the very bedrock of imperial security, the will to power of the metropolis, and the acquiescence of subject peoples in an imperial rule which they had regarded as permanent. The retreat from Kabul in 1988–89 was a historic event indeed, though subsequent events in the war in Afghanistan make it abundantly clear that Moscow was not simply cutting and running. Moscow's client-ally in Kabul may well come to a sticky end, but, unlike U.S. malperformance in South Vietnam and Cambodia, the Soviet government has supplied (and is supplying) its local security dependents with all of the munitions and machines of war that it can use.

The CPSU is being run over by the locomotive of history, but Soviet defense professionals do not appear to be confused as between the nonoperational political concepts which dominate strategic discourse in the West—deterrence, stability, parity, escalation control, and the like—and the serious business of planning, training, and equipping to win any war which the political authorities command them to wage. This is not to deny that Soviet military doctrine is in a state of flux, even transition.[2] But the transition at issue lends itself to military-professional, as well as to political, explanation.

STATE AND EMPIRE

Great Russian émigrés are prone to argue that the Soviet Union is an extraordinary anomaly in Russian history which, eventually, will give way before the basic character and allegedly enduring qualities of the Holy Russia upon which it has been imposed. The question of whether the U.S.S.R. is more Soviet or more Russian may appear to be the kind of issue which strictly is of interest only to scholars in pursuit of truth, and not to officials or policy scientists in quest of useful knowledge. Such an impression would be false. The key to the future of the U.S.S.R. must lie significantly in its past. If officials do not understand how to interpret the course of Soviet (Russian?) history, they cannot be well placed to make educated guesses about its future.

The makers of U.S. national security policy have no choice other than to be interested in the possible or probable future course of Soviet history, and in identifying the kinds of goals for which Soviet leaders are most likely to strive. At least three generic positions are tenable on the question of the Russian versus Soviet nature of the U.S.S.R., each of which has implications for U.S. national security policy. First, one may argue that the Bolshevik Revolution of 1917, and the subsequent crisis period of War Communism (1918–20), effected a radical discontinuity in Russian history. In this view the servants of a transnational ideology seized a country, which happened to be the Russian Empire, and set about organizing that country for the forwarding of a historic mission in support of the spread of socialism. This view does not deny the fact of some allegedly superficial similarities between Czarist and Soviet statecraft and style in governance, but argues that what is uniquely Soviet is more significant for policy than what is distinctively Russian. By definition this perspective attributes a high quality of menace to Soviet intentions, a menace endemic to the character of the regime and to the basis of its claims to legitimacy.

Second, the view may be sustained that the U.S.S.R., far from comprising a radical discontinuity from the Russian experience, actually is a logical development of that experience. In this view, the effect of Russia on (international) socialism was far more profound than was the effect of socialism on Russia. The distinctively, though not uniquely, despotic and oppressive nature of Soviet state socialism is not, in this argument, a commentary on socialism—it is a commentary on the (Asiatic, non-Western) Russian soil in which it was implanted. Lenin may well have thought of himself simply "as a humble disciple of Karl Marx,"[3] an instrument of a quasireligious transnational movement; but in action he solved immediate Soviet problems in a very Russian way and set his dictatorial stamp on all which was to follow. There was no Bolshevik "Revolution," at least not in 1917. In Petrograd, Lenin and his coconspirators seized control of a bourgeois revolution that had lost the ability to defend itself.

Third, one may seek the golden mean and argue that while the U.S.S.R. cannot be understood outside the framework of Russian history and culture, neither can it be assessed sensibly without paying due and considerable regard to its uniquely Soviet features. On balance, this discussion reflects the second view expressed above. In this perspective ideology has been a legitimizer for the Soviet state, but has nothing of much note to tell us about Soviet foreign and defense policies. Theories of power politics and of the dynamics of empires are fully adequate to explain Soviet international conduct.

It is probably most useful to think of the Soviet Union as a classical continental empire.[4] Marxism-Leninism has not inspired, indeed could not inspire, a distinctively socialist foreign and defense policy. The prerevolutionary texts of the prophets did not anticipate the establishment of socialism in one country, a situation obliging that country to protect its "national interests" (albeit in the name of the interests of the working class everywhere). Whatever the Bolsheviks may have believed that they were achieving in 1917 (creating the spark in Russia, the weakest link of capitalism, which would ignite the prairie fire of socialist revolution in the advanced industrial West), in practice they and their successors inherited and came to augment an old-fashioned continental empire.

There are many possible motives for empire, but the most enduring has been the defensive search for a preclusive security. Everything in an empire protects everything else. The empire seeks to expand— hegemonically, at least—because that appears to be the most prudent course. If an empire cannot safely divest itself of a troublesome province or client, it is obliged to construct a new buffer zone beyond that province or client. In this narrowly defensive perspective, until very recent times the Soviet Union had sought better to protect itself at home by the threat of force in Eastern Europe. The recent, indeed contemporary, Soviet experience of imperium is that instability in the territorial empire has destabilized, indeed destroyed, the hegemonic empire in Eastern Europe. The price of a serious bid for reform at home has been a loss of effective grip upon formerly obedient client-states, a loss of grip which—coming full circle—has led to radical domestic political change.

The critical assumption behind any grand design for the military disengagement of the superpowers in Europe has to be a genuine willingness on the Soviet part to forgo the attractions of hegemonic empire as a price well worth paying for the conclusion of the costs of such empire. What transpired as the Yalta-permitted system of Soviet and U.S. spheres of influence in Europe had many imperfections, and broke down under (incredibly, Soviet-ignited!) popular pressures in East-Central Europe. But, that system has kept the international peace—a cardinal virtue in any accounting. If a replacement system of security in Europe is replete with every virtue *except* for the ability to keep the general peace, then those virtues (satisfying national aspirations, and the like) would have been purchased at too high a price. As of the time of this writing, the familiar Soviet hegemonic empire in East-Central Europe is no more (it was destroyed, *seriatim,* in 1989), but the U.S.S.R. remains the dominant power in the region.

Soviet international conduct is fully explicable in terms of defensive motivation. However, that behavior fits no less well with a long-term policy drive intended to achieve global primacy (for defensive reasons?). In truth, it really does not much matter why Soviet leaders behave as they do. The fact is plain that, reasonably enough, they seek as much security, or as favorable a correlation of forces, as the outside world will tolerate. It has been the Russian Imperial and the Soviet experience that international history is a record of armed struggle and that periods of peace are really periods of relative rest and refit for the renewal of that struggle. With some tactical adjustments for nuclear facts, Soviet statecraft to date has embodied the principle that in its international relations the U.S.S.R. perpetually is in a state of (political) war with actual or potential adversaries beyond its imperial frontiers. Gorbachev may be in the process of altering systemically the Soviet/Russian approach to imperial security, but the evidence is not yet in on whether his *perestroika* pertains to policy goals as well as to near-term means and methods. Given the number of times in the twentieth century that optimistic people in the West have proclaimed the arrival of a permanent peace, the burden of proof does not rest with the skeptics today.

As Richard Pipes explained in great detail in his controversial classic historical study, *Russia Under the Old Regime,* the state in Russia *owned* society. Notwithstanding the radical shift in political imagery and language since 1917, it happens that Soviet Russia is no less patrimonial than was Czarist Russia. Old habits of mind and practice die hard, if at all. The CPSU has thought and behaved as if it owned Soviet society—a fact which Gorbachev noticed and deplored for its inexpediency. In practice, the dictatorship of the proletariat, always a dangerously slippery concept, meant the dictatorship of the vanguard of the proletariat (the CPSU, itself not exactly a democratically run organization save in an ironically Orwellian sense) over the proletariat.

In one form or another the Soviet/Russian empire is an enduring menace to its neighbors and hence to the U.S. interest in the balance of power in Eurasia. Nonetheless, one needs to remember that Soviet power, for all its negative aspects, also provided an order and predictability in a region not known for those qualities. For a century, the Balkans were a byword for anarchy, violence, and misgovernment;[5] they comprised most of the raw material for what nineteenth-century diplomats knew as "the Eastern Question" concerning the devolution of power from the crumbling Ottoman Empire. Also, as current events attest, imperial devolution in the East leads inevitably to contending definitions of the German Problem (or opportunity!).

Soviet statesmen do not need education in the unpleasant grand-strategic choices which may face them. They can hope that the erosion or even the breakup of NATO would leave the reorganization of a security system for Europe very much at Soviet discretion, or mercy. However, it is a possibility, remote though it may seem, that a Western Europe cast adrift from its transatlantic security anchor would respond to the looming regional imbalance of power not by bandwagoning with the new-look, slimmed-down Soviet empire, but rather by finding a new—indeed a long presaged—security identity as an emerging superstate. One should recall the old advice to beware of one's wishes because they might come true. Early in the twenty-first century, Soviet self-congratulation over a dissolution of NATO which Moscow had plotted and schemed for decades to encourage, could be more than offset by a grim realization that their superpower foes now included China (and Japan?), a new European defense community, and a United States with military means and (much reduced) security commitments in far better balance than at any time since the 1950s.

Assessed strategically, Gorbachev's policy is obviously dedicated to the restoration of a tolerable match between available means and traditional ends. As with Lenin and his New Economic Policy in the early 1920s, Gorbachev's *perestroika* requires a benign international environment while the domestic home of the Soviet empire is re-trained and refitted for effective competition in the future, albeit at the probable cost of the demise of the U.S.S.R. (as contrasted with a Russian empire). Setbacks and concessions can be accepted *pro tem,* precisely because they can be offset or withdrawn in the future as new opportunities for Soviet competitive advantage beckon. Naturally, Gorbachev has to be exceedingly careful, to the degree that he has any practical choice, that in the course of fuel-injecting the engines of reform he does not permit the Soviet/Russian state to lose authority that cannot safely be regained. When one rides the tiger, one may—or may not—alight safely with all key parts intact. East-Central Europe already is lost—lost, that is, beyond easy retrieval—while the Baltic, transcaucasian, and transcaspian peripheries are in various stages of nationalist revolt.

GRAND STRATEGY

Both Marxism-Leninism and Russian historical experience bequeathed to the U.S.S.R. an understanding of political life that has
the idea of struggle as its centerpiece. The insecure empire of the
Soviet Union must justify the past and present of domestic brutalities,
shortages, and inconveniences with reference to the sacrifices required for the good of the state and the forwarding of its mission, its
"sustaining myth."[6] Similarly, the ideological postulation of external
danger served to justify those measures of domestic mobilization
which facilitated the control of the CPSU over its patrimony. For
decades, the Soviet system at home and in Eastern Europe virtually
defined itself with reference to foreign enemies and the putative dangers posed by the ability of those enemies to poison minds at home.

Soviet leaders are not thugs in a hurry, after the fashion of the
Nazi leaders of the 1930s. The Soviet state has been at war with the
West ever since it came into very shaky existence in 1917. Broadly
understood politically, the idea of war is as central to the Soviet system
as a narrowly military idea of war was central to the Nazi system.
Any and all manner of near-term, tactically convenient agreements
with the West are possible. But Soviet leaders—both as good Imperial
Russian statesmen and as worthy heirs of Lenin—do not seek what
U.S. political culture would recognize as a stable world order. The
Soviet Union can recognize no "national" interests as inherently legitimate, other than its own. After all, in the Soviet worldview "national" interests are really the interests of the ruling class and, by
definition, Soviet "national" interests really are the interests of all of
progressive mankind.

Ideological and religious fashions have come and gone, and weapons technologies have evolved, but international politics have remained much the same from the days of ancient Greece to the present
time. Soviet leaders, as the faithful custodians of a generally lapsed
continental European tradition in statecraft, regard major war as
likely, though not certain. War has to be judged likely because of
the history of statecraft and the stakes in the Soviet-American contest
(global hegemony), not to mention the objective menace posed by
(a revived) Soviet power to the interests of the ruling class in the
West. Since statecraft is statecraft, regardless of ideology or religion,
Moscow has not been seeking to pursue a socialist foreign policy
(whatever that might mean, beyond appealing to the working class
in capitalist countries over the heads of the local governments).

Rather it has been seeking, in classic imperial fashion and notwith-standing periodic severe setbacks, to achieve bicontinental hegemony in Eurasia on entirely traditional lines.

There has been an absence of haste about Soviet policy which has yielded valuable leverage against the typically short-term focus with which the policy instruments of the Western democracies are applied. In company with their partial progenitors in statecraft from medieval Byzantium, Soviet leaders typically have given the appearance of believing that time was on their side.[7] Save for briefly under Khru-shchev and again under Gorbachev, the Soviet state has never acted on the premise that it had to deliver substantial benefits of any kind— material comforts, military glory for the general enjoyment—*today*. Military power has been so prominent an instrument of the Soviet state because the country is a great continental power; because of the embattled course of Russian and Soviet imperial history; because the military realm is an area of competition wherein Moscow enjoys important comparative advantages; and because appreciation, indeed generation, of international dangers tends naturally to focus attention upon military matters. However, it would be wrong to suppose that the Soviet Union has a highly militarized view of international politics. Unlike the fascist regimes of the interwar years, the Soviet Union does not romanticize war. Soviet political leaders are fully aware that the only challenge to their authority which could be effective would have to flow from, or at least would have to neutralize or coopt, their military establishment. So long as that establishment remains polit-ically loyal, the problems of unrest and dissaffection among particular nationalities pose generally manageable difficulties capable of reso-lution by traditional methods of bribery and repression.

On balance, real and imagined nuclear dangers were useful for Soviet statecraft because they served as a near-perfect political in-strument for assault upon the center of gravity of Western democratic societies. That center of gravity, as Ho Chi Minh appreciated all too well, was popular support for collective action and, indeed, the quality of civic virtue. In time of war the authority of the Soviet state and its society may well be at least as vulnerable to nuclear damage as are Western states and societies. But in peacetime and crisis time there has been no comparison between the respective ability of fright-ened Soviet and U.S. citizens to influence the course of public policy.

The arguments and judgments presented thus far in this section are deeply unfashionable from the perspective of the balance of con-temporary opinion. It is true that the Soviet state just characterized is radically different from the Soviet state that Gorbachev has been predicting. However, the Soviet Union in this text is the Soviet Union of past and present. As noted already, if there is an issue of burden of proof, that burden lies with those who predict a Soviet polity dramatically different from that which is known and which is the logical product of at least half a millennium of distinctive historical experience.

V. I. Lenin was an admiring student of Clausewitz's writings. There are many threads of method and content in *On War* which Lenin found familiar and appealing. Clausewitz was very much a scholar of his time, writing in the somewhat confusing genre of ideal types[8] (*après* Kant) then fashionable among German philosophers. Clausewitz would not be obscure to people reared on Hegel and on Marx's use of the dialectic. Clausewitz was respected by Lenin because *On War* explored persuasively the connections between war and policy and provided theoretically irrefutable support for the dominance of the latter over the former. Also, Clausewitz touched a responsive chord in Lenin with his emphasis upon the role of military "genius" in seizing advantage from situations of confusion. Exemplifying genius, the elite Leninist party of dedicated and disciplined professional revolutionaries would "make the revolution." The thoroughly political view of armed struggle which Clausewitz conveys fits very well the spirit of the Leninist or Soviet approach to statecraft. Soviet military and arms-control policies are as persistently political in their inferable intended effects as U.S. military and arms-control policies tend to be apolitical.

In the absence of clarity over goals, flexibility of policy means translates inexorably into an erratic opportunism. However, while admitting to some doubt about Gorbachev, it is true to say that the U.S.S.R. has enjoyed clarity of goals. Consistent with not recklessly hazarding domestic stability, the Soviet state has sought geostrategic bicontinental primacy in Eurasia. That goal involves expelling, or helping organize the expulsion of, U.S. influence, and hindering the evolution of any new regional superstate in Europe or Asia. From a multiregional base in Eurasia, Soviet leaders would be well placed to prosecute the struggle between continents for the closer and closer confinement of the United States to North America.

The geography behind grand strategy really has meaning as plain to the Soviet Union as it is to the United States. Soviet commentators demean "geopolitical theory as a basis for the United States' global expansionist plans and the strategy of a Cold War against the Soviet Union," and claim falsely that "it makes an absolute of the influence exerted by the factors of physical geography and population on the world sociohistorical process,"[9] but the geographical referents for strategy are clearly understood in Moscow. Obviously, standard-bearers for Marxism-Leninism cannot grant much explanatory value to rival grand theories; still less can they be seen to endorse the idea that Soviet strategy might be susceptible to geopolitical interpretation. Nonetheless, anyone broadly familiar with the pattern of sea-power and land-power conflict from the late sixteenth century until the close of World War II is well-equipped to comprehend the basis of the geopolitical dimension of Soviet-American rivalry. Through the patient conduct of war in peace, the Soviet Union has sought to deprive the United States of continental allies in Europe and Asia. The Soviet grand-strategic purpose is no different from that of Napoleon when he invaded Spain, Portugal, and ultimately Russia, or of Imperial Germany when it sought to cripple Russia in 1915 and France in 1916—to isolate the maritime power and deny it both continental access to friendly territory and a plausible theory of success.

With the exception of the traumatic, but brief, civil-war period, the Soviet Union has no Napoleonic tradition of military seizure of power, and has a history and culture of civilian supremacy no less plain than that of the United States. Unlike the United States, however, with its civilian Office of the Secretary of Defense, the Soviet Union has not of recent years developed a civilian party institution parallel to the General Staff. While grand strategy, or political-military doctrine, unarguably is securely in the hands of civilian political leaders, military strategy is wholly a professional military product. However, from time to time—particularly in the period immediately prior to World War II—Soviet political leaders have attempted to regulate and control military decisions through the operation of "political administrative" organs functioning parallel to, or rather in tandem with, the chain of military command. This phenomenon, literally of "dual command," operated as far down the military pyramid as company level. The military impracticality of dual command was recognized under pressure of dire necessity in 1941, and *edinonachalie* ("single command") was reinstated. Of recent decades, the CPSU's principal organ of control over the military establishment, the Main Political Administration, has not ventured into the realm of military decisions.

Resource-allocation decisions affecting the armed forces and the management of the weapons-acquisition process are influenced heavily by extramilitary perspectives. But "doctrine of war" (how to fight) is an area of competence firmly under military control. One need hardly add that "theory of war" (how to wage and win a particular conflict), though probably developed almost wholly from ideas provided by military professionals, requires contributions from policy far in excess of simple enemy identification and timely issuance of a "go" or "no-go" order. It is commonplace to observe of the Soviet worldview that the conduct of war is the realm of strategy, whereas the political parameters of the fight are the responsibility of doctrine. For example, the *Soviet Officer's Handbook* instructs its readers as follows: "In wartime, military doctrine [meaning national security policy] drops into the background somewhat, since, in armed combat, we are guided primarily by military-political and military-strategic considerations, conclusions, and generalizations which stem from the conditions of the specific situation. Consequently, *war, armed combat, is governed by strategy, not doctrine.*"[10]

There is at least some possibility—one cannot be more definite—that Soviet grand strategy could suffer important "disintegration" in military action as a result of the apparent system of civilian control by broad political direction from the top. The dominance over military strategy, and—of course—over military-operational options by the General Staff could leave political leaders with scant real power for the direction of the course of a war. However, political leaders usually have confined their roles in wartime to the provision of policy guidance, the setting of strategic objectives (on military advice), the identification of broad terms of engagement (e.g., do not sink American ships), the selection of senior military commanders, the allocation of resources (on military advice), and the political mobilization of the populace. The question of interest, given that politicians are not professionally competent to instruct soldiers as to how they should fight, is the extent to which Soviet political leaders would permit a unified General Staff view to shape the character and course of a war conducted either with nuclear weapons or in the shadow of nuclear possibilities. It seems unlikely that Soviet political leaders in effect would hand the keys of the empire over to the General Staff in time of war, but the extraordinary degree of monopoly of military expertise by military professionals might just have that unintended result.

It should be noted that some, at least, of Gorbachev's new thinking on national security issues would seem to have originated in the ranks of civilian defense intellectuals from the world of the institutes in Moscow. This may be true, but before Western commentators wax overly enthusiastic about the apparent expansion of the marketplace for strategic ideas in the U.S.S.R., they should reflect on the sources of strength of the Soviet General Staff as *the* local authority on military science. The Institute of the U.S.A. and Canada and the Institute of World Economy and International Relations may enjoy some access at the highest level at present, but Soviet political and strategic culture is fundamentally unfriendly to the evolution of an influential body of genuinely civilian defense and arms-control experts who would provide recommendations competitive with those from military professionals. The point is not that such a development cannot occur, but rather that it is not likely to endure.

Western identification of possible Soviet problems in the higher direction of the conduct of war may reflect nothing more than the cultural conditioning of the observers. Specifically, the idea of the military instrument being unleashed to do its job—which is to say, to win a war—on its own expert professional terms is a concept so alien to the strategy cognoscenti of Western Europe and the United States that it tends to be treated either as a fundamental Soviet error (as dangerous for us as for them) or as a prescription which would not be followed in practice. On balance, Western observers would appear to be correct in pointing to the likely absence in wartime of strategic, let alone operational, advice for Soviet civilian leaders distinct from that emanating from the General Staff. However, it is more likely than not that the civilian leaders share with their military advisers the strategic cultural notion that the conduct of war is, and should be, virtually wholly a military matter. The preeminently political concepts which dominate what is called strategic theory in the West—stability, for the leading example—have exercised no apparent operational guidance over Soviet military planners.

The good of the state has been the ultimate value in Soviet policy. In order to protect their political control, historically Soviet leaders have proved themselves capable of any act. Unremarkably, Soviet leaders obey an ethic of consequences; their morality is the morality of prudent statecraft for the protection and advancement of their political system. But nothing is prohibited. If Gorbachev can discard the CPSU as *the* engine of political authority, then truly all things are possible for the purpose of retaining real power and in the interest of the political integrity of the state. It would not be true to claim that the autocracy of Imperial and later Soviet Russia somehow was learned from the Byzantine *basileus* or from Tatar overlords; the full development of that autocracy in the sixteenth and seventeenth centuries almost certainly can be traced to indigenous Russian conditions and impulses. Nonetheless, a distinguished historian's characterization of Byzantine political culture looks remarkably similar to Soviet realities.

> The ruling circles of Byzantium regarded the state as the highest value in society. They did not admit that the actions of the state were subject either to law or to morality. Nor could they attribute any political validity to such concepts as "humanity" or "the unity of mankind," since they saw the world around them in terms of disconnected and conflicting parts. In the tradition of Byzantine statesmanship no moral opprobrium attached itself to war and no intrinsic value inhered in peace.[11]

In a very real sense, the CPSU has operated a considerably lawless state in the U.S.S.R.[12] The state is accountable only to its own best interests as its contemporary servants choose to interpret them, and to the verdict of a "history" which is forever rewritten according to the precepts of political expediency. Even Gorbachev's willingness to reopen some key historical questions is largely a willingness only to permit historical reinterpretation "by official commission." With the security of fixed ultimate goals, and a policy-making system which still enjoys a typically permissive domestic environment, the Soviet state, if in bold hands, can be exceedingly agile in its statecraft. A Soviet leader simultaneously can brandish "sticks and carrots" and can reverse the tactical designs of past years without need for explanation or apology. (When, remarkably, fault is acknowledged—as by Eduard Shevardnadze over the Krasnoyarsk radar violation of the ABM treaty—the purpose is transparently tactically political, to advance the prospects for START, not to show respect for truth. In short, it became critically inexpedient for Moscow to continue to deny that Krasnoyarsk was an arms-control violation.) A Soviet leader is obliged to deliver some tangible successes, but he is not at all obliged to be consistent, scrupulous, or honest. It is only results which count. Poor performance by the state can be explained away as the product of errors committed by particular individuals, not as the product of a fatally flawed political system—a proposition that Gorbachev denied for years with great vehemence.

There is some sense in the familiar claim that the U.S.S.R. is a one-dimensional (military) superpower. Certainly it is true to argue that the Soviet empire, territorial and hegemonic, is a great military empire (as generally has been true of continental empires). Soviet weight in international relations is felt almost exclusively through the influence of its instruments of coercion, overt and covert. To an uncertain but probably extensive degree, Soviet authority at home in the U.S.S.R. rests importantly upon the awe in which the will to power of the state is regarded. The enterprises of government and public respect for the state hence are interlocked in ways that have no close Western parallels. The United States could lose, or appear to lose, an unpopular war (and in good measure the Vietnam War was unpopular because it appeared to be unsuccessful), and Britain could lose a worldwide empire, yet the legitimacy of their domestic political systems was not shaken as a consequence.

A system of political authority whose public legitimacy stems heavily from popular respect for its effectiveness in action, and particularly in coercive action, has to be exceedingly protective of its domestic reputation for successful application of the will to power. When respect for the coercive power of the state is the ultimate basis for acquiescence in the orders of government, policymakers have to be very careful not to risk weakening that respect in gratuitous adventures. Soviet leaders cannot know how robust their empire would prove to be in the face of severe and undeniable military setbacks, but they have to be worried that their enemy next time would not be at all politically analogous to the Nazi Germany which proved to be its own worst enemy in 1941–42.[13] Gorbachev's stewardship in the period 1988–90, in the apparent hesitancy of its will to rule, showed an insensitivity to the reputation and prestige of the Soviet state which was fundamentally incompatible with the needs of imperial governance.

As an instrument of grand strategy, Soviet propaganda functions jujitsu fashion to turn the strengths of Western societies into exploitable weaknesses. That propaganda can appeal to the selfishness of Western businessmen and labor leaders, and hence of many elected politicians, and to the fears and anxieties of ordinary citizens, as well to the hopes for a better future which are entertained universally. Because of their relative lack of popular domestic accountability, Soviet leaders can be cynical and pragmatic in their attempts to manipulate public opinion in the West—an opinion which is able to influence governments only in the West. In terms of Western political values, Soviet political calculation is utterly amoral.[14]

The true cutting edge of Soviet grand strategy, just as it is the central pillar of security and stability at home, is the KGB (Committee of State Security). The scope and scale of KGB activity is well documented, but is culturally so alien to Americans that its menace tends to be discounted. It is rather like deception as a principle of military art, recognized in the West, but not practiced seriously save in desperate circumstances—as by Britain in World War II. The respect accorded secrecy and surprise in Soviet military history is as natural to Russians living in an authoritarian political culture as it is unnatural to Americans. (It might be noted that the great and persistent success of the British in deception operations in World War II provides instructive illustration not only of the axiom that necessity is the mother of invention, but also of the value of geographical isolation and of the closed character of British officialdom.) Attempts at deception are integral to all Soviet military activity in peace and war.

Because of their political culture, as a general rule Soviet leaders are able steadily to pursue a policy abroad which looks to reward and advance the interests of their friends and to punish their enemies. In the tradition of great empires, the Soviet Union proved for nearly forty-five years to be a competent organizer of a client-states system. The collapse of the hegemonic empire in Eastern Europe in 1989 was a consequence of the economic, and hence social and political, crisis in the U.S.S.R. itself. As an imperial power, Moscow has shown itself to be tolerant of local foibles, generally staunch in support of those prepared to behave in ways compatible with Soviet definition of its interests, and usefully secure in its ability to provide assistance (directly or indirectly) in ways minimally embarrassing to obedient local clients. In 1988–89 Eastern European leaders could not keep pace with the policy line set by Gorbachev, nor could they find the local power to resist and survive.

Both superpowers have severe problems of strategic reach. With the satisfactory closing of its continental frontier by 1890, the United States turned to the oceans to expand its influence and enhance a national security no longer menaced in the Americas. After the manner of preponderant sea powers throughout history, the United States has employed its maritime strength to ensure that the sea is a defensive moat and not a highway for enemies; to knit together a mixed maritime-continental coalition; and as the interior lines of communication to forward-located allies whose territory abuts, and hence potentially grants access to, the imperium of the adversary. With U.S. strategic nuclear power functioning as a counterdeterrent and with the U.S. Navy enjoying a working command of the Atlantic and Pacific, Soviet defense planners have problems of useful strategic access to the North American center of gravity of the Western Alliance that are unprecedented in their history. Save with regard to their instruments of intercontinental bombardment, the Soviet Union cannot reach its most powerful enemy. Furthermore, the Eurasian elements of the

Western Alliance provide massive distraction for Soviet military power from a contiguous geographical base that cannot be ignored, and serve directly to impede Soviet access to the wider world beyond the Eurasian landmass. Furthermore, the very probable loss of East-Central Europe as a forward staging area must pose unwelcome problems of time and distance for Soviet operational planners. It would be no easy matter to "lunge" for the Channel from a starting line on the Soviet-Polish border.

With the exception of Britain in the 1850s and Japan in the early 1900s, Russia has always been able to conclude wars with the use of its preferred military instrument, the army. As with the United States through most of the nineteenth century, the Soviet Union has had a preponderantly continental focus in its national security policy. The Soviet geostrategic condition is not a healthy one and is worsening precipitately with the pending necessity to withdraw forces back to the U.S.S.R. itself. The Soviet defense establishment must plan on fighting a major land campaign in the West, while being prepared for combat simultaneously in the East. Furthermore, the geography of their central bicontinental position *vis-à-vis* an enemy who would enjoy global agility in power projection, means that Soviet planners have to anticipate being placed on the defensive by U.S. raids in the far north as well as in the south from the Mediterranean and possibly from the Indian Ocean and Arabian Sea.

The home base of the U.S. adversary cannot be reached except through what likely would be the self-defeating use of strategic nuclear weapons. So long as the United States maintains a suitably deterring strategic nuclear force posture, the Soviet Union is obliged to discount the practicability of effecting the political-military overthrow of U.S. power via a surprise homeland assault. It is most plausible to maintain that, current troubles discounted, Moscow has a two-step geopolitical grand design which follows that of Nazi Germany (save with reference to timing), and for the same reasons of strategic geography. As a first step the Soviet Union must dismantle, or prompt others to dismantle, the mixed maritime-continental coalition which both grants the United States strategic access to Eurasia and denies the U.S.S.R. bicontinental hegemony. Second, with a tolerably secure base in Eurasia undistracted by contiguous landward political-military problems, the Soviet Union would move out into the wider world to effect the political, economic, and even military strangulation of North America. In the medium run, the loss of its unwilling client-states in East-Central Europe may well be of net security benefit to Moscow. That massive development both helps the West redefine "the Soviet threat" and creates a huge vacuum of power (that Moscow will not permit a united Germany to fill).

As aspiring hegemons, Nazi Germany and the Soviet Union have shared some of the same geostrategic problems and opportunities. Both have sought to establish an unassailable supremacy in Eurasia. Until that bicontinental supremacy can be established, all distant ventures must be subordinate to the first-step problem of excluding the influence of the maritime powers. Continental empire cannot bid seriously for a global primacy unless first it is truly secure in its Eurasian continental base. In their historical turns, France, Germany, and then the Soviet Union could all appreciate the logic in the following words of Adolf Hitler: "For me, the object is to exploit the advantage of continental hegemony. It is ridiculous to think of a world policy as long as one does not control the Continent. . . . When we are masters of Europe, we have a dominant position in the world."[15]

The continental Heartland situation of the Soviet empire is a source of both geostrategic strength and weakness. It is a source of strength in that the logistical reach needed to project power into Western Europe is far shorter for the U.S.S.R. than for the United States, though at present it is becoming longer by the month. It should be remembered that the central problem of U.S. defense strategy since the late 1940s has been how best to extend deterrence, so as to afford protection for allies located on the doorstep of the Soviet imperium. But the central continental location of Soviet power is a limiting condition in that that power can be landlocked so long as the Eurasian periphery comprises, in critically important cases (Britain, Iceland, Norway, Denmark, Turkey, Japan), allies of the United States serving as barriers to Soviet military egress from the continental domain. Furthermore, the contiguous landward proximity of Soviet power which can be a source of influence over anxious European and Asian minds, also provides incentives to resist.[16]

Notwithstanding the current period of enforced imperial retrenchment, at some time in the future Soviet leaders may be tempted to improve their standing in the superpower correlation of forces by limited military conquest in peripheral Eurasia. Among the factors which might deter them would be recognition of the possibility of vertical (nuclear) escalation, and a sensible concern as to the possible or probable character of their victor's inheritance. Territorial conquest likely would be achieved only at the price of widespread damage to the assets seized, to the political cohesion of the Soviet empire itself, and possibly to the Soviet military machine. The U.S. and NATO-European interest in stable deterrence requires that Soviet leaders should be very anxious about the quality of their possible victor's inheritance. A Pyrrhic victory in Europe by definition should work to the long-term strategic disadvantage of the U.S.S.R. Needless to add, perhaps, there is no guarantee that a Soviet victory in Europe would be Pyrrhic in character—any more than there is a guarantee that the current era of good feeling will outlast the current Soviet time of (domestic) troubles.

As a matter of strategic assessment, the grand strategy of the Soviet empire is not difficult to identify and dissect—despite the confusion invited by Gorbachev's "new thinking." For the better protection of their political system, even for the better defense of their homeland, and certainly for the robustness of the sustaining myth of the Soviet Union as a political community, Soviet leaders have been condemned or obliged to wage permanent struggle (war in peace) for the enhancement of hegemonic empire. The U.S.S.R. has not sought, indeed responsibly in its own terms cannot seek, an even balance of power. The Soviet idea of empire has been Roman or Napoleonic, driven by a concept of absolute security. It cannot be the Soviet ambition to find tolerable security in a reconstructed, *multipolar* balance-of-power system. An unchallenged, and perhaps unchallengeable, geostrategic primacy throughout Eurasia is scarcely to be compared in attractiveness with the perils of a new balance of power wherein the Soviet Union, the United States, China, Japan, and Western Europe—or, worse still, "Europe," or, worst of all, a German Fourth Reich—would jockey for advantage in shifting three–two combinations. However, at present Moscow is both the second most ailing player (after China) and is the lonely minority team in a game that not implausibly could be aligned one–four.

Western political commentators and defense experts are not in the habit of reasoning dialectically. In their typically linear, unidirectional view of the course of history, the Soviet Union plainly is evolving, or effecting a transition, to some variant of a much kinder, more gentle, and distinctly less menacing polity. One should not dismiss that attractive vision quite out of hand, but neither should one confuse one's hopes with the tactical necessities of a Soviet leadership struggling to save imperial Russia, if not the Soviet system for who knows what purposes in the twenty-first century.

THE MILITARY INSTRUMENT

As a very large land power facing a succession of other large land powers, Russian governments have both needed and had available military manpower on a massive scale. Until very recent years, the Soviet military establishment was obliged of necessity to pursue quantity over quality. Consequently, it has been the Russian way to rely heavily upon mass, upon brute arithmetic—albeit intelligently applied—to achieve operational results. Through the middle years of this century the Soviet Union remained fundamentally a peasant society, whose work force and military personnel were deficient in engineering, and indeed all technical, skills. Recognizing this reality, the Soviet military establishment was geared in peace and war to the production of rugged but effective "no-frills" weaponry in the very large numbers facilitated by relative simplicity of design, construction, and maintenance. It acquired very large numbers of military end-items that were believed to be good enough in quality to do their job, given the quantity of them available for use on the battlefield. However, times have changed. While the United States has embraced a parity principle in SALT and START and in the INF treaty which contradicts the strategic logic of flexible response, the Soviet Union has worked at what amounted to a frenetic pace to improve the quality, while not weakening the quantity, of its military instrument of decision for continental warfare. Recognizing that the *sine qua non* of a continental strategy is a tank component to combined-arms forces of undiminished effectiveness, the Soviet Army has remained ahead in the complex armor-antiarmor competition. The competition is not simply a matter of relative technological excellence; rather it is about the tactical effectiveness of tank forces in a combined-arms setting as an instrument of an offensive (if, in the future, perhaps a *counter*offensive) deep operational design. Technology is critically important; but so also is procurement in large numbers, so are combined-arms tactics, and so is a concept of operations which matches the likely scale of attainable military prowess.

Because of the limited tactical skills of Soviet conscript soldiery (including NCOs and junior officers), the Soviet military establishment has long emphasized flexibility in the skills and routines of command at the operational and strategic levels of conflict, in tandem with tactical inflexibility. The basic fighting quality of the Russian soldier ("moral fiber" in combat and physical resilience) is not at issue, but his tactical agility certainly is. The Soviet Union has worked around this fact by asking relatively little of its non-elite combat arms beyond the ability to perform tactical drills with great proficiency in the face of tough opposition (the similarity with the British Royal Navy in the eighteenth century is quite striking). Initiative will be exercised at the army, front, and theater (*Teatr Voyennikh Deystviy,* or TVD) levels, not by divisional and lower-echelon commanders.

The traditional dominance of problems of land warfare has produced a powerful, land-war oriented, combined-arms tradition. How well that tradition has adapted to the novel circumstances of potentially global war must be a matter for speculation. The Soviet Union has never conducted independent "strategic" operations by naval and air forces as complements to, let alone as substitutes for, land warfare. Soviet operational art and tactics have seen many changes as the country has industrialized, as the armed forces were educated in the field by the Wehrmacht, and as the science of war has been impacted by nuclear and, most recently, by advanced conventional weapons.

As an example, the operational, and just possibly the strategic, significance of recent developments in Soviet tank design (weaponry and [overdue improvements in] protection) is that NATO's covering forces for far-forward defense should be much reduced in their ability to slow down and attrite a Soviet tank-led offensive—pending arrival of distant reinforcements and redeployment for the exercise of counterattack options. With reactive armor negating perhaps 90–95 percent of NATO's infantry antitank weapons, and with a new Soviet tank (the FST-1, or future Soviet tank-1) equipped with a sure-tank-killing 135-mm gun and well protected by composite and *multi*layered reactive armor, the Soviet army of the late 1980s became a credible instrument for decision in continental warfare. However, for both political and military-technical reasons, the Soviet army is in the process of down-tanking its divisions and dispersing its Operational Mobile Group (OMG) super divisions. Nonetheless, in its military-technical dimension Soviet military doctrine is very much in a state of transition, not to say lively confusion.

The Soviet doctrine of war—in the sense employed in this book of how to fight—has shown a remarkable longevity, notwithstanding Stalinist interruption in the mid and late 1930s, a challenge from Nikita Khrushchev in the late 1950s and early 1960s, and pressures today to adjust to a new revolution in military affairs—including the adoption of a more defensive posture. This long-standing Soviet doctrine in essence is Napoleonic. With the aid of deception, decisive campaign victory has been sought through the conduct of very fast-moving offensive operations throughout the length and breadth of the theater. This is the concept of "deep battle" or "deep operations." The lightning conventional war (Blitzkrieg) option which in the 1980s was associated most closely with the names of N. Ogarkov and M. Gareev plainly had its provenance in the writings and teachings of V. K. Triandafilov and M. Tukhachevsky in the 1929–32 period.

The popular image of Soviet military power as a steamroller which can be applied to grind down an enemy by attrition is seriously mistaken. The Soviet belief in mass is not at all akin to the belief by many senior members of the British General Staff (and some politicians) in 1915–17 that the enemy would be beaten tactically in detail, casualty by casualty, in a "wearing out struggle" preparatory to the decisive battle. Instead, the Soviet armed forces respect the concept of mass in its Napoleonic sense, of applying superior, and preferably overwhelming, force at the decisive point for the achievement of operational-level victory. Moreover, by the prompt reinforcement of tactical victory, with a view to translating it into operational victory, the agile application of mass should create a decisive point. When fighting the Germans, this continentalist concept of "deep operations" in land warfare—with naval- and air-power adjuncts—was fully satisfactory as a theory of victory in war. But by definition the concept is only of limited applicability against an enemy coalition whose center of strategic gravity is offshore. That is not to say that the concept is invalid, only that for geostrategic reasons it cannot easily encompass operations likely to achieve victory against an enemy who cannot be reached by the continental instruments of deep battle. A theater-strategic operation may secure continental victory, but a continental victory need not be synonymous with victory in war as a whole.

Military style in peacetime defense preparation and in the conduct of war cannot help but reflect the culture of a particular society and political system. For that reason a good fraction of the public U.S. debate on the subject of military reform in practice has been irrelevant, because it was devoted to seeking improvement in performance by methods which either were fatally un-American or were incompatible with the political objectives of critically important segments of allied opinion. The Soviet Union, in practice, would be no less constrained to wage war in a manner *feasible for Russians* than the United States would be constrained by the limitations of its society and culture, even though Western studies of the Soviet army in the 1980s pointed to impressive improvements on many figures of merit.

There is a seriousness about Soviet defense preparation in peacetime which is not generally matched by the Western democracies (with important exceptions, e.g., the U.S. Air Force's Strategic Air Command [SAC] and the U.S. Navy's submarine and carrier operations). This fact is attributable to a character of political system which has posited, ideologically, a permanent state of war in peace; to a historically based strategic culture which inclines its legatees to make pessimistic assumptions about both the preventability of war and the scale of military disaster that can follow from deficiencies in prewar defense preparation; and to a society which accepts partial defense mobilization as the normal state of affairs. Soviet leaders were obliged not to believe that the march of history could be arrested by nuclear weapons. But their ideological and pragmatic commitment to winning the contest with the United States was (just about) compatible with the idea that political-military incompetence could produce defeat.

There has been an unresolved, perhaps unresolvable, tension between the official Soviet belief that their polity was uniquely sanctioned to be the executive agent of progressive historical change and the belief that objective forces (capitalist contradictions and the like) are working their purpose out. One might recall the knotty problem which confronted would-be revolutionaries early in the 1900s: was it their duty to make the revolution, or should they merely interpret, express, and lead an objectively revolutionary situation when (or if) such a situation should arise?[17] The Soviet practice of grand strategy has abjured the cardinal sin of adventurism, though adventurism is only identifiable reliably in retrospect, as bold moves which did not work (unlike the adventurism of Lenin's *coup de main* on November 7, 1917).[18] Whatever Soviet leaders may really believe about the blessing of their executive agency by "history," fortunately they do not subscribe to the proposition that the success of their historic mission is infinitely fault-tolerant with reference to the quality of Soviet statecraft and strategy. There is merit in James Sherr's assertion that "[T]he U.S.S.R.'s philosophy of history disciplines her philosophy of politics."[19] It should be recalled that Adolf Hitler's philosophy of history, to risk dignifying the astrategically grandiose, was emphatically Alexandrian. Hitler's philosophy of politics as a guide to action was dominated by his perceived need to win the race for empire against the time constraint imposed by his own mortality.

A rather foolish debate has simmered in the West for fifteen years over the question of whether or not the Soviet leadership believes that a nuclear war could be won. Soviet leaders would appear to endorse the view that war can be won or lost; that a violent "exchange" of nuclear arsenals most likely would produce the outcome of a bilateral defeat; and that therefore war, while to be waged ruthlessly for decisive results, would have to be pursued decisively for limited objectives—if political-military primacy in Eurasia can be regarded as a limited objective, that is! There is no way in which Western statesmen possibly can know for certain what their Soviet counterparts believe about the likely outcome of a nuclear war. More to the point, there is no way in which Western intelligence communities can predict what a particular Soviet leader may choose to believe on that subject at some moment of acute political crisis in the future.

A yet more foolish debate is brewing over the sincerity or otherwise of the much-trumpeted radical changes in Soviet military doctrine. Radical changes in strategic culture do occur; witness the cases of Sweden in the eighteenth century, and Japan, Germany, and perhaps even Britain in the twentieth. But those radical scales of change were the forced products either of defeat in war or of a dramatic change in relative power position. It is difficult to cite persuasive cases of a very substantially voluntary restructuring of strategic culture.

It is unlikely that the ideas of a "reasonable military sufficiency" and a defensive strategy, which have been bruited about by Gorbachev and by Defense Minister Dimitri Yazov in particular, will prove to have a lasting military, as contrasted with a tactical political, significance. That political significance pertains to the linked issues of the Soviet desire to lower Western perceptions of threat, and to the leadership's need to have some doctrinal justification for reducing near-term resource allocations for defense. A truly inoffensive Soviet deterrent with reference to ground and to strategic forces would remove from the board of international competition the sole source of comparative Soviet advantage at a time when the future strength of the Soviet economy is very uncertain; would signify the conclusion (*pro tem,* at least) of Soviet endeavors to influence by the threat of negative sanctions the evolution of new threats in the forms of an erratically modernizing China, a rearming Japan, and possibly a uniting Europe (and Germany); and generally would constitute a denial of the central tenets of the traditional Soviet science of war. That Soviet science of war long has stressed the importance of offensive operations, *conducted abroad,* for the seizure of the initiative when war appeared inevitable.

If and when the Soviet military establishment verifiably transforms itself wholly into a territorial defense force, this author will be as ready to give credit for assuredly inoffensive policy intentions as he will be amazed. At the present time the Soviet armed forces are postured in expression of both offensive and defensive operational ideas. Even if Gorbachev is sincere when he talks about "a change in the entire pattern of armed forces with a view to imparting an exclusively defensive character to them"[20] (a subject on which the jury is likely long to be out), Soviet military professionals are certain, indeed are obliged, to resist him in the name of military science, as well as of their basic responsibility to the security of the state. In other words, should war occur, policymakers certainly would demand that the armed forces seek military success, and military success could not be secured strictly by defensive actions. For example, the Deputy Chief of the Soviet General Staff, M. A. Gareev, has written: "The experience of the war [1941–45] demonstrated that a combination of the offensive as the main type of military action and the defensive is an objective pattern of warfare and, like any pattern, it operates with the strength of necessity and it is very dangerous to disregard it."[21]

To read some of the childlike gushings of the Western mass media today is to find evidence of the quite unreasonable hope that a Russian political and strategic culture developed over half a millennium, with a Soviet overlay, is in the process of being swept away. While alert for genuine signs of change, and particularly for genuine signs of change that may be of benefit for Western security, the fact remains that in its capabilities dimension Soviet defense policy thus far is only a pale reflection of the political rhetoric of "new thinking." It is true that Gorbachev has spoken of a sufficient security and a reasonable sufficiency as goals for Soviet defense endeavor, and it appears to be true that Soviet defense expenditures have begun to turn downward (from an exceedingly high level); but students of Soviet affairs must advise that the West keep its powder dry and work hard to develop and deploy better antitank weapons. "Defensive defense" is a concept that truly illustrates "the perils of amateur strategy."[22] The concept can only have political, not military-technical, meaning.

Without seeking to emphasize novelty for its own sake, important trends in Soviet military science are identifiable. Some of these are of long standing. Overall, the traditional Soviet preference for a continentally oriented combined-arms approach to war is being re-emphasized at the expense of blue-water maritime ventures and distant power projection in general. Of very recent years, the Soviet Union has made organizational and personnel changes designed to forward the complementarity of land and sea operations and of the wartime activities of tactical aviation and homeland air defense. Nuclear use options, while available as suppressive fire and as "door openers," would be preferred to function as a counterdeterrent, intended to hold the ring square for decisive regional action on the part of nonnuclear forces. In the interest of achieving rapid success on land in the face of a NATO enemy armed increasingly with smart weapons which might (though on current trends, more likely would not) function as a great equalizer against Soviet AFVs, in the 1970s and 1980s Moscow trained and equipped (some) forces for true *Blitzkrieg* combat. After the fashion of Erwin Rommel's Seventh Panzer Division in May 1940, five division-strong OMGs were tasked to exploit ruptures effected in NATO's defenses and race to the rear for the unhinging and unraveling of the enemy's front in a campaign of great encirclements. Unilateral Soviet force reductions, not to mention possible CFE-mandated cuts, may not hinder Soviet ability to conduct theater-strategic operations anywhere near as much as some NATO circles are hoping. It would seem to be the case that, quite aside from the political (i.e., economic) imperative for force (and particularly tank) reductions, Soviet defense professionals were persuaded by the mid-1980s that their ground forces had become muscle-bound and vulnerable, too bulky for agile maneuver and control in the terrain of West-Central Europe, and too easily targeted by NATO's advanced conventional munitions.

The concept of deep operations may indeed be characteristically Russian, and not merely Soviet, but the focus in exercises in the 1980s on envelopment and encirclement operations looked distinctly Teutonic.[23] *Desant* (airborne assault) forces of several varieties would contribute usefully to the attack upon the cohesion of NATO's defense, as would *Spetsnaz* (special purpose forces) troops of all kinds. In order to achieve maximum effectiveness and optimum flexibility from the top down in war, the Soviet Union has organized for prospective operations by TVDs—incorporating the assets of several fronts (army groups)—and has a truly combined-arms notion of strategy and operations (albeit a notion geared overwhelmingly, if understandably, to the prospective needs of continental campaigning in Eurasia).

In response to political demands as well to the menace predicted to be posed by NATO's advanced conventional munitions organized in "reconnaissance/strike complexes," the military-scientific aspects of Soviet military doctrine appear to be changing in favor of a posture less capable of taking the offensive *rapidly*. There can be no doubt that the Soviet ability to unravel NATO's Central Front defenses rapidly will be damaged when the five OMGs in East Germany and Czechoslovakia are withdrawn and disbanded, and when the tank holdings of regular rank and motorized rifle divisions are radically downscaled—*other things being equal* (i.e., NATO's defenses remaining much as they are at present). But one need hardly add that if the trenches on the other side of the line appear to be emptying, a coalition of democracies is unlikely to sustain a formidable collective military posture, let alone the political coherence necessary for such deterrence and collective defense as a crisis may require.

Deception continues to be required in military planning as a short-term force multiplier. Indeed, the cavalry spirit of daring thrust for deep operations which has been emphasized in the Soviet military literature for more than a decade must have deception (at all levels) as a centerpiece if it is to achieve operational, let alone strategic, results. It would seem to be the Soviet aspiration that the mixture of surprise (by deception), skill in operational art at the top married to an organization of command most suitable for the conduct of theaterwide conflict, and an abundance of firepower and mobility assets, will compensate for the lack of professionalism to be expected of the short-service mass of military personnel. Also, true to its societal parent, Soviet military science is governed in its planned activities to a quite extraordinary degree by a requirement to achieve performance norms *(normy)*.

Analytically derived rules and plans lie at the heart of contemporary Soviet military science. The fascination of the U.S. defense establishment with quantification and pat formulae pales into tepid interest in contrast to the Soviet faith in military calculation. The "correlation of forces and means" is not just a Soviet verbal formula; it is a mathematical method for calculating the objective strengths of opposing forces and is used as a critical aid to military decision. At the sharp end of war, Soviet commanders quantify the estimated military effectiveness of tactical units—Soviet, Soviet-allied, and enemy—as a crucial decision aid. Clausewitz would be appalled!

The Soviet Union has, or at least aspires to, what amounts to a classical strategy familiar from prenuclear times, set firmly within the parameters of politically provided doctrine (national security policy).[24] Pending undesired revelation by experience, it is an open question just how much influence the grammar, or military dynamics, of war would exert upon Soviet operational strategy. For that matter, it is an open question just how much influence military calculations and procedures actually would exert upon the U.S. government in time of war. For all its seriousness about war, indeed perhaps as a result of that quality, the Soviet Union can be trusted to engage in combat only for very compelling political purposes. Whether or not the manner and style of Soviet combat would be tolerably compatible with those purposes is an important, but analytically intractable, subject for Western speculation.

If fight it must, the Soviet Union would prefer to wage nonnuclear war. War is uncertain enough without rolling dice for a new dimension to conflict. Nonetheless, it is also plausible to argue both that the Soviet Union does not intend to be the second party to have resort to nuclear weapons, and that any Soviet nuclear use would be intended to achieve, or directly facilitate the achievement of, decisive results at the theater level of war. Whether or not the Soviet government would permit its military establishment to use nuclear weapons as a staff solution to break a theater *impasse,* rather than settle for a process of conventional attrition or for a negotiated outcome, is not predictable with confidence. On balance, on a complementary matter, the evidence suggests that Soviet forces would be far less reluctant to use chemical than nuclear weapons.

Neither side's officials are in need of education on the subject of the probable horrors of a nuclear war. Similarly, the possible difficulties in the exercise of real-time political control over nuclear operations are not exactly analytically unknown territory.[25] Save for the transparently obvious objective of engendering fear among Western publics, nuclear holocaust—unilateral, let alone bilateral or multilateral—is operationally uninteresting if it masquerades as strategy. Whether or not holocaust would be avoidable is, of course, another question. For Soviet, as for U.S., strategic nuclear targeting staffs, the engines of long-range nuclear bombardment are, and really have to be approached as, weapons, not as agents of apolitical and astrategic destruction. The political value of threats of holocaust for prewar deterrence is not the responsibility of the military professional.

Unconfused by unduly systemic, evenhanded theories of deterrence, the more serious Soviet military literature (by way of contrast to the disinformation texts and speeches which some Western scholars are wont to raid for evidence of new thinking when it suits them) has not found virtue in the concept of *mutual* deterrence. After all, how could the socialist camp require deterring? But the concept of mutual deterrence and its practical application and consequences are appreciated no less in Moscow than in Washington. From the early 1950s to the present day the Soviet Union has been constructing, in different guises, counterdeterrents to possible U.S. nuclear initiatives and has itself been seeking to escape from the straitjacket imposed by U.S. counterdeterrence. For the most persuasive of self-regarding reasons,

Soviet leaders recognize that central nuclear war would be a self-defeating enterprise. It is prudent to assume that the Soviet Union would elect to wage a large-scale nuclear war were its leaders convinced—absolutely convinced, that is—that the United States was about to launch a nuclear assault on the Soviet homeland. Moscow would "go first in the last resort," even though its strategic forces are no longer vulnerable to attack. But it is vastly improbable that the U.S.S.R. is confident that it could wage a central nuclear war and profit by the deed.

Soviet leaders have never been casualty-shy. A state with the record in mass murder *(of its own people)* of the Soviet Union does not have ethical scruples against nuclear use. However, U.S. defense analysts would err in an elementary way if they were to suggest that those leaders are indifferent to Soviet civilian suffering and damage. For the most strategic of reasons, although the Soviet state cares most for its political leadership and its means of coercion, the wrecking of the urban-industrial U.S.S.R. would be fatal for the power of its system. If the societal patrimony is blown away, burned down, or poisoned, what is the future for a safely bunkered leadership or a relatively safely dispersed military machine? The prospect of an army without a country can hardly be an appealing one, even to Soviet leaders prone to take a brutally instrumental view of the value of their citizenry.

The Strategic Rocket Forces (SRF) is the premier armed service in the U.S.S.R. and the heir to a great artillery tradition. The political primacy of the SRF rests upon the same calculation which accords, or should accord, the strategic nuclear forces of the United States premier status. It is the one category of force for which there can be no functional substitutes from other military instruments. War might be won or, more likely, lost at that level, while resort, or the credible threat of resort, to central war could reverse the verdict of some lower courts of combat. Western experts of various political hues have woven many speculative theories over the past twenty years concerning Soviet purposes in the course of development chosen for the SRF. Today, a quarter century after Secretary of Defense Robert McNamara affirmed in 1965 that the Soviet Union was not racing the United States in strategic nuclear arms, the record of modernization and augmentation of the SRF quite literally speaks eloquently for itself. In keeping with its own distinctive style in research and development and weapons acquisition, the Soviet Union: has developed whole families of fourth- and fifth-generation missiles; has registered partial generation advances as each system acquired has been improved *in situ;* and has been neither deterred nor restrained by arms-control agreements from acquiring a nuclear arsenal as militarily effective as the available technology and the resources allocated permitted. Gorbachev's "new thinking" has yet to manifest itself in any visible change in nuclear strategy or substantially altered direction to the strategic forces' posture.

President Reagan's SDI generated great alarm in Moscow, not because it threatened to render nuclear-armed ballistic missiles "impotent and obsolete," but—in good part, one may surmise—because it threatened to render such (Soviet) missiles impotent and obsolete as *reliable military instruments.* Such a reduction in reliability threatened to reduce drastically the political utility of Soviet long-range ballistic missiles. Other parts of Soviet anxiety have to do with their fears (in a classic case of projection) that the United States: might *add* reasonably effective defenses to very effective offensive forces; might develop hybrid defensive-offensive weapons (a space shield with a long reach becomes a "space strike" weapon); and will register widespread gains in military effectiveness as a result of the technology advances likely to be produced by the broad-brush SDI research and development program. The SDI options which the United States could exercise for deployment in the 1990s, domestic politics, budgetary guidelines, and arms-control obligations permitting, would include having the operational character of helping to protect the U.S. strategic nuclear forces for retaliatory missions. Paradoxically, such deployments would strike directly at the heart of Soviet strategy and, indirectly and ironically, possibly at the heart of U.S. and NATO strategy also.

SDI defense of U.S. strategic forces and of the strategic command system should render a Soviet ICBM-artillery *kontrpodgotovka*—that is to say a preemptive "breakup" barrage against an enemy believed to be about to strike—even more impracticable than it is today. Far more reliably than other means for rendering strategic offensive forces more survivable,[26] active defenses should render the outcome of a counterforce blow beyond useful calculability by the numerate analysts on the Soviet General Staff, with their mathematically based pseudoscience of war. Rather more useful even than in its contribution to the protection of U.S. strike-back capability, SDI and adjunct air-defense deployments could provide a heavy, preferential defense of those handfuls of targets (ports, airfields, major bases) in the United States which would be critical for the military projection effort for global war.

The paradox and irony cited above lie in the probable fact that new Soviet strategic defenses which U.S. SDI deployment would license could hardly help but undermine still further the credibility of the U.S. extended-nuclear deterrent. The prospective operational policy and strategy contexts for the SDI debate comprise a condition wherein the Western Alliance anticipates a need to exercise the nuclear initiative in an endeavor to restore deterrence in the face of regional military defeat in Europe. Ever more competent Soviet strategic defenses must render Western long-range offensive forces a more and more blunt, and hence unprofitable to employ, military instrument. As a practical matter, if peace continues to break out in the 1990s the United States will choose not to invest heavily in SDI deployment, while the Soviet Union will be unable to afford to deploy important new elements of its "Red Shield."

It is certainly understood in the Soviet Union that the SRF might function as a quasiindependent strategic instrument of political-military decision, notwithstanding the prominence of combined arms in their military thinking. However, given the strategic geography of Soviet-American security relations, it is more reasonable to suppose that the primary combined-arms function of the SRF is to operate so effectively as a terrifying counterdeterrent that the West would be obliged to wage regional conflict strictly with nonstrategic means. It follows that even if U.S. strategic forces cannot serve reliably to intervene in, and reverse the verdict of, a regional campaign, at least they should be capable of preventing the Soviet Union from calculating that it could win a central nuclear war in the event that the Soviet army failed to deliver victory promptly in Eurasia.

At the present time a wide range of predictions are more or less plausible concerning the future course of Soviet foreign and military policy. The reasoning in this book cannot thoroughly and reliably unlock the mysteries of Soviet policy-making. But, a book such as this examining strategy and statecraft, which views *strategies* as theories of victory expressing *strategy*—the mutual accommodation of means and ends—can provide some healthy protection against "Gorbaphobia," "Gorbaphilia," or whatever the fad of the month happens to be.

It should be recalled that this text has five themes pervading the argument and historical examples: the unity of strategy and war; the salience of geography, history, and culture for strategic attitudes, choices, and behavior; and the implications of an ever dynamic technology. These themes allow for, indeed help explain, change. But, they also inoculate against the merely faddish. It is quite evident that civilian and even some military leaders in the U.S.S.R. are talking about a dramatic change in Soviet military doctrine. However, the geostrategic logic of continental empire still holds. That logic must address the potential for war on two or more land fronts, not to mention maritime and long-range air, missile, and eventually space-based threats as well. The promise to reduce the immediate offensive potency of the Soviet army may well be entirely genuine. The questions of interest pertain to the operational goals of the policy of which military doctrine is one expression, as well as to what the West might attempt in order to exploit this current—and possibly temporary—shift in Moscow's course.

The more careful students of Soviet affairs will notice, first, that the U.S.S.R. is not seeking to construct a truly inoffensive defense (*à la* Switzerland). Soviet land power should look distinctly less menacing as its divisions lose some of their currently overabundant armored assets. But given sufficient time to mobilize, particularly in the possible context of a NATO adversary far from formidable in resisting power, the Soviet army still could perform its traditional offensive missions.

Second, given that Soviet statecraft and defense policy-making inhabit a world wherein politics rules, the focus in this book upon the *unity* of strategy with statecraft directs attention holistically to the total effectiveness of the U.S.S.R. in its (again, unified) domestic and external policies. If one harbors the notion that Soviet leaders prior to Gorbachev truly were interested in overrunning Western Europe, it is easy to be overimpressed with arguably benign interpretations of the policy meaning of the announced changes in Soviet military doctrine and posture. The unarguably offensive posture of Soviet forces in Central Europe through the 1980s was a reflection of a grand and substantially erroneous (which is why it is being retired) design for the coercive achievement of influence over the minds of those who are not courageous, not the reflection of a purposive design for war. It follows that the partial down-tanking of Soviet divisions may carry a lot less policy meaning than might be supposed.

Third, it would be well to remember that the recasting of Soviet military-scientific doctrine in ways that place more emphasis upon defense already was well under way before Gorbachev's "new thinking" assaulted the doctrinal bastions manned by the General Staff. Air-Land Battle (now "Army 21"), Follow-on Forces Attack (FOFA), conventional retaliation, the U.S. Navy's maritime strategy, and the potential of the SDI to produce space (-based)-strike weapons, in a general context of perceived, almost across-the-board technological inferiority, were driving the Soviet General Staff toward the upgrading of defensive (as in defense, then counterattack) capabilities long before defensive sufficiency and the like attracted political blessing. As Michael Donnelly has argued, a great deal of what the Soviet Union can attempt to pass off as purposeful evidence of good international intentions in fact will be little more than sensible doctrinal-postural adjustment to changing times. This point can be overemphasized, admittedly, but thus far it remains underappreciated by somewhat credulous Western commentators.

Fourth, the Soviet Union plainly requires a breathing space in the form of a condition of relaxed international tensions. Such a breathing space may enable Moscow to restore its fitness to compete effectively in technological arms competition. Geographical, cultural, and historical factors all suggest, on balance very strongly, that the prospects for the emergence of a truly much kinder and gentler U.S.S.R., in short a U.S.S.R. all-but-unrecognizable from Russian history to date, cannot be rated as very promising.

COMPETITIVE STRATEGY: THE ARMS-CONTROL WEAPON

As typically appreciated in the United States, the arms-control process is wholly a Western fiction. Popular discussion implicitly posits this so-called process as a struggle by the superpowers against the alleged dangers of the arms competition. The Western capacity for self-deception—the ability to believe that the enemy is the arms race rather than Soviet imperialism (or, in abstract geopolitical terms, the distribution of power)—enables Soviet policy to turn some of the virtues of Western democracy into vices. The strategic history of East-West relations over the past twenty years demonstrates beyond a reasonable doubt that the arms-control process is either an irrelevance or is dangerous to international security. The reason for this is plain enough to see. Arms programs are driven by politics and not vice versa. If the politics of international rivalry can be treated to general satisfaction, then arms programs scarcely matter. If arms programs are treated through arms-control negotiations while the political basis of rivalry festers untouched, the outcome of an arms-negotiating process is very likely to be advantageous to the country best able to arm both while it is parleying and more or less covertly while nominally under legal restraint.

In the theory and practice of Soviet statecraft, arms-control diplomacy of all kinds can serve as an offensive or a defensive instrument of grand strategy. Arms control is attractive as a policy instrument because it defines a political realm wherein Moscow, or indeed any strongly authoritarian polity, enjoys great structural competitive advantages over democratic rivals. Given both the unique political vulnerability of democratic states to the "lulling" promise of arms control and disarmament, and the systemic disadvantages of the Soviet Union in the economic and technological bases for military competition, "it is no accident" that arms control figures prominently in Soviet grand strategy. Understanding that international politics is the conduct of war in peace, Soviet leaders can strike at what Stalin termed "the stability of the home front" in the West, the popular consensus necessary to sustain a competitive level of counterarmament. For their part, Soviet leaders have not been constrained by the need to build and constantly to maintain a domestic political consensus on the difficult subject of the complementarity of arms and arms control.

The Soviet Union does not want, indeed for reasons of imperial political stability probably cannot afford, an *enduring* "real peace" with the West. But the Soviet Union does want to avoid competition, crisis, or war *on disadvantageous terms*. In that Moscow is completely sincere. And as with Japan, Italy, and Germany in the interwar years, and for some of the same reasons, the U.S.S.R. sincerely desires to achieve agreements labeled as manifestations of arms control. The U.S.S.R. seeks arms-control agreements which: diminish the pace of Western military effort through action against the political consensus necessary to sustain arms-competitive behavior at a high and expensive level; help psychologically to disarm democratic societies; and help alleviate or resolve some Soviet military (and economic, and hence social and political) problems. In and of itself, arms control and the process thereto associated has no normative value in the Soviet political pantheon. In its own official estimation, at least pending the definitive dethronement of Marxist-Leninist ideology, the Soviet state is engaged inalienably in a struggle to ultimate decision between antagonistic social systems and their political and military superstructures.

The public debate in the United States about the value of an allegedly legal framework for the mutual restraint of arms development has said far too little about the absence of law in the U.S.S.R. A Soviet state that still knows little law beyond expediency, and which recognizes in practice no absolute legal rights for its citizens *vis-à-vis* a still arbitrary and all-powerful government, is not exactly a state inclined by political culture to respect the legalisms of arms-control constraint with reference to obedience to law as a value.

The idea that the superpowers can build a working relationship for greater systemic security through an arms-control process is simply ludicrous in Soviet perspective, though not in the rhetoric which Moscow provides for the gullible. For a mix of balance-of-power and ideological reasons, the United States is an enemy of the Soviet state, albeit an enemy with whom Moscow is determined to avoid engaging in overt military hostilities. A multilevel East-West military balance and associated political security system which truly would be judged stable and to the mutual benefit by realistic elements in the United States would likely be a catastrophe for the stability of the Soviet empire (territorial and residual hegemonic). If the military dimension to East-West rivalry effectively could be retired, how could a grossly economically disadvantaged U.S.S.R. compete successfully for influence in the world? It follows that any Soviet signature to a Western strategic-conceptual credo needs to be treated with skepticism. For example, there is nothing in Soviet operational doctrine or military-postural practice which can provide independent verification of their signature to a preamble to the INF treaty which asserts that the high contracting parties are "[g]uided by the objective of strengthening strategic stability." Needless to say, perhaps, this affirmation undoubtedly is sincere—only it affirms a notion of stability distinctly alien to the technocrats in the U.S. arms-control community. The Soviet ICBM and tank-modernization programs speak eloquently to the authoritative Soviet definition of stability.

As a distinctive subject, Soviet arms-control policy is without integrity and definition—would that this were true for the United States also. What appears as Soviet arms-control policy is an instrument of Soviet propaganda and defense policy, generally of grand strategy. The Soviet approach to international negotiations is firmly in the Leninist tradition, with the competitive or noncompetitive circumstances in which Soviet leaders find themselves determining just how accommodating they choose to be. Agreements to the mutual advantage can be secured, though the historical evidence in support of that optimistic claim is woefully weak. However, Western negotiators should not allow their hearts to triumph over their heads and imagine that in negotiating on security topics of any kind with the U.S.S.R. they are joining with a negotiating partner, rather than an adversary, in attempted resolution of common problems. In the Soviet view, your problems are strictly your problems—notwithstanding Gorbachev's words to the contrary.[27]

Lenin understood the Western democracies all too accurately. "Useful idiots" in the early 1920s, as in the ranks of the U.S. Arms

Control Association today, could be relied upon to think the best of Soviet (mis)behavior (remember Krasnoyarsk!) and motives and perennially to hope for better things to come. The practice of arms control has translated repeatedly into common restraints uncommonly observed. The pattern of Western self-restraint and Soviet advantage-seeking is as unmistakable as it is regularly dismissed as relatively unimportant by apologists for Soviet misbehavior. Where many Western arms and arms-control experts believe that through an arms-control process they are addressing pragmatically essentially technical issues in the necessary technical manner, the Soviet Union is engaging in political theater and seeking to inhibit the will of the enemy to compete. In the United States, it is *de rigueur* to claim that arms-control policy is a subordinate and fully integrated component of foreign and defense policies for the national security, writ large. In the Soviet Union, that claim is the reality of actual practice.

Strategy is not a craft to be applied by experts regardless of societal political setting. Robert McNamara was demonstrably foolish in asserting that in Vietnam the United States was learning how to wage a limited war (and was teaching the enemy how such a war should be waged). Similarly, conservative critics of the arms-control malpractices of Western governments would be wrong if they believed that they could design an arms-control policy *suitable for official implementation* which really would protect Western interests. The conservative critique of Western arms-control theory and practice is now mature, amply documented with Soviet evidence, but is largely irrelevant to the course of Western statecraft. The authors of this critique, this writer included, have done their duty to truth as they have seen it; but culturally based yearnings for the imprecise benefits of the arms-control process are far stronger an influence upon public policy than are the strategic warnings of experts. If the Reagan administration could negotiate an INF treaty which is not verifiable; against the backcloth of probable Soviet lies about its missile inventory; in the context of continuing Soviet cheating on other arms-control regimes; which subverts the very basis of NATO strategy; in ignorance at the highest level of the difference between verification and enforcement; and knowing nothing about the real prospects for structural changes in the balance of conventional forces in Europe, then plainly one should not be optimistic over the ability of democratic polities to negotiate competently.

The purpose of this section has not been to castigate the U.S.S.R. for perfidy as an arms-control "partner," or to charge Soviet leaders with using arms control as a tool for the promotion of other agenda items. One must assume that the Soviet state will seek its own good as it finds it expedient, and that the competent Soviet conduct of what appears on the surface to be arms-control activity will yield political gain *vis-à-vis* a Western world ever prone to discern the dawning of the era of eternal peace. Moscow behaves strategically in arms control—and so should we. The means available to prosecute policy ends include the political theater of arms control, as well as the tangible forces that are the formal currency of negotiation.

In case after appalling case, the United States and NATO perform tactically, not strategically, in the arms-control arena. NATO has never believed that in this nuclear age the relationship between the military inventories of East and West bore any close relation to the probable success of deterrence. Rather what mattered for deterrence was that Soviet leaders should perceive an intolerable nuclear danger in any large-scale military fracas. That being the case, indeed that being the heart of the uncertainty principle which overhangs NATO's concept of flexible response, how could one possibly endorse the antinuclear double zero of the INF treaty of 1987? Similarly, NATO's arms-control *strategists*—if any such should prove to exist—need to ask themselves whether a CFE agreement actually would tend to work to subvert the emergence of a new security order in Europe, rather than to support it. Specifically, CFE is very likely to license large-scale Soviet force deployments in Eastern Europe. Nonetheless, the point is that viewed strategically CFE is not, finally, about reductions in forces. Instead, CFE is about the consequences for security—a slippery concept—of reductions in forces. The difference is that between tactics and strategy.

COMPETITION FOR POWER: THE SOVIET HAND

As Soviet statesmen and defense planners recognize explicitly both in their dynamic concept of the correlation of forces and in the inclusiveness of their military doctrine, choices in strategy must express the totality of the state's competitive position *vis-à-vis* adversaries with particular strengths and weaknesses. There is a fairly distinctive Russian way in warfare, traceable in a first-class artillery tradition, and shown operationally at its peak in the destruction of Germany's Army Group Center (Operation *Bagration,* June 22–July 10, 1944) and of Japan's Kwantung army in the Manchurian campaign (August 9–17, 1945). Overall, though this characterization can lend itself to misunderstanding, Peter Vigor makes an important point when he argues that

> the Soviet Union believes it highly desirable to deliver as weighty a blow as possible on each and every occasion, and against any and every enemy. In Soviet thinking the concept of economy of effort has little place [this is not really true, provided one remembers that Soviet strategic culture understands "economy of effort" differently from ways standard in the West: CSG]. Whereas to an Englishman the taking of a sledgehammer to crack a nut is a wrong decision and a sign of mental immaturity, to a Russian the opposite is the case. In Russian eyes the cracking of nuts is what sledgehammers are clearly designed for.[28]

The Russian, now Soviet, way in warfare, though very much the operational product of a professional general staff system, is rooted firmly in the strategic culture of an insecure bicontinental empire. Soviet strategy cannot usefully be explored solely with narrow reference either to the technical elements discernible in the evolving Soviet science of war, or indeed with regard strictly to military subjects, virtually no matter how expansive the domain of such subjects is understood to be. Whether or not modern war is waged for unlimited ends, its conduct is a general test of the capacity for collective action by a whole society or coalition. The discussion which follows rests upon recognition of the saliency of Vigor's argument that

> according to the Russian way of thinking, if it came to a long war the Soviet Union would almost certainly *lose*. As Marx, Engels, Lenin and all their successors have continually hammered into the Soviet consciousness, war is essentially a function of economics; and victory in war generally accrues to him who has the greater economic potential, *provided, of course, that the war continues long enough for that greater potential to be realized.*[29]

Soviet military strategy gives every appearance of expressing the doctrinal belief that it must win a short war lest it lose a long one. The history of continental-maritime conflicts over half a millennium suggests that on the one hand Moscow is wise to recognize its vulnerability in protracted conflict, but that on the other hand it may seek in vain for continental Blitzkrieg-offsets to the grand-strategic disadvantages of continentally confined imperium. The trend of the 1980s toward a better balance between defensive and offensive capabilities suggests that Soviet soldiers themselves came to doubt the operational promise of the tank-led Blitzkrieg, at least as it had developed through the 1970s.

As with the United States, many of the competitive strengths of the U.S.S.R. also, paradoxically, are a source of weakness. In principle at least, the central planning and direction of state socialism can permit a society to identify and rigorously apply priorities in its investment decisions, and as a consequence extract the maximum benefit from scarce assets. But in practice the centralization characteristic of state socialism has worked efficiently neither in time of war nor peace. Although the Soviet economy performed adequately in World War II under desperately difficult circumstances (of evacuation of plant, some enemy interference, material and labor shortages, and transportation problems), the British and American economies were models of efficiency in comparison (though the latter, admittedly, did not have to contend with disruption caused by enemy action). It was the Axis economies which functioned very poorly, in good part because fascism was a heavily militarized political system deeply suspicious of capitalist industry.

Today is a particularly difficult period from which to make judgments about the long-term competitiveness of the U.S.S.R. The changes heralded and partially introduced by Mikhail Gorbachev are the most radical since 1917, and there is no way in which any Western (or Soviet) expert can predict with confidence the likely success, durability, and effect of those changes. Moreover, the Gorbachev campaign to revitalize the Soviet economy is heavily impregnated with tactical political considerations that bear at least as much upon the consolidation of his personal power base (i.e., *his* patronage system) as they do upon the needs of the country as viewed reasonably objectively by the new leader. By way of a modest accounting of factors important in the competitiveness of grand strategy, contrasting annotated checklists of Soviet strengths and weaknesses are provided below.

Contiguity of imperium. With only trivial quite recent exceptions, the Soviet empire—territorial and what remains of the hegemonic—is a consolidated, contiguous landmass. All of this empire, by virtue of territorial contiguity, can be policed and defended more or less easily by the Soviet military instrument of excellence—the army. The extent of the empire certainly poses awesome logistical problems, but those problems are familiar (recall how Russia sustained by a single-track railroad a large-scale, if limited, war in Manchuria and Korea in 1904 against Japan). Soviet logistical problems in the West need to be compared with the transoceanic difficulties of a U.S. superpower.[30]

Command economy. Some U.S. claims that the Soviet economy is a "basket case" easily can mislead. The Soviet Union is a very large economy which has demonstrated steadily that it is well capable of producing efficiently those goods judged most important by the state (e.g., missiles, tanks, and so forth). This is not to deny that Soviet pessimism over their ability to sustain an open-ended technological arms competition has been *the* principal element fueling Gorbachev's drive for *perestroika*. However, it would be a serious error to endorse the caricature of the U.S.S.R. as "Upper Volta with nuclear weapons."

Authoritarian policy-making and policy execution. When in capable hands, the Soviet state can direct change effectively from the top downward. The Soviet government has shown repeatedly that it is capable of any degree of ruthlessness in order to achieve those goals which must be achieved if the authority of the state is to be sustained (including purposeful destabilization of its ally-clients in Eastern Europe). The Soviet system is critically overdependent upon initiative from the top—a condition amply illustrated by Gorbachev himself. It very much remains to be seen whether a newly pluralistic Soviet Union can shed its cultural dependency upon authoritarian rule.

Economic (near-) autarky. Unlike the United States, which is a fully (or even over-) developed mature economy, the Soviet Union remains greatly underdeveloped, particularly in Asia. With the critically important exception of food (depending upon the weather for the harvest), the U.S.S.R. needs little beyond high technology know-how from the outside world. Of all the great continental empires with whom sea powers have contended in modern history, the Soviet Union is uniquely, though not totally, invulnerable to economic pressure or warfare (including blockade).

Will to compete. Soviet ideology may be tired, but it is voluminous, ambiguous, suitable for continuous revelation, and noncritical to the actual practice of day-by-day rule. The will to power (at home) of the political elite *as leaders of the CPSU* plainly has eroded. But that elite is showing no erosion of its will to real power. *Perestroika* and the resolution of the debate over the future of the party show that when power is at stake nothing is sacred. Relatively untroubled thus far by the need felt by Western politicians to accommodate very seriously the sentiments of citizens on such subjects as defense burdens, the perceived justice in Soviet international behavior, and the like, Moscow has been at considerable liberty to pursue an agile *Realpolitik* without popular domestic political inhibition. Some Western experts argue that ideology limited critically the adaptiveness of Soviet grand strategy, obliging it, for example, to seek and retain imperial rule in Eastern Europe, rather than settling for an influence derivative simply from the prestige of perceived power. This argument is interesting but thoroughly unpersuasive—as the events of 1989 attested. Soviet empire-building in East-Central Europe may well have been a case of redundant causation, with ideological considerations playing a part. But it is difficult to believe that any Russian state, faced with the temptations of 1945 to ensure reliable hegemonic imperium, voluntarily would have withdrawn its legions. The Europe of 1945 was not the Europe of 1814–15. The current Soviet loss of effective power in Eastern Europe illustrates the point. Attempting what has to be attempted to restore the competitiveness of the U.S.S.R., the resulting destabilization, then effective termination, of the imperium in Eastern Europe is a bearable price that simply had to be paid (at least for a while). The enduring facts of geopolitics suggest strongly that the story of effective Soviet dominion over Eastern Europe is unlikely to have been settled for all time by the political Chernobyl of 1989.

Steadiness in grand strategy. Since fashions in domestic public opinion do not play strongly in Soviet foreign policy-making, and since Soviet leaders are not confused by their political culture into believing that "real peace" might break out if only this or that policy were changed, Moscow is able to be tactically flexible in (dogmatic) pursuit of security objectives which are held steadily over decades. Moreover, since strategy is a matter of relating ends to means, Soviet leaders have enjoyed a great advantage over their U.S. counterparts in their political ability to be steady in development of the means for strategy expression and execution.

Notwithstanding its several strengths, readers today scarcely need reminding that the Soviet Union has problems which are likely to prove resistant to substantial alleviation. Indeed, some of those problems pertain to the very nature of the Soviet imperium as currently constituted. In Paul Kennedy's words, "The problem isn't in the system—it *is* the system."[31] The paragraphs which follow itemize some of the leading difficulties which beset Soviet grand strategy.

Inefficient economy. Military strength is founded in part upon economic strength. If the latter develops a severe case of entropy, so eventually will the former. There are severe practical limits to what any reform campaign can achieve in the U.S.S.R., so long as the government declines definitively to imperil its centralized political authority. If Gorbachev remains unwilling to take the severe political risks of sanctioning real and comprehensive movement toward truly market mechanisms, the Soviet economy is likely to be permanently hindered in its ability to produce the surplus wealth of which, in theory, it is well capable. A careful contemporary Western prediction—by the CIA—for the future of the Soviet economy holds that even success in *perestroika* would produce an economic growth rate averaging only 2.7 percent through the 1990s. That figure, which is very optimistic, falls far short of the Soviet planned, and predicted, growth rates of 4–5 percent. A growth rate averaging 1.7 percent is at least as likely as 2.7.

Unwilling (even absent) client-allies. In an age of nationalism, empire is always deemed illegitimate by those ruled, or ruled through local agents, from abroad. The ties of threat that bound Eastern Europe to the U.S.S.R. were ever potentially challengeable by local dissension, while Soviet performance in hegemonic imperial rule always had possible ramifications for the stability of rule at home. It is an irony of recent history that, contrary to all expectations, it has been the U.S.S.R. that destabilized its client-allies. In time of war with the West and particularly of protracted war, probably all of the Soviet "allies" in Eastern Europe would be thoroughly politically unreliable, at best. Should Warsaw Pact forces fail to achieve Blitzkrieg success, most of their non-Soviet elements, even if not actively in revolt, would need either physically to be disarmed or at the least to be watched very closely (and overawed) by superior Soviet forces. Indeed, as of today the Warsaw Pact is not a functioning instrument at all. The Pact, it should be recalled, has always been a political charade. In reality, the "Pact" is a Soviet military command system.

Problems of political legitimacy of multinational empire at home. Great Russians may identify the Soviet state as their country and as the heir to many of the traditions that they value, but it is plain enough that close to 50 percent of the Soviet peoples feel no such affinity for the Soviet empire. In conditions of peacetime normalcy the uncertain domestic legitimacy of the U.S.S.R. has posed only manageable difficulties for central authority. But in a period of very great, let alone protracted, crisis, Soviet leaders would have to fear for the stability of the integrity of their empire at least as much from forces of internal political fission as from U.S. nuclear warheads. Moscow has bitter memories of its mid-century period of acute and sustained crisis. In the early period of the Great Patriotic War, the national minorities in the European U.S.S.R. typically either collaborated or defected *en masse* as Nazi-German opportunity beckoned, or, at best, provided only a low level of participation and support for the Soviet war effort. *Glasnost* and *perestroika,* and particularly the official tolerance (even encouragement) of popular demands for true political independence in Eastern Europe, have led to the 1990s opening with a condition that is far from normalcy. Inadvertently, Gorbachev has lent encouragement to nationalist, ethnic, and religious fission on such a scale that the unity of the U.S.S.R. is threatened.

Landlocked strategic condition. At the present time Soviet maritime power can move onto the high seas only on the sufferance of the Western Alliance. Given that transoceanic military operations of any size must depend (90 percent–plus) upon seaborne supply, Soviet strategy effectively can be landlocked. Writing of Soviet perception of NATO's strengths, Donnelly attributes to Soviet officials recognition that "[t]he geo-strategic position of the U.K. and that of the U.S.A. may make victory in the Central Region inconclusive, and make it difficult for the Soviet Union to bring a war to the necessary speedy conclusion."[32] As the extra-European world modernizes, the strategic consequences of a landlocked political geography become more and more serious. Less and less of the gross world product is within the combat/logistical reach of the Soviet army in Europe, and it is difficult to see how the Soviet Union could enhance its security by endeavoring to absorb through conquest the advanced industrial societies of Western Europe (let alone the backward economies of its former client-allies).

Geostrategic position flanked by potential superstates in West and East. The "flip side" of the benefits of central continental location is the potential vulnerability to territorially contiguous threats on several flanks. Over the course of the next half century, a painfully modernizing China is certain to attain at least some of the qualities of a superstate (in an unpredictable relationship with a well-armed Japan), while Western Europe (or Germany) might realize some of its political-military potential in forming a regional superstate that could function as a security successor to the NATO of today. Trouble may be coming for the United States on its southern border, but such potential trouble is placed in suitable perspective when one considers the worsening strategic problems of imperial primacy, and even just of security, which beset the U.S.S.R. on the bicontinent of Eurasia. Soviet leaders would be delighted to trade Germans, Shi'ite Moslems, and Chinese for Canadians and Mexicans as neighbors.

Vanishing vitality of ideology. This unmistakable fact is of uncertain consequence. But it is undeniable that in theory the privileged position of the CPSU—along with the political legitimacy of the U.S.S.R.—derived wholly from public acceptance of the claims to validity of the ideology which the party espoused. The U.S.S.R. is but the latest historical example of the fusing of a secular impulse to empire with a religious or ideological mission. Militant Islam and the counterrevolutionary (counterreformation) empire of the Habsburgs are other examples of the genre. The vitality and longevity of those enterprises demonstrate how powerful the synergism can be between the will to conquer and rule and the urge to bear witness to a creed through action. When it occurs, ideological demoralization tends to be fatal to the mind-set necessary for the statecraft of empire. As A. P. Thornton has written, "Empires are not built [or long maintained: CSG] by men troubled by second thoughts."[33] The formal disestablishment in 1990 of the CPSU's leading role amounted to a repudiation of the ideological pretensions of the U.S.S.R. itself.

Safe-siding society and bureaucracy. The penalty for error in the Soviet Union can be high (if no longer acutely painful), and the reward for successful initiative can be nonexistent or at least uncertain. Gorbachev may yet change some of this, but the inertia in the system is so powerful that one should be skeptical. It is more likely than not that the dead hand of a bureaucratic political culture, married to appreciation, or memories, of the coercive proclivities of the state, will continue to depress social and economic performance.

It is open season for speculation on the future of the continental Great Russian empire that is the U.S.S.R., though genuinely strategic assessment tends to fall early victim to the wishful thinking which overreadily perceives the transformation of the U.S.S.R. into a relatively constructive partner in the politics of international security.

Either gradually or by military coup in peace or war, the U.S.S.R. might revert to its Great Russian origins and take at least the semblance of a bold step backwards to the Mother Russia which many people affirm, or hope, is waiting to be reactivated. The patriotic *Pamyat* (memory) movement is an apparently important expression of Great Russian chauvinism. The movement reportedly enjoys important, if generally silent, backing from significant figures in the great institutions of the state. *Pamyat* expresses Russian ethnic hubris, spiritual arrogance (the Third Rome syndrome), and traditional affection for the smack of very firm central government (by way of contrast with the flabby and confused style of the would-be reformers currently in high office), as well as healthy patriotic sentiments. Behind the transethnic, Marxist-Leninist, and multinational U.S.S.R., a Great Russian imperialism lurks none-too-quietly in the background.

Alternatively, the U.S.S.R. may fail to revitalize itself economically, socially, or politically (notwithstanding Gorbachev's discarding of the CPSU), and instead could proceed down a path of more or less graceful relative decline. There are any number of historical examples of countries great and small which have been sufficiently robust as to avoid dramatic domestic upheaval, while their international standing steadily has diminished. It is improbable that the Soviet Union has the political resources to enable it to organize and reorganize with sufficient flexibility to compete effectively with the Western world and with the rapidly rising powers of East Asia. The military options of contemporary Soviet superpower, if exercised, most likely would compound rather than alleviate, let alone solve, Soviet competitive difficulties. However, recognition of that point might not suffice to deter desperate Soviet leaders from rolling the military dice.

After the generic fashion, though not on the model of, the Austro-Hungarian Empire, the U.S.S.R. could decline very ungracefully; indeed, it could decline in a manner so ungraceful as to render it the equivalent of a loose cannon on a rolling deck. A Soviet leadership convinced that it faced the choice between foreign adventure and gradual but inexorable decline in international standing (and domestic respect) might decide that the prudent course was the military one. A mix of contemporary military optimism and deep pessimism over the future can be profoundly encouraging of near-term risk-taking. There is much to recommend Paul Kennedy's view that

> there is nothing in the character or tradition of the Russian state to suggest that it could ever accept decline gracefully. Indeed, historically,

none of the overextended, multinational empires which have been dealt with in this survey—the Ottoman, the Spanish, the Napoleonic, the British—ever retreated to their own ethnic base until they had been defeated in a Great Power war, or (as with Britain after 1945) were so weakened by war that an imperial withdrawal was politically unavoidable.[34]

If Gorbachev should succeed in reforming the Soviet economy, the likelihood that that success will translate into better performance in the qualitative arms competition has to be judged to be quite high. The issue of guns today versus guns tomorrow can require a country to depress investment in near-term military equipment in favor of investment in capital stock for the eventual production of more, or better, weapons in the future. Mikhail Gorbachev's major investment drive for the modernization of capital goods in the (defense-related) machine building sector of the Soviet economy has to be interpreted as an intention to invest in a more competitive position many years in the future. In peacetime the Soviet Union practices the kind of armament in depth which the United States and Britain have practiced only on the brink of, and during, war. The enormous quantities of military equipment of all kinds which the Soviet Union produces regularly probably cannot be explained rationally and fully strictly with reference to political-military doctrine or indeed to strategic reasoning. In addition, one has to factor in the operation of astrategic aspects of political culture. Unlike the U.S. political system, the Soviet political system has been geared to the maximization of state power and not to the maximization of opportunities for individuals to pursue "happiness" (practically translating into private wealth). Great depth of armament, as contrasted to a showcase of weapons with minimum reserve inventories, is not really an economic and social, let alone a political, burden on the Soviet system—*assessed in terms of traditional Soviet political culture.* In substantial measure, the production of tangible military strength, far from being a diversion of Soviet wealth, rather has been its true purpose and expression. Gorbachev appears to be challenging this view of the world, but the jury remains out on whether or not he will succeed. Moreover, to proceed one step further, a large question mark has to hang over the subject of what use he and his successors would make of such success (whether or not they are popularly elected).

Soviet competitive performance in the future, as in the past, is certain to be flattered as a consequence of the constrained political ability of its enemies (adversaries, confused partners) abroad to compete at any level close to their truly awesome combined potential. By far the greatest strategic asset of the Soviet Union is the subject of the next chapter of this analysis: the difficulties faced by its rivals, or potential victims, in realizing sufficient security in the context of coalition politics.

CHAPTER 8

The Perils and
Pleasures of Coalition

---

*Personally I feel happier now that we have no allies to be
polite to and pamper.*

—KING GEORGE VI, 1940[1]

STATECRAFT AND generalship of an unusually high order are
required for the successful conduct of coalition warfare. Virtually by
definition, a coalition will function with divided counsels, with variable commitment to particular enterprises, and on the basis of a
mixture of common policies that are a compromise among alternatives
and of particularistic national policies which other coalition members
choose to tolerate. Notwithstanding historical changes in weapons
technology, there are lessons of enduring worth to be gleaned from—
for leading examples—the management of the Grand Alliance whose
forces Marlborough led against the armies of France (and Bavaria),
the Fourth Coalition of 1813–14 (comprising sixteen members, as
with NATO today) against Napoleonic France, and the coalitions
which defeated Germany twice in this century. It is particularly instructive to study not only those coalitions which succeeded, as did
the four just cited, but also the coalitions which failed (for example,
the First, Second, and Third Coalitions against France in the 1790s
and 1800s, the Central Powers in World War I, the Anglo-French
Alliance of 1939–40, and the Axis in World War II).

Perhaps paradoxically, prominent among the greatest strategic assets of the U.S. superstate are those continental allies in Europe and

Asia whose strength provides local complements to the power of the far offshore United States, and distracts Soviet attention massively toward regional continental issues. From the eighteenth century to the present day, continental statesmen have sought to exploit European resentment against the balance-of-power proclivities of geostrategically detached Britain (and later America). For the other side of the coin, the insularity of strategic mind which can flow from (Eurasian) offshore location has encouraged a stream of policy belief in Britain and America to the effect that continental alliance entanglements are as unnecessary as they are expensive. Many continental Europeans have been as suspicious of the policy motives of the offshore maritime powers as many opinion leaders in the maritime powers have had difficulty understanding the relevance of the outcome of continental squabbles to their insular security. R. B. Wernham has written that "there was built into English foreign policy a duality of ocean and continent. In normal, peaceful times the dominant influence, the dominant attraction, was that of the ocean. In times of European crisis, when the continental balance was upset, the influence of the continent was the more powerful as questions of home defense came uppermost in Englishmen's thought."[2]

NATO is an extraordinary phenomenon in the modern history of coalitions, both because of the degree of preponderance of one of its members and because of the nuclear factor which makes alliance both potentially more perilous in its consequences and more cheaply rewarding (to date) than generally has been the case. Nonetheless, with the unusual features of a hegemonic coalition leader and of nuclear dangers and benefits freely admitted, still there is much in the NATO experience which is very familiar to the student of the history of grand alliances.

THE MAKING AND BREAKING OF COALITIONS

Weapons change, but the terms of international political life do not. States, particularly democratic states, acquire what seem to be natural and then traditional enemies, and in this century at least are prone to believe that if only that traditional enemy can be overthrown or otherwise strictly contained, a condition of permanent peace can be enjoyed. The fallacy of the last move to peace is a recurring fantasy. The fallacy was harbored by popular opinion in the democracies with regard to the peace settlement imposed on Germany in 1918–19; it flowered again briefly over the Kellogg-Briand Pact of 1928 (by which the signatories renounced war as an instrument of policy); it reappeared in noble aspirations for the United Nations Organization; and, more recently, it can be found in the wider-eyed sector of Western arms-control theory and Soviet area expertise.[3]

The common element across time in last-move-to-peace thinking is the hypothesis that there can be a radical break point between the bad old past and present, and a bright new tomorrow. The details vary from case to case, but the central proposition is "if only" we can: beat the enemy of today (Kaiser Wilhelm II [or Prussian militarism], Adolf Hitler [or Nazism]); settle (what are believed to be) the outstanding political issues—satisfy national aspirations for statehood, end world hunger, and so forth; stop deployment of the weapon-ogre of the day (ABM, MX, ASAT, SDI, and one day, no doubt, antimatter weapons)—all things desired become possible. But in practice there can be no last move in the politics of international and hence national security.

People may dream of a world without frontiers, but the evidence suggests overwhelmingly that the only way such a world might occur would be through the agency of a universal empire established and sustained by coercion: thereafter one could anticipate with high confidence the eruption of civil wars on a massive scale within the universal empire. Bids for expansive imperium are a perennial feature of world politics. It follows that the making, unmaking, and remaking of antihegemonic coalitions similarly are perennial. Hegemony-intending states always arise, as do hegemony-opposing coalitions. The rival hegemonic-antihegemonic "teams" will change over decades and centuries, but those are details. Moreover, strategic geography all but mandates the persistence of particular systems in statecraft and defense preparation. Offshore Britain required a first-class navy and first-class continental allies, whether the threat of the period was from Spain, France, or Germany. Similarly, the United States will continue to require a first-class strategic-forces posture, no matter how the geometry of the now-global balance of power may alter.

U.S. opposition to the grand strategy of the Soviet empire is required geostrategically by the threat posed by Moscow to the balance of power in Eurasia, not by the political malpractices of the Soviet variant of oriental despotism. The United States and Imperial Russia for balance-of-power reasons were objective friends throughout most of the nineteenth century, briefly were cobelligerents (Alexander Kerensky's Russia) in 1917, and were allies easily within living memory of today (1941–45). Neither alliance nor enmity is eternal in international politics.

Ideologues in all periods have neglected to acknowledge the merit in the argument that the enemy of today may be needed as an ally tomorrow. Metternich and Castlereagh were alarmed in 1813–15 lest the ending of the Napoleonic hegemony simply would be replaced by an Imperial Russian hegemony; this was not an unreasonable fear since Alexander's Russia could field 800,000 soldiers and the Czar was more than willing to play the role of gendarme of Europe (on behalf of the Holy Alliance for the dynastically legitimate order). A century earlier, British statesmen were prepared to ride roughshod over the interests of some of their allies in order to ensure that the War of Spanish Succession was not prosecuted to the point of the total ruin of France.

No better illustration can be provided of the harmful consequences of prosecuting a conflict to the point of total military overthrow than in the linkage between the demise of German power in 1945 and the inevitable onset of the Cold War. This is not to say that the Western Allies had any very practicable alternatives to the war aim of unconditional surrender. But geopolitically and geostrategically there is no question that Britain and the United States lost World War II as a consequence of the manner in which they won it. Metternich and Castlereagh's nightmare anxieties of 1814 finally had come true: the deposing of one continental hegemon had elevated a yet more powerful successor. Britain and the United States went to war in order to restore the balance of power upon which security in Europe, and ultimately their own security, rested. The practical outcome was the elimination, for many decades at least, of any possibility of there being a European balance of power at all. It is by no means obvious that the Western Allies could have waged World War II simply to effect a correction in the balance of power. So strong was Nazi Germany that the statesmen of West and East surely were correct in placing highest priority upon the immediate goal of what, with some exaggeration, was called the Grand Alliance—the defeat of Germany. It is unlikely that either the Western Allies or the Soviet Union alone could have brought down Nazi Germany, while the nature of the Nazi enemy precluded Washington and London even from considering seriously any possibility of a negotiated settlement.

Just as Hitler's errors in statecraft cumulatively produced Germany's no-win military context of 1943–45,[4] so it was only through statecraft in the form of an effective political countercoalition strategy that he might have saved his Reich. Unfortunately for future international security, the Western Allies could not negotiate with the Hitler of that late date; in practice no wartime successor regime was possible in Germany; and the geopolitical legacy of the policy of unconditional surrender was by no means as clearly perceived in the West as should have been the case.[5]

Alliances are contracts of convenience. The convenience may be asymmetrical, while certainly it will fluctuate over time and over different issues. There is variable normative value attached to fidelity as an ally, but there should be no normative value pertaining to the fact of alliance itself. The basis of alliance has to be a tolerable congruency of interests. But the common, or complementary uncommon, interests which bind allies together usually do not extend very far into the realm of ways and means for the accomplishment of common objectives. As a general truth about alliances, one can assert that it is in the interest of each alliance member to contribute as little to the common cause as is compatible with the alliance generating enough security overall as to fulfill its essential functions for that member. It goes without saying that the selfish profit-maximizing principle easily may conflict in practice with the requirements of the notion of fair shares. In time of war the calculation can be a close one as to whether the current and waning enemy poses a greater threat to the national security than does the ally whose military and political fortunes are waxing strong.

The formal and informal global coalition led uneasily by the United States conforms to a classic pattern of coalition-making. Geographical contiguity breeds antagonism, yields motives for expansion, and provides ease of access for action. Neighbors *tend* to be antagonists, while neighbors-but-one tend to have strategically objective security interests in common. For example, in the fifteenth century England allied with Burgundy against France; in the eighteenth century Britain allied with Austria or Prussia in order to keep French attention focused on the Rhine; in the first half of the twentieth century Britain allied with France and Russia to keep Germany heavily occupied in two directions on land; and today the United States and its security dependents in NATO-Europe are allied functionally with a China which poses a latent menace to Soviet territory and interests in Asia. Should the U.S.S.R. enter a time of very deep internal troubles and decline precipitately in its relative power standing—in other words, should the current trend continue—and should China and Japan cooperate as an emerging alliance of complementary superstates, then the United States would become very interested indeed in forging new security ties with Moscow.

Individuals may decide to act on "forlorn hopes,"[6] but statesmen responsible for the future of a country are not at such liberty to choose the near certainty of national demise over the dishonor of a humiliating accommodation. National leaders will elect to resist hegemonic pressure only when they can believe in a theory of victory for resistance. There are always exceptions. However, for every quixotic Poland there is a bevy of prudent, if unheroic, Czechoslovakias. The option of coalition with a great power or superpower does not so much give courage to a small country as it makes such courage useful as contrasted with prospectively dangerous to the point of suicide. In long-term perspective, although the United States might survive with its political institutions intact in the event of the reorganization of security in Eurasia by, and on behalf of, a single power, it is very much in the U.S. interest to keep hegemony there disputed.

NATO formally is an alliance among sovereign equals. In practice, though decreasingly so, NATO is a U.S. client-states system with the countries of NATO-Europe enjoying the status of security wards of a superpower guarantor. This is only a modest exaggeration. Certainly it is not an exaggeration *vis-à-vis* the bilateral relations between the United States and each individual ally. The operative terms of alliance are not to be found in the deliberately ambiguous founding documents of NATO, but rather in long-established precedents and habits of behavior. Roles and style in behavior have a way of outliving the material circumstances which first forged them. "Who does how much" is an enduring and unavoidable issue in, and really a condition of, alliance management. Much of the public U.S. debate about NATO and the U.S. contribution thereto appears to be innocent of recognition of the enduring political realities of coalition maintenance.

The security generated *in toto* by a coalition of sixteen countries (NATO) has the important quality of being what economists call a "collective good." Each member of NATO does not receive security strictly on a sliding scale which measures the amount of effort expended by that member in the common cause. For geostrategic as well as political reasons, NATO, and particularly the United States as its largest contributor, is motivated to tolerate even gross underperformance on the part of some members. For the most obvious example, the U.S. interest in protecting the security of Canada is rooted immovably in geography. Even if the United States were able selectively to fine-tune its security protectorate over Canada according to some measure of the Canadian defense effort (percentage of gross domestic product for defense, *per capita* cost of defense, and so forth), it could not be in the U.S. interest actually to do so (though to threaten to do so may be another matter). Similarly, particularly strategically located allies, such as Norway, Britain, Germany, Turkey, and Japan, either have or could have the strength of weakness over U.S. policy. These countries, by geopolitical gift from the past to the present, occupy territory critical to the U.S./Western command of principal Soviet geographical axes of military threat.

Unlike the loose and shifting coalitions which fought the wars of the French Revolution and Empire intermittently from 1792 until 1815, NATO has a member relatively so preponderant as to invalidate some of the traditional theory of alliance behavior. Strangely, the potentially most damaging consequences of alliance (mis)behavior tend to be alleviated in the NATO case not by the exercise of strategic rationality, but rather by very astrategic U.S. domestic politics. The scope for "free (or cut-rate) riding" by medium-size allies of the United States is reduced, though far from eliminated, by the appreciation that the U.S. Congress, probably immune to strategic arguments, may have a strategically incalculable threshold of tolerance for perceived allied underperformance.

The dominant position of the United States within NATO, indeed the client-states character of the alliance, on balance has worked to minimize the ill effects of the buck-passing impulse for free-riding which afflicts all coalitions. Realistically or otherwise, as relative economic circumstances have altered to diminish U.S. dominance over the course of four decades, there has never been any doubt as to which country was the last line of the common defense. The United States has paid fairly willingly what amounts to a leadership premium in its contribution to security in Europe. The very structure of NATO has discouraged the preponderant member from attempting to pass the buck to medium-size allies, while the damage wrought by buck passing on the part of the smaller members has been only very modest, if that. In a coalition among, say, four or five roughly coequals, the extent and consequences of buck passing tend to be much higher and far more serious. Furthermore, the oceanic separation of the United States from Europe also has encouraged the United States to overperform in its tangible forward deployments, in order to help offset the potential for dangerous Soviet (mis)perceptions of the quality of U.S. political commitment.

Paradoxically perhaps, the novel nuclear facts pertaining to U.S.

alliance leadership and guardianship have helped incline the United States to maintain large general-purpose force deployments in Europe. Those deployments have been an element critical for the (U.S.) aspiration that nuclear weapons might not need to be used. Additionally, those nonnuclear forces have the status of an *effort de sang* so massive as to sustain the plausibility of the idea of U.S. strategic nuclear use *in the last resort*. It should go without saying that each member of NATO is likely to entertain a distinctive definition of what ought to constitute *the last resort*.

The still critically bipolar security structure for international order increasingly is out of synchronization with economic realities. In political form and military substance, the United States continues in a global hegemonic role which no longer fits the objective context. The United States finds itself with a security challenge of commitments which cannot be alleviated radically by any measure of strictly national military reform, nor, realistically, even by a geostrategically prudent shift in national military strategy. The problem is not really for the United States to conduct its military affairs more efficiently or more cleverly (in the realms of tactics, operational art, and strategy), but rather for it to manage what would amount to a paradigm shift in its *grand* strategy. Following the British example in the first decade of this century, the United States need abandon none of the geostrategic principles critical for its security. But the United States should work to redefine its global security role in ways which would encourage rather than discourage the reemergence of a bicontinental balance of power in Eurasia—a momentous development which would enable, indeed require, a radical reshaping of U.S. military strategy. The current troubles in the Soviet empire which are fueling downward revision of threat estimates in the West facilitate change in U.S. grand strategy, yet also encourage thoroughly astrategic shifts in U.S. and allied defense policies.

Western Europe and East Asia, which geopolitically must be considered in tandem with respect to the balancing of Soviet imperial power, either have already, or are certain to obtain, virtually all of the assets necessary for the maintenance of security in their regions on tolerable terms.[7] The critical asset that is lacking both in Europe and in Asia (with reference to Japan, though not of course to China) is the political will to effect a transition from military dependence upon the declining hegemony of the distant United States to an uncertain and unknown future. There is no necessary and absolute correlation between economic and military strength, the intervening factor of political mobilization is all-important. But, even if one or two of the great economic powers of the early twenty-first century choose not to realize very much of their military potential—Western Europe and Japan for leading candidates—it is improbable that all three of the rising economic superstates or communities would decline to become rounded superpowers.

The NATO Alliance and the bilateral U.S.-Japanese security pact have served the Western world very well indeed in the past and have vital future roles in discouraging U.S. isolationism and providing security for a period of coalition restructuring. Nonetheless, those treaty ties also are major hindrances on the road to greater self-reliance in regional security. It is not suggested here that the United States is economically incapable of persisting with the global guardianship role. The point, rather, is that in a very relaxed climate of East-West relations the U.S. electorate assuredly will be unwilling to tax itself heavily for the purpose of providing a very substantial military establishment. The issues are ones of strategic need and of popular political will.

Although he did not develop this argument, Edward Luttwak's thesis (in *Strategy*) on the paradoxical logic of strategy is complemented by recognition that an alliance created to alleviate or solve a problem eventually itself can become a part of the problem. The U.S. military commitments to NATO-Europe which date from 1950–51 (the initial period of general rearmament) and from 1954 (by way of prospectively permanent tangible guarantees to European allies nervous about the planned German military contribution to the Alliance) should have been regarded sensibly as arrangements for the interim period between the condition of NATO-European near-defenselessness and full NATO-European recovery. The Eurocentric focus of U.S. military strategy has had the consequence of dramatically diminishing U.S. capabilities for action elsewhere in the world, retarding the evolution of a Western European political and defense identity, and encouraging NATO's retention of an impracticable faith in an unduly nuclear-oriented security stance. On the basis of the ever-evolving distribution of economic power and recognizing the monumental uncertainties about the future course of Soviet policy, the United States certainly should be associated tangibly with security in Europe. However, no longer should the United States provide security for Western Europe via a strategy of flexible response which, in the name of deterrence, if ever tested might well function as a holocaust machine.

It is important not to forget the geopolitical fundamentals which explain the enduring success of NATO as a coalition. Although the existing, and in some measure seemingly frozen, political forms and operational habits of NATO serve as a brake upon the evolution of the Western security order, it is well to remember that, as it is (warts and all), NATO: keeps U.S. military power intimately involved in European security (which, historically, is no mean achievement over a forty-year period); resolves the problem of Western leadership for security in Europe (admittedly not in a way that is constructive for the long term, but certainly in a way that works for the time being); and is a huge obstruction to ultimate success for the inferable, geo-strategically logical, Soviet system of statecraft—which looks to continental consolidation, or "fortress *greater* U.S.S.R.," as a base for *Weltpolitik* (either if and when current weaknesses are corrected, or perhaps as a desperate bid to offset those weaknesses).

In addition to the brake that the NATO habit applies to the positive evolution of security arrangements in the West, the Alliance can also work to hinder forms of evolution that would be dysfunctional for international order. The United States is relatively more powerful than ever Britain was in its two and a half centuries of great-power status (roughly from 1700 to the mid-1950s), but the geostrategic interests which mandated the conduct of coalition statecraft for Britain apply also to the United States. No state that is wisely led chooses to be a mere spectator of international security politics if, by intervention at tolerable cost, it can help shape the course of those politics so as to preclude the emergence, or at least moderate the dimensions, of foreign dangers. A dilemma for Soviet policy has to be the consideration that there may be no reliable solution to its burgeoning European insecurity problems. Intended solutions to the problems posed by NATO that fall short of a true Soviet hegemony over all of Europe—a condition far removed indeed from that extant—sooner or later are likely to require that risks be run with an overly strong reunited Germany.

This discussion may seem strange to some readers, given the fact that Moscow today appears to be willing to redefine its security relationships with its erstwhile client-allies in *Eastern* Europe on whatever terms it can receive. There is no question that Mikhail Gorbachev has taken fearful risks in Eastern Europe—in accepting the delegitimization and then the termination of Soviet imperium—because of his twin domestic needs. Those needs are first (the *sine qua non*) to maintain his personal power, and second to bull through some of the reforms necessary if the U.S.S.R. is to remain close to first-class superpower status. It is possible, even probable, that in the course of scrambling much of the existing architecture of Soviet power, Gorbachev will produce a U.S.S.R. or Russian successor state that would be content *for a while* to be passive in world politics.

At present, several Soviet possibilities are open, if not equally probable. The logic of geopolitics, which includes a general prudence on the part of national security communities, and the current priority attached in Moscow to domestic reform, should serve to alert the West to the prospective longevity of the problems that NATO has been sustained to alleviate or resolve. Similarly, in Soviet geopolitical perspective, once the domestic crisis is resolved—as it surely will be, one way or another—the logic of geography and of strategy is bound to promote historically characteristic statecraft from Moscow.

A coalition of democracies (in particular) can be broken in three ways. First, it can be broken as a consequence of its success. Once-perceived threats that have been long-deterred may be forgotten. The wartime variant of this point is that coalitions which cohere well enough to wage war successfully will necessarily lose much of the incentive to continue to cooperate as the common danger, though still actively in the field, plainly becomes less menacing than are one or two coalition partners. Second, a coalition can be broken by failure. Diplomatic failure will encourage some states to reconsider the net benefit of coalition membership; while unfolding, but still incomplete, military failure certainly will fuel arguments in favor of a separate peace. Third, a coalition can be broken if the costs in external effectiveness incurred for reasons of the internal logic of alliance politics are too high. Simply stated, the price of tolerable coalition coherence may be paid in a security product which cannot meet the traffic of external danger. Delays in decision-making, undue buck passing, divided and confused military doctrine, particularist military deployments, and overmuch political reassurance against war at the expense of military deterrence[8] are all typical costs of coalition.

The fact of some objectively common interests provides no absolute guarantee of alliance cohesion. Alliance ties can be sundered by popular perceptions of allied malperformance (undue "free riding," or gross infidelity, or disloyalty in behavior), or by behavior by allies which is believed likely to increase the risk of war. Moreover, alliances can grow old and unravel cumulatively as a product of generational change, evolving diverging attitudes toward external dangers, and shifting sentiments about alliance partners. A point may come when Atlanticist forces in Europe and North America productively cannot simply circle the NATO wagons yet again, as contrasted with reexamining the viability of the alliance forms and procedures dating from a past era. It is no criticism of NATO per se to note that some of its less flexible enthusiasts give the appearance of being afraid of change, lest the whole enterprise should fly apart as the unintended consequence. Similarly, it is no criticism of NATO to observe that the U.S. nuclear protectorate over Western Europe ought to evolve into a more even transatlantic security relationship which would both make more military sense and would encourage, rather than discourage, collective regional self-defense.

If political confidence in the deterrent or war-fighting success of a coalition is lost, then there can be a veritable race to defect—to bandwagon with the power or coalition perceived to be irresistibly in the ascendant. The earlier the defection is arranged, the greater its value should be to the side which is joined, and hence the greater the prospect of securing reward and the lower the risk of punishment. Punishment can take the minimal form of rewards not offered by the side to be joined, may include negative sanctions imposed for the past error of having been on the wrong side, and may encompass rough handling by the side which has been abandoned but which still is in a position to cause hurt (witness the sad, if richly merited, predicament of Italy in 1943–45). This phenomenon is familiar in the arena of U.S. presidential politics. To adopt the Clausewitzian concept, there is a culminating point of victory for an opinion leader considering when to declare his support, or to change his affiliation, beyond which the bandwagon for the most popular candidate will not much profit from the new adherent.

Rank opportunism can be prudent though still dangerous behavior, and may even warrant description as a system of statecraft—in the cases of Italy and Rumania in the two world wars, for example—but alliance-changing often has expressed more than just self-regarding calculations of *Realpolitik*. At least in modern times, the weight of continental empire has tended to lay much more heavily upon ally-clients than has the weight of sea-based empire. It is a general rule that by its very nature sea-based imperium is less intrusive and less promoting of popular resentment than is continental imperium. Apart from the obvious incentive to avoid being on the losing side, the ally-clients of visibly failing continental empires frequently have accumulated massive quantities of deeply felt popular—and sometimes even official—resentment against their imperial masters. For example, both Napoleon's and Hitler's failures in Russia triggered ultimately comprehensive defections from the new imperial security orders forcibly established by those rulers. The very different characters of the Soviet and U.S.-led coalitions have major implications for the theories of deterrence and of war best suited to them. Individual members of NATO might calculate that a separate peace would be the path for responsible policy, but there are no NATO countries which can be predicted plausibly to be eager defectors or neutrals.

For most countries in most periods, and especially so for the great powers of the day, the case for or against particular alliance affiliation has been reasonably clear. However, for those polities which have found themselves in situations where a genuine choice in security affiliation appears to be available, history suggests some rules, or perhaps principles, which should guide policy. First, identify the side which will win (particularly if one plans to defect from an alliance led by a state certain to be motivated to engage in exemplary punishment for perfidy—the sad case of Capua at the hands of a vengeful Rome in the Second Punic War [in 211 B.C.] serves as a brutal illustration of principle). Second, if a country's alliance selection is judged likely to affect the outcome of a war, it should pick the side whose dominance of the succeeding period of peace will bear down the least heavily upon it. Third, there can be no evading the complex need to attempt to intervene sufficiently early in a war so as to make a difference valued highly by new allies, but not so early that undue national effort is required to be expended nor so late that the currency of adherence is greatly devalued. Fourth, when in serious doubt stay neutral. Fifth, statesmen should never forget that the more glittering the prizes offered as a reward for coalition membership, the less likely they are to collect them. Only winners gain prizes, and not always then—as resentful Italians discovered in 1919. The statesmen of belligerents in desperate straits are prone to promise whatever fits the bill for greedy and ambitious policymakers in neutral, or hostile, countries. Sixth, even if a country picks the winning coalition, the path to eventual coalition-wide victory in war as a whole may still accommodate that country's very painful defeat. Finally, history teaches that great powers truly are greater than small powers, and that promises solemnly made to minor allies in time of war may be negated by contradictory promises made to other allies, may prove simply to be too inconvenient to consummate, or may just be abandoned in the interest of the higher good of a new postwar security order.

In common with the principles of war, these elementary principles of statecraft for alliance adherence can be almost impossibly difficult to apply with any confidence in particular cases. The historian looking backwards knows, for example, how disastrous was the Turkish decision to join the Central Powers in 1914, how unwise was the Italian decision to join the Allies in 1915, how suicidal was the Rumanian intervention in 1916, how imprudent was the Italian declaration of war in 1940, and how sensible it might have been for Japan to ignore German discouragement as well as the pessimism of its own General Staff's intelligence division and attack the U.S.S.R. in 1941.[9] But this is the wisdom of hindsight, and—in the Japanese case—a very arguable wisdom at that.

THE GUARDIAN: AMERICA PREPONDERANT

The costs of alliance to a superpower coalition leader include: the danger of involvement in war over the defense of other nations' territories and interests;[10] the need to shape policy for workable compatibility with the interests of allies; the loss of some flexibility in the design, deployment, and doctrine for use of national military forces; and the financial costs of an inevitably disproportionate contribution to a supposedly common defense enterprise. In contrast, the benefits of alliance should be viewed in the first instance in broad geopolitical perspective. The wellspring for the U.S.-organized global coalition has not been the joy of a form of imperium; rather it has been the perceived need to balance Soviet power and influence. There can be little doubt that a U.S. return to isolationism after World War II would have set the scene for the U.S.S.R. to move on from the conquests achieved by its army in 1944–45, and the political consolidation registered by 1948, to achieve a position of unchallengeable authority throughout Europe, the Mediterranean, and eventually much of the Middle East also. If it was not to turn its back on the more fundamental (balance-of-power) reasons why World War II was waged, and was not to dishonor those Americans who were casualties in that struggle, the United States had no practical alternative to throwing its weight behind the organizing of the peace for a more stable international order.

There is an outside possibility that Western Europe, via the Brussels Treaty, the Monnet Plan, a European Defense Community, and the Common Market, might have stabilized the German Problem and forged a regional security community which could have resisted Soviet pressure. Indeed, some people argue that U.S. leadership of NATO on what became a hegemonic pattern, and particularly the rearmament of Western Europe (including the Federal Republic of Germany) upon which the United States insisted as a condition for its active partnership, helped generate an East-West military confrontation which substantially might have been prevented. The argument is not noteworthy for its plausibility.

Overall, by far the most probable alternative to a U.S.-organized, subsidized, and directly defended containment around the Rimland of Eurasia would have been a great expansion of the Soviet Union's informal hegemonic empire, not the creation of a "third force" Western Europe standing as a buffer between the superpowers. The historical record is plain enough: the countries of Western Europe did not merely acquiesce in the emergence of a U.S. nuclear protectorate; they were desperately eager to encourage the United States to play the hegemonic role that its economic and atomic power permitted. If the Western security system was an example of mild imperium, it was an imperium welcomed by the dependents. Whether or not the security of the West truly required the rapid evolution of NATO into an integrated military alliance (1950–51) whose protection was guaranteed by U.S. air-atomic striking power, one can never know. But there is no doubt that the responsible statesmen in Europe at the time certainly perceived no superior available alternative.

U.S. grand strategy was tentative and ill-armed in the immediate postwar years. That fact fitted ill with the brief popularity of Halford Mackinder's geopolitical theory in the United States from 1939 to the end of the war,[11] and with the widespread perception by 1946 that in Stalin the Western Allies had a former coalition partner who aspired like his czarist predecessor, Alexander I, to function as the gendarme for a new brand of Moscow-defined political legitimacy. The spatial concepts of the geopoliticians seemed to have been overtaken in significance by the belated fulfillment of the newly absolute promise of strategic air power, courtesy of the atomic bomb. In the late 1940s the United States had the defense-industrial infrastructure, the mothballed equipment, and the recently trained people with which to generate enormous military power after a period of mobilization, but its ready combat power was woefully small. In 1948–50 the United States uniquely was *the* superpower, but that superpower reposed in economic strength (the U.S. economy delivered more than half of the total world manufacturing product), in political prestige, and in a small atomic arsenal.[12] The unimpressive initial combat performance of the U.S. Army in Korea in 1950–51 demonstrated how comprehensive a decline in military competence had been produced by five years of peace.

The shape and enduring detail of the U.S. grand coalition strategy of which the NATO of the past four decades has been the most prominent feature took the better part of a decade to emerge in full. The period of unplanned, though still real, U.S. preponderance in world security affairs lasted for nearly twenty years, roughly from 1950 to 1970. If not actually a golden age of U.S. freedom of grand-strategic action, this was nonetheless the golden age of U.S. global guardianship (and from 1955 to 1965 was also a golden age for U.S. strategic theory).[13] In many matters of local and regional security, the United States was both too muscle-bound and too fastidious in its willingness to use its power to function as *the* superpower could have done. However, through most of this period the Western Alliance was not an alliance of much prospective military value to the United States in time of major war. In the 1950s, as David Alan Rosenberg has documented, nuclear weapons were "in effect, a weapon of first resort."[14] The U.S. Air Force and the carrier attack aviation of the U.S. Navy would have bombed the U.S.S.R. back to a very radioactive stone age virtually at the very outset of a conflict in Europe. The Great Deterrent that was SAC certainly was going to defeat the Soviet Union, though whether it could win for the United States was another question. By 1961–62, when U.S. satellite reconnaissance revealed what the Soviet Union had and had not built, it was plainly apparent that the United States enjoyed a truly splendid first-strike capability. Although Western Europe probably would have suffered severely, there can be little doubt that a U.S. (and British) surprise attack on the U.S.S.R. in 1961–62 would have achieved a truly definitive military victory.

It did not much matter by the mid- to late 1950s whether NATO-Europe fielded large forces or small forces. Indeed, radioactive fallout from the Carthaginian nuclear peace which SAC planned to impose probably would have been a greater hazard to U.S. allies than would Soviet military prowess of all kinds. Provided a state has an absolute end in view—the definitive elimination of a Carthage, a Corinth, a Jewish revolt, a Nazi Germany, a Soviet Union—absolute means are not incompatible with strategy. To "create a desolation and call it peace"[15] may not sit well with humane sentiments, but such sentiments have tended not to override the perceived necessities of statecraft, Roman or American (or much in between—Rome was a very bad enemy to acquire and the Roman way in warfare was brutal and ruthless to a degree that the Greeks of the third and second centuries B.C. found to be literally barbaric). What mattered for the future was that the golden age of U.S. superpower forged and consolidated attitudes and habits of guardianship and wardship, with their associated conveniences, that would not easily be adjusted to the different grand-strategic context of the 1970s, 1980s, and beyond.

The Great Deterrent had diminishing value as a compellent, and even as a credible deterrent, as Soviet nuclear striking power rendered nuclear deterrence more and more mutual an enterprise. The progressive neutralization of the positive utility for statecraft of nuclear threats has re-created some parts at least of the geostrategic context familiar from former contests in modern history between continental and sea-based coalitions. As strategic forces reverted in the 1960s to the role of shield rather than sword, NATO could choose among: the frank recognition of cumulatively radical change in what Soviet analysts call objective conditions and a return to some variant of the ideas of 1950–52 (entailing provision of very large conventional forces against the backcloth of a presumed nuclear deadlock); a pretense that nothing of essential significance had changed, given a conveniently optimistic notion that the deterrence of major war was an existential fact of the nuclear era; a redoubling of effort to regain military advantage in the strategic balance; elevation of a strategic theory of coercive diplomacy to the status of strategy; or adherence to the comforting proposition that the pathetic fallacy was to be avoided in consideration of "the Soviet *threat,*" and that Soviet leaders really needed little deterring. In worst coalition fashion, NATO found it expedient not to exercise a clear choice among its strategy alternatives—an outcome which was beneficial for the political coherence of the Alliance in peacetime, but which could well have fatal consequences in times of crisis or war.

There is a critical difference between a situation characterized by a security guarantee provided by a superstate to its wards, and a situation wherein the superstate coalition leader has essential need of allies to provide a continental sword—the classic geostrategic requirement of a sea-based great power. The declining operational salience of nuclear weapons for military strategy has returned the United States, *faute de mieux,* to the latter road, though ironically in a context where threats of all kinds from the East are looking less and less fearsome. The NATO allies in Europe provide the United States with geostrategic access to the region, while their status as security clients ensures, at a minimum, that their assets are denied direction by and for Soviet purposes. Soviet defense planners can draw the appropriate geopolitical lesson from Germany's successive two- (plus) front war problems, as well as from Hitler's failure to provide a well-defended perimeter on the Atlantic which could not easily be turned. Unlike the leaders of the German navy, Hitler failed to appreciate the geostrategic significance of the North African littoral as an axis of advance for U.S. military power.

Since the nuclear arsenals of East and West seem more and more likely to neutralize each other in times of crisis and war, the relative strengths of the warmaking potentials of the economies of East and West are, or should be, increasingly important factors for deterrence. But the economies of the Western world are strictly nominal warmaking assets unless they are knitted together by a secure system of maritime transportation, protected against nuclear punishment or intimidation by nuclear deterrence (or defended by thoroughly reliable strategic defenses), and safe from military seizure or neutralization.

ALLIES AS PROBLEMS AND SOLUTIONS

In peace and war, allies function both as problems and as solutions in statecraft and strategy. By definition, the United States as a superpower has interests of differing intensities in many regions. Similarly, the United States is an ocean away from its "barrier allies" and can, indeed is obliged to, consider properly the security concerns of a particular ally only with reference to global considerations. On geopolitical grounds, there is no way in which the United States is able fully to share, say, German, Turkish, or South Korean views of their security requirements. Of necessity, there is an absolute quality to a country's attendance upon its own perceived security needs which no other country will, or should be expected to, share. With finite defense resources, the United States cannot make decisions about its military commitments in Northeast Asia, for example, without as a consequence making decisions about its planned contingent behavior in Europe or South Asia. The overwhelming precommitment of the U.S. armed forces to the defense of Europe must have a radically constricting effect upon U.S. freedom of strategic choice elsewhere in the world (in the same time frame for action). The point here is not necessarily to criticize the extant European focus of most of U.S. military effort; rather it is simply to indicate that a U.S. decision to wage all the war that may be needed in defense of Europe would also be a decision not to wage very much war in other regions of the world. That might be a sensible course in policy and global strategy, but it would be only one of the feasible courses in policy and strategy.

Pending a lengthy period of mobilization, the United States could not conduct and sustain ground operations on a major scale in more than one geographical theater at a time. Understandably and *to a degree* appropriately, Europe is a magnet for U.S. combat power because of its inherent importance, because of the ready access to allies already in the field and heavily armed, and of course because the infrastructure—logistical and political—for the productive reception of additional U.S. forces already exists. It is a canon of continentalist military science that military effort must be concentrated with unwavering determination upon the defeat of the main body of the enemy's military strength in the principal theater of war; all else is evasion. Contrary to some readings of the history of British strategy, the archetypal maritime power of modern times did not often dissent in practice from this canon. In the words of British official historian (of World War I—Britain's greatest continental commitment) Cyril Falls:

> When we had allies who could stand up to the enemy we sent our armies to join them. When not, we turned to theaters less crowded with triumphant foes. We did not adopt a peripheral strategy for love of the conception, but for want of sufficiently sturdy allies. After all, the traditional British campaigning theater was not the Iberian Peninsula, or Italy, and least of all North Africa. It was the Netherlands: the very antitype of the periphery, the cockpit of Europe.[16]

The problem for the United States, as it was in the early 1700s for Marlborough's Britain, for example, is where to strike the balance between the continental commitment to the main theater of operations which is necessary to sustain the coalition, and the strong desirability of distracting enemy attention and pressuring him on his flanks. The issue is not whether the United States should plan to fight in Europe, but—first—whether that effort prudently could be sufficiently modest as to leave a healthy margin of disposable military power available for use elsewhere, and—second—whether the use of military power beyond Europe could promise strategic effectiveness superior to the opportunity cost of not using it in Europe. It is no criticism of coalition or alliance per se to note that the obligations undertaken limit freedom of policy decision and action. Moreover, alliance obligations vary very widely; from a commitment merely to exchange information and consult, through to a military guarantee pertaining to more or less clearly specified circumstances, to what amounts to a "blank check" for political and military support.

The advantage of alliance always is a *net* advantage. There is always some price to be paid for a political arrangement of reciprocal advantage that can be called an alliance. Even the pseudoalliance that is—barely today—the Warsaw Pact, undergirded with a series of bilateral mutual security treaties between Moscow and its clients, is not totally one-sided to the client's disadvantage in all cases. For example, Poland may need the security of Soviet protection against German irredentism, as may Rumania against the Hungarian claim on Transylvania. If there ceases to be a net advantage to all concerned, then an alliance which has been freely contracted will end or decline in authority more or less gracefully.

Historically speaking, there is no discernible pattern in the implications of alliance for the policy behavior of the geostrategically most exposed members. International politics and strategy are always specific to concrete historical cases. Grand theory can function as policy science, for example, concerning the proclivity of states under threat to balance or to bandwagon: it can help explain the structure of a subject at a high level of generality. But one cannot proceed competently from grand theory to specific policy advice without first interrogating the local facts of the situation. Alliance with a great or superpower certainly is itself no guarantee of safety, as Poles discovered in 1939, but neither is the absence of such alliance, as Belgians and Norwegians can attest. Moreover, the accretion of very dependent allies can be an important net minus for a great power, as Hitler's Germany discovered with its Italian security connection. To a potentially significant degree, the greater power in an unequal alliance is obliged to assume some responsibility for defending the vital interests of its dependent allies, as those allies see fit to define those interests. Only in an alliance that is a political cover for the reality of empire is the great-power leader at liberty to treat the vital interests of its clients with disdain.

The United States does not have a tradition of outstanding skill in statecraft. As a popular democracy with a poor sense of historical awareness and a rather short-term view of the future, the United States can rouse itself magnificently to solve an immediate problem. Great dangers, whether or not accurately perceived, typically will generate late but—thus far—effective policy responses. The most pervasive reason for the United States to persist with its existing alliances is that they are a settled bequest of entanglement from the past which are still valuable for maintenance of the balance of power and, more generally, for order. Those alliances could not easily and reliably be resurrected in a timely fashion were they to lapse. Although there are powerful, if rather abstract, geostrategic reasons for the current architecture of the U.S. multilateral alliance system, that system is kept alive more by historical momentum ("happy inertia") than by contemporary enthusiasm. If NATO did not exist today, it would not be reinvented short of the occurrence of some security emergency which might unfold so rapidly that provision for common defense could not be organized in time. Historically, insular countries have been in the habit of dropping in and dropping out of the mainstream of international power balancing. NATO, for all the stresses, strains, and complications which it imposes upon the United States, helps mightily to facilitate the United States to perform its still necessary guardianship duties. That guardianship pertains not only to the narrow, traditional role of protecting Western Europe against (the apparently departing) threats from the East, but also to protecting the process of change by which Europe will choose to reorder its security arrangements. Such European choice can never forget the inconvenient geopolitical fact that the U.S.S.R. is a quasi-European superstate. Unlike the United States, the U.S.S.R. cannot choose to be other than present on the ground in Europe.

POLITICAL CONFIDENCE AND THE DISTRIBUTION OF RISKS

It is a military axiom for the tactical and operational levels of war that because of the enemy's locally divided order of battle, the boundaries between formations tend to offer profitable axes for attack. Similarly, it is a grand-strategic axiom that coalitions are vulnerable to fission over issues liable to elicit separate responses from coalition members. "May all your wars be waged against coalitions" is an ancient military blessing with many variants. Divide and influence, or divide and conquer piecemeal, is the obvious strategy for any power confronting a hostile coalition whose nominal total slate of assets is formidably large. As with an individual country, a coalition has a center of gravity or pivot to its security system. Politically regarded, the center of gravity of a coalition in peace or in war is the confidence felt by members concerning the commitment of all essential partners to the particular, agreed common goals of the coalition. This is not a matter of trust analogous to that between individuals. The confidence in question flows from the calculation that allies discern strong net benefit from remaining as allies, a calculation reality-tested against the evidence of performance.

Political confidence among allies is the glue of NATO. This confidence has to function as trust, since there is no reliable way in which any member physically could be prevented from seeking individual national safety in time of acute crisis. The basis for political confidence among the NATO allies is the calculation that there is greater safety in balancing Soviet power than in bandwagoning with it. Important allies are believed to be unlikely to leave one isolated and exposed to face maximum danger alone. Also, there is a sense of security in, a reassurance from, the familiarity of long-accepted roles in an alliance.

Though with much creaking of old hinges, NATO still works. As though in a time warp, and notwithstanding some efforts to reflect shifting political fashions—as with the Harmel Report of December 1967, which sought to establish NATO as an instrument of détente[17]— NATO is looking more and more like a medieval castle in the early days of the age of gunpowder. The difficulty is that the Alliance has been afraid to experiment with its structure, terms, and strategy— preferring the risk of political and military obsolescence to the risk of outright dissolution which could attend any thoroughgoing attempt to implement radical reform. NATO has worked politically both because of the willingness of the U.S. superpower to tolerate the costs of what amounts to a client-states structure, and because the clients have been willing to tolerate the political costs of clienthood to some of their interests and to their self-esteem. The client role is resented in Europe, but there have been no available superior alternatives. Coalitions are bound together by the perceived necessity of accomplishing a task that single members are unable or unwilling to undertake alone. Classically, coalitions dissolve when the enemy is so far beaten (or is believed to be so, accurately or otherwise) that individual members are no longer under the discipline of fear of defeat. When a leader is convinced that his forces alone can impose the peace that he desires, his incentive to play the cooperative ally will evaporate rapidly. Instructive examples include the misbehavior of Czar Alexander I in 1814 and of Stalin in 1944–45.

NATO generally has not suffered from divisive debate over the character and reality of Soviet power; at least not at the official working level. But, the diverse political geography of the Alliance does mean that a fairly common understanding about that Soviet power inevitably is not mirrored in a common definition of the stakes for the several national securities. The geography of NATO renders the notion of equality of risks among members nothing more than an important concept; it cannot be a full-fledged reality. Of course,

U.S. or Soviet strategic choices could make a catastrophic reality of the doctrine of equality of risks. But the superpowers share an obvious common interest in recognizing their national frontiers as a political-geographic threshold of great strategic importance. In peacetime the Soviet Union profits by telling Americans that a war which erupts in Europe certainly must spread to encompass North America, and by telling Western Europeans that their U.S. guardian would strive to wage a war of limited national liability and restricted (non-American) geographical scope. The enduring popularity in Europe of the idea that French or British strategic forces could function to superpower catalytic effect attests to the sense in this Soviet theme.[18] In wartime, by way of contrast, the Soviet Union should discern the most pressing of reasons for inducing the United States to cooperate in respecting superpower territory as sanctuary from attack (always provided the Soviet Union was winning a regional conflict).

Any number and scope of devices can be specified to promote confidence among allies. But realistically and contrary to the policy logic behind NATO's strategic concept of flexible response, confidence should derive from arrangements which would be in the best interest of members actually to implement in action. Whatever a country's leaders may affirm in peacetime for the sake of securing favorable allied press notices, if the affirmations amount to promises to take wholly unreasonable actions, they will certainly be ignored in the event of war. On the political front, confidence flows from positive appraisals of the record of allies in steady behavior tolerably compatible with one's national security. Allies must not believe that they are being used for, or exposed to dangers because of, the policy of an ally which serves no ends beyond its own. Naturally, since the United States is by far the largest net producer of security within NATO, it is the (variable) confidence that NATO-European countries repose in Washington which tends to be most important. That confidence pertains to the firmness and steadiness of the U.S. commitment to extend protection, to the perceived wisdom in U.S. policy, and to the skill with which U.S. policy is executed and explained.

The late 1980s saw periods when Washington both appeared to its allies to be too eager to conduct serious arms-control business with Moscow, and—subsequently—seemed a little slow to recognize that the old security order in East-Central Europe was dissolving. As coalition leader, the United States must lead from a position at least within short tactical reach of the positions of its principal European allies. If those allies should come to believe that the United States had become a major net problem for European security, then NATO would indeed be in peril. Similarly, thinking of Germany, NATO would be in peril if an important member came to believe that the Alliance was a barrier to legitimate national aspirations (for unification via self-determination for all Germans).

The countries of NATO-Europe are allies of the United States in a legal sense, and their security association with Washington unquestionably is voluntary. But the relationship is more like one between protector and client than between approximately equal partners. The relationship of great inequality was inherent in the internal conditions of the allies in the early years of NATO's history, and has been sustained by the continuing political fragmentation of Western Europe. Moreover, "the nuclear tie between the United States and Europe is the very core of European security 'made in USA.' "[19]

The nominal obligations of superpower guardianship are plain enough: first, to exert any and every effort required to protect allies who endeavor vigorously to help protect themselves; and, second but of equal importance, so to manage political relations with Moscow that the Soviet interest in peaceful relations is maximized. But the United States is a world power whose NATO allies endeavor to exert influence over their protector often from a narrowly regional, European perspective. Also, important though the political independence of Western Europe from Soviet contrôle is to U.S. security, in practice NATO obligations are substantially unidirectional in favor of the non-U.S. members. This is not a complaint; it simply recognizes an existing condition. The public rhetoric of partnership and the like to one side, NATO effectively remains a unilateral, and critically nuclear-focused, superpower guarantee organization.

Because of fears of guilt by association, there is a permanent unease in U.S.-European relations over the extent and the legitimacy of superpower prerogatives. The enemy of our guarantor may treat us as enemies also. The United States has the prerogative to suggest major changes in Alliance-wide policy, but not the prerogative to override deeply held allied objections. This is the prerogative to exercise leadership by persuasion and example, but not further than the more important clients themselves wish to go. Over the past three decades, with the arguable exception of the double-zero terms of the INF treaty, the United States has not been ultimately successful in pressing its European allies on any major issue about which those allies had very serious reservations, or to which they were flatly opposed. This judgment applies particularly to East-West strategic trade and to the recurrent surges of discussion over the desirability of strengthening the conventional forces of the Alliance. In practice the compromise outcomes on the regulation of East-West trade and on conventional-force modernization invariably have been compromises tilted heavily in the favor of long-standing European preferences. One cannot criticize NATO-Europeans for standing up for their several national, and sometimes even their collective regional, interests as they see them. But one can criticize American leaders for being unduly conciliatory over issues central to U.S. national security (for example, strategic trade important for the military competitiveness of the Soviet economy, and the early nuclear dependency of NATO's forces on what used to be called the Central Front).

The persisting, though now really politically obsolescent, debate over relative burden-sharing demonstrates that this is a supremely political subject totally beyond usefully conclusive assault by economic, or any other kind of analysis. A superpower with the global interests and responsibilities which pertain to, indeed help define, that status is bound to spend a lot more on defense functions than are medium-size or small allies. Every ally can claim to be distinctive in the approach needed properly and fairly to assay its level of effort. Three tentative conclusions on the burden-sharing issue suggest themselves.

First, by the time a reasonable person makes suitable, if statistically uncertain, allowance for the leadership premium paid fairly willingly by the United States, a powerfully simple, certain, and quantifiable case proving European underperformance has flown out of the window. Moreover, calculation of Alliance contribution is complicated further by recognition of the cost of capabilities important to the United States almost regardless even of the existence of allies in Europe, by acknowledgment of the low financial but high social costs of (most) NATO-European conscript manpower, and by registration of the host-nation support provided for U.S. forces in Europe and Asia.

Second, notwithstanding the multiple and cumulative statistical uncertainties, a few allies unarguably are persisting, gross underperformers. The leading examples are Canada and Japan. Both of these countries can "free-ride" with seeming impunity because of the "barrier" character of their geographies for U.S. strategic interests. The United States must defend Canada if it is to defend itself, and Japan is key both to the United States having any forward strategy whatsoever in Northeast Asia and to the landlocking of Soviet maritime power in the region. The case of Japan is unusually complex. Although the United States would welcome a Japan better armed for national and regional security, neither Washington nor U.S. allies and friends in Asia are ready for a Japanese military superpower. Nonetheless, unwelcome though the near-term emergence of a superpower scale of Japanese armament would be, there is resentment in the United States that the competitiveness of the Japanese economy in international trade is noticeably, even perhaps measurably, a function of the modesty of the scale of Japan's diversion of high-technology talent to military purposes.

Third, radical improvement in the quantity or quality of allied defense contributions will not be achieved through the diplomatic event of nominal agreement on identified numbers for real increases in defense expenditure. Indeed, radical improvement will not be achievable by any means as "peace breaks out" in the 1990s. However, if NATO were serious about an endeavor to share defense burdens more evenly, it would alter its failed past approach of agreed percentage increases in measurable inputs. Instead, NATO would work the problem backwards from an estimate of the ready and reserve forces needed to achieve what the allies agree should be achieved, to allocation of national responsibilities for provision of those forces. A problem with this military-requirements approach to burden-sharing is that it would require the Alliance to confront precisely those central issues of strategy and theories of deterrence which have been fudged deliberately and conveniently for so long by the all-enveloping concept of flexible response. One need not be a professor of statecraft to predict that NATO countries will discern, and prefer, an arms-control to a unilateral-military-effort route to regional security improvement. It appears to be so much cheaper.

As the Soviet threat is perceived to wane, the seemingly perennial burden-sharing debate will change its terms. In a period of unprecedented uncertainty over the future security order for Europe, strategy questions for NATO change in detail, but not in kind. Similarly, whether the Soviet threat is believed to be waxing or to be waning, the central coalition question of "who does how much of what" remains.

From time to time, both U.S. and European statesmen have aired the proposition that NATO ought to develop along the lines of "twin pillars," or even—unfortunately—of a "dumbbell," with Europe and North America roughly balanced in their relative weight in Alliance counsels. Apart from the risks many people have discerned in the external security performance of such a hypothetical NATO, in practice it transpires that few countries actually would favor it. Canada would be a beaver in bed with an elephant in North America, while the smaller European members have no wish further to institution-alize their status as minor players behind the regional medium powers of Britain, France, and Germany. Moreover, thus far at least, each of the major European members of NATO has placed quite extraor-dinary value on its individual, bilateral relationship with the United States, and has been unwilling to place that relationship at risk in return for the highly uncertain benefits to be derived from chipping in to a European identity and voice in NATO.

STRATEGY AND PROTECTION

The protection of clients is an activity as old as organized conflict. Edward Luttwak expressed the nub of the matter when he wrote, "Superpowers, like other institutions known to us, are in the pro-tection business. When they cannot protect clients, they lose influ-ence, not just locally but worldwide."[20]

Although military strategy and the East-West balance of regional and strategic forces have changed greatly from the time of the signing of the North Atlantic Treaty on April 4, 1949, the most characteristic element in the protection extended by the United States over its European client-allies has remained nuclear. Indeed, the concept of extended deterrence has always meant extended *nuclear* deterrence.[21] The reason for this is not difficult to identify. The U.S. nuclear arsenal was transformed from a condition of scarcity to one of relative abun-dance from the late 1940s to the close of the 1950s. (In July 1948 the United States had just fifty Mark 3 "Fat Man" implosion bombs, while by December 1960 U.S. SIOP-assigned forces alone had close to 3,200 nuclear weapons—the total nuclear arsenal comprised 18,000 weapons.)[22] Through the 1950s the United States had an ever-growing lead over the Soviet Union in size of nuclear arsenal and in the means of delivery. For better or worse, though certainly inevitably under the circumstances of the period, NATO formally hitched its strategy wagon to the U.S. nuclear guarantee in December 1954 when it adopted MC-48—"The Most Effective Pattern of NATO Military Strength for the Next Few Years"—which reflected in detail the nuclear-oriented New Look in U.S. defense policy introduced by the Eisenhower administration in late 1953. The cheapest, most potent way for the United States to guarantee its allies against aggression was through the extended deterrent of the U.S. "long suit" in "air-atomic striking power." This power was viewed as the Great Deterrent, the ready equalizer against the canonical 175 divisions of the Soviet army. Notwithstanding the growing complication of Soviet nuclear striking power, through the 1950s the United States, with allied concurrence, planned in the event of war to wage nuclear combat *à l'outrance* against the Soviet homeland: NATO's regional defenses were to function as a tripwire for the nuclear initiative and just possibly as a shield minimizing loss of territory.

Fortunately, the question of whether or not the United States could have waged and won a nuclear war in the 1950s must forever remain a subject for speculation only. Certainly the trend in official U.S. net assessment from mid-decade onwards was not very encouraging. By 1957, for example, U.S. government estimates of probable American fatalities in a nuclear war (prompt and delayed—that is to say, as a result of fallout) were beginning routinely to lie in the 50–100 million range. In the event of a U.S. disarming first strike, that range would be lowered radically. However, there was general agreement that the United States could wage intercontinental nuclear war virtually with impunity on behalf of its forward allies only if the Soviet Union obligingly declined to place its long-range nuclear strike forces on alert in the course of an acute crisis (in fact they were this obliging in October 1962).[23] The relative nuclear advantage of the West in the 1950s was so large that probably it conveyed both political and military benefits, notwithstanding the growing significance in the minds of statesmen of the absolute damage that alert Soviet nuclear forces could impose. The Soviet Union would have lost a nuclear war waged at any time in the 1950s, though there was a growing danger that a Soviet strike back would have produced, at best, a Pyrrhic victory for the West. Richard Betts is correct in his historical assessment that "[e]ven with advance warning of attack, U.S. vulnerability to countervalue strikes [against cities] was judged to be extremely high by the late 1950s."[24]

The ideas of a nuclear sword and a conventional shield were reversed in the 1960s under the pressure of a deteriorating military balance. Nuclear (and particularly strategic nuclear) weapons were to be weapons of last, rather than first, resort. However, amidst the vicissitudes of doctrinal evolution, changes in weaponry, and cumulatively massive alteration in the relative strengths of allied economies, the latent threat of the U.S. nuclear guarantee for the extending of deterrence has remained central to NATO strategy to the present day. This persisting fact is a convenient habit which has become a burden of history upon the Alliance, as well as a symbol critical to political confidence among allies. Extended nuclear deterrence is the only doctrinal mechanism by which the immediate hazards of war truly can be shared between allies who lie an ocean apart.[25] Also, it is claimed to mean that the superpower guarantor will not tolerate the conquest of its allies without exerting every effort, and accepting every risk, to prevent completion of that event.

However, there is an obvious contradiction, or tension, between the value of equalizing risks among NATO members in aid of persuading Soviet leaders that an attack on one would be an attack on all, and the operational requirements of the protection business. The credibility of superpower protection logically should repose in an inequality of risks among Alliance members. On the one hand a condition of limited liability for protective action may weaken deterrence and strain an alliance as friends and foes wonder whether the offshore guarantor is really very committed to uphold exposed allies. On the other hand restriction of the potential costs of protective action ought to encourage superpower leaders to fulfill commitments.

For extended nuclear deterrence to be a sensible pillar of coalition strategy, one or more of three conditions must obtain. The protecting power must be able to disarm the enemy of virtually all of his ability to retaliate; or he must be convinced that the enemy assuredly will suffer and tolerate military defeat and will choose not to retaliate massively when he could do so; or he must be satisfied that even threats which are thoroughly incredible in terms of strategic logic will deter reliably for reasons of their awesomeness. It is obvious why extended nuclear deterrence should have worked in the very early 1950s, before the Soviet Union acquired an operational nuclear strike force by 1954 which might just have navigated itself successfully on one-way missions against the United States. Similarly, if the SDI one day should restore a very clear measure—insofar as these things could be calculated—of operational military advantage to a U.S. strategic posture balanced as between offensive and defensive prowess, then extended nuclear deterrence ought to be rejuvenated as a consequence. But if restorative action for extended deterrence is sought only via the revision of doctrine and the greater accuracy of weapons, it is less than obvious how operational success is to be achieved. The Commission on Integrated Long-Term Strategy sought salvation through the advanced technology which should render greater selectivity in assault both feasible and credible. What has not been explained is how a discriminate deterrent could deter or defeat the enemies of the United States. "Discriminate deterrence" is a counterfeit strategy; it is tactics and technology masquerading as strategy.

Given that there has been no war in Europe, the deterrent strategy of NATO can be said to have succeeded—though whether or not it has ever really been tested is a matter strictly for speculation. As an issue of military prudence one might judge that NATO long has been dangerously overdependent upon nuclear threats, allegedly of declining credibility, but how can one argue very convincingly with success (or the absence of failure)? The nuclear centerpiece of NATO's strategic concept of flexible response is sustained importantly by two considerations. First, it appears to work well enough. Second, in the words of Henry Kissinger, "Conventional deterrence rarely works."[26] Ancient, medieval, and modern history is replete with cases of the failure of conventional deterrence. Critics of NATO's nuclear dependency, no matter how cogent their strategic arguments, can point only to *hypothetical* dangers for that dependency.

International security requires a nuclear-armed Soviet Union to feel the weight of *nuclear* dissuasion. The policy issues for NATO do not pertain to nuclear deterrence per se, but rather to the function of such deterrence in its strategy and to the practical arrangements for its organization. For the United States there are two issues. First, is it practicable any longer for deterrence—i.e., is it sufficiently credible?—to guarantee distant allied territory by threats of central nuclear action in the last resort (whatever that may mean)? Second, are such threats, credible or not, either necessary or desirable? The problems of credibility which long have exercised officials and theorists of nuclear strategy may have been considerably exaggerated. U.S. intervention in the two world wars, forty years of coalition leadership in NATO, more than 300,000 military personnel still (if not for much longer) deployed forward in the region, and pervasive political, economic, social, and cultural ties should provide as much of a basis for credible commitment as any reasonable person could ask. Moreover, Soviet leaders can reason as well as can we that their conquest of NATO-Europe would constitute a geopolitical and geostrategic setback to the United States of truly historic proportions, whatever the expanded problems of internal security it brought to such an inflated Soviet empire.

Overall, the likelihood of the United States being willing to take at least some nuclear action over a losing campaign in Europe, even to and beyond the point of licensing Soviet strikes against the U.S. homeland, prudently has to be calculated in Moscow to be quite high. So much is not really arguable. What is arguable is whether that credibility of U.S. commitment to exercise the strategic nuclear initiative is either high enough to stand the required deterrent traffic in the context of a desperate Soviet military adventure, or would or should be matched by U.S. operational behavior. A robust-seeming deterrent, as with the edifice of NATO's strategy today, looks to be much less robust only in one quite extraordinary context. That context is when the Soviet risk-benefit calculus has been transformed by a radical narrowing in the direction of belligerency of Moscow's perceptions of its available options. Unfortunately, far from being the exception which proves the rule (that NATO's deterrent strategy is good enough), this limiting case instead is precisely the case, indeed is the only case, when NATO would need its strategy to work for deterrence in the forefront of Soviet minds. All too often, Western discussion of the requirements of a stable deterrence are utterly insensitive to the highly variable political intensity of the threat. A Western combination of military capability and political will as perceived in Moscow may be more than adequate to deter aggressive moves designed by a confident Soviet Union to improve its geostrategic position. But that Western combination could fail to deter in the face of a Soviet calculation that the status quo—translating dynamically into a declining security—is intolerable. A Soviet Union facing the imminent reality of precipitate decline could be a very dangerous Soviet Union indeed.

The basic answers to the question of what deters are the responses "an insufficient prospect of success, or an unacceptably high prospect of painful failure." However, denial of victory and intolerably painful failure as dissuading prospects may not be interchangeable for deterrence. NATO could craft its regional nonnuclear forces for the purpose not of deterrence by the threat to ignite a central nuclear conflagration, as at present, but rather with a view to persuading Soviet defense planners that military victory was unlikely. By limiting the consequences of military failure for the Soviet Union, NATO might drastically and critically weaken deterrence. As the former U.S. Under Secretary of Defense for Policy, Fred Iklé, has advised, one has to be careful lest in the search for a more credible deterrent with less apocalyptic consequences in the event of failure, one strays into the field of enunciating what could amount to a "dogma of immaculate aggression."[27]

To an unknown degree, awesomeness in the potential pain which might be suffered can be substituted for credibility in the likelihood of that pain actually being inflicted. At least, that judgment should be true for the typically cautious style of Soviet leaders; it would not hold for a political leader who was an inveterate gambler, or who believed he had exhausted his nonbelligerent options. Deterrence cannot function in a relationship where the intended deteree is truly irrational, which is to say when he does not consider the consequences of his actions and does not operate in a strategic mode relating means to desired ends. The historical record suggests that deterrence is far less technical a condition than contemporary defense analysis could mislead one into believing. States go to war when, rightly or wrongly, they believe that their vital national interests are at risk. Contrary to much popular mythology, the great powers of Europe did not stumble by accident into World War I, any more than the European and Pacific conflicts of World War II were the products of technical malfunctions in the deterrent mechanisms of the period. In both cases the responsible statesmen consulted their countries' interests and decided to fight. What is important here is the need to recognize that the key to stable deterrence lies more, though certainly not exclusively, in the realm of political interests than it does in the details of strategy and forces. Debate over U.S. and NATO deterrent strategies hovers around the point that policies intended sensibly to limit the liability of society to damage, both as a worthy and ethical end in itself and as an aid to the credibility of threatened contingent action, also have the unfortunate consequence of limiting the liability of the aggressor.

From the time when the first SIOP (SIOP-62) was revised in 1961 (SIOP-63, adopted in 1962) through to the present day—though far more rigorously in the 1970s than in the 1960s (leading to SIOP-5 of 1976 and SIOP-6 of 1983)—the fundamental problem for extended nuclear deterrence, Soviet second-strike capability, has been handled by development of a generally inexplicit theory of intrawar deterrence. In order to evade the unacceptable binary choice between suicide and surrender, elaborate schemes have been woven for the more or less timely, measured, and discriminating application of strategic nuclear firepower by forces which, today at least, assuredly could be commanded and controlled in an operational nuclear environment. Then–Secretary of Defense James R. Schlesinger emphasized the low end of the newly fashionable idea of "limited options" for central war in 1974 and 1975, while the higher end saw the light of public focus in the discussion and testimony which succeeded the Carter administration's explanation of PD-59 in the summer of 1980. The trend has been to fine-tune the extended nuclear deterrent, both with reference to the quantity of firepower to be applied and to the target sets selected. This was, and remains, an entirely healthy development—even, one might say, a development motivated by a pressing need to bring genuinely strategic considerations to bear upon planning for central war. In the case of PD-59, an outstanding purpose was to key central nuclear systems to the needs of theater commanders (long-range fire support), a purpose that did not fit very compatibly with the concept of the SIOP, the central nuclear plan.[28]

What was wrong with U.S. planning for central nuclear war was not the belated quest after very reliable command, control, communications, and intelligence (C^3I) to maximize the prospects for the controlled use of nuclear force, or the determination to slice strategic nuclear force into more and more options for presidential choice, or—least of all—the search for targeting options informed by sophisticated analyses of how the Soviet empire is believed to function. Instead, the problem lay with the weight of the deterrence burden which continuing deficiencies in NATO's regional fighting power placed on the U.S. strategic forces. NATO's authoritative strategic concept of flexible response has at its core the notion of a "great chain of deterrence." The concept subsumes the theory that military aggression, if not deterred at the planning stage, could be arrested in midwar by Soviet recognition that NATO would wage an ever more destructive conflict. In other words, the decision to escalate—on the battlefield, then to the rear area in the theater, and then to the homeland of the enemy superpower—successively would be a string of NATO/U.S. decisions. Needless to add, perhaps, preemptive Soviet nuclear action might well intervene between a Western decision and Western execution. Repeatedly, if deterrence were not restored promptly by some symbolic nuclear "shots across the bow," it would be a U.S. President (possibly in consultation with sensibly terrified allied leaders) who would be requiring his nuclear forces to function coercively in order to compel the Soviet Union to step back from very recently, and presumably expensively, acquired gains.

The Achilles' heel of extended nuclear deterrence in support of deficient conventional stopping power is the absence of a thoroughly reliable way for the United States to insure itself against an unacceptably destructive Soviet strike-back. U.S. strategic offensive forces should function magnificently as a *counter*deterrent, dissuading the Soviet Union from taking central-war initiatives, except by way of preemption, of course. But, unless the United States is near certain of achieving preclusive offensive and defensive counterforce success, how could it expect to prevail in an escalating spiral of competition in the acceptance of pain, given that the burden of the initiative to escalate would be on the shoulders of the U.S. President?

Scarcely less troublesome than the difficulty of finding a plausible theory of success in war in the more violent reaches of flexible response is the nontrivial possibility that Soviet nuclear strategy would be guided by principles incompatible with the model of measured escalation which finds cultural favor among leading U.S. defense analysts.[29] Those Western analyses of probable Soviet nuclear strategy which are the most careful in trying to avoid ethnocentric bias point to a Soviet style in the conduct of war which does not fit well with NATO's hopes for the success of flexible response in action.[30] Specifically, the Soviet Union appears to aspire to secure strategic warning of nuclear escalation by NATO in Europe, and to be ready to preempt such escalation with a large-scale nuclear forestalling blow of its own. Similarly, the Soviet Union would be maximally alert for strategic notice of escalation to central war and, on receipt of such warning, would function as best it was able in a damage-limitation mode. Striking preemptively, on the principle that it is better to fire first than to fire second, the Soviet Union should be expected to endeavor to win a central nuclear war.

The details of Soviet operational nuclear strategy certainly should vary with the context (was the strike preemptive in a condition of regional conflict, that is to say when Soviet strategic forces were fully generated on alert, or were Soviet forces responding in a second-strike mode?). The point of importance is that the military strategy— and the theory of deterrence which it expresses—of NATO described here, that of flexible response, is the product of the political structure and terms of alliance of the Western coalition. Flexible response is virtually totally innocent of serious consideration of its likely implications if applied in war. The continental tradition in statecraft and war which the Soviet Union represents, augmented by the poignant lessons of 1941–45, is extraordinarily sensitive to the dangers and advantages of surprise; is determined to wage war as the visiting, rather than the home, team (notwithstanding the political concept of defensive sufficiency); and plans to wage war, if fight it must, to a military conclusion. In the event, and if they have the time, Soviet political leaders might improvise and contradict the central themes in Soviet strategic culture, but the designers and operators of NATO's military strategy cannot afford to assume that that would be the case.

For an extended nuclear deterrent to work as reliably as it can for the prevention of war, it should backstop a forward defense sufficiently formidable that Soviet defense planners would calculate that most likely they could not win a war against NATO strictly at the regional level. Alternatively, if the prospects for assembling truly first-class regional defense capability are deemed less than encouraging, then the only prudent course consistent with the U.S. national security concept of forward containment would be to attempt to add first-class strategic defenses to the strategic offensive force posture. Further refinement of the capabilities of the strategic offensive forces toward an ever greater selectivity in possible execution, treated in isolation from the synergistic strategic value of defenses, simply cannot meet the mail. Though desirable in itself, a truly discriminating deterrent needs to be incorporated in a robust theory of success in war. A mixture of unilateral and negotiated asymmetrical reductions in the Soviet ground forces may yet transmute the base metal of NATO strategy into gold: this would prove that strategic folly (NATO's nuclear dependency) can reap wholly unearned rewards. However, it is distinctly possible both that the Soviet army will restructure itself so that it is leaner, meaner, and more agile, and that NATO will fumble its historical opportunity to achieve conventional parity.

Although there is much about NATO for which there are approximate historical precedents, the fact of mutual nuclear deterrence highlights as never before the dilemmas for policy and strategy of what amounts to a military protectorate. *Pour encourager les autres* is a familiar rationale for military action in an alliance context. Motives usually are mixed, but the very protracted British campaign in the Iberian Peninsula from 1809 to 1814, Russian and British offensives from 1914 to 1917, and the Anglo-American assault upon Italy in 1943 were all conducted for purposes which included that of encouraging beleaguered allies to remain actively in (or return to) the field. However, there is no historical precedent for the contingent promise by the United States to take nuclear action on behalf of allies which is judged more likely than not to have suicidal consequences. Lovers may die for each other, but there is no record of countries choosing to do so.

Throughout the First World War Britain retained large forces at home against the improbable contingency of a German invasion (over an uncommanded North Sea!). In 1940 Britain placed very severe limits upon her commitment of fighter squadrons to the continental campaign, and was not overly troubled at leaving her continental ally to fight on alone, albeit very briefly (not that Britain had any practicable alternative by early June). Similarly sensible were the successive Ango-American decisions in 1942 and 1943 to defer the launching of the Second Front, no matter how insistent the demands from Moscow. No coalition in history has asked, let alone expected, what NATO-Europe demands of the United States by way of an allegedly fair distribution of risks. In the interest of perceived transatlantic political coupling for stable deterrence and to reassure geo-graphically exposed NATO-Europeans, the United States has promised to place the survival of its society immediately on the line rather than acquiesce in a military defeat for the coalition in a cam-paign in Europe. That, starkly, is what flexible response is all about as a theory of deterrence. Many NATO-Europeans too fearful of Libyan terrorist retaliation to be willing to associate themselves with U.S. military action in that connection, nonetheless have seen nothing strange in expecting Americans at home to be prepared to die by the tens of millions rather than tolerate the Soviet conquest and occu-pation of Western Europe.

It is no answer to cite, correctly, the vital interests of the United States in thwarting presumed Soviet geostrategic ambitions for the unilateral organization of security in Europe. In the context of global strategy the United States does not have survival-level interests at stake in Europe. One may eschew apocalyptic visions of nuclear war, and choose to believe—with Albert Wohlstetter, for example[31]—that the superpowers could and would wage both theater and central nuclear conflict in a highly controlled and discriminating fashion. But still it remains self-evident that the quality of risk to the principal (offshore) protecting power has escalated by orders of magnitude from all other coalition cases in history, not excluding the threat and reality of aerial bombardment in World War II.

STRATEGY AND POLITICAL COHESION

There is persisting merit in the politically infelicitous axiom coined by NATO's first secretary general, Lord Ismay, that NATO has three essential functions (everything else of value being only desirable ex-tras): to keep the Americans in, the Russians out, and the Germans down. While the 1990s are proving to be open season for German reunification, there is no very plausible way in which the new Ger-many can be suitably disciplined (in the minds of nervous neighbors) save through the agency of coalitions led by the rival superpowers. NATO, for all its troubles and imperfections, provides a structure of security almost certainly greatly superior to any currently feasible alternative. Many of the Alliance's root-and-branch critics on both sides of the Atlantic neglect to notice that the worth of an institution has to be assayed in the context of available alternatives, given that the problems which the Soviet Union poses for the balance of power in Europe, although they wax and wane, are not transient in kind. Both NATO-Europe and the United States see value for security in the very fact of NATO. A library of specialized studies on the military problems of the Alliance generally suggests otherwise, but it is a first-order truth that the political leaders of NATO, particularly in Europe, are vastly less interested in the prospective combat prowess of the coalition than they are in maintaining a political cohesion founded upon mutual confidence among the members in peacetime. That cohesion is valued virtually regardless of the cost to military common sense. This strand of thinking is very frustrating to people who discern, and seek to correct, the more manifest military deficiencies of the coalition. It is not particularly helpful for improvement in the military stopping power of NATO for European leaders, first, to endorse what amounts to the idea of an existential political deterrent (after the fashion of the British government's reasoning in the spring of 1939 *vis-à-vis* its guaranteeing of Poland's frontiers),[32] and, second, to prefer a regional defense posture which is almost designed to fail after waging a good fight for a few days or weeks.

With regard to NATO forces and strategy, as for the U.S. strategic nuclear forces, there are sharply divergent schools of thought on the critical subjects of "How much deterring might the Soviet Union need?" and its corollary, "What deters?" However, the divergence between those who take a preponderantly political view of deterrence and those who assert that reliable deterrence must rest upon a robust military denial, or so-called war-fighting, capability is less a clash of attitudes and philosophy than a clash between less and more careful analyses. The war-fighting approach to deterrence holds broadly that if there is not some plausible and discernible rough fit between threats issued and threats which would make political and military sense actually to execute in action, the results could be catastrophic. Given that a massively punitive approach to deterrence ought to be a bluff, since its implementation would leave an enemy with no incentive to exercise self-restraint in his strike-back, it is a prescription for the paralysis of the will to resist. Alternatively, if the ridiculous idea that it can be rational to threaten to act irrationally (on a slippery slope, or the edge of a cliff, to prompt or delay nuclear Apocalypse) truly were not a bluff, but were called as if it were, then the punitive deterrent would produce the end of Western (and Eastern) civilization.

The Soviet-calculated military strength of NATO in action almost certainly is not important for deterrence in what may be termed normal times, let alone the extraordinary times when the Soviet empire is almost wholly self-absorbed by its internal troubles. Deterrence is going to fail in Europe neither because Soviet military planners can devise operational plans which express more or less plausible theories of victory nor because those planners adhere to offensive ideas for the conduct of war. Nothing in Soviet history, distant or recent, suggests a cultural proclivity for military adventure. The critical issue is political motive. When liberated from domestic preoccupation, or—heaven forfend—if that preoccupation ever should lead to a military policy of desperation, Soviet leaders will want to deny their superpower enemy geostrategic access to Eurasia. Needless to add, perhaps, Soviet leaders—desperate or not—should be presumed to be highly motivated to avoid the necessity of waging a very large war to secure that ambitious goal. The military prowess of NATO, in prospective detail, has to be presumed important for deterrence in that unpredictable situation when the political velocity of Soviet threat makes a quantum leap upwards. Today, it seems that the Soviet Union can be deterred without Western effort. But, one day, desperate and hence very determined Soviet leaders could require a great deal of deterring. The U.S.S.R. might come to believe that it faced problems of imperial instability which could not be resolved by prudent appeasement or domestic repression. Furthermore, a condition of apparently inexorable decline in relative Soviet power might threaten. In such conditions what today would be deemed a military adventure or a reckless gamble could become the prudent and conservative policy of choice—perhaps to attack NATO, or to seize control of the lion's share of the world's easily accessible oil reserves in the Persian Gulf region. The reasons why such military gambles on the Soviet part should have the net effect of worsening the Soviet political and strategic situation are so obvious as not to require stating. Indeed, the leap from the U.S.S.R. of today to the U.S.S.R. of Tom Clancy's *Red Storm Rising* is so large that its very implausibility should arouse interest.[33] History rarely follows the course scripted by optimists.

It is no revelation to argue that NATO's guiding strategic concept of flexible response has the virtues of its vices. Moreover, the virtues of flexible response, at least until today, have been the virtues which counted for the most in the peacetime management of the Alliance. The literature on the defense of NATO-Europe is stocked superbly with the carefully drafted schemes of military purists of one or another strategic, operational, tactical, or even simply technological persuasion. Much of that literature is as irrelevant as it is well intentioned and quite possibly narrowly militarily sound. The difficulty lies in identifying those military improvements in coalition defense which are affordable and do not challenge the political terms upon which the common coalition enterprise is conducted. Since there is no scientific basis upon which threat analysis can proceed,[34] the scale of NATO's regional defense problems is subject to a wide variety of not-implausible definitions. From a common data base, would-be reformers of NATO's unreconstructed defenses can argue, alternatively, that a Soviet invasion would fail as did Imperial Germany at the Marne in September 1914, or succeed as did Nazi Germany in May 1940. The use that NATO governments would or would not make of political and strategic warning time and their willingness to respond tolerably in unison are much more important as factors bearing upon short-term success than are the quantifiables of rival orders of battle—a point that all schools of thought endorse. No amount of defense analysis can resolve in advance the difficulties for NATO which a ragged political response to ambiguous evidence would produce. Indeed, the ever-arguable prospective net military prowess of NATO is being rendered yet more arguable as a consequence of the doctrinal ferment and postural evolution in the East, the loss of the Soviet control mechanisms of the Warsaw Pact and local Communist Party rule, and the major uncertainties that radical measures of disarmament would introduce.

There are ample military-technical grounds for uncertainty as to how best NATO could defend in Central Europe. However, in the real peacetime political world of a sixteen-member coalition comprising highly self-regarding nations, by far the most critical problem for coherence in defense is the incompatibility of the objectives for that defense preferred by key members. The continental European members of the coalition do not want an architecture of defense which should enable the offshore coalition leader to function in wartime after the historical pattern of the British conduct of European war. It was ever the British spirit in its conduct of continental campaigns to operate in light of the knowledge that, so long as the Royal Navy commanded the narrow seas, its army could fight and run away to the ships—to fight again another day.

NATO-Europe understands that it must expend sufficient effort on defense as to satisfy the U.S. Congress concerning its performance in satisfaction of the transatlantic bargain. But in European perspective, provision of larger conventional forces: would encourage the U.S. Congress to favor the proposition that a large, permanent U.S. ground commitment is no longer needed (a proposition that both the executive and legislative branches of the U.S. government are certain to endorse in the 1990s); could well have the unintended effect of decoupling, in Soviet minds, the NATO-desired perceived connection between a European battlefield and central nuclear war; would be utterly out of tune with the times, as the Soviet Union moves unilaterally both to reduce the weight of its tank-heavy threat and to redeploy most of its erstwhile front-line forces back to the U.S.S.R.; and would be very expensive—economically, socially, in domestic politics, and possibly in the diminution of regional security. Americans are not always as sensitive as they might be to the consequences of two protracted world wars for the cultural "debellicization" of Western Europe.[35] For prewar deterrence NATO-Europe favors provision of relatively large denial forces designed to function as not wholly incredible triggers for potentially catastrophic nuclear war. The overriding, indeed exclusive, NATO-European objective for military security is the deterrence of war. In this view, the NATO military requirement is to provide "a level of defense that it would require a major attack to breach."[36]

For geopolitical reasons the United States has a risk-interest calculus very different from that of its forward-located allies. Awesome near-term nuclear possibilities make some kind of sense as a feature of defense strategy desirable for countries which would stand to lose everything in a war. For the United States it might be the case that a functionally, if not purposefully, punitive nuclear strategy connected by a very short fuse to conflict in Europe would be a superior deterrent to war. But the uncertain benefit for deterrence easily would be overborne for policy by the extent of pain to be suffered in the event deterrence should fail. This discussion touches upon a complex subject of concern traceable through several decades. Specifically, there has long been debate over the priorities appropriate as between endeavors to deter war, efforts to limit the possible damage should war occur, and the logic which holds that nonapocalyptic threats are more credible, but perhaps critically less frightening, to the deterree. Should an East-West war occur, it would be very much in the U.S. (survival-level) interest for that war to be waged strictly abroad. Plainly, the idea of sanctuary homelands for the superpowers is potentially erosive of prewar deterrence. Indeed, superpower sanctuaries are fundamentally incompatible with the logic of NATO's concept of flexible response and—if believed in Europe to be the U.S. operational intention—would be fatal to NATO's political cohesion.

A good deal of the real and apparent incoherence in NATO strategy is the product of a number of coalition members who know quite clearly what they want to achieve, but whose interests are incompatible. In summary form: NATO-Europe does not want a strictly regional defense capability, while the United States would like NATO to be so strong in regional stopping power that a war just might be confined to the regional level. Inevitably, the outcome of this geopolitically rooted disagreement on strategy is a compromise and a good deal of incoherence. NATO has ready-deployed, and readily deployable, a lot more conventional strength than really would be needed simply to register the fact of a major attack and to guarantee a very large war. But to date NATO hasn't had conventional defenses, particularly in the realm of staying power, so competent as to render a nonnuclear invasion attempt a truly reckless gamble (though certainly it would be a gamble), let alone an utterly forlorn hope. Through Soviet unilateral reductions and withdrawals, as well as through the CFE process, the military balance in Europe may be transformed in favor of the defensively motivated coalition that is NATO. Even though CFE, in principle, should yield net benefit for NATO (indeed, perhaps because of such prospective benefits), Western democracies are entirely capable of failing to modernize their military ideas and their forces as an arms-control regime allows.

Flexible response can be defined and explained in ways compatible with both U.S. and European preferences. There are some grounds for asserting either that the concept and its expressive force levels is a happy compromise, or exactly the reverse. Frequent public reference is made to the "NATO triad" of conventional, tactical nuclear, and strategic nuclear forces. A balanced NATO triad means that undue prominence is not accorded the role in deterrence of strategic forces, which has been unacceptable to the United States since 1961; while undue burdens are not placed upon conventional forces, which is unacceptable to NATO-Europe. The concept of the NATO triad, like flexible response itself, is sufficiently slippery in its implications that the important goal of political cohesion in the Alliance is not embarrassed by its promotion. Just how slippery flexible response can be may be gauged from the words of an official report on strategy: "While emphasizing our resolve to respond, our policy is to avoid specifying exactly what our response will be. This is the essence of our strategic doctrine of 'flexible response,' which has been United States policy since 1961 and NATO strategy since 1967."[37]

The absence of genuinely strategic rationales for the INF treaty, for the pending START treaty, and in support of a transition from strategic offense-dominance to defense-dominance should suggest to the wary that the avoidance of specificity lauded in the quotation above is really a case of finding virtue in confusion. A mountain of collateral evidence presses the conclusion that a doctrine of war and a theory of war *recognizably strategic in character* may both be lacking, behind the doctrinal smoke screen of flexible response.

Major initiatives have been launched, NATO-wide and by the United States unilaterally, which could, paradoxically, both diminish the military utility of nuclear weapons and, if successful, increase (Soviet) incentives to use those weapons as their nonnuclear prowess diminishes. Specifically: in 1983 President Reagan announced what (in 1984) was to become the SDI; in 1984 NATO's Defense Planning Committee adopted the (SHAPE-developed) FOFA (Follow-on Forces Attack) concept as a basis for long-term planning for European defense; while, beginning in 1985, a Conventional Defense Improvements (CDI) initiative was launched by the Alliance. For the purposes of this discussion, the details of the CDI and of the nascent European offshoots—or parallel programs (antitactical ballistic missiles [ATBM] for "extended air defense," for example)—from the U.S. SDI are less important than are the several geopolitical contexts which have educated the approaches to NATO strategy described above. Amidst the shifting sands of fashionable ideas (the good, the bad, and the arguable), emerging technologies, and the like, an opposition persists. On the one hand the United States always is looking for ways in which NATO could provide a regional defense which really defends. On the other hand NATO-Europe wants a regional defense posture capable of imposing a major war upon an invader, but which—in effect—is all but programmed to fail after a matter of days or weeks. This preference is not the inadvertent consequence of undue funding for the welfare, as contrasted with the security, functions of NATO-European societies. Rather is the European preference the persisting exercise of choice in favor of a regional defense coupled with the U.S. strategic-nuclear arsenal by its very inability to sustain successful local protection, let alone throw an invader out.

There is no shortage of candidates for the short-list of factors responsible for conservatism in NATO strategy. One can nominate the sheer number of separate national security communities in the coalition (a large convoy to organize and herd for a change of course), the fact that existing arrangements appear to work well enough (particularly as the enemy's trenches are emptying), the plethora of options for military improvement and the uncertainty over which to pick and how best to exploit them, the perennial issue of "who pays what," and so on. However, the most formidable barrier to substantial change in the basic architecture of NATO's strategy for deterrence is more political than it is military. NATO-European interpretation of the terms of the transatlantic bargain requires a coalition strategy which appears to equalize the risks of resisting aggression as between the two sides of the Atlantic. Since, possibly unfortunately, there is no U.S. national territory in peninsular Europe, European governments favor a coalition military strategy design to couple the transoceanic home territory of the United States with continental Europe. Any defense initiative which increases the prospect of NATO being able to defend successfully in Europe will be resisted, no matter how attractive it is on narrow military grounds. NATO-Europe wants to deter war, not to be able to wage war successfully, *at home*. Europeans tend to believe that some reasonable prospect of the latter could damage the former. This enduring political consideration in strategy for the Alliance is being neglected as defense analysts seek to calculate how Gorbachev's unilateral force reductions and withdrawals should improve NATO's ability to defend the Central Front—if, that is, NATO continues to have a recognizable Central Front.

For the next several decades at least, the United States must continue to pursue a coalition strategy if there is to be a balance of power in Eurasia. The U.S.S.R. is a deeply troubled empire at present, but it is very far from being *hors de combat*. An important part of the price to be paid for the geostrategic benefits of coalition is the lack of untrammeled national control over the terms and conditions of deterrence and defense. The United States cannot intervene effectively on the continent except when operating in conjunction with continental allies.[38] If those continental allies fail in the field, or if their societies lack the will to fight, then the offshore power similarly cannot succeed—pending manifestation in continental overextension on the part of the enemy of the consequences of the familiar "victory disease."[39]

National security policy and its implementation in grand strategy are about more than the narrow generation of war-fighting capability. The determined U.S. quest after U.S.-defined excellence in NATO's regional defense prowess rapidly generates sharply diminishing—and even negative—returns to marginal effort. The analytical wing of the U.S. defense community persistently fails to recognize that its pursuit of the best NATO military posture can be the enemy of a posture which ought to be good enough. For reasons of geopolitics, culture, and history, the countries of NATO-Europe define the requirements of their security more broadly in political terms than is usual in the United States.

The differences in outlook on grand strategy as between the United

States and its European allies are attributable in good part to their respective placings in the power hierarchy of states, as well as to the location of their national territories. Europeans measure their security less with reference to their national or multilateral contributions to the variably common defense effort, and more with regard both to the reliability of the U.S. political commitment to security in Europe and to the dampening of possible political incentives to undertake military enterprises on the part of the U.S.S.R. The European allies frequently are less than enthusiastic for American-authored proposals for the reform of Alliance military practices. The allies are fearful of their exposure as campaigning ground; they recognize that the extent to which their own military efforts can generate more national security is distinctly limited; and they are anxious lest an absolute increase in NATO's regional fighting power should have the paradoxical consequence of producing less security for reason of its negative consequences for policy on the other side of the hill. Because the United States is *the* net security producer for NATO, able (and indeed obliged in the interests of its own national security) geostrategically to consider Western Europe as a theater of war, it is scarcely surprising that U.S. policymakers, uniquely among the allies, tend to be willing to treat military questions as military questions.

Sooner or later, and probably sooner, the view will prevail in American politics that the United States is attempting to produce too much security for too many prosperous countries who could afford to share the burdens of a common defense on a more equitable basis than is the case today. Moreover, more and more Americans will share the view that they are paying to provide a quality of security for their allies that those allies may well not need. U.S. allies in Eurasia are reluctant to pay what most Americans would judge to be their fair share toward Western defense not only because of the negative implications for local prosperity and welfare, but also because a disproportionately American military effort is believed healthily to maximize deterrence. This agreeable economical opinion travels none too well with popular resentment at the perceived arrogance of superpower. European politicians find it convenient to be able to blame Washington for being unimaginative as the Cold War rhetorically, and in some large degree practicably, is interred. A United States holding on to sustain security in Europe relieves European policymakers of some of the domestically unpopular need to do the same.

Because this book is about strategy and statecraft in general, rather than about the future (if any) of NATO strategy, this chapter has confined its analysis fairly rigorously to actual historical examples of coalition behavior, past and present. Nonetheless, it is appropriate to close this discussion with some reference to the possible, even pending, strategy challenges of the 1990s. Specifically, as Soviet forces withdraw from East-Central Europe, where—if anywhere—is NATO's "Central Front"? Furthermore, although flexible response remains all but holy writ to NATO as a whole, and certainly in Washington, D.C., German leaders are indicating that a nuclear-oriented flexible response is simply too menacing to the newly non-Communist societies that *were* the Soviet hegemonic empire. Just as NATO will have to redefine itself politically if it is to survive the 1990s, so also will it need to find a new military strategy.

CHAPTER 9

Nuclear Weapons and Strategy

The study of nuclear strategy is therefore the study of the nonuse of these weapons.

—LAWRENCE FREEDMAN[1]

As the tradition of nonuse grows stronger, the role of atomic diplomacy necessarily shrinks.

—MCGEORGE BUNDY[2]

AS EARLY as the fall of 1945, commentators of all shades of opinion and in many countries agreed that the atomic bomb was a weapon radically different from all other weapons. Description of the years from 1945 to the present as "the nuclear age," or era, is as noncontroversial as it has become a cliché through familiarity and unreflective repetition. The only plausible candidate-precedent in history for the introduction of nuclear weapons was the coming of gunpowder, and that came slowly through trial and refinement over the course of two hundred years from the early fourteenth to the early sixteenth centuries. For a weapons technology to be held to be politically and militarily the dominant characteristic of a period, as in "the nuclear age," one has to believe that that technology has had very important structural consequences for major institutions (e.g., war, diplomacy).

Virtually regardless of one's substantive preferences in policy and strategy, there is no substitute for identifying the right questions to ask. Legitimately enough, Lawrence Freedman finds little strategy in what passes for nuclear strategy. Indeed he concludes his *magnum opus* with the arguably pejorative claim that *"C'est magnifique* [the present state of nuclear plans and doctrine], *mais ce n'est pas la stratégie."* Whether or not one agrees with Freedman that what passes for nuclear strategy in the official designs of the Western Alliance is "more the antithesis of strategy than its apotheosis,"[3] his writings have the rare virtue of being founded upon an accurate appreciation of what strategy is and is not. He is exactly right when he argues: "The question of what happens if deterrence fails is vital for the intellectual cohesion and credibility of nuclear strategy. A proper answer requires more than the design of means to wage nuclear war in a wide variety of ways, *but something sufficiently plausible to appear as a tolerably rational course of action which has a realistic chance of leading to a satisfactory outcome."*[4]

Freedman deems it unlikely that such an answer can be found. He may be correct, which is why the proper subject for study should be war writ large, and not nuclear war. Furthermore, the still absent "tolerably rational course of action" to which he refers should be approached as being synonymous with the broad and inclusive concept of a theory of war, not with an exclusive theory of nuclear war.

On the admittedly negative evidence available to date, nuclear weapons have functioned very much as the friends of peace with security. Those weapons play in the total mosaic of strategy and should not be treated as though they stood apart from, and overshadowed, the broad themes which have been analyzed in this book thus far. References to nuclear strategy abound in public debate and in the literature on contemporary defense issues. Bowing to the convenience of adhering to common usage, this discussion also refers from time to time to nuclear strategy. Strictly speaking, however, there is no nuclear strategy; the concept of nuclear strategy asserts a false distinction. All kinds of forces, nuclear-armed or otherwise (or even dual-capable), have strategic effect as instruments of national or coalition military strategy and serve the objectives of grand strategy.

Uncertainty, fear, confusion and a sense of guilt all work to hinder honest and responsible discussion of the proper place of nuclear weapons in policy, strategy, and tactics. People are uncertain as to whether or not a nuclear weapon is a weapon in the traditional meaning of the word; they are fearful that errors in policy, strategy, or tactics might open the Gates of Hell for the human race;[5] they are confused about the political-military roles of nuclear weapons; and they feel guilty that their acquiescence in the nuclear dimension to national and coalition strategies may prove to be signature to a substantially voluntary Faustian pact. The final point requires some explanation. Some residual dependency upon nuclear threats—as a counterdeterrent to discourage first nuclear use by an enemy—is as necessary in a nuclear-armed world as it may be ethically unpalatable. But what is one to make of a Western Alliance which collectively chooses to remain conventionally underarmed for decade after decade, in part for reason of the high economic and social costs of nonnuclear forces?[6] Moreover, that Western Alliance which chooses to be nuclear-reliant resolutely declines to address the strategic implications of its practical pronuclear preference.

The moral questions which occasionally assail the laagered wagons of the theorists on nuclear deterrence and nuclear war have a way of touching raw nerves and uneasy, if not actually guilty, consciences. It is symptomatic both of the spirit of the age and of a desire to evade recognition of inconvenient realities that countries no longer have war departments; instead they have departments of defense. Of course, war has long been an affront to the liberal conscience. Moral philosophers and strategic thinkers generally inhabit very different intellectual universes. The former are concerned with decision rules for right conduct (though most of them acknowledge that those rules cannot responsibly be determined or applied in isolation from consideration of their consequences), while the latter are the servants of Leviathan and inhabit a world which they perceive to be bounded quite tightly by necessity.[7] For example, some very decent human beings, functioning as the servants of perceived necessity (a strategic imperative?), claim to find no discomfort in a system of mutual deterrence which, purposefully or incidentally, quite literally holds tens of millions of the innocent as hostages to the good judgment of governments. The threat of the Carthaginian Peace is justified morally with reference to its beneficial consequence—the preservation of peace (by what amounts to a punitive theory of deterrence).

Discussion of moral questions generally has been avoided in this book. The work has not been designed as an extended marketing brochure for a particular, allegedly better—let alone more just— strategy. However, a chapter which focuses upon nuclear issues must recognize the salience of ethical matters. Rather than replay familiar arguments on the subject of the morality or immorality of nuclear deterrence, or of particular strategic choices pertinent to the threat or use of nuclear weapons—subjects already treated competently in the public literature—a few observations on the broad topic of morality and strategy may be helpful to readers.

First, ideas on what constitutes right conduct in war certainly have changed over the centuries, but it is not self-evident that anything resembling a uniform progress has been achieved. For example, treaties are no longer secured by the formal exchange of hostages (e.g., the children or other relatives of political leaders), military leaders who fail are not crucified, and prisoners of war have important and widely recognized rights. But within living memory machine-age mass warfare has been conducted with a brutal, if arguably practical, indifference to nice distinctions between soldiers and civilians which even the unsentimental and distinctly inhumane Carthaginians, Romans, and Mongols likely would have found to err on the side of excessive zeal. The USAAF (upgraded from a corps in June 1941) entered World War II passionately devoted to the theory and practice of precision daylight bombardment of legitimate military targets. In the spring and summer of 1945, that same USAAF systematically and intentionally set about the wholesale burning of flimsily constructed Japanese cities.

Second, as noted already in this text, it is probably true that quantity has a quality all its own. It is a fact that nuclear weapons have come to be regarded with a unique moral distaste. The virtual taboo which surrounds these weapons, created in good part by a forty-five-year-long tradition, if one can call it that, of nuclear nonuse, has reinforced the belief that these devices are morally (or immorally) unique among the military instruments of potential inhumanity.

Military history tells us that casualties in war tend to be a function of time (i.e., duration of period of risk), the capacity of states for sustained collective action, and choice of operational methods and styles of combat (which are influenced by technology). Those variables produced total fatalities in World War II very imprecisely calculated to have been in the region of 41–55 million.[8] A war in which nuclear weapons are used could produce a level of fatalities, prompt and delayed, many times fifty or so million, but—scarcely less persuasively—it may have a casualty rate far below the level of 1939–45.[9] There is probably something to be said for the argument that a particular moral opprobrium should attach to weapons whose extensive use *could* result in casualties and damage unarguably both disproportionate to the political values at stake in the conflict and incompatible with any reasonable definition of success in war. However, essentially quantitative moral arguments are not really very satisfactory. Many people, including scholars of defense questions, seem to find some common-sense merit in distinguishing between more and less morally acceptable weapons, as they do between so-called offensive and defensive weapons. Nonetheless, it is the view of this author that both of these claimed distinctions generally reflect flabby thinking which confuses rather than clarifies. If there is an evil it is war, not particular weapons. Strategists occasionally stray into deontological box canyons, asserting that particular options are absolutely wrong (regardless of arguments of alleged necessity, let alone expediency). But, the general run of strategists' reasoning is consequentialist, or prudential, and is compatible with reasonable interpretation and application of the guidelines provided in the Christian just-war tradition.

Third, although defense professionals behave and talk among themselves as though consequentialist logic applied to nuclear, as to other, weapons, those "experts," and particularly their political masters, do not talk to the general public as if nuclear weapons were weapons. It is not suggested here that the general public is wrong to have an unrestrained fear of the damage that might be suffered in a nuclear war. There is no question that nuclear war could write *finis* to "civilization," if not actually to much of life on earth. The public is entirely right to be fearful. The consequentialist logic of strategy, which relates means to ends and requires that ends be selected for their attainability at bearable cost, suggests strongly that nuclear weapons would be used extremely carefully in a manner calculated to forward, not to negate, the achievement of war aims. But no one can guarantee that that would be the case or can provide assurance that the necessarily very uncertain costs of nuclear war would be judged by its survivors to have been worth the results obtained. Indeed, recorded history attests persuasively to the general inability of experts to predict the course and outcome of future war.

In the present relatively very benign strategic condition of the Western Alliance, there is a strange contrast of considerable policy importance between two rival theses bearing upon burden-of-proof arguments. On the one hand, prudential logic can be held to require that the burden of proof should fall upon those who assert or argue that a nuclear war could be controlled, limited in its scale and scope, and, if need be, prosecuted to a politically satisfactory termination. On the other hand, prudential logic can point to the absence of general war since 1945 and therefore to the inferable positive influence of nuclear deterrence for that absence of war. Hence one can reason that the burden of proof must rest upon those who point to the allegedly unacceptable dangers in the contemporary nuclear dependence of the West. After all, the system has worked, no matter what hypothetical risks may lurk within it. Indeed, the postwar security system may have worked as well as it has precisely because of the near-universal perceptions of those nuclear risks.

Moral qualms about nuclear deterrence, whether deontological (absolute) or consequentialist (instrumental) in nature, have not had any very noticeable impact upon the behavior of the practical people who understand that strategy is a pragmatic business. No strategy is sustainable for long in a democracy if it offends public standards of right conduct. Admittedly, those public standards are somewhat variable with circumstances, but they enjoy cultural significance and can play importantly in national strategic style. Nuclear dread is probably an absolute, and does not vary with reference to a modest scale of war-fighting nuclear options for direct military effect, as contrasted with the monumentally punitive horrors of assured societal destruction (presumably because the former could escalate to the latter).

Politicians and defense professionals endeavor to finesse the culturally unacceptable face of nuclear threats by a strategy of denial, evasion, and appeasement via a visible arms-control process. The habits of denial and evasion have become so deep-rooted, even instinctive, that the practitioners in question may not even be aware when they are obfuscating. Consequently, writings on the nuclear thread in strategy tend to be heavily front-end loaded: that is to say they focus upon the prevention of war by nuclear threats intended to deter, at the expense of careful treatment of the possible course of actual war.

As a security community, the United States and the coalition on whose behalf it may act do not really discuss what is known as nuclear strategy. Beyond the threats which should deter there is a politically and morally expedient blur. Moreover, although that blur can be justified with reference to the fog of war as well as to political expediency, in addition it is attributable both to a lack of moral courage and to a deficient understanding of the requirements of strategy. Readers will look in vain in the pages of President Reagan's report *National Security Strategy of the United States,* or in the text of the report *Discriminate Deterrence* produced by the Commission on Integrated Long-Term Strategy, for an explicit system or theory of war from which grand or national military strategy could be deduced. How does the United States succeed in deterring or actually defending? Those reports advertised the merits of flexibility, of threatening what the enemy is believed to value most, and overall in having "the Soviets understand that they cannot gain their objectives through nuclear warfare, or nuclear coercion, under any conceivable circumstances."[10] What has occurred is that strategy worthy of the name has escaped attention for reason of an unfortunate synergism. On the one hand there is moral cowardice (prudence?) on the part of political leaders, who know that the electorate's political tolerance for contemplation of what lies beyond the veil of nuclear use is practically nil. On the other hand there is incompetence on the part of many defense professionals who confuse the tactical application of force with strategy. Public discussion of what passes for nuclear strategy thus has a way of being about virtually everything except strategy. Strategy indicates how particular means are to be applied for the achievement of particular objectives: the set of problems for which only a theory of war can provide suitable guidance.

The discussion of strategy in the United States all too easily degenerates into a flight into technicism (an undue focus upon weapons), into the seemingly pragmatic realm of tactical style in operations (the extolling of the virtues of being flexible and discriminate), and into political or even technical surrogates (the elevation of the arms-control process as a vehicle which can seem to remove the need for strategy). The problem is neither that people seek military advantage through the threat or discriminate application of new weapons nor that they look to alleviate some military (and political) difficulties through arms control—both of which are reasonable ambitions. Rather, the problem is that people, perhaps unknowingly, evade contemplation of the strategic questions which should give meaning to their technological and tactical concerns and preferred solutions. The relative paucity of genuinely strategic debate ensures a lack of strategic discipline in the controversies over particular weapon systems, force deployments, and arms-control proposals. Debate over contentious items in the ICBM modernization program, for example, proceeds with scant reference to what it is the United States requires its ICBM force to accomplish, why, and in what circumstances. Moreover, if that issue is addressed it is likely to be handled with reference to desired target coverage and not to how such target coverage should promote the prospects for success in war as a whole (and hence how it should strengthen pre- or intrawar deterrence).

THE NUCLEAR AGE

Today, in the fifth decade of the nuclear period, important disagreements among would-be opinion leaders in the West over the meaning of nuclear weapon (and delivery system) technologies continue to hinder rational debate on national security policy. In one form or another, the running debate over basic assumptions figures in every important controversy over strategy, weapon research and development, weapon procurement, and arms control. For the sake of clarity, it is useful to identify the two contrasting, extreme poles of the debate. On the one hand, as discussed, there is the view that nuclear weapons are not weapons in any traditionally meaningful sense; instead they are instruments of mass destruction whose actual employment must transcend in their awful results the importance and relevance of any strategic goals or policy objectives. On the other hand there is the view that nuclear weapons are weapons like other weapons in most important senses. The first view holds that there can be no nuclear strategy and that nuclear war would not be war as war has been understood historically. The second view recognizes the possibility that nuclear war could become a holocaust beyond analysis in Clausewitzian terms. But that second view also asserts and argues that nuclear weapons could, and almost certainly would, be used with discrimination according to the calculations of a self-regarding prudence for the achievement of particular military objectives. In the total absence of historical experience, one must record that the jury is still out on whether or not nuclear weapons, nuclear strategy, and nuclear war are or are not, operationally, contradictions in terms— or, if one prefers, whether a "Scotch verdict" of "not proven" obtains. However, the case for the utility of nuclear weapons as power, or latent force, and indeed for the value of nuclear strategy in time of peace, is a persuasive one.

Philosophical discussion of nuclear weapons helps formulate the attitudes and opinions which find concrete discrete expression over the particular issues of the day. But it is as plain as anything can be that the constant of human nature and the enduring logic of geopolitically grounded interstate politics vastly constrain the bounds of responsible policy choice on the part of the U.S. government. The past is not in detail a reliable guide to the future, but the sum total of the human experience with organized conflict cannot summarily be dismissed as having been cast into irrelevance by a step-level jump in the destructiveness of weaponry. What humankind ought to do is a fit topic for prescriptive *Moralpolitik* on the grand scale, but strategy is a practical business. Within the confines of an unchanging human nature, albeit with variable standards of right conduct ("situational ethics") and an organization of global politics which has evolved recently with scant regard to the possibility of nuclear holocaust, there is no obvious way for a U.S. government to proceed from the "here" of mixed international conflict and cooperation as usual, to some radically different "there" wherein nuclear war would be impossible. There is an extrarational element in the public policy debate which confuses the strongly desirable with the safely attainable. Beyond doubt, nuclear conflict could be so horrible that it is not difficult to comprehend why all obstacles to the root-and-branch reformation of human political organization tend to be dismissed by some people as inconsiderable trivia.

While recognizing our true ignorance of the probable course and outcome of a nuclear conflict, nonetheless it is sensible to remember that it is contrary to the logic and dynamics of applied scientific inquiry for particular weapons, no matter how potent, permanently to assume a plausibly dominant position. Indeed, the very measure of their real or apparent dominance motivates the search for counterweapons and tactics, or as Luttwak argues forcibly in the case of nuclear weapons, for an operational style which simply circumvents the problems of aggrandizement which could be posed by the new technology.[11] Furthermore, there is nothing inherently uncontrollable about the use of nuclear weapons in war.

The ongoing debate over nuclear weapons and strategy is heavily populated by commentators who would seem to have misread their Clausewitz. A very selective reading of *On War* might lead one to the reductionist conclusion that the (Kantian) ideal type of an absolute war of absolute violence is in the very nature of war. The philosophical method of the dialectic lends itself to severe abuse. At some risk of being unduly optimistic, there is a great deal, even an overwhelming amount, to be said for the position that humankind will do—and indeed has been doing—what it has to do in order to tame for strategy and policy a stream of weapons technologies which cannot be abolished. The possible horrors of nuclear war should not diminish appreciation of the arguable salience of the following judgment by Robert Gilpin: "We are but a few decades into the nuclear age, and it is far too early to conclude that there will not be a Gaius Marius, Alexander, or Napoleon who will develop tactics and strategy to make nuclear weapons and the nuclear threat effective instruments of national policy."[12]

Gilpin's point is well taken, in that the nuclear age indeed is still young, but the problems which nuclear weapons pose for national policy can no more be reduced to a need for innovative strategy and tactics than they can to a need for militarily more effective technologies. Gilpin's role models certainly were skilled in strategy and tactics, but the *sine qua non* of their success was their ability to mobilize their polities for the sustained collective action which they (generally) competently directed. If strategy does not work well in its domestic social dimension, it cannot work well for external security. Having said that, it is important to recognize also that, in somewhat Leninist fashion, by success in action policy and strategy can create the objective domestic conditions which forward further success. However, as President Johnson demonstrated in Vietnam, if a theory of war and doctrine of war are selected with regard to their likely domestic acceptability, but in substantial disregard of their fit with the objective needs of the conflict in question, then the result is going to be a military failure in the field which must erode, and eventually destroy, the willingness of society to stay the unsuccessful course.

In terms of the genealogy of doctrine, Anglo-American professional military thought and plans on nuclear strategy were the obvious descendants of the Combined Bomber Offensive of 1943–45. The atomic bomb was the fulfillment of the long-heralded promise, and incomplete application in World War II, of independent strategic air operations. The SIOP, created in part for the subordination of the U.S. Navy's *Polaris* force to the SAC worldview, as an idea for the centralized, coordinated, and single-pulsed application of force, embodies the heart of air-power doctrine. Civilian theorizing about nuclear strategy in the United States has manifested the symptoms of belief in limited liability which are endemic to insular polities. This is not to confuse American with British strategic culture. Save briefly, of necessity, in 1916–18, official British strategic thought has never made a virtue of hard fighting (by *British* soldiers) on land for the purpose of defeating the principal military strength of a continental enemy. Following their misreading of Ulysses S. Grant's ideas, but their correct reading of his practice in Virginia in 1864–65, leading American soldiers—certainly through 1945—believed that clever strategy could never substitute for hard fighting (an emphasis on an attritional style in the conduct of war).[13]

However, the United States is heir to a mixed insular-continental tradition. The insular thread in U.S. statecraft and strategy tempts Americans to believe that they can retire at will from a contest whose rules or course they do not like. Readers should recall the serious anxieties of Churchill and Roosevelt lest undue frustration of popular American wishes for the conduct of the war in Europe in 1942 and 1943 might oblige the U.S. government to shift its fundamental policy from "Germany First" to "Japan First." Similarly, the first rumblings of contemporary U.S. debate over the fundamentals of its national security policy are imbued strongly with the voluntaristic spirit of limited liability. Because of its transoceanic geography, and always provided it can avoid being held massively to nuclear account at home for its Eurasian security commitments, very many Americans believe that their country can choose how much, or how little, it will risk in foreign fields. This attitude finds expression in U.S. strategic theory, as it does also in the murmurings of isolationist and unilateralist sentiment over foreign policy.

In the Soviet Union, unsurprisingly, in light of its strategic geography, historical experience, and culture, thought on nuclear operations has been influenced most heavily by artillery thinking in the framework of a land-oriented, combined-arms theory of conflict. Realistically or otherwise, the Soviet Union has not viewed nuclear weapons as though they comprised a *deus ex machina* which transcends military calculation for strategic effect. Of recent years Moscow has evinced a clear preference for the waging of nonnuclear, theater-level warfare. However, this apparent trend does not mean that the Soviet Union is convinced that a nuclear war could not be won, nor should one assume that the tilt toward a nonnuclear preference must be permanent. It is the very essence of strategy that military preferences will alter as the putative enemy finds plausible-looking solutions to the intensity and character of threat perceived in yesterday's posture and doctrine. The prospect of NATO succeeding in fielding a nonnuclear, high-technology, 1990s version of the system of defensive war which denied operational mobility for most of the First World War on the Western Front, has prompted Soviet defense planners to search earnestly for new, or refurbished old, operational designs for theater victory. In due course that search may come to identify a prominent role for nuclear weapons as a possible solution to the predictable defeat or stalemate of a conventional offensive or counteroffensive. Indeed, as noted already, it may be the case that the current restructuring of Soviet divisions away from armor dominance that Gorbachev is advertising as proof positive of a truly defensive posture (and intent), in fact expresses a good part of the findings of the Soviet military in their search for answers to the threat posed by NATO's advanced conventional munitions (actual, imminent, but largely only possible).

In its defense policy the Soviet Union has acted on the premise that it is the duty of the state to make such preparations as it is able for survival and recovery. A punitive character to the threats for nuclear deterrence was accepted by the U.S.S.R. in the 1950s as the best that could be achieved *pro tem*. But, since the later 1960s the Soviet Union has provided thoroughly convincing evidence of an unswerving commitment to secure such military utility from its evolving nuclear arsenal as competitive prudence, technology, and available economic resources would allow. The Soviet approach to nuclear strategy was explained by General Mikhail Milshtein when he posed the rhetorical question "Without war-fighting [capabilities], what is deterrence?"[14] Milshtein's question might be refined by Herman Kahn's conceptual scheme so as to ask, "Without war-fighting, what is Type II deterrence (the deterrence of provocative acts other than direct attacks upon the United States)?"[15] Everyone who finds utility in nuclear deterrence adheres to some war-fighting notions. In its restricted meaning of countermilitary targeting preferences, a so-called war-fighting orientation is the only practicable choice for a country which aspires to be in the protection business with extended nuclear deterrence. But relatively little even of the literature on U.S. nuclear strategy which recognizes the folly of society-wide threats attempts to make the transition from issues of nuclear targeting to the subject of strategy. In the context of this discussion nuclear targeting policy is operational art. Targeting should express a theory of war and a strategy, but it cannot itself be such a theory or strategy.

Edward Luttwak, with some reason, assigns targeting to the level of grand strategy and he notes that choices in targeting are a "fit subject for *national policy*."[16] Given the independently decisive potential of air and missile bombardment, Luttwak's argument is not implausible at first glance. Nonetheless, he is wrong. More to the point, one would be well advised to behave as if he were wrong. The issue is not what in some philosophical sense is true; rather it is to find that which works well enough. The proposition that targeting guidance is really high policy or grand strategy positively encourages the confusion of means with ends, of technology and of style in tactics and operational art with strategy. Luttwak would not commit these errors, but some of his readers might. Those few members of the strategic studies community who have endeavored to grapple constructively with the much underexamined subject of war termination in the nuclear age should be particularly well qualified to appreciate the fallacy in the reductionism which effectively and conveniently— but erroneously—equates targeting with strategy. However, there is some small danger that the same cultural urge to flee from politics and strategy into administrative technique which produced theories of "crisis management" may be at work encouraging Americans to believe that they can learn how to terminate wars. Those prenuclear theorists and official executors of "strategic" air bombardment who (for example) saw civilian morale as the primary target committed the same error which is under discussion here in a nuclear context. They failed to explain the causal connection between a fearful and presumably demoralized populace and victory in war. Advocates of this or that scheme for nuclear targeting have to explain how the posing of technically credible threats to particular targets—or the actual destruction or disabling of those targets—would help produce success in the war as a whole. Vague expostulations with the character of "it stands to reason . . ." will not suffice, at least not if one is determined to treat strategic questions seriously.

Classical or traditional strategy pertains to a context wherein a state defends itself actively in the process, and as a consequence, of fighting and beating an enemy's armed forces. By way of contrast, the new wisdom that is dogma in the liberal theory of arms control holds that strategic stability reposes in the standoff between two punitive deterrents. In a curious reversal from prenuclear times, the leading Western school of arms-control wisdom holds that offense has become defense and defense has become offense (conveniently ignoring the situational qualities of particular weapons which render them more or less "offensive" or "defensive").

Defensive weaponry or other related programs are judged to be destabilizing because they may deny the rival power confidence in his power to deter via credible threats to destroy his adversary's society. Offensive weaponry, by way of sharp contrast, and provided it is not potent in the counterforce role against an enemy's offensive weapons, is held to be stabilizing because it holds society hostage to the prudent behavior of its leaders. On this expert, though scarcely popular, logic, states in quest of stability in their "strategic" relationship should strive to develop only offensive weapons incapable of delivering military victory. Furthermore, those states should eschew defensive weapons which might hold damage anticipated to be suffered in retaliation down to a very modest level. These may appear to be burdensome restrictions upon defense planning, but it has long been believed—not without some good reason—that modern weapons technology, married to elementary prudence on the part of policymakers, really permits of no technical strategic condition other than the deadlock just described.

However, notwithstanding the overall grand- and military-strategic value of such a deadlock for Soviet policy, Moscow has never been reconciled to the proposition that the only military victory available via nuclear war would not be worth the winning. If a classical approach to strategy is not adopted (whether or not its goals can be realized in action is another matter), a state is tying its hands against taking the nuclear initiative because it would lack the means to limit the damage which could be suffered by the enemy's retaliation. If some freedom of nuclear action is strongly desirable, as it must be for a NATO still dependent upon extended nuclear deterrence, then the merit in a classical approach to strategy is not easily denied. Combined arms would be of no relevance to a war that was a holocaust. If one or both superpowers were to suffer what would amount to a history-stopping, indeed erasing, level of damage, then questions pertaining to the tactical and operational handling of complementary military instruments for land, sea, air, and space warfare would be of no interest. However, if nuclear weapons either are withheld or are used carefully only for precise military purposes and on a modest scale, then combined arms would retain most of its traditional value as the superior approach to the employment of individual elements of force.

It was a historical coincidence, no more, that atomic weapons appeared at the very moment in the mid-to-late 1940s when the international system was transformed from the oligarchic character of the previous half millennium to a bilateral condition. The coincidence of the nuclear era and the appearance of two superstates has promoted confusion in the minds of people who have succumbed to the temptation of overemphasizing the significance of weapons technology and undervaluing the importance of new rigidities in world politics. The phenomena both of superpower and of (superpower dominance in ownership of) nuclear weapons have diminished, but certainly not ended, the strategic importance of allies. Indeed, the relative decline of the superpowers will continue to loosen alliance ties, really ties of dependence (as the relatively less super superpowers are deemed to be less dependable, as well as perhaps less necessary as guardians), while—paradoxically—making allies more important as power is concentrated less heavily upon two principals. In one of their more inspired passages, the authors of *Discriminate Deterrence* argue:

A world with three or four major, global military powers would confront American strategic planners with a far more complicated environment than does the familiar bipolar competition with the Soviet Union. In any such multipolar world, the United States would have to manage relations with several different global powers and form appropriate coalitions with them. Wars might break out between powerful nations not aligned with the United States. *Alliances might shift.* The next twenty years will be a period of transition to this new world of several major powers.[17]

One cannot be certain that nuclear weapons are capable of being employed in action for strategic effect. While acknowledging the possibility that there may be a "grammar" of nuclear war which is not amenable to discipline by the logic of policy or the objectives of strategy, still there is good reason to suspect that dangers and opportunities of self-fulfilling beliefs and preparations lurk about this question. So wide is the technical range of military capabilities for flexible nuclear employment for carefully circumscribed operational and strategic goals, and so strong should be the incentives to exercise restraint in weight and choice of targeting, that popular fears of nuclear-war-as-holocaust probably—though only probably—have been much exaggerated.

The idea remains widespread that the very fact of nuclear armament has provided what may be called metastability. Allegedly, such superstability is based upon an existential deterrence which pertains not only to initiatives with nuclear weapons, but also to all diplomatic or military activity which plausibly might escalate to the realm of nuclear conflict. This view is indifferent to arguments about the balance, or lack of balance, between rival strategic nuclear armaments. The point is made that in prenuclear days a lead in battleships or in trained and rapidly mobilizable soldiers had implications for likely victory or defeat; but to be behind or ahead in the nuclear arms competition is an arguable fact beyond exploitation by statesmen or generals. If whole societies would be destroyed in nuclear "war," can it matter whether or not some figures of relative military merit favor one side or the other?

Variations upon this theme pervade the public debate over the modernization of strategic nuclear arms and over arms-control policies. If an official goes halfway to appease the idea of an existential deterrent, acknowledging that nuclear war *could* mean mutual holocaust, it can be difficult to argue, for example, that the difference between fifty MX ICBMs and one hundred is important. The official is in some danger of appearing to conventionalize nuclear arms if he argues for the military, and hence political, merit in particular weapons. What is the wider context? Is he claiming that a general nuclear war, as with other kinds of war, actually might be won—that the United States could prevail? To reject forthrightly for policy the idea of an existential deterrent which would render all-but-irrelevant the weighing of the strategic balance for advantage is not to claim as a fact that such net assessment assuredly has important implications for policy choices. Instead, the argument is that one cannot be sure that Soviet perception and calculation of some strategic nuclear advantage could not have a malign effect over policy choices. President Reagan's 1988 report on *National Security Strategy* explained, albeit somewhat disingenuously, that "we must deter an adversary who has a very different strategic outlook from our own—an outlook which continues to place great stress on nuclear war-fighting capability."[18] One must say somewhat disingenuously, because the logic of nuclear war-fighting prowess *for deterrence* has been ever more dominant in official U.S. thinking over the past decade and a half. Moreover, in its January 1988 report, the semi-official Commission on Integrated Long-Term Strategy recommended a doctrine for nuclear use *in Europe*—though, by logical extension, also elsewhere—which is really a celebration of the war-fighter's (or Soviet) thesis. The commissioners advised that "The Alliance should threaten to use nuclear weapons not as a link to a wider and more devastating war [*sic transit gloria* of flexible response]—although the risk of further escalation would still be there—but mainly as an instrument for denying success to the invading Soviet forces."[19]

The problems which this attempt to rewrite the military terms of U.S. extended deterrence must pose for the political cohesion of NATO were apparent immediately. In a prompt trinational reply, three distinctly Atlanticist opinion leaders from Britain, West Germany, and France warned that "it [the war-fighting recommendation for NATO's use of nuclear weapons in Europe] could be misunderstood to undermine the most important basis of alliance: the community of risk."[20]

The case for approaching nuclear arsenals in a manner which rejects in practice, though recognizes in principle the significance of, the existential deterrence hypothesis may be summarized by the presentation of eight interconnected points. First, holocaust, while possible, lies only at one end of the spectrum of potential horror of nuclear war. Second, the threat to unleash nuclear action is, and prospectively long will remain, an essential element in the structure of threats which deters, or may restore deterrence. Third, decisions concerning nuclear conflict are not totally in Western, let alone strictly U.S., hands. Even if NATO could remove much of its current dependency upon nuclear threats, nuclear initiatives by the Soviet Union still would need to be deterred.

Fourth, nuclear weapons are now a permanent fact in international politics. Consciously to tailor a nuclear force in size and quality so that it could only strike plausibly at large urban areas, quite apart from the likely adverse consequences of such a policy for deterrence, would be to ensure that should nuclear war occur the possibility of holocaust would become a certainty. Fifth, without denying that nuclear weapons are not as other weapons, still it is a fact that they could be used on a scale and against targets such that holocaust would not result (at least, not by comparison with the measure of destruction which could be inflicted). Sixth, although Soviet political leaders probably harbor most of the same fears of nuclear war as do U.S. leaders, Soviet strategic culture is not inclined to be passive in the face of technological change. Still less is Moscow inclined to be passive when it must cope with changes which could be argued to have adverse implications for the art of war, the power of war to achieve political decision, and the prospects for success of the Soviet Union or Russia as a competitive superpower in the game of nations. The extraordinary political risks that Gorbachev is taking with *glasnost* and *perestroika,* and his willingness to accept what may be more than just a temporary cancellation of imperial writ over East-Central Europe, provide eloquent testimony to the length to which the U.S.S.R. will go in order to avoid falling too far behind as a modern technology-dependent society.

Seventh, even if it is impolitic to recognize this publicly, both Moscow and Washington know that nuclear war could be waged against the rival war machine in such a controlled way that holocaust would be an unlikely result. Finally, given the admitted possibility of a general catastrophe which would transcend the traditional meaning of war, still there may be leverage for deterrence securable through holding at risk, fairly discretely, those elements of state power known to be judged most important by the adversary's political leaders. If the Western powers were to subscribe to the theory that the quest for military utility in nuclear forces was merely an atavistic conventionalization in thinking about a threat that is by its nature apocalyptic, then they might find themselves critically self-deterred in face of an enemy who, wisely or not, regarded nuclear weapons as weapons. In addition, since the geography and political cultures of the West disincline it to prepare for conventional war *à l'outrance,* the shortfall in deterrence which a truly apocalyptic frame of nuclear reference could produce would be much more likely to weigh in the Soviet than in NATO's favor.

The power to be balanced through nuclear arms competition is both the calculated military efficacy of Soviet strategic forces as a potential instrument of decision in war and the power of those Soviet forces over the minds of people in the West in time of peace (or acutely troubled peace—i.e., crisis). No matter how disastrously one may believe a bilateral nuclear war would proceed, it is essential that people believe that Soviet nuclear (and conventional) threats can be neutralized if they are to have the political confidence necessary to resist accommodation to Soviet pressure. Since arms competition functions generally as a substitute for war, what the United States is balancing with its military forces is the influence of Soviet arms over political decisions in the West.

The United States is obliged to pose nuclear threats on behalf of an overall defensive policy because of the geography of the Western Alliance, as a legacy of the past history of NATO strategy, as a reflection of the contemporary—though admittedly shifting—balance of advantage as between NATO and Soviet conventional forces, and for the purposes of maintaining allied perceptions of there being a true community of risk. U.S. strategic nuclear forces cannot readily defend West German territory directly, though they could impose such damage upon logistical and other military targets in Eastern Europe and the Western U.S.S.R. that the tip of the Soviet spear in Germany would lack combat endurance. But the very existence of those strategic forces, connected to West Germany by local U.S. military deployments still on a large scale, carries the message that the United States might well choose not to acquiesce in an unfolding military defeat in Europe. Security guarantors throughout history have been in need of the ability to project military power abroad in order to protect their clients, a need which implies the requirement for an offensive strategy.

NUCLEAR STRATEGY: CONTRADICTION IN TERMS?

Is nuclear strategy a contradiction in terms? Of more practical significance, is it prudent for responsible officials to assume that nuclear strategy is a contradiction in terms? In the minds of many generic critics of nuclear weapons and nuclear strategy it is an open question at best whether there can be competent, as contrasted with incompetent, nuclear war plans. If the U.S. body politic is not thoroughly convinced that nuclear weapons are *weapons* for military application, then the relevance of military expertise to planning for their use may be questioned. Furthermore, whether or not there are militarily correct ways of waging nuclear wars of different kinds, would the political leaders of both sides permit nuclear employment according to "staff solutions" to problems in the grammar of war? A well-regarded British theorist, Lawrence Freedman, is less than impressed with the intellectual accomplishments of those who have sought to render nuclear strategy true to the meaning of strategy: "By the mid-1980s, therefore, four decades after the destruction of Hiroshima and Nagasaki, the nuclear strategists had still failed to come up with any convincing methods of employing nuclear weapons should deterrence fail that did not wholly offend common sense, nor had they even reached a consensus on whether or not the discovery of such methods was essential if deterrence was to endure."[21]

Freedman could be guilty of misrepresenting personal judgment as fact. Furthermore, he is writing about nuclear strategy from the perspective of a citizen of a small island. These points do not mean that Freedman is in any absolute sense incorrect, but they should alert one to the possible influence upon opinion of the geostrategic context from which opinions flow. One should expect perspectives on nuclear weapon employment policy to differ somewhat as between a continental-size superstate which is in the overseas "protection business" and small countries with only a modest ability to influence by their own efforts the quality of their national security.[22]

The question which heads this section—is nuclear strategy a contradiction in terms?—does not admit of a simple, let alone a conclusive, answer. However, it is possible to provide definite answers to variants of the question rephrased for greater specificity. First, can nuclear-armed forces make positive contributions to the securing of political goals in times of peacetime normalcy or crisis? The answer cannot be quantified or documented beyond scope for argument, but it has to be in the affirmative. After all, strategy—grand, national military, or coalition military in kind—works as much, if not more importantly, in conditions other than those of active hostilities as it does in time of war. Deterrence is about nothing if not the influencing of minds in time of peace, or at least in the absence of war. Those ideas for the contingent use of nuclear-armed forces which are more or less accurately expressed in actual plans and military capabilities comprise strategy in (latent) action for deterrence or compellence.

If the concept of nuclear strategy truly was an oxymoron the political objectives of states could not be served by nuclear threats. Such a position would be logically implausible, as well as contrary to reasonable interpretation of the historical record.

Second, is it the case that nuclear strategy must be a contradiction in terms with reference to the actual use of nuclear-armed forces in time of war? The common-sense hypothesis behind this question is the argument that nuclear war—a shorthand term which requires some careful interrogation—must be so destructive that the nuclear grammar of war would overwhelm in gross disproportion to damage suffered and inflicted the political integrity of any and every war aim. Since there have been no bilateral nuclear wars, one is confined agreeably to the realm of speculation. In the unsatisfactory region of what is conceivable and what is logical, there is no very convincing reason to deny the compatibility of nuclear weapons with strategy. As a defensive alliance, NATO's overriding and minimum essential war aim undoubtedly should be the negative one of repelling an invasion. This aim does not mandate a defensive mode in the conduct of war, nor need it preclude the sensible ambitions both to punish the aggressor for his aggression and so to weaken him that at least any near-term recurrence of his aggression should be militarily impracticable. However, purposeful pursuit of the "best" war aim of bringing down the Soviet Union may well be to compromise the prospects of achieving the "good enough" aim of defeating a Soviet invasion at a cost tolerable to the Western Alliance. Also, the breakup of the Soviet Union might have the unwelcome consequence of leaving the power of Chinese and Japanese superstates unduly unbalanced in Asia (not to mention German power in Europe). The carefully controlled use of nuclear weapons against Soviet military forces relatively early in a war might—but only might—have the *strategic* effect of denying Soviet leaders the military capability to conquer Western Europe (or the Persian Gulf); the threat of much more to come might have the effect of persuading those leaders that their gamble had failed and that an escalation of the violence would prove self-defeating.

At the level of homeland-to-homeland conflict between the superpowers, it is possible that constrained countermilitary strikes by nuclear-armed forces would have the effect of restoring deterrence and securing the political objectives for which one or other of the superpowers were contending. Deterministic theories of nuclear-war-as-Apocalypse may be sensible. Perhaps it is strongly desirable that political leaders should not be optimistic over the strategic utility of nuclear operations. But honest analysis, and particularly honest analysis empathetic to the geopolitical and political-cultural constraints upon Western policy and strategy, cannot be satisfied with arguments which are simplistic, logically and technically unsound, and effectively indifferent to the distinctive burdens which Western policymakers place upon their military establishments. The problem is that even if one chooses to pretend to believe, contrary to logic and at least to a major thread of common sense, that nuclear war *must* mean a general holocaust, enemies could reason differently. Those enemies are likely to perceive that Americans do not believe what they claim to believe, and—in the dread event of a breakdown in deterrence—the West could come face-to-face with the fact that its overarching nuclear canopy to defense preparations had no operational integrity. U.S. and NATO strategy could be exposed as a bluff born of peacetime expediency and the optimism generated by more than forty years of apparent success with nuclear deterrence.

The problem of how best to think about nuclear weapons as a factor in tactics, military strategy, grand strategy, and high policy highlights the interrelatedness of the elements which have occupied the attention of this book. The Western coalition led by the United States is obliged to consider nuclear weapons as an instrument of its strategy, not as a substitute for strategy. Moreover, although they are a military instrument, nuclear weapons have symbolic political functions critical to the peacetime cohesion of NATO. The stream of technological innovations which produced the multifaceted nuclear problem in statecraft and strategy has also produced other weapons which could, in the right circumstances, both tame the tactical application of nuclear weapons and provide efficient nonnuclear substitutes for them.

The engineering mentality which has found a congenial calculability in the bloodless studies of very large scale nuclear "exchanges"—as it did in the plans for strategic air bombardment in the interwar years—is very much alive and well and has resurfaced in the attractive promises of emerging smart technologies as *the* answer to masses of Soviet armored fighting vehicles. In the latest variant of the "Kentucky rifle syndrome," NATO's high-technology marksmen would pick off enemy targets at long range, in all weathers, amidst the confusion of battle, and in the face of a wide range of countermeasures (including direct assault upon NATO's real-time intelligence gathering assets, weapon delivery platforms, and command and control apparatus). The point of these skeptical observations is not generically to denigrate technology, but to claim that marginally superior or inferior technology—which is to say *vis-à-vis* an enemy who is technologically at least a worthy foe—does not win or lose wars as a quasiindependent factor. It is no advance for the quality of Western policy and strategy if imprudent reliance upon an ultimately apocalyptic nuclear threat is replaced by another overly technological vision of the dynamics of deterrence and war. The emerging (smart) technology school of thought on NATO's defense in Central Europe seems to have as its aspiration the idea of rendering much of the territory of Germany the equivalent of the no-man's-land which was operationally, though not tactically, impassable for much of 1914–18. Standoff smart weapons would function as the latter-day machine guns and artillery which would deny operational-level success to invading armies. What is required is an inclusive theory of deterrence and war which asks of high technology that which high technology is likely to be able to deliver, that which NATO countries are likely to choose to afford, and that which in action should not contradict the objectives of strategy or the purposes of coalition policy. Whether or not Europe will need defending is, of course, another question.

The domestic and interallied politics of NATO countries, including what Michael Howard has termed the neglected social dimension of strategy;[23] the limitations of technology; rival strategic theories; and fears of the consequences of friction in crisis and war all combine to deny Western defense establishments the possibility of finding correct, let alone scientific, general staff solutions to the problems posed by nuclear weapons. In order to identify what is worth debating on the subject of the role of nuclear weapons in strategy, it is important to specify the broadly agreed assumptions from which productive exploration can flow. Amidst all of the sound and fury of public controversy over nuclear questions, four assumptions make up the bedrock of what must pass for a body of knowledge.

First, the prenuclear world is lost beyond retrieval. Preferences in military strategy may reject or embrace the prospective employment of nuclear weapons, but any and every preference must accommodate a role for those weapons, negative or positive or both. Arguments for and against the abolition of nuclear armaments are neither right nor wrong; they are simply irrelevant and hence foolish. Whether nuclear arsenals be large, small, or supposedly prohibited (but capable of reconstitution), they are of permanent concern for policymakers and strategists.

Second, since nuclear weapons exist or could be built again if once dismantled under the terms of some inconceivably effective compliance regime for disarmament, they have to be fitted into national or coalition military strategy. Even if Western national security communities comprehensively and genuinely were to reject first use of nuclear weapons as a matter of policy, their nuclear-armed forces would require strategic, operational, and tactical direction for second-use duties. The very fact of nuclear armament demands thought, plans, and technical preparation for contingent employment. Everybody who accepts the necessity for national or Western-coalition nuclear armament for the sundry purposes of deterrence, *ipso facto* sanctions contingent nuclear use. Furthermore, everyone, from Catholic bishop to SAC colonel, who recognizes nuclear weapons as a more or less regrettable necessity endorses some notion of "war fighting" for those weapons, which is to say, some idea of how those weapons would be used in war. The ends cannot be endorsed honestly if the means are not also accepted. If a nuclear element in deterrence is essential, as it is today beyond argument, because only nuclear weapons can deter nuclear use (to ignore CBW), then there is no evading the admittedly complex issues of how the use of those weapons should be threatened, over which issues, and how they should be used. Since everybody readily can agree that it would be far better to deter than to wage war, there should be no dispute over allegedly war-fighting versus deterrence theories (a case of a false contrast).

Third, there are no disagreements over the wisdom in the prevailing superpower practice of investing heavily in the technologies for the reliable command and control of nuclear-armed forces. Furthermore, it is not controversial to favor the adoption of very careful operational procedures for the control of nuclear weapons, either to backstop technology or to substitute for it in circumstances when connectivity with central command might be tenuous. To endorse the controllability of nuclear-armed forces is necessarily neither to predict with very high confidence that those forces would be centrally controlled in their tactical application in war nor to affirm the feasibility of very limited nuclear conflict. This third general assumption is really a simple rule of prudence, or common sense. If nuclear-armed forces were capable of being commanded strictly *en masse* and by means of a "go—no-go" signal, then their owners would have constructed what easily could amount in operational practice to a Doomsday Machine. Clausewitz's philosophical idea of absolute war would be made manifest. Such a highroad to societal oblivion may lurk inadvertently in the consequences of the intersecting plans of the nuclear forces of today, but it is of no *operational* interest to policy or strategy.

The strategic merit of latent Doomsday threats for inducing restraint in statecraft—of "utility in nonuse"[24]—is arguable, and long has been argued. But there can be no argument over the prospective idiocy in contingent action of a "strategic" nuclear threat which would render all matters strategic strictly moot. It is worth noting that many of the people who worry about the potential wartime fragility of U.S. strategic command, control, and communications have a failure of the strategic imagination when it comes to estimating how great a risk of catastrophic failure Soviet attack planners must judge that they themselves would be running with a countercommand assault.[25]

Finally, although there may be some strategic value to the limited employment of nuclear weapons in time of war, as there would be strategic value to nonnuclear naval, land, air, and space operations, the nuclear arsenals of the superpowers cannot be regarded as instruments of military decision. There is no reason in principle why wars in which nuclear weapons are used cannot be won. But it is equally certain that a war between the superpowers in which nuclear weapons are used in the thousands against each other's homeland must terminate in bilateral defeat. The degree to which the unknown and incalculable danger of explosive escalation to SIOP-level nuclear use should discourage the measured employment of nuclear weapons is a matter for policy judgment. There is no "science of nuclear war or strategy" which can educate political or military leaders as to the correct course of action.

To worry about the endgame or the trailing edge of war is to be concerned about the outcome of war. Evidence of such concern on the part of officials or theorists easily lends itself to vilification as planning for the winning of a war which could well be partially, if not terminally, nuclear in character. The Reagan administration was subjected to ridicule and abuse when it was reported in 1982 that the government "planned" to prevail in any future conflict, even in a protracted nuclear conflict. In response to the predictably bad press they received on the subject of their alleged views on nuclear strategy and nuclear war, the President and other high officials adopted the safe and reassuring verbal formula that "a nuclear war cannot be won and must never be fought."[26] The delegitimization of the classic notion of victory in war, however sensible a reaction to nuclear possibilities, poses awesome strategic problems for U.S. and NATO military planners. If a nuclear war cannot be won, does that mean that all nuclear use must be presumed to be self-defeating? Then what remains of the integrity of NATO strategy? Even if nuclear use were ruled self-defeating, might not the vigorous and successful prosecution of conventional operations press the aggressor dangerously close to nuclear temptation? Then–Secretary of Defense Weinberger talked around the question of the trailing edge of war in the following way:

> But should deterrence fail, our strategy is to secure all U.S. and allied interests, and deny the aggressor any of his war aims. We would seek to terminate any war at the earliest practical time and restore peace on terms favorable to the United States that secure all our aims and those of our allies and friends.
>
> In seeking the earliest termination of war, the United States not only would act to defeat the aggression, but also try to convince the attacker that his continued aggression would entail grave risks to his own interests.[27]

U.S. strategic thinkers and planners face the perennial difficulty of having to guess as to what kinds of wars their country may be compelled to wage. Through most of the postwar era to date the dominant paradigm has been of a superpower conflict both brief and probably maximally intensive. But over the past decade this paradigm of a swift gallop to Armageddon has come under growing challenge. Recognition of the value of endurance for strategic forces and their command, control, and communication, as well as what amounted to a revival of (offensive) maritime strategy in the 1980s, at least pointed to possibilities dramatically different from the long-standard scenario of a war which "explodes" radioactively from NATO's (erstwhile) Central Front. Changes in Soviet military doctrine over the past decade appear to be somewhat congruent in their implications with the diminution in Western expectation of early nuclear use in war. However, Marshal Nikolai Ogarkov's revolution in Soviet military doctrine was geared primarily toward the achievement of swift conventional success in theater operations. It is far from certain that a Soviet army in the early stages of reorganizing in favor of a more defensive posture—as required by a military doctrine reshaped by Gorbachev's "new thinking"—*given time to mobilize,* will be much less capable of unraveling NATO's defense in Central Europe than is the Soviet army of today. It is easy to persuade oneself that the Soviet army of the late 1990s and beyond should be dramatically less capable of surprise attack from a "standing start" than was its predecessor in the 1970s and 1980s. Nonetheless, should the Soviet army restructure very intelligently, and key NATO countries restructure their armed forces very unintelligently—in a pell-mell rush to save money—the net result may not be a happy one for military stability in Europe, even if Soviet forces would have to transit Poland in order to reach their Western foe.

Debates on what is called nuclear strategy appear to be endless, almost cyclical, notwithstanding the changes in weapons technology. General recognition of a body of knowledge authoritative beyond variants on the four general points registered above is as remote as ever. The truth of the matter is that no one knows, really knows, that is, what role nuclear weapons would play in war. In addition, no one knows, really knows, what role nuclear weapons have played in the long peace to date. Historical experience is consistent with the proposition that nuclear weapons have deterred, or helped deter, major East-West conflict. But it cannot be demonstrated that the presence of nuclear weapons was critical for the peaceful outcomes to crises. Still less can it be demonstrated that specific capabilities and doctrines for nuclear employment made any specific difference to broad decisions to wage, resolve, or desist altogether from crisis, or to eschew military adventure. Common sense suggests that nuclear weapons have been important for the stability of the security structure in postwar Europe, but it is difficult to claim much more than that with any precision.

When it comes to selecting force structures and doctrines for the contingent use of nuclear weapons, strategic preferences can fly without fear of authoritative contradiction. In the absence of assistance from a science of strategy, what can the nominal experts—actually specialists—advise about nuclear weaponry, targeting doctrine, and strategy? By overwhelming majorities, the expert-specialists did not predict the swift Prussian victory of 1870–71, the protracted conflict of 1914–18, the Anglo-French military *débâcle* of May–June 1940, Soviet survival in 1941–42, American failure and humiliation in Vietnam, or Soviet withdrawal from Afghanistan in 1989. The scope for error is so wide in predictions for the course of a World War III which would involve the use of realistically untried conventional weaponry, possibly the employment of nuclear weapons, and certainly the massive political straining of rival coalitions of states (if, indeed, there would be a coalition on the Soviet side), that one cannot help but pity the leaders and officials who are obliged to make choices for national and coalition defense. The "right strategy" cannot reliably be deduced by logic (anchored upon axiomatic, great-strategic truths), derived from the scientific study of past wars and campaigns (which ones? and whose interpretation?), or revealed by common sense (understood as practical wisdom).

The limits to the pragmatic utility of common sense are none too difficult to illustrate. For example, common sense suggests strongly that nuclear-armed states and coalitions would make war, if at all, much as scorpions are required to make love, very carefully. By extension, it should be true that neither East nor West would launch nuclear attacks on a scale and of a character which would deprive the enemy of its ability to conduct a nuclear campaign in a very careful and controlled manner. Similarly, attacks should not be launched which would deprive the enemy of his incentive to exercise restraint—lest his leaders be left with the conviction that they had nothing left to lose and so could "go for broke" with no additional penalty for failure. If this is a fair representation of a pragmatically useful workaday truth, does it mean that nuclear weapons can be used for limited purposes, with little risk that the enemy would execute explosive escalation to a society-threatening level of violence? Does not common sense, inconveniently perhaps, also suggest—again bereft of anything which would warrant ascription as reliable supporting evidence—that nuclear war truly is *terra incognita* and that the only safe level of nuclear use is complete nonuse?

To proceed further, does not common sense also suggest that there can be no clash even of nonnuclear arms between nuclear-equipped states which should be judged by reasonable people to be tolerably safe from the dangers of nuclear escalation to holocaust? Statesmen would need to guess, one cannot say calculate, whether the certain self-interest of the enemy in not inviting his own destruction should so constrain the character of his reply to a limited nuclear attack that such an attack could be ruled an acceptable risk. The statesmen upon whose shoulders fell the burden of decision for or against first nuclear use would, one must suppose, have been educated about the salient features of the enemy's strategic culture and style; would be alert to the unpredictable operation of Murphy's Law; and would have in mind the total course and needed outcome of the conflict. On this last point, for example, there is little doubt that nuclear use at sea would be tactically expedient for a Soviet navy which is likely to be hard-pressed. But as Donald Daniel has argued persuasively, it is improbable that a continentally oriented group of Soviet leaders who would define victory with reference to campaigns on land would risk compromising the prospects for continental success simply at the behest of their naval advisers.[28]

The limits of common sense also may be tested with reference to the perennial topic of "how best to deter?" Common sense pulls in opposite directions. On the one hand it seems eminently reasonable to argue, albeit apparently tautologically, that only credible threats can deter. What is a credible threat? It is a threat which the enemy believes that one could *and would* (or just might?) execute in action. Threats which after execution would leave the enemy with little left to lose should be as frightening to their executors as to their recipients. On the other hand, it is scarcely less reasonable to argue that in many cases literally the more credible the threat, the less likely it is to deter. If, for example, the United States is judged to be certain, or near certain, to execute a particular nuclear threat precisely because its military impact would be very far from system-threatening to the Soviet Union, the dissuasive value of such a threat has to be assessed to be modest.

Leaving theory aside, it is a political fact of coalition life that the ever-renewed U.S. quest for a more credible deterrent raises NATO-European anxieties over the sufficiency of deterrence. In their shot-gun blast of criticism of the American-authored report *Discriminate Deterrence,* Howard, Kaiser, and de Rose argued:

> Of course, every effort must be made to avoid uncontrolled or automatic escalation once nuclear war has started, but unless there is at least the perception of that danger clearly in the mind of the opponent Europe becomes a zone of guaranteed limited nuclear war [presumably this is an intentional exaggeration: CSG]. It is one thing to be better prepared, as the report suggests, for a local aggression with limited objectives, but quite another to define strategy in such a way that it gives the aggressor the assurance that his actions will result for him only in military losses that will not affect his vital interests.[29]

It may well be that in the real world of frightened politicians and conservative defense planners the tension in the relationship between credibility and deterrence really does not exist. Thus, contrary to the assertion by Howard, Kaiser, and de Rose, no matter what NATO's defense strategy may be said to be, the would-be aggressor will never believe that he has any "assurance that his actions will result for him only in military losses that will not affect his vital intersts." It is unlikely that a Soviet General Staff respectful of military history, probably somewhat chastened by its experience with Afghanistan, and suspicious of the loyalty of conscripts from the national minorities, will be overly optimistic regarding its ability to foretell the course and outcome of a major war.

In its social and political dimensions, the role of nuclear weapons in strategy has to be acceptable at home as well as effective for deterrence in the minds of identified likely enemies abroad. Moreover, "at home" for the United States embraces the domestic politics of at least the more important members of a sixteen-member-strong (or weak) NATO Alliance.

National and coalition military strategy should be developed in the context of grand strategy. Furthermore, military strategy should not be synonymous with one particular military instrument, unless that instrument alone either is very plausibly capable of delivering victory in war at acceptable cost, or if circumstances temporarily preclude alternatives. Periodically during the wars of the French Revolution and Empire, Britain was reduced to the waging of a strictly maritime-colonial conflict against France. Generally speaking, it was not expected in London that France could be brought down solely by the very slow working of sea power against her, but for temporary want of continental allies in the field maritime pressure was the only kind of pressure that Britain could apply. German military strategy in both world wars was reduced to a repeated endeavor to wage and win multienvironmental conflicts through tactical and operational excellence in land power alone. German air power fairly strictly was a tactical adjunct to the army, and the U-boat campaigns, though unexpectedly significant, were not accorded in either war the necessary measure of timely resource allocation for them to stand a very good chance of functioning to strategic effect as the instrument of victory.

In their effect on the course of a war, it is probably sensible to view nuclear weapons as likely to be as constrained in their utility as sea power and land power respectively have been for maritime and continental states and coalitions. Just as neither sea power nor land power could secure a fatal grip to force a decision in war against enemies militarily preeminent in the other environment, so nuclear-armed forces in their turn cannot be entrusted with the full burdens of national and coalition strategy. It may be objected that NATO strategy accommodates the working of a triad of conventional, short-range nuclear, and so-called strategic nuclear forces, and not of nuclear-armed forces alone. But the debate over strategy in the Western Alliance which briefly was rejuvenated by the INF treaty signaled as clearly as could be that NATO strategy in action is expected rapidly to be reduced to the nuclear dimension. Unsurprisingly, the all but collapse of the Warsaw Pact, against a background of a massive arms-control agenda, has served to snuff out the small flame of strategic argument that the perpetration of the INF treaty had begun to blow into life.

Nuclear threat and, if need be, controlled nuclear use, has been the final argument of a NATO coalition which has not expected to hold a Soviet invasion of Western Europe for more than a matter of weeks (or, *mirabilis mirabile,* for a month or two). Indeed, as observed previously, NATO-Europe has not really wanted to be able to hold a Pact invasion for months. As configured at present, NATO's grand strategy and military strategy are driven by the principle that defeat in Europe literally would be intolerable. Therefore, NATO's strategy can be reduced to total dependence upon the restorative merits of nuclear coercion. Unlike the historical cases of sea power against land power and vice versa, nuclear-armed forces would have reliable access to the enemy's center of gravity, and hence—technically—could secure a decision. But in an age of reasonably secure second-strike forces (unlike the Soviet nonalert condition circa 1961–62), the consequences of pressing for such a decision by nuclear coercion most likely would be suicidal (no matter how measured and well controlled were the individual steps taken in the escalation of nuclear violence). Obviously there is a theory of deterrence, even a vague theory of war, implicit in NATO's nuclear-heavy concept of flexible response. However, it is not self-evident that the contemporary U.S. and NATO willingness (or pretense of willingness) to wage nuclear war would be likely to succeed in its strategic purpose of overturning promptly and at bearable cost an adverse decision on land in Europe.

U.S. and NATO strategy is acceptable socially precisely, indeed perhaps strictly, because political leaders and general publics are persuaded that war will never come. Objectively very risky strategies, in stock market speculation or in nuclear dependency, are not perceived subjectively to have a high-risk character all the while the weather is fine. Moreover, the longer the fine weather endures, the more unthinkable is the notion of a day of reckoning. People come to have confidence in confidence alone, to borrow a line from *The Sound of Music.* Widespread faith in an ever-upward stock market may not be wholly dissimilar from the phenomenon of a NATO Alliance which, in practice to date, has related the stability of the European security system very closely to political cohesion among allies.

The role of nuclear weapons in U.S. and NATO strategy overwhelmingly, and sensibly, is to deter war. The official theory for the deterrence of war does not rest importantly upon the persuasion of Soviet leaders that an invasion of Western Europe would fail militarily. Instead, deterrence is held to flow from Soviet belief that a war with NATO would be likely to assume a nuclear character, and that the historically uncharted trail of nuclear use in war could well lead to a general holocaust. For reasons of political sensitivities (domestic, West-West, and East-West), as well as for the preservation of strategically desirable mystery (the virtues of uncertainty in enemy minds), there is little careful treatment of the issue of what to do should deterrence fail: how would a war be fought and terminated? Presumably, and it is difficult to be more precise, deterrence would be restored and Soviet invaders would withdraw as a result of a process of Western-led nuclear escalation. How this would happen and why a Soviet Union sufficiently motivated to attack NATO—or its vital interests more broadly—would permit itself to be bested in a competition in resolve and pain acceptance remains obscure. This is one view of the reality of NATO and U.S. strategy.

It should not be forgotten that NATO can draw upon four decades of historical experience with the demonstrable reality of a deterrence system which works (or, at least, which demonstrably has not failed). From this perspective, people reason that a search for a radically better strategy may place in peril the integrity of an existing strategy which to date unarguably has been good enough. Indeed, even to question publicly the sense in U.S. and NATO strategy, as with well-intentioned expressions of doubt about an ever-upward stock market, can have the effect of undermining the stability of the extant system. There is no intention here to ridicule the proposition that NATO's strategy is unlikely ever to be field-tested. No less an authority than Michael Howard advises:

> the record shows that as technology has developed, so wars between powers, at least between powers of a comparable stage of economic development, have become psychologically less attractive, increasingly expensive and difficult to wage and, above all, appalling in their results for victor and vanquished alike. The general realization of this has, in consequence, made the incidence of such wars increasingly rare. *It is quite possible that we shall never see another.*[30]

Readers must decide for themselves whether or not they are sufficiently worried about the probable inutility of existing strategy and forces *in time of war* as to wish to consider genuine, though only arguably available, alternatives. The inutility of strategy refers to a condition wherein the designated nuclear means are unlikely to achieve the political objectives set for their accomplishment. Also, strategy designs which are superior in principle may not be politically tolerable, may require a military instrument well beyond the current state of the technological art, and may well ask more of U.S. allies than there is good reason to believe would be forthcoming. Any bold American strategy innovator has to take full account of the following mainstream European view:

> . . . the recommendation [of the report on *Discriminate Deterrence*] to strengthen the conventional posture of NATO and to use modern technologies is to be welcomed. But the report's proposition "that the alliance could defeat the Soviet army, or at least fight to a standstill, without having to reach for nuclear weapons" not only prescribes the impossible—the West conventionally is vastly inferior—but also the unacceptable, since Europe would be in ruins.[31]

If modern weapons technology and the dynamics of arms competition deny the West the plausible ability to wage and win a nuclear campaign at tolerable cost, and if an all-conventional conflict is fundamentally unacceptable to NATO-Europe, then—inevitably—one is reduced to some close variant of the familiar strategic concept of flexible response. The point is not that flexible response is the best strategy (to stretch terms somewhat), and certainly not that it would be likely to prove good enough in an hour of real need, but rather that it may be the best—and perhaps the only—strategy available to the Alliance in peacetime. Readers might care to consider the proposition that whatever the 1990s may bring by way of changes in the military dimension to international security, the prospects are truly minimal that NATO will seize the opportunity created by what may be only a temporary Soviet entropy to put its strategy house in order. When peace breaks out, even though history teaches us that peace always breaks down eventually, great democracies do not make a habit of "catching up" with the errors in strategy (means-ends relationships) that accumulated over four decades of Cold War.

The broad theoretical alternative to flexible response would be to construct a theory of deterrence and war which reserved for nuclear weapons the roles fairly strictly of counterdeterrent and, just possibly, of limited counterforce instrument for modest tactical or operational effect. The United States still would require a very menacing arsenal of nuclear-armed forces, but the operational purposes of those forces overwhelmingly would be the dissuasion of Soviet (or other) minds from exercising their nuclear options. This theory of deterrence and war would cease to rest upon the hopes for the efficacy of Soviet fears of holocaust or its functional Soviet equivalent—total loss of political control at home. Instead, Soviet leaders would be deterred, in the foreground, by the calculation that to wage war upon the Western

Alliance—initially either in Europe or upon its vital interests else-where—would be to wage what would likely be a global and pro-tracted war against an economically vastly superior enemy coalition. In the background, as a deterrence makeweight, would be some irreducible Soviet anxiety that a nuclear holocaust could well occur as a result of the unpredictable dynamics of such a major conflict. Regardless of the formal reshaping of Western strategy and defense preparation away from its erstwhile nuclear dependence, residual nuclear dread should help deterrence even in a less markedly nuclear era.

CHAPTER 10

Seeing the Problem Whole

Having conducted the [Seven Years'] war during four years, he [William Pitt the Elder, Earl of Chatham] had come to understand the connection between all its parts. He saw that a diversion in Germany kept busy French troops and money that would otherwise be employed in Flanders, Portugal, or an invasion. He understood the necessity of a financial strain which he believed we [the British] could bear and France could not. He insisted on the totality of the war.

RICHARD PARES[1]

IF A pervasive villain has been identified in this text, it is the error of essentialism. This is the error, or the important partial truth which positively invites error, which leads a commentator to argue, for example, that *essentially* the Roman Empire in the West fell because its army lost its tactical edge over the barbarians;[2] *essentially* the Byzantine Empire endured for a thousand years (with only a brief hiatus: 1204–61) because the site and fortifications of the imperial capital of Constantinople rendered the city impregnable; *essentially* the Byzantine Empire declined and fell because the catastrophic defeat of the imperial army at Manzikert in 1071 by the Seljuk Turks led inexorably to the loss of the empire's heartland in Anatolia— whence came most of the soldiers and the revenue of the Empire;[3] *essentially* it was the offensive military doctrines of the Great Powers which produced the European cataclysm of 1914–18; *essentially* the

323

logic of strategy, really of conflict more broadly, is "paradoxical"; and *essentially* great powers rise and fall as the economic base of their resources expands and shrinks relative to that of their rivals (if stated too simply this essentialist argument becomes a tautology).[4]

Essentialisms come at all levels of analysis, from the technical and tactical (it is fighting spirit and cold steel that win battles), to the grand-strategic (the longer purse wins wars), to the omnilevel workings of the logic of conflict *("the entire realm of strategy is pervaded by a paradoxical logic of its own")*.[5] From the admittedly limited perspective of the student of strategy—to repeat, a person strongly inclined to seek, if not actually charged with seeking, *useful* knowledge—sweeping essentialist arguments can be recognized to be as generally true as they are unhelpful. As examples: Kennedy's and Luttwak's analyses can be combined to produce the argument that there is a paradoxical logic in the rise and fall of great powers. The price paid for current military greatness is the eating of the economic seed-corn which will be needed if that relative greatness is to be sustained far into the future. Walter Lippmann, Paul Kennedy, and Samuel P. Huntington, most prominently amidst a host of commentators, have advised that statecraft (policy and grand strategy) *essentially* is about the effective balancing of capabilities of all kinds with commitments.[6] What that amounts to is really nothing more than a restatement of any competent definition of strategy. The fact that the restatement may well be politically necessary, given the abundant historical evidence of cases of imperial overstretch, should not obscure the truth that what has been discovered, or rediscovered, is something less than a dazzling insight, let alone—necessarily—the basis for useful advice for policymakers and military planners.

It should not be supposed that the reciprocal adjustment of means and ends, critical though that is, encompasses the totality of strategy and statecraft. Although strategists and statesmen must be presumed to be pragmatists, determined to attempt only those things which their countries should be able to achieve, still they are required to decide where the objectives of policy shall sit on the spectrum from modest to heroic. A state may be exceedingly well directed in statecraft in the strategic sense that what it sought to achieve was well within the bounds of attainability. But that state might have attempted to accomplish too little for its own security. Properly viewed, statecraft and strategy must accommodate questions of purpose as well as issues pertaining to the means-ends nexus. There will be no plaudits awarded by historians to a national leader who wonderfully accomplishes what future events reveal to have been the wrong tasks.

GEOGRAPHY AND THE STRATEGY MOSAIC

The many references in this book to the strategic relationship between sea power and land power have been mandated by its pervasive and long-enduring significance for the history of conflict. However, that thread also stands as extended illustration of a concern that the unity of necessary preparation for the deterrence and waging of conflict should be accorded its due. If there were states or coalitions of states whose strategic cultures and grand strategies had been shaped very significantly by dependence upon air power or space power, then this book might have analyzed the strategic problems and opportunities of "eagles" *vis-à-vis* "tigers" and "sharks," rather than just the latter pair. Air power and space power effectively were relegated to adjunct status. That relegation assumed, arguably, that strategic nuclear forces are not very interesting as a usable military instrument of decision, which is to say that the decision they might impose is judged to be too costly.

To denounce essentialism, or undue reductionism, is not to deny a need for the selection of priorities. Some interests, military objectives, military capabilities, and individual weapon systems plainly are more important than others. Moreover, even if clear decision rules for the determination of relative importance are absent, all governments operate in an economic universe, which is to say in a realm where choices have to be exercised in the allocation of scarce resources.

Proper design, assembly, and maintenance of the mosaic of strategy particular to a distinctive state or coalition require a coherent vision of how war can be deterred and, possibly the same subject, how war could be prosecuted to a politically successful outcome.[7] The strategic implications of geography alter as adversaries and allies change, perhaps as national territory expands or contracts, and as transportation technologies (and hence weapon platforms) evolve. Nonetheless, national systems of statecraft and strategy have persisted over the course of centuries, even in the face of radical changes in international alignments and technology.

The strategic brain which collectively orchestrates the instruments of grand and military strategy requires a total framework of understanding of how the separate pieces of the mosaic fit together. This understanding is of a "system of war" (conceived within a system of statecraft), a clear idea of how to deploy the total assets, including the combined arms, of the state or coalition.

At the level of national military strategy, both superpowers must design mosaics which fit together the same major pieces—land power, sea power (and their tactical air- and missile-power adjuncts), "strategic" nuclear power, and space power. The total size of the mosaic and the choice among competing capabilities—to enlarge some pieces at the expense of others (perhaps nuclear forces because they are cheaper than conventional forces)—will be influenced by "the Kennedy factor" (in *The Rise and Fall of the Great Powers*), the great equation between economic weight and military security. Furthermore, the total, elaborate pattern of interlocking pieces requires the functional political support of a compliant populace, as well as the technical support of logistic, intelligence, and communications services, backed by a financial, industrial and trading economic engine of appropriate size and quality.

The pieces that make up the strategy mosaic, though largely common across frontiers, have different sizes and shapes from security community to security community. Consideration of the specifics of geopolitics and geostrategy suggests, or should suggest, different designs in the strategy mosaics of rival powers. For an important example, consider the relative significance for the Soviet Union and for NATO of the INF and shorter-range missiles which are being withdrawn and destroyed, asymmetrically, to a double zero. The basis for the bargain of the INF treaty has to be the assumption that like (NATO's INF) is being traded for like (Soviet INF). But is this *strategically* true? Plausibly, Samuel P. Huntington claims not: "The Soviet Union does not need nuclear weapons to conquer Western Europe; NATO does need them to deter and to defeat a Soviet attack."[8]

Beyond the INF issue, if the Western Alliance elects for geostrategic and social-political reasons not to change its strategic concept from flexible response to preparation for global and probably protracted conventional war, then it requires that the long-range nuclear-armed forces of the United States should be able to exert coercive strategic effect as an extended deterrent. Arms-control regimes, or any other developments which tend to depress the relative coercive value of superpower nuclear-armed forces, geostrategically must function to the net disadvantage of Western security. As Huntington suggests, NATO requires more strategic effect of its nuclear-armed forces than does the Soviet Union.

Although all of the military pieces of the mosaic are important, they are not equally important for all states. Moreover, no state in modern times has been so preeminent in the economic basis of its military power that, given its distinctive geostrategic circumstances, not to mention its unique traditions, it could afford to purchase true excellence in all the environments in which conflict could occur (to the degree to which such excellence really is for sale). Thus inevitably, the superpowers are obliged to assign top priority to their nuclear-armed forces. Unlike the recurring historical situation of a standoff between superior land power and superior sea power, strategic air and missile power could be an independently decisive war-winner or war-loser for any state, regardless of its primary geostrategic orientation as between a continental or a maritime focus. The geostrategic detail of the East-West conflict yields nuclear-armed forces a potentially larger strategic role for NATO than for the Soviet Union: those forces could trump any impending regional military decision achieved by conventional arms, or perhaps upset the card table altogether.[9] Also, as the United States apparently demonstrated for the better part of two decades (1949–c. 1969), albeit not unambiguously, perceptions of a superior weight and quality in nuclear-armed forces probably can substitute for absent combat prowess at lower levels of violence.

Assuming that the nuclear balance is satisfactory, a still effectively insular United States must attach relatively greater weight to its maritime power than to its land power, just as a still continentally challenged Soviet empire must prefer its land power to its maritime power in resource allocation decisions. However, for the time being the United States has to generate and sustain sufficient land power— both garrison and expeditionary in kind—to encourage its formal and informal allies around the Rimland of Eurasia to stay in the field and provide the bulk of the ground fighting forces needed for the continental confinement of the land-power superstate (or perhaps in the 1990s for the stabilization of an increasingly politically uncertain European security condition). Similarly, aside from the significance of its sea power for the projection of power in peacetime, the Soviet Union requires sufficient naval power to deny its maritime enemy at least some of its theoretical options for the imaginative conduct of offensive sea-based operations in time of war. The Soviet Union cannot afford to ignore the hoary old strategic truth that military decision against a maritime coalition can be achieved only by action at sea (again, assuming that intercontinental nuclear coercion is judged to be unprofitable). The Alexandrian and Roman option of commanding the sea by holding the shore would not be available to the U.S.S.R.

Of recent decades a new piece has been added to the strategy mosaic that is not at all well understood. Specifically, the prospect of war in the fourth dimension, of operations conducted to, in, and from outer space, generally is recognized to be a certain feature of future superpower conflict. Space is a geographically unique environment for war, characterized (*inter alia*) by vast distances, featureless "terrain," enormous costs of operation (because of the distances involved, the need to provide sufficient energy to climb the "gravity mountain" or out of the "gravity well"), and the generally predictable movement and positional (rather than maneuverable) nature of space vehicles which must obey the laws of orbital mechanics.

Simple, if not simplistic, approaches to space as an environment for conflict recognize that they are dealing with the new high ground and that command, or control, of the upper reaches of the gravity mountain may confer the same kind of military advantages conferred by elevated terrain on earth. However, the relatively primitive state of space weaponry (with the exception of long-range ballistic missiles which, though not deployed in space, function as space vehicles through most of their flight regimes), the utter strategic novelty of space as a battlefield, and the parochial—as well as legitimate—concerns of terrestrially focused and bureaucratically well entrenched armed services, thus far have combined to frustrate development in the West of persuasive and coherent stories which seek to explain the strategic meaning of space.

Heated public debate over the merits or otherwise of this or that variant of (partially) space-based strategic defenses has overshadowed professional study and discussion of the much broader question of space as an environment for conflict. For example, a public attentive to the rumbling, great SDI debate may well not know that the fulminating protagonists have only the dimmest grasp of the probable terms of combat which flow from the distinctive character of the space environment. It is no exaggeration to say that the advocates of limitations upon antisatellite weapons quite literally are recommending—and indeed legislated for several years—that particular military capabilities should not be developed (in the guise of space test constraints), even though they do not understand the nature of war in space. One is reminded of the total impracticality of the pre–World War I endeavors to legislate international control regimes for constraint of the ways in which submarines and aircraft might be used.

Because of its scattered global geography, it is often alleged that the Western Alliance has a greater stake in the free use of the spaceways in time of war than does the continentally consolidated Soviet Eurasian empire. Nonetheless, whether that is true or false—and it is probably a plausible fallacy—on the fairly convincing evidence of actual space programs, the Soviet Union has long had a more consistent appreciation of the military importance of space passage in time of war than has the United States. In a 1987 speech the Chief of Naval Operations, Admiral Carlisle Trost, advised as follows:

> At a time when space technology is almost begging us to use it, we are still wrapped in our earth-based security blanket. We are thinking in terms of the millions of square miles of opaque ocean when we should be thinking in terms of a planet seen as the size of a basketball.
>
> We are falling farther behind in a space race that affects not only ASW and naval warfare but our very national security. Today we know that in wartime, even in a conventional war of limited duration, the two superpowers would fight a battle of attrition in space until one side or other had wrested control. The winner would then use the surviving space systems to decide the contests on land and sea. Today, that superpower would probably not be the United States. . . .
>
> In short, the Soviets are prepared to go to war in space, and we are not.[10]

Given the total absence of historical experience with war conducted in and from space, there is no way of knowing for certain whether or not the admiral is correct. However, his statement has the rare, outstanding merits both of seeing the space environment as a whole, and of considering the strategic effects of a battle for control in space upon war on earth. As can be said of the oceans and the airways, space is a place rather than a mission. However, each geophysical environment is better viewed as both place and mission. While the seat of policy purpose in statecraft and for strategy is on land, space as a place (like the sea and the air) can be used for the advance of military purpose on land only if it is treated as a mission in its own right. In other words, the United States would need to fight for the right to use the spaceways in wartime—this is the mission of space control—for the same reasons that its rights to air and maritime passage would be contested. The RAF and the USAAF fought for control of the air in Europe in 1943–44 not because there was anything in the air worth winning, but rather because they could only function effectively against the enemy on the ground if they had first defeated the Luftwaffe.

Exactly how and why the control of space inexorably must, or even should, lead to control on earth tends to be left unexplained, presumably as a self-evident truth beyond need of explanation. It is not difficult to understand how space control—meaning space denial to the enemy—would facilitate the efficient conduct of military operations of all kinds.[11] But, with one important exception, the idea that a working control of the spaceways must function as the key to military victory should be treated with the skepticism suitable to all such reductionist, dominant-instrument and strategically monistic arguments. The important exception pertains to a context wherein one state or coalition could deploy in space a highly effective, mission-survivable strategic defensive shield for the thoroughly reliable protection of whole societies. *In conjunction with* offensive nuclear threats against which an enemy defeated in space could not defend itself, such a shield truly would warrant ascription as a decisive military instrument. However, viewed in isolation, a space-based defensive shield would not be a war-winner. It would keep many enemy missiles and aircraft away from the protected territories, but that might have the operational effect only of neutralizing a military instrument which the enemy had neither wished nor expected to employ anyway. Synergistically as always in strategy, the space-based defensive shield would contribute significantly to wartime success only if either it permitted the threat and execution of nuclear threats unanswerable in kind; or if it quarantined long-range nuclear bombardment from active military interest and thereby liberated superior conventionally armed forces to win their war.

Space poses a historically familiar kind of challenge to statecraft and strategy. In the late sixteenth century, the England of Elizabeth I struggled with mixed success to understand the novel problems of how its (largely) private and public naval power might best be wielded as an instrument of national policy.[12] Maritime power as an instrument of grand strategy was as unfamiliar an idea to Elizabeth and her counselors as air power and space power for her functional successors in the twentieth century. Then, as now, people knew about ships (or airplanes, or satellites). But how ships and landward support for ships (bases, colonies, and so forth) could function strategically as *sea power* (or airplanes as *air power,* or satellites as *space power*—both requiring very extensive terrestrial support systems), and how that sea power should be exploited in relation to national and allied land power, could be determined only on the basis of much trial and error and careful reflection upon historical experience. Furthermore, the incipient sea power of Elizabeth's England was massively constrained by the manifest financial weakness of the crown and the logistical limitations which must discipline attempts to pursue a sustained offensive at sea. Then, as now, too much too soon was envisaged or promised for the strategic benefits allegedly certain to accrue from what a later age was to call command of the sea (or air, or space). Then, as now, independently decisive (strategic) results were advertised as the glittering prize which would follow from: an effective blockade of Spanish sea-lines of communication to the Americas and the Baltic—for the purposes, respectively, of interdicting the annual treasure convoy (the *Flota,* a principal basis of Habsburg credit with its Italian bankers) from the Americas[13] and denying naval stores to the Spanish navy; the demoralization of undisciplined urban civilians by aerial bombardment; and, most recently, the control of space.

The strategist's world grows ever more complex. In the first half of the twentieth century statesmen and military planners had to come to grips with the strategic meaning of air power and with the possible strategic opportunities opened by the internal combustion engine in the form of trucks and armored fighting vehicles directed by adept operational artists. Events appeared to demonstrate that superiority in the air, however exploited, probably could not be an independently decisive, truly strategic, factor prior to the development of the atomic bomb. But history did show that in regular naval and ground warfare success was very unlikely in the absence of a working command in the air. This is not to deny that on occasions a mix of favorable terrain, skilled engineering, inclement weather, and outstanding fighting spirit and tactical agility could substantially offset gross inferiority in the air. The German defense, successively, of the Gustav and the Gothic lines in Italy in the winters of 1943–44 and 1944–45 illustrated all too clearly that there are limits to the military advantages conferred even by total control of the skies. For another case, the French airhead that was established to be the fortress of Dien Bien Phu was destroyed in 1953–54 in a classic cauldron battle by General Giap's Viet Minh who held the surrounding high ground—notwithstanding the fact that the French enjoyed a command of the air space contested "only" by antiaircraft fire.[14] The Germans had learned at Crete in 1941 and at Stalingrad in the winter of 1942–43 that a working command of the aerial "high ground," having been exploited as an operational enabling agent, could be exercised as a tactical adjunct to beleaguered ground forces (air-inserted in the Cretan case) only at a prohibitive price in the face of very determined ground-based opposition.

Conventionally armed air power has speeded the operational victories of excellent ground forces (the Germans from 1939 to 1942), and has enabled less-than-excellent ground forces to achieve operational (in the case of the U.S. Army in Vietnam, tactical) successes which otherwise would have been beyond their power (the Anglo-American armies from 1942 to 1945, the U.N. forces in Korea, the U.S. Army in Vietnam).[15] Superiority in the air probably would not have saved the French and the British in May 1940 from the fatal implications of their operational errors, but it was critical for the Allies in North Africa, Sicily, Italy (with reservations), and France. The brief history of air power provides additional support for the general argument that has long been understood to apply to geostrategic stalemates between superior land power and superior sea power. Namely, to date at least, very great land power cannot secure victory in war against a sea-power enemy whose control of the maritime environment cannot effectively be contested. Similarly, no measure of advantage at sea, no matter how exclusive the degree of command achieved, in and of itself can bring down an enemy who is continentally supreme. With regard to land combat, advantage—even great advantage—in the air can only affect campaign outcomes if friendly ground forces are fit to be helped. If those friendly ground forces truly comprise what amounts to a rabble in arms, no measure of overhead assistance will reverse for long the course of the terrestrial fighting.

That very wide distribution of military value among separate targets in land warfare which constrains the impact of air power does not obtain in the maritime environment. As early as May–June 1942 it was evident that sea power subsumed, and *absolutely* required, air power at sea (at least in the most maritime of all theaters of war, the Pacific). The very narrow base upon which major military value is distributed in capital—and other important—naval platforms (targets) rendered rapid decision against surface fleets as practicable an objective of naval air power as it was for naval gunnery. On reflection, the U.S. Navy in the Pacific in World War II probably overadjusted to the arrival of the naval air age: the gun power of the fleet was underused tactically and operationally.

Ships, tanks, airplanes, and satellites attract a vast literature devoted to their technical functioning and anticipated tactical effectiveness. That literature is important, but for statecraft and strategy it is a part of the basis for policy and strategic discussion; it is not that discussion itself. Technical and tactical competence, if not excellence, is essential for operational success and strategic effectiveness,[16] but such competence is no guarantee of effectiveness at the strategic level. Tactical and even operational success at sea, in the air, and in space has no inherent strategic meaning save with reference to the conduct of war as a whole, with particular and ultimate reference to its typically territorial stakes. Even operational victories in land warfare which pertain directly to the territorial prizes of conflict lack comprehensive strategic meaning if they are juxtaposed with unsatisfactory terms of combat at sea, in the air, and in space. Victories on land may have the status only of temporary campaign successes if an enemy is operationally at liberty to recover and reorganize for a renewal of continental combat behind and under the shield of superior maritime power, air power, and space power.

The idea employed here of a strategy mosaic has been linked umbilically to a combined-arms view of the synergisms among military instruments oriented toward combat in four geophysically distinct environments. Individual strategic thinkers will prefer distinct frames of reference for the explanation and exploration of the complexity of the subject. There is certainly no single correct way in which to think strategically and explore strategic problems, though there is an abundance of wrong ways. What matters is that the objective unity of statecraft and strategy be recognized, and that diplomatic and military analysis and planning be conducted within a holistic frame of reference.

HISTORY AND CULTURE

In the kingdom of the pragmatic strategist, wherein strategy is the art of the possible, skill in strategy can come to be regarded as the philosopher's stone which renders success probable, if never quite certain. Richard Betts has referred to "strategism" and "strategic romanticism,"[17] the error of identifying in almost intuitive strategic reasoning "an autonomous art, a genie that should drive defense planning, unhobbled by managerialists."[18] My concern here is somewhat different from that expressed by Betts, though it is complementary to his analysis. Strategy is no more detachable from the fighting quality of its tactical instruments and the efficiency of the logistic support for those instruments than it stands apart from the cultural preferences of the geographically organized, historical security communities which must design and apply it. The mix of socially transmitted attitudes, beliefs, and preferred modes of operation—as well as the institutions which express them—in short what is known as culture, is very much the product of the historical experience of the society in question.

History is not the mere chronicle of events, but rather an explanation of why events occurred and what the consequences were. There is some limited merit in Oscar Wilde's observation that "Any fool can make history, but it takes a genius to write it."[19] The perils for the student of strategy in trying to learn lessons from history are so familiar as to require no extensive commentary. All history is written from a particular cultural vantage point, grounded temporally in the frame of reference of the age in which it is composed. Moreover, all history necessarily is written as communication to a particular society—one whose dominant political ideas, standards of right conduct and the like the historian is likely to share. It is for these reasons that much written history is at least as informative about the author and his times as it is about the subject of his scholarly inquiry. It may be unhistorical to explain strategic behavior in distant periods with reference to modern concepts, but if those concepts help explain what was attempted, no great harm is done. Indeed, there is no particular virtue in interpreting the past as faithfully as possible in the terms familiar to that period, if modern ideas and theories can help understanding. For a *reductio ad absurdum,* just because medieval commentators were culturally predisposed to discern the Will of God in the unfolding of events, we are not obliged to follow them out of a misplaced determination to achieve historical empathy. Serious error creeps in, of course, if the historian, or the strategist looking backwards, neglects, or recognizes and then just disdains, the mental worldview of historical characters. For example, the ease with which Islamic Arab armies overran the easternmost provinces of the Byzantine Empire (in the 630s and 640s) is substantially explicable with reference to the exhaustion of that empire in its late, great (albeit ultimately victorious) war with Persia. But behind the strategic explanation lay the fact that Egypt, Palestine, and Syria had long been theologically exceedingly disaffected from Constantinople's Orthodoxy (and indeed pretensions to theological primacy). Because of their Monophysite preference—a belief in the strongly divine character of Christ—the empire's subjects in the east were not inclined to resist the arrival of a fairly tolerant Islamic rule.

Historians can forget that as a general rule (at least for modern times) they know what the consequences were both of action and inaction on the part of historical principals, and of the seemingly inexorable working out of broad social, economic, political, military, and intellectual trends. But the historical figures whose behavior and foresight come under the judgmental pen of the historian necessarily lacked the advantage of knowing what happened next. It is far more difficult creatively to identify practicable, alternative "might be's"—

the real-time problem for the policymaker and the strategist—than it is to provide with impressive scholarship so convincing a rationale for what was that the reader has difficulty even conceiving of alternative tracks of historical development. Thus the contemporary strategic thinker actually may have a skill bias in his professional techniques for coping with uncertainty (i.e., the future), which renders him more sensitive to the real dilemmas of historical figures, institutions, and polities than is the trained historian. Also, the historian may be so locked into the science of the particular, and so professionally fearful of condemnation for arguable and unhistorical generalization, that he will eschew a level of explanation of events which might have some meaning in contemporary terms—or, dare one suggest, some *relevance* for today and tomorrow.

The value of history for strategic thinking today is more often simply asserted or denounced than it is debated rigorously as an issue to be demonstrated or refuted. Two responses to this question are offered here; one objective and the other distinctly subjective. Objectively speaking, whether or not interpretations of historical experience from far distant eras should be deployed in contemporary discussion, it is a fact that they are so deployed. People will continue to decorate their arguments on current issues in strategy with more or less plausibly relevant historical examples and anecdotes. It follows that there is no point discussing solemnly the legitimacy or otherwise of, for example, citing prenuclear cases in illustration of points bearing upon nuclear-age issues; or the sense in referring to cases from the period prior to the emergence of the modern nation-state for the illumination of today's policy dilemmas. In practice, the only choice is between more and less careful historical illustration of argument. Subjectively, as this book reveals in abundance, this strategic thinker finds that the study of history—ancient, medieval, and modern—educates his strategic imagination and, he believes, helps interrogate contemporary problems in policy and strategy with the variable aid of an almost infinitely rich reservoir of human experience.

The content of strategic reasoning is always to a degree culture-specific and historically particular, but strategic reasoning per se is value-free. Naturally, the two interpenetrate. The dynamic mixture of unbridled personal ambition—and historically rarely paralleled competence—and newly released national political energy which produced the Napoleonic way of war ran afoul both generally of the means-ends centerpiece to strategy and specifically of the problems peculiar to continental empire-building. For enlightenment through strategic exploration, it is really unimportant whether policy and strategy have been viewed by contemporaries as being in the service of God—with success or failure attributable to the mysterious workings of Divine Providence—in the service of the personal and dynastic interests of ruling families, or in the service of the interests of a security community which conceived of itself as a nation. Strategy is strategy. Motives for war will direct the choice of strategic objectives and the style of operations. Those motives have ranged, on the positive side, among glory and political prestige, personal redemption, material loot, the control of trade routes, the seizure of territory, fulfillment of some ideologically mandated historic mission, and even the purchase of divine favor through the capture of prisoners for blood sacrifice (as in the Aztec conduct of war).[20]

There have been many significant changes in the technologies of war, or in the technologies useful for war, as also there have been in the ability of security communities to mobilize and motivate their people either to fight or to pay for those who must fight. Those changes have had drastic effects upon the range of the tactically feasible, hence upon the sensible scope for operations, ergo upon the attainable scale of ambition for strategic objectives, and ultimately upon the character of policy goals. Nonetheless, classes of policy and strategic problems (and their solutions), as well as the generic warp and woof of the "mechanism of war," have remained substantially unaltered through the ages.

Of course the introduction of very expensive siege artillery employing gunpowder had profound implications for the military importance of thin-walled castles and other places so fortified, and hence for the political organizations whose material basis for independent decision was thus rendered obsolete (though the connection easily may be exaggerated).[21] But were the problems of grand strategy or military strategy very different from period to period, as technologies and political forms changed? In all periods the central problem for the strategist has been the mutual adjustment of means and ends. Alliance and counteralliance, threats, bribes, and exemplary punishments, diplomacy and war, intelligence, technological and tactical innovation, logistics, the skills of statesmen and generals, the ability to pay (or make war self-financing through requisition and plunder), popular enthusiasm or at least acquiescence at home, the willingness of soldiers actually to stand and fight—not to mention the enduring significance of terrain and climate—the history of factors relevant to strategy is as near constant as makes scant difference from ancient times to the present. Discipline and morale were as critically important for the feasibility of the strategist's grand designs in the days of the Roman Republic as they are today for armed forces who must train to fight in the shadow of nuclear and chemical dangers.

Strategic problems and opportunities in the effective conduct of war between maritime- and land-power coalitions are as well illustrated in the experience of the Greece of the fifth century B.C., and of the Rome and Carthage of the third century, as they are by the wars of the French Revolution and Empire or the British record of anticontinental-hegemonic behavior in the twentieth century. The geostrategic context for statecraft and generalship in the West shifted radically from the European-Mediterranean theater of ancient and medieval times to a (barely) global dimension in the sixteenth century. However, with the all-too-obvious atomic exception, it can be difficult to specify an algorithm which makes much sense for the division of historical experience between that which should be included and that which should be excluded, as worthy or unworthy of study by the contemporary strategist in pursuit of useful knowledge (by way of contrast to the contemporary strategist merely indulging antiquarian interests).

For the frustration of small and tidy minds, the periodization of history can be as arbitrary as it is arguable. The Roman Empire in the West was never the same after the calamities of the 400s (culminating in the first sack of Rome—by Alaric's Visigoths from August 24 to 30, 410), even though the final "fall" of the *Roma aeterna* of the ancient world was not registered, with a whimper rather than with a bang, until 476. But the Roman Empire in the East did not fall until 1204 (to plunder and land-hungry Franks, and Venetians in search of preclusive security for their trading empire)—or was it until 1453? If great political events are an unsatisfactory basis for the drawing of clear lines between the strategically relevant and the strategically irrelevant—Rome was cited merely as an illustration of the problem—perhaps one would be on firmer ground with political forms. Again, there are awesome difficulties for the scholar. The pace of political modernization has been uneven among political entities: from feudal monarchy to some rough approximations of the modern state, though still with dynastic rather than truly national interests guiding policy, and from the dynastic state to the unquestionably modern nation-state. Also, local political forms and culture have been considerably variable among the grossly oversimple categories of feudal monarchy, early modern (dynastic) state, and modern nation-state.

If one still believes that the historical experience accessible to the contemporary strategic thinker and planner can usefully be divided into the antiquarian and the relevant, then one is most likely to reach for some technologically founded algorithm. One must acknowledge the landmark status of, for example, the stirrup, Greek fire, the crossbow, the oceangoing sailing ship, gunpowder, the breech-loading repeating rifle, the machine gun, quick-firing recoilless field artillery, steam transportation, the internal combustion engine, and heavier-than-air flight—to mix the engines of war with transportation platforms useful in war. But some of these have problems of historical uncertainty of date of introduction, all of them were improved over time, and they all helped define an era in the context of combined arms. How much simpler it is just to draw a historical marker through the calendar for July 16, 1945, with the successful test at Alamogordo, New Mexico, of the first atomic bomb (or one might prefer August 6, 1945, for the date of the first use of an atomic bomb in war).

Unfortunately for the historical depth in American strategic education, the unquestionable importance of the atomic events of 1945 and the plainly technological dimension to those events coincided fairly precisely with U.S. emergence as a superstate in world politics. In short, an American culture not characterized by a friendliness toward historical reflection (or, in a pejorative vein, toward nostalgia) has been encouraged by the novelty of its own geopolitical preeminence to believe that the strategic universe was made over by the meaning of Alamogordo. Now, in the fifth decade of the nuclear age, the apparently radical break point of 1945 looks to have been less of a chasm than is still widely believed. The apocalyptic aspect of the nuclear (really atomic, until 1952–53) age, though heralded as such from the outset, was not a military—though it was a psychological—reality until the hydrogen bomb entered superpower arsenals in the mid-1950s. Should one then identify what strategically is meant by the nuclear age as the period after, say, 1955–56?

Although technology builds many of the military means used by strategy, technology and weapons in themselves are not synonymous with strategy and policy. An apocalyptic premise to strategic thinking and military planning is extreme and implausible—though admittedly it is irrefutable and well worthy of generating prudential prophylactic measures so as to render it a self-negating prophecy. Paradoxically, the very same possibility of nuclear Apocalypse whose appreciation has moved people to disdain the strategic experience of prenuclear times has triggered changes in policies and strategy intended to evade the full potential horrors of the nuclear possibility. Indeed the consequences of the nuclear standoff for the stalemate of mutual nuclear deterrence have led to the situation described in the following words by Richard K. Betts: "But except for the long-shot eventuality of near-perfect defense of the United States combined with sustained Soviet vulnerability to U.S. nuclear attack, *nuclear forces of all sorts are likely to remain far less strategic (in the proper Clausewitzian sense) than is conventional military power."*[22]

Nuclear armament is a novel complication for strategic theorists and planners, but can it be said to pose difficulties so different in kind from those familiar to the theorists and planners of earlier periods that strategy has changed its meaning or its relevance? The operational orchestration of armies and navies (and air forces) for strategic effect is as important today as ever it was, unless one believes that the strategy-negating possibility of nuclear Armageddon has (or should have?) dominated statecraft and military planning. As a matter of record, nuclear-armed states have not abandoned strategic designs (though they have been very cautious with respect to action), large and small, under the influence of nuclear dread and despair. The terms of warfare change constantly at all levels—tactical, operational, strategic—with the evolution of weaponry, but the great strategic problems have a way of enduring.

For example, nuclear weapons notwithstanding, the Western Alliance in the 1980s sought new, or rediscovered some old, solutions to its strategy dilemmas in Central Europe. The maritime coalition of the West investigated how best it might exploit its superior sea-based power for the purpose of applying pressure for war termination upon the continental empire of the Soviet Union. This same problem exercised the minds of British and French statesmen and military leaders in the somewhat misleadingly called Crimean War of 1854–56. Popular Crimocentric analysis of that passage of arms focuses unduly upon the campaign in the Crimean peninsula, thereby misunderstanding the *strategic* course of the conflict. The truth of the matter appears to be that Russia lost the war not so much, and certainly not only, because her Black Sea fleet base of Sebastopol fell on September 8–9, 1855. In addition, Russia faced an intolerable threat early in 1856 in the Gulf of Finland from a massive Anglo-French fleet (as well as the prospect of Sweden and Austria entering the field against her).[23] The newly steam-driven navies of the allies could move an army from Britain to the coast of Finland and the approaches to St. Petersburg in ten to fourteen days. By way of contrast it would have taken three months for Russia to transfer forces from the Crimean theater to the Baltic coast, traveling at the rate of ten miles a day, "and they would arrive exhausted and in rags."[24]

Tactically, the relationship between sea-based and land-based military power has been transformed since the 1850s to the disadvantage of the former, as the continental states purchased agility in landward military movement through the construction of railroads and the application in road transport of the internal combustion engine. Operational relationships and their strategic implications for the conduct of war are always historically specific. In an absolute, technical, and tactical sense, troops can move much more rapidly by rail and road (let alone by air) than they can by sea. But sea-based power can still raid or seize and occupy with the benefit of surprise—provided arms control or budgetary follies do not deny the maritime coalition the services of the antisatellite weaponry necessary to deny the continental enemy fairly reliable, wide-area ocean surveillance. Moreover, the ability of the continental power to redeploy and reinforce rapidly by land (or air) depends critically both on relatively undamaged rail lines and roadways (and airfields) and on his not being distracted massively on land elsewhere. That distraction may take the form of active fighting fronts, of armies of observation of potential belligerents, and of forces withheld from fighting for the purposes both of safeguarding lines of communication and discouraging domestic and extended-imperial insurrection. In the 1850s the Russians were obliged to "observe" the Austrians, as well as discourage revolt, with an army of 200,000 men deployed in Poland, while in the 1990s the Soviet Union at least has to "observe" the Chinese.

Nothing could be plainer than the cultural distinctiveness of national signatures in defense thinking. This distinctiveness owes little, if anything, to the psychological experience of nuclear danger. Whether or not the Russian Imperial experience in statecraft and strategy is judged worthy of study by strategists in pursuit of useful knowledge, the fact remains that Soviet political and strategic culture today, including Soviet attitudes toward nuclear issues in security politics and military planning, has been shaped by a uniquely Russian and Soviet history.

THE UNITY OF STRATEGY AND THE DANGERS OF TECHNICISM

From time to time, the argument in this book may appear to have swayed perilously between the polar opposites of determinism and indeterminism. The emphasis upon geography and culture may seem to suggest that historical polities have acted out a drama on a stage already set and with a script already written. At the opposite pole, the argument that everything relates to everything else, that statecraft and strategy are a unity and that combined arms deter or win wars, may seem to imply that all factors bearing upon strategic performance are of equal importance. The question of determinacy and indeterminacy points to the heart of the argument. The geographical circumstances of a polity cannot help but contribute significantly to the shaping of the attitudes toward statecraft, defense preparation, and preferred style in the conduct of war. Insular countries will go under if they are unable to secure, or find allies who can secure for them, a working control of the maritime approaches to their homeland, or if they cannot ensure free passage over the sea-lines of communication essential to their economic functioning. Such maritime dependency mandates national or allied naval excellence. That excellence typically needs to be supported by the continental distraction of large land-power enemies so as to depress their ability to forge a first-class navy. Similarly, continental states, to survive—let alone to prosper—require some combination of superior landward fighting ability, excellence in diplomacy, and preferably maritime allies to distract maritime enemies.

To argue that there really is no key, no single essential thread to strategy which explains all as with a blinding light, may appear to reflect an absence of robust thought on the part of the writer. If this book has presented a single big idea, it is that strategy is a unity; it may be visualized as a mosaic whose patterns will vary according to the geographical and historical circumstances of the polities in question. Historical experience and speculative theory both suggest that the unity of statecraft and war is exploited by particular polities in endeavors to secure maximum strategic effect from their relative strengths, and to provide what is hoped to be at least adequate compensation for their weaknesses. The strategist true to his calling seeks to maintain a judicious balance between commitments and resources. Within this view of strategy, one can accept easily Edward Luttwak's thesis that much of strategic behavior expresses a paradoxical logic, and—with considerable caution—Edward Gibbon's (and Paul Kennedy's) argument that the price of "immoderate greatness" may be future relative debility.[25]

To argue that statecraft, strategy, and war are unities and that all of the elements which must be orchestrated for their successful conduct are important is not to argue that every element has to be viewed as equally important, nor is it to deny that each security community has some latitude in the implementation of trade-offs between elements of weakness and elements of strength. Unduly formalistic treatment of policy, grand strategy, military strategy, operational art, tactics, and technology risks sacrificing understanding of the creative, compensatory relationships among these levels of analysis. It may seem logical to compare security communities by means of the conduct of net assessments, level by level, or like with like. Again, one could conduct comparative analyses of Soviet and American policies, grand strategies, and so forth. Unfortunately for such an approach, the very nature of strategy is its creative balancing of ends with means. It follows that the quality of, for example, U.S. national security policy cannot be compared intelligently with the quality of Soviet national security policy, as in a beauty contest, save with extensive reference to the quality and quantity of instruments available for direction by grand strategy to secure the purposes of policy.

Clausewitz tells us, *"War is thus an act of force to compel our enemy to do our will."*[26] That act of force compels the enemy to do our will because of the sufficiently coercive net strategic effect of our instruments of war (in action or in the persuasive threat of action yet to come). It is not the intention at this late juncture to revisit the realm of argument over the relative importance of men and machines. Rather, the purpose here is to highlight the confusion of means with ends which a fascination with technology can encourage. This confusion has no better illustration than in the popularity of the fallacy which refers to U.S., or Soviet, "strategic" nuclear forces as the U.S. "deterrent" or the Soviet "deterrent."

Weapons purchased for the purposes of deterrence and defense attract such great interest as technologies (Will they work?), as cases in procurement (How efficiently have they been purchased?), and as tactical instruments (What can they do?) that little time and energy are left for discussion as to why the weapons are being acquired. It is probably accurate to claim that most of the people—officials, legislators, and others—who comment upon new weapon systems have no clear notion of strategic, as contrasted with other kinds of, argument. This means that the absence, or incompetent formulation, of strategic argument tends to pass unremarked. Collateral evidence in support of this assertion was provided by the public debate over the INF treaty and a prospective START treaty. The net strategic effect of these agreements could be seriously adverse for the West, but considerable labor is required in order to find any genuinely strategic commentary on them (positive or negative).

Schemes of military strategy and operational art ultimately depend upon the fighting worth of the tactical instrument. As Charles Callwell wrote in his minor classic on nineteenth-century colonial warfare: "Strategy is not, however, the final arbiter in war. The battlefield decides."[27] Callwell was following, rather crudely, the quintessentially Clausewitzian dictum that "The decision by arms is for all major and minor operations in war what cash payment is in commerce."[28] Recognition of the truth in these statements becomes dangerous if one neglects the superordinate point that "Strategy [is] *the use of engagements for the object of the war.*"[29] Naturally, strategic effect is built upon tactical prowess. It matters if an important weapon system has a technical-tactical weakness (e.g., if Turkish horse-archers can unhorse heavily mailed knights by shooting the knights' chargers out from under them, or if American tanks are vulnerable to a wide range of antitank weapons [as in 1942–45]). That is the reason why particular weapon systems fight in combined-arms teams: crossbowmen helped to keep horse-archers out of range of mounted knights, and infantry and artillery alleviate the dangers to tanks. However, in addition to the necessary efforts for improvement in the tactical instruments of war, there is no substitute for careful thought about their strategic value—albeit ultimately for political effect. The error of technicism is not the study of technical issues, but the study of technical issues in the mistaken belief that those issues themselves are issues of strategy. The claim that virtually all contemporary issues in strategy have technical referents in abundance is both true and beside the point.

For the sake of balance, it is only fair to note that the error of technicism coexists with such errors as strategism, the faulty use of history, and the placing of overmuch reliance on diplomatic skills and processes. Strategism is the error of attaching undue importance to the skills of the statesman and the general, at the expense of the military instrument which must do the fighting. The faulty use of history includes exaggerated claims for the utility of the study of historical experience for the education (or even the guidance) of policymakers and military planners today. The appeal of diplomacy is not difficult to identify: it is enormously cheaper than war. In general, diplomacy may be characterized normatively on the Western model as the processes of representation and negotiation by means of which polities mutually adjust their behavior for the purpose of maintaining international order compatible with their vital interests. However, as with flexibility in relation to strategy, diplomacy inherently is empty of content save for that provided by foreign policy. The error lies in the confusion of diplomacy with foreign policy, even in attempting to substitute one for the other. The skillful practice of diplomacy can mislead its practitioners into the strategic error of failing to notice that in their absorption with the diplomatic means of grand strategy, somehow the purposes to be achieved by those means have slipped from view.

These four classes of error are not, however, of anything approximating equal significance as dangers to the quality of U.S. statecraft and military preparation. Occasionally, ventures in strategic thinking, in historical scholarship, or in diplomatic virtuosity are applauded loudly and widely, but the U.S. defense community and those domestically who observe that community closely are in general not predisposed to concentrate unduly on matters strategic, historical, or diplomatic. The most characteristic American error is the neglect of the strategic implications of weapons technology: the error in believing, for instance, that competitive schemes for research, development, and procurement are really "competitive *strategies*."

This book was not conceived, and certainly has not been executed, as a quest after some El Dorado either of strategic theory or strategic advice. A professional Athanasian Creed for the strategist would be as unremarkable, even commonplace, as its items suffer neglect or are forgotten in the attempted practice of strategy. The broad policy goals (free Jerusalem from the infidel, defeat Germany, contain Soviet power and influence, maintain a friendly government in Saigon, or whatever) which license strategy will vary widely, but the central problem of strategy remains the same: the selection, preparation, and direction of means appropriate to secure the objectives instrumental to achieving the purposes of policy. The purposes of high policy are not above the pay grade for examination by the strategy professional, because if those purposes are unpopular in a democracy, domestic society will not tender its necessary support. Moreover, if the use of force is required, policy which falls short of popular endorsement will undermine the combat effectiveness of the tactical instrument, and hence will reduce the prospects for success in strategy.

Strategy is a practical art, comprehensible by everybody; it is not an arcane discipline with mysteries which can be revealed only to a chosen few. An education in strategy is inherently neutral as among the political values that inform policy choice, or as between rival schools of doctrinal thought. That education, rather, should train people to be able to probe rigorously all three elements in the means-ends nexi that define strategy (the suitability of ends, the availability of means, and the tie between the two). People educated to reason strategically will ask, "How do we win (achieve our objectives)?" Such people think in terms of a theory of war, which is to say a theory of how a particular conflict is to be brought to a successful conclusion. Strategists, as strategists, do not want to be told, for example, that the U.S. Navy could dominate the Norwegian Sea at the outset of a major East-West conflict. Instead, strategists would want to know (among other things, e.g., the absolute military cost and the operational opportunity costs) how such regional domination would influence the probable course and outcome of a war.

The door to strategic wisdom is opened by the posing of a simple basic question (which is not to say that it is easy to answer). The questioner, concerned citizen or strategy professional, inquires after the value—the expected *net* strategic effect—of a particular tactical instrument for the achievement of specified objectives. For example, the questioner as strategic inquirer does not want to know that a force of three hundred nuclear-armed sea-launched cruise missiles (SLCMs) can cover "X" number of Soviet military targets, leaving only "Y" undamaged (given platform survivability, readiness, reliability, and defense attrition calculations), albeit only at a relatively leisurely pace. Those may be important data, but they are not strategic data. The strategic question asks after the value of the threat or actual use of three hundred SLCMs in terms of the likelihood of the United States achieving its foreign policy goals or its war aims. In other words, what is the expected connection between a particular threat or application of force and the desired political outcome to the conflict?

As noted, if strategic sense is to be made of the many instruments of grand strategy, and if those instruments are to be employed coherently, there has to be a total vision, or theory, of success in deterrence and war. If a comprehensive theory of deterrence and war is missing, then the mosaic of strategy cannot purposefully be assembled and employed as a whole. In the absence of an authoritative conception of how an enemy (a particular enemy, that is—not some notional Red Team) is to be deterred, if need be coerced, and ultimately defeated, there are no standards by which military doctrine, priorities among different kinds of military power, force levels, or arms-control proposals can be assessed intelligently. A habit of strategic thinking should ensure that the consequences of action, or lack of action, are properly considered. In the face of a competent adversary, coherent strategy will not offer wonder formulae or magical keys for the achievement of cheap success. But well-crafted strategy enables a state to make the most of limited resources.

Above all else, strategy is a state of mind which demands to know the reason "why."[30] All levels of concern for debate and analysis are important, but there should be no confusion over the facts: that policy is more important than grand strategy; that grand strategy is more important than military strategy; that strategy is more important than tactics; and that tactics, in its turn, is more important than technology. Americans wondering how to approach the national security puzzle might begin with appreciation of this top-down logic: policy decides what to do; grand strategy decides what mix of assets (military, diplomatic, and so forth) to use; military strategy explains how force will achieve politically useful military goals; tactics specifies how forces should fight; technology is about tools.

Solutions—plans, tactics and technology—to military problems are only as interesting as the problems themselves. For example, as a matter of tactics and technology, long-range unmanned drone vehicles operating in a reconnaissance-strike mode may be able to conduct very low altitude searches of Soviet forest areas for mobile ICBMs. But at the level of operations is it efficient to hunt for such missiles— or should the United States prefer to attack those missiles (rail-mobile SS-24's and road-mobile SS-25's, to date) with missile defenses after they launch? At the level of military strategy how interested should the U.S. government be in the efficient conduct of a central nuclear war? The U.S. theory of victory in a great war with the U.S.S.R. might postulate simply that Soviet leaders would be deterred by U.S. long-range nuclear forces from using their ICBMs (mobile and fixed-site). At a still higher level of concern, it might be decided as a matter of U.S. grand strategy that the best solution to the problems posed by Soviet mobile ICBMs would be their elimination under a negotiated arms-control regime. This ascending litany of solutions to the problems posed by Soviet mobile ICBMs (strategic relocatable targets, in U.S. perspective) must be capped with the thought that policy may decide that the U.S.S.R. intends the West no harm: such a policy determination would have the inevitable effect of encouraging defense professionals simply to lose interest in agile *Soviet* ICBMs.

Statecraft at the highest levels embraces policy choice and grand-strategy design. If those top categories of official responsibility are mishandled—as they were by the British government in its treatment of Germany in the 1930s—it is all but impossible for (generally selective) excellence in the narrowly military aspects of national security to provide suitable and timely compensation.

Afterword: Sharing the Load/Shedding the Load: U.S. Strategy for the Twenty-first Century

If a single postulate could be found, a kind of core reality underpinning American attitudes about how one should approach the world, it is that the postwar world is over.

—MICHAEL VLAHOS[1]

THE PRACTICAL people who must make strategy work, day in and day out, perpetually face the future incrementally, short run by short run. It is the nature of political and bureaucratic life for there to be near-permanent fires in the in-basket. That is the reason why truly long range planning approximates a bad joke in the folkways of bureaucracy. Official endeavor in the United States is particularly inimical to the practice, let alone the implementation, of such planning, because of the glorious chaos enshrined in the constitutionally mandated separation of powers. Two centuries of the practice of what amounts to a form of feudal government, which political scientists overly dignify with the title of the policy-making process, have made worse some of the problems already embedded in constitutional forms. It should be needless to say that the institutional forms and practices which inhibit agility in U.S. policy also inhibit a foolish agility resting upon ephemeral evaluations and desires. Given the

347

tendency toward lunges for instant gratification in the short-term focus of U.S. politics, on balance it is perhaps no bad thing that truly bold changes in policy and grand strategy are greatly hindered by the separation of powers and the openness of U.S. policymakers to influence from outside.

This book has not extended its analysis very far into the murky regions of the making of strategy. The complex relationships among political setting and the making and implementation of strategy generally have been subsumed for the specific purposes of this discussion under the rubric of the concept of culture. It must be conceded, if that is the appropriate idea, that the process by which strategy is made has a nontrivial effect upon the content of the strategy which emerges. However, there is no need to concede that it is sensible to examine the content of strategy very largely with reference to the domestic and parochial interests of the players in the strategy-making process. One may detect the overheavy hand of the Admiralty (not to mention colonial, trading, and shipbuilding interests) in the British policy process which repeatedly made inadequate provision for the conduct of continental warfare. But no great perception is required to appreciate that a country dependent for its economic well-being and even for its political survival upon the friendly command of its sea-lines of communication is much more likely than not to have maritime interests very well represented in the domestic processes which produce policy and national military strategy. Military activity of all kinds inevitably generates domestic constituencies.

"Waste, fraud, and mismanagement" are always possible; indeed they are as characteristic of human activity as they are a reflection of human frailty. However, such pathology of defense preparation typically (though not invariably) is of small importance for the quality of national security. Systemic venality (according to the well-scrubbed mores of contemporary America), however morally reprehensible, has been characteristic of many military systems. The greatest importance that it has is not of the kind usually identified—villainy, the waste of taxpayers' money, weapons that do not work, and so forth. Rather, the rigorous and highly repetitive quest after detailed sins of official and industrial commission and omission displaces the consideration of strategy. Politicians and journalists would seem to find better reward in the minute examination of the procurement process than in the investigation of the suitability of hardware and procedures for the objectives of operations and strategy and the purposes of policy.

To return to the thought expressed at the beginning of this "After-word," the practical people who must make strategy work are in the day-by-day business of management. They must manage the strategy enterprise which is the national security of the United States with overwhelming reference to the threats which are perceived to be the most immediate and pressing. Those threats usually are not of Soviet aggression, but rather of withdrawal of legislative support from major programs. The level and content of U.S. domestic debate inexorably and very substantially are set by the level and content of the challenges to which officials must respond (on peril of their budget). Notwith-standing recent congressional insistence upon more explanation of national military strategy, the law of supply and demand drives the market for defense information and argument. If the Congress, se-riously and persistently, were to demand the supply of strategy ra-tionales, then the executive branch of government assuredly would attempt to provide it. What is more, an appreciation by officials that some important legislators were becoming adept at strategic argument could not fail to raise the quality of official strategic thinking. By way of a rather sad analogy, the armed services of necessity responded in kind in the 1960s to the mania for quantified defense analysis which dominated the management style and procedures of Robert S. McNamara as Secretary of Defense.

Poor U.S. strategy could well result in defeat in war. But poor U.S. strategy tends to pass unpunished by a Congress, by opinion leaders in the media, and by NATO allies, who in peacetime are not really very interested in the strategic consequences of the tactical performance of American arms. Plainly, on the evidence of the ab-sence of major war, that peacetime performance has to be judged good enough for its superordinate purpose of deterrence. Such common-sense logic liberates the legislator or journalist from the exacting necessity of demanding answers to questions on strategy. Instead, he is free to explore the costs of hammers and coffeemakers, to worry about the international legality of a weapons-test program, or to attend, very properly, to the anxieties of a distinctly astrate-gically minded domestic constituency.

It should not be supposed that the author is dismissive of those nonstrategic defense issues which occupy so much attention in public discussion. The point simply is that the mighty noise and the heat which is generated by the ongoing debate over issues of defense (and Alliance) management distract attention from, indeed preempt, ques-tions of strategy.

Paul Kennedy's morality tale, *The Rise and Fall of the Great Powers,* with its relentless explanation of the way in which the pride of empire eventually is humbled by intolerable burdens of imperial security, penetrates to the core of what should be meant by strategic thinking. The book is probably best viewed as a flawed masterpiece. It is flawed in that it takes too far the basically sound argument that state power has to flow from economic strength (anyone who disagrees should contemplate the brief and exciting story of Il Duce's New Roman Empire). As in Marxist theory, Kennedy's insistence upon the primary importance of economic factors can lead him seriously, if unintentionally, to understate both the importance of unquestionably noneconomic factors and the extent to which noneconomic factors have a way of producing economically significant consequences. Nonetheless, Kennedy's book does provide a masterly historical education for the stimulation of genuinely strategic enquiry.

What might be said about the future of U.S. strategy, viewed in the spirit of this book, which is to say approached more as an exercise in concrete, historically grounded strategic thinking than as advice or prediction? More particularly, what might be said about the strategy journey from the here of the very late twentieth century to a there arbitrarily identified as a period twenty to thirty years hence?

It would be analytically convenient to assert, as do Soviet commentators, that strategy is an accurate reflection of objective conditions. In practice, strategy is founded upon a mix of perceptions of objective conditions—i.e., subjective appraisals (guesses)—and calculations of expediency by policymakers. Any treatment of U.S. strategy must begin with identification of the purposes which that strategy is charged by high policy (or, in contracted form, by politics) to achieve.

By far the most important purpose of U.S. national security policy—identified at a level that still has operational meaning (i.e., not peace or freedom, which defy useful translation into strategy)—remains, as President Reagan argued, the prevention of domination of the Eurasian landmass by any "hostile state or group of states."[2] The qualifier, "hostile," is strictly redundant. U.S. grand strategy and military strategy since 1917 have been directed actively, with one long lapse in the 1920s and 1930s, to the pursuit of that purpose. The task of strategy has been the coordination and guidance of national (and allied) assets of all kinds for the achievement of objectives which promoted the political goal of a divided Eurasia. At present, much of the public debate in the United States is trapped conceptually and emotionally in what amounts to a time warp dating from the early 1950s. American political and strategic culture transferred its experience-based assumptions and expectations of hegemony from the Western Hemisphere to the world at large in a period when objective conditions were permissive for such transfer. In the 1940s, 1950s, and through much of the 1960s, American hegemony worked well enough. In opposition to the inferred Soviet threat in those decades to achieve domination of the World-Island of Eurasia, U.S. means were broadly adequate to support U.S. strategic objectives in pursuit of the political ends identified.

The strategy problem for the United States does not lie in the economic impracticality of the identified purposes of its national security policy. Those states with the strongest of interests in denying the Soviet empire bicontinental dominion (to assume, pending unambiguous notice to the contrary, that the U.S.S.R. remains a major player in the traditional game of nations, albeit a player in need of a lengthy rest and retraining) are amply provided with the economic strength from which more than adequate countervailing military power could be mobilized. Indeed, it is incredible that the "declinist" fad of the late 1980s could have led people to draw partial comparisons between the contemporary U.S. superstate and the Imperial Spain of the first half of the sixteenth century, or the British Empire of circa 1900. Throughout the 1980s it was commonplace for thoughtful defense commentators to charge the Reagan administration with a neglect of strategy, in that, allegedly, it declined to adopt priorities and generally sought to accomplish too much with too little. The (temporary?) retreat of Soviet strategic ambition, in face of domestic-imperial difficulties almost totally unexpected by the West, has promoted a like retreat in the salience of the charge of imperial overstretch against U.S. defense policy.

By a bizarre dual paradox of history, first, it is the current superstate rival to the United States which faces, and has acknowledged in the most unmistakable of terms that it faces, the possible disintegration of its strategy under the pressures of an economic base in very serious relative decline. Second, the relative decline in U.S. economic leverage in the world has practical meaning primarily *vis-à-vis* current U.S. allies, not *vis-à-vis* putative U.S. enemies, at least not in the near term. In the long term all things are possible, including some shifts of status among current friends and foes.

The long-claimed disequilibrium between U.S. foreign security commitments and the U.S.-grown strength of all kinds pertinent to meeting those commitments—the inspiration for Kennedy's charge of "imperial overstretch"—is in active process of being turned on its head. The strategy question is being redefined as "How little is enough?" It remains to be seen whether defense drawdown in the 1990s will be accomplished in any more strategically rational a manner than was the defense buildup of the early 1980s. The U.S. government, and certainly its critics on the left, is behaving as if it has borrowed the old British "ten-year rule." That was the planning assumption, adopted by Britain in 1919 (and dropped in 1932), that the country would not be obliged to wage a major war for at least ten years. Not excluding NATO, the bequests of the past to the present and future are a hindrance as well as a source of help. The United States needs to effect a paradigm shift in its own—as well as encourage such a shift in its allies'—thinking about the structure of the international security order.

A strategy dilemma for the Western world today, and predictably for the next several decades, is that the solution to the dilemma of Eurasian Rimland security—the United States stepping in to redress the continental imbalance of power—itself has become an important part of the problem. Conceptually, institutionally, even culturally, the Western world and its Asian geostrategic extensions still remain wedded to an obsolescent, though probably not yet obsolete, security structure. In aid of maintaining yesterday's architecture of international order, the United States has borrowed heavily from the financial markets of allies in order to help pay for the defense of those allies. In addition, ever more ingenious technological, tactical, and operational fixes are adopted or proposed for the armed forces of the West, though for the U.S. armed forces in particular, in attempts to evade confronting the problem of international security strategically.

It will not be necessary, desirable, or possible (socially and politically, rather than narrowly economically) for the United States to continue for long with an approximation of the rather lonely (the allies were clients, not partners), if heroic, balance-of-power role which historical circumstances bequeathed to it in the 1940s and early 1950s. However, in no important sense should a major downward revision in the security-producing burdens placed upon the U.S. armed forces be regarded as a *retreat*, let alone as dereliction of duty. Provided contraction in U.S. military duties is paced realistically with a compensatory shift in the locally determined balance of power in Eurasia—admittedly a nontrivial qualification—the change in U.S. grand strategy envisaged here would not be a repudiation of

the U.S. hegemonic experience, but rather would herald its vindi-
cation.

The U.S. hegemony of the third quarter of the twentieth century
was very much a trusteeship role in guardianship. In the late 1940s
and early 1950s, the U.S. military role in the defense of Europe was
viewed, in America at least, as a regrettable and temporary necessity,
pending Western European recovery from the war (and possibly
pending some politically definitive resolution of East-West security
differences in Europe in general, and over the future of Germany in
particular). The overriding purpose of postwar U.S. national security
policy to date has been the containment of the Soviet empire in a
condition far short of Eurasian dominance, not the pursuit of U.S.
glory or profit. That being so, one would think that the still distant
but now dimly visible prospect of a substantially autonomous balance
of power in Eurasia would meet with more enthusiasm than as yet is
evident among those American strategy professionals who are rightly
anxious about means-ends dilemmas.

In its social, and hence domestic political, dimension, a condition
of U.S. military power which places impracticable demands on an
extended nuclear deterrent, and which envisages the United States
as *the* principal defender of Western interests all around the periphery
of Eurasia, will prove as intolerable as it should be strategically unnecessary. Symptomatic of the gradual disintegration of Western
strategy is the authority of the strategically nonsensical proposition
that NATO's political coherence requires a rough equality of risk
among its members. How could it be that a United States totally
vulnerable at home would be as reliable a nuclear guarantor as a
United States whose homeland effectively enjoyed sanctuary status?
Relative U.S. means have declined since the late 1950s as the Soviet
Union acquired the full panoply of military superpower, while policy
ends, and the paradigm for security from which they derive, have not
altered. Opposition to those ends, which is to say Soviet menace, is
slackening, but no one can know whether that is an interruption in
competition as usual or a trend of much longer term significance. At
the present time the United States has begun what will prove to be
a cumulatively radical downshifting of its defense effort, a redefinition
of the means-ends problems of strategy as a result of an overwhelmingly political reassessment of threat. It should not be forgotten that
in order to sustain its military guardianship role in the guarantee
treaty that continues to be NATO, the United States still is obliged
to pretend that it would assume risks of nuclear catastrophe which

are an offense against the logic of statecraft and strategy. Contemporary political-military trends in Europe as a whole certainly favor NATO. Nonetheless, Gorbachev's peace dividend to a West unduly euphoric over the proclaimed end of the Cold War easily could overturn whatever benefits should accrue from unilateral Soviet force reductions and from CFE. The Soviet, or Russian, threat to European security truly is written in geography.

It is very much in the U.S. interest that no single power should dominate Eurasia. But it is also true to say both that the United States does not owe the taxpayers of Europe and Asia their security, and that the terms of U.S. security production for foreign clients should not offend grossly against U.S. strategic—i.e., means-ends—reasoning. Both the United States and its security dependents in Eurasia are clinging to objectively outdated systems of strategy and war (for deterrence). Those systems are expedient, which is to say they have been shown to work well enough, and there is an enormous political cost sunk in them. Alternative security systems enjoy only a speculative nature and a theoretical effectiveness. Those facts oblige policymakers to move only with great caution from a global coalition structure guarded somewhat precariously by the United States, to some new structure wherein linked regional balances provide the lion's share of ordering effect for security. It would be the height of folly for the United States precipitately to "scuttle and run" from the forward Eurasian military duties it has performed in so steadfast, *and successful*, a manner since the late 1940s. Wisdom does not lie down the path of a strategic-accountancy exercise whereby the United States selectively would disengage its pledged word, or deployed forces, from erstwhile military commitments. What is required is a paradigm shift, a new or much revised holistic appreciation of the strategy problem, and not a process of quick-fix pruning within an unchanged edifice.

The means-ends dilemma that is the universal problem of strategy can be resolved satisfactorily for the United States by the measured returning of regional security production to the states in those regions, as and when they are able to assume, or resume, control over their own security futures—and in the light of changing political assessments of threat. It is ridiculous to anticipate there being a strategic need for the United States to continue indefinitely to place upon its armed forces the heroic scale of burdens for global security guardianship which the early 1990s have inherited from the radically different conditions of the early 1950s. Moreover, it would be an affront to strategic common sense, as well as to elementary prudence, for the United States long to continue to have nuclear coercion as the centerpiece of its overseas guardianship strategy for no better reason than because now-wealthy regional clients prefer that arrangement.

Some readers may object that it is inconsistent for a book which has emphasized the fact that strategy is a practical art to close on what at least appears to be a somewhat fanciful note. Such an objection would not be well-founded. It is not practical, realistic, or even very expedient to assume that anything approximating the current range and weight of military burdens will be required of the U.S. armed forces very far into the twenty-first century. That century undoubtedly will witness the slow emergence of China as a great military power (albeit regionally focused in its security objectives); certainly will see the augmentation of the (again, regional) military power of the economically gigantic trading empire that is Japan; likely will register the ever firmer arrival of India as a regional great power; and may see the Carolingian revival of a Western European defense entity hinged on the Paris-Bonn (or, more likely, Berlin) axis—and associated economically at least with some of Moscow's erstwhile security clients in East-Central Europe. Even if one boldly predicts some modest success for economic reform in the Soviet Union, it is evident that the security world as tentatively just sketched is very different indeed from that in which the grand architecture of current U.S. national military strategy is intended to be effective.

The Eurasian-Rimland states which variably perceive themselves to be menaced, if ever more latently, by the geostrategically contiguous and still consolidated continental empire of the Soviet Union will be as reluctant to shed their American security blanket as American policymakers will be fearful lest visions of a new, and much less U.S.-dependent, balance of power in Eurasia should prove to be no more than the products of wishful thinking. It may be attractive to cling to the known, if creaking, security structures and arrangements of the past. But those structures and arrangements must suffer cumulative entropy as the United States becomes, and is perceived ever more plainly to be, a *primus inter pares* in the great game of nations, and not itself effectively *the* Western end of the global balance of power. Equilibrium can be provided for U.S. strategy not so much by new technologies, tactics, and skill in operational artistry—valuable and important though these can be—but rather by objective reduction in the demands for strategic effect, a reduction which will place a more modest burden upon strategic supply.

It is too early to say whether or not the Western coalition truly will confront an "empty trenches" opportunity, or problem, as Mikhail Gorbachev endeavors to translate more and more of his "new thinking" into the practice of altered military posture. When the Soviet Union completes the withdrawal and disbanding of its tank-heavy, superdivision OMGs from Central Europe, and when it "down-tanks" its other divisions, will the Western Alliance maintain a collective defense posture that has adequate military integrity? More to the point, if, or perhaps when, Moscow ends virtually all of its forward military deployments in Eastern Europe, and if (when?) the Warsaw Pact and even the bilateral security treaties linking Moscow to the states of Eastern Europe become obviously totally dead letters, could—indeed should—NATO survive, and if so in what form and for what purposes?

The message of this book is that the key to national and international security is not the ability to predict the future with perfect foresight; nobody can do that. Instead, it is argued that if the U.S. government can function strategically, which is to say can mutually adjust policy, strategy, and means—military and others—as political circumstances alter, one need have little fear for the safety of the Republic. Much of the discussion of the U.S.S.R. in these pages reflects the U.S.S.R. that demonstrably has been, and that remains today. The author is agnostic, leaning skeptical, over Gorbachev's prospects for success as a reforming czar. But, if Americans can function tolerably strategically, it will not much matter whose guess about the future course of Soviet history was more nearly correct. The United States will be able to adjust and to cope well enough. U.S. policy, grand strategy, and military strategy will never be things of beauty; they will lack Byzantine subtlety and the ruthless logic of the policy and strategy of the Roman Republic—but they will do their jobs. The Super Bowl of international security politics, like the Super Bowl of the National Football League, is about winning: there is no requirement that success be achieved prettily. Writing in 1944 on the subject of "the American Way in War," D. W. Brogan argued as follows:

> For Americans, then and now [i.e., in the 1750s and in 1944], the battle is *always* the pay-off. . . . Victory is the aim, and the elegance of the means is a European irrelevance, recalling the days when war was the sport of kings. To Americans, war is not the sport of kings but the most serious national and personal concern which they like to fight in

their own way and which, when they do fight it in their own way, they win.[3]

Nuclear dangers have bred a pressing need to be careful in defining terms of victory, but—lightly adapted for today—Brogan is correct. Winning matters, in conflicts of will in time of crisis (deterrence) as in defense in time of war, and victory is probable only when Americans compete or fight in a manner that is true to American culture.

Notes and Sources

A brief selection of particularly important sources is cited after the notes for each chapter. Also see the Selected Bibliography. It is my intention here to effect a tolerable compromise between the scholarly pedantry of foot-noting and the opposite sin of requiring readers wholly to guess as to the sources for claimed facts and asserted opinions.

INTRODUCTION: FIVE THEMES

1. John R. Galvin, "What's the Matter with Being a Strategist?" *Parameters,* Vol. 19, No. 1 (March 1989), p. 2.
2. James H. Billington, quoted in Ann Geracimos, "New Librarian Called Fundamental Scholar," *The Washington Times,* September 14, 1987, p. E3.
3. Francis Fukuyama, "The End of History?" *The National Interest,* No. 16 (Summer 1989), pp. 3–18. Fukuyama's hypothesis, or perhaps one might say his mischievous speculative inquiry, is to the effect that modern times may have witnessed the conclusion of the long historical struggle among contending schools of thought over mankind's preferred form of political and social organization. Lest one be accused of caricature, let Fukuyama speak for himself. "What we may be witnessing is not just the end of the Cold War, or the passing of a particular period of postwar history, but the end of *history as such* [a troublesome, subjective concept if ever there was one]; that is, the end point of mankind's ideological evolution and the universalization of Western liberal democracy as the final form of human government." P. 4. This pretentious nonsense is suitably treated in Samuel P. Huntington, "No Exit: The Errors of Endism," *The National Interest,* No. 17 (Fall 1989), pp. 3–11.
4. Henry Kissinger, "Superpowers and the New Europe," *The Washington Post,* October 10, 1989, p. A21.
5. Huntington, "No Exit," p. 5.
6. The cases of great wars among great powers which dominate these pages yield a rich harvest of evidence of varying quality on the broad subject of strategy. In principle, though probably not adequately in practice, the same issues of strategy could have been treated here via the mech-

anism of examples of "small wars," raids, and the like. Strategy is strategy and deterrence is deterrence, regardless of the size of the conflict, the character of the weapons, or the identity of the players. Deterrence applies to partially miscalled low-intensity conflict (it is high intensity to those at the sharp end—dead is dead, in World War III or in a skirmish in remote, rural Colombia) as it does with reference to central nuclear war. It just so happens that deterrence is much more difficult *vis-à-vis* Colombian drug lords or Shi'ite death squads than it is with regard to surprise nuclear attack by a superpower.

7. Allan R. Millett, "The United States Armed Forces in the Second World War," in Millett and Williamson Murray, eds., *Military Effectiveness,* Vol. 3: *The Second World War* (Boston: Allen and Unwin, 1988), p. 77.

8. Edward Gibbon, *The Decline and Fall of the Roman Empire,* 7 vols. (J. B. Bury, ed.) (New York: AMS Press; reprint of 1909 ed.). The volumes of the first edition were published over the period 1776–88.

9. Barbara W. Tuchman, *The Guns of August* (New York: Macmillan Company, 1962).

10. Paul Kennedy, *The Rise and Fall of the Great Powers: Change and Military Conflict from 1500 to 2000* (New York: Random House, 1987).

11. Alfred T. Mahan, *Naval Strategy, Compared and Contrasted with the Principles and Practice of Military Operations on Land* (Boston: Little, Brown and Company, 1919; first pub. 1911), quotations from pp. 161 and 9, respectively.

On the Byzantine history referred to in this chapter, see George Ostrogorsky, *History of the Byzantine State* (New Brunswick, N.J.: Rutgers University Press, 1969, rev. ed.; first pub. 1940); Peter Charanis, "The Byzantine Empire in the Eleventh Century," in Marshall W. Baldwin, ed., *A History of the Crusades,* Vol. 1: *The First Hundred Years* (Madison, Wis.: University of Wisconsin Press, 1969, second ed.; first pub. 1955), pp. 177–219; Romilly Jenkins, *Byzantium: The Imperial Centuries, A.D. 610–1071* (Toronto: University of Toronto Press, 1987; first pub. 1966), Chapters 23–26.

CHAPTER 1: STRATEGY

1. Jeffrey Record, *Beyond Military Reform: American Defense Dilemmas* (Washington, D.C.: Pergamon Brassey's, 1988), p. 4.

2. Fred C. Iklé, "The Challenge of a New Era," *The World and I,* Vol. 4, No. 41 (April 1989), p. 22.

3. Christopher N. Donnelly, *Red Banner: The Soviet Military System in Peace and War* (Coulsdon [U.K.]: Jane's Information Group, 1988), p. 19.

4. Unlike the Western Allies' great amphibious expedition to seize the Dardanelles in 1915. This scheme was probably operationally sound,

but it was tactically infeasible given the contemporary material deficiencies of the British Empire and French troops and—above all else—given their lack of fighting and leadership skills. The best study is Robert Rhodes James, *Gallipoli* (London: Pan Books, 1984; first pub. 1965).

5. J. F. C. Fuller, *The Decisive Battles of the Western World and Their Influence upon History,* Vol. 1: *From the Earliest Times to the Battle of Lepanto* (London: Eyre and Spottiswoode, 1954), p. 75. This quotation is provided as an example of clear strategic argument, not as a sound judgment on Athenian policy motives, or policy premises, in 415 B.C. To say that Fuller greatly oversimplified would be generous. Athenian motives would appear to have been as mixed and arguable as were U.S. motives in the great overseas expedition of the mid-1960s. See Donald Kagan, *The Peace of Nicias and the Sicilian Expedition* (Ithaca, N.Y.: Cornell University Press, 1981), Chapter 7. In his treatment of the much-debated question of whether or not Pericles had intended to attempt a maritime blockade of the Peloponnesus in the Archidamian War that began in 431 B.C., Donald Kagan notes that "it is far from clear that imported grain was necessary for the survival of the Peloponnesians and that the deprivation of imported grains would have been more than an annoyance." *The Archidamian War* (Ithaca, N.Y.: Cornell University Press, 1974), p. 29.

6. Shelford Bidwell and Dominick Graham, *Fire-Power: British Army Weapons and Theories of War, 1904–1945* (London: George Allen and Unwin, 1982), p. 56.

7. Adda B. Bozeman, *Politics and Culture in International History* (Princeton, N.J.: Princeton University Press, 1960), p. 200.

8. Michael Howard has observed somewhat censoriously that "while making all allowances for the atmosphere in which the decision was taken and the immediate motives which inspired it, one may still conclude that the announcement was made without any of the forethought and careful consideration which should have gone to the framing of so major an act of Allied policy." *History of the Second World War, Grand Strategy,* Vol. 4: *August 1942–September 1943* (London: H.M.S.O., 1970), p. 284. Howard concludes his anaylsis with the rhetorical point that "Allied leaders might have reflected a little more deeply on the question, whether total victory is necessarily the surest foundation for a lasting peace." P. 285.

9. "President's Speech on Military Spending and a New Defense," *The New York Times,* March 24, 1983, p. 20.

10. President Ronald Reagan, *National Security Strategy of the United States* (Washington, D.C.: The White House, January 1987); *National Security Strategy of the United States* (Washington, D.C.: The White House, January 1988). Samuel P. Huntington notes that in American usage immediately after World War II, national strategy was the peacetime equivalent of grand strategy. *American Military Strategy,* Policy Papers

in International Affairs No. 28 (Berkeley, Calif.: Institute of International Studies, University of California, 1986), p. 54.

11. The contrast is between the urge to establish, or re-establish, a universal preclusive territorial imperium (after the pattern of Rome), and the more modest goal of managing a hegemonic imperium, dependent upon the subsidization and political-religious cultural manipulation of barbarian clients.

12. Stig Förster, "Facing 'People's War': Moltke the Elder and Germany's Military Options after 1871," *The Journal of Strategic Studies,* Vol. 10, No. 2 (June 1987), p. 225.

13. Carl Von Clausewitz, *On War* (Michael Howard and Peter Paret, eds.) (Princeton, N.J.: Princeton University Press, 1976; first pub. 1832), pp. 88–89. Clausewitz's reference to the "grammar," contrasted with the policy "logic," of war is on p. 605.

14. Maurice Matloff and Edwin M. Snell, *United States Army in World War II, The War Department: Strategic Planning for Coalition Warfare, 1941– 1942* (Washington, D.C.: U.S. Government Printing Office, 1953), pp. 267–73. Marshall suspected the British of favoring a peripheral strategy in Europe which would amount to an "indecisive encirclement" of Germany rather than efficient preparation for delivery of a "body blow" to achieve a clear decision. See Kent Roberts Greenfield, *American Strategy in World War II: A Reconsideration* (Baltimore: Johns Hopkins Press, 1963), p. 59. Marshall's suspicions were not groundless and his military reasoning was impeccable. The problem was that the Western Allies were not ready in 1942, or 1943 for that matter, to take on the German army and air force *in France.*

15. Caspar W. Weinberger, "The Defense Policy of the Reagan Administration," address before the Council on Foreign Relations, New York, June 17, 1981, text in *The New York Times,* December 17, 1986, p. B-10.

16. Caspar W. Weinberger, *Annual Report to the Congress, Fiscal Year 1983* (Washington, D.C.: U.S. Government Printing Office, February 8, 1982), p. I-10.

17. David French, *British Strategy and War Aims, 1914–1916* (London: Allen and Unwin, 1986), p. xiii.

18. Bidwell and Graham, *Fire-Power,* p. 15. The Frenchman was General Langlois. The subject of British military doctrine is handled with great sophistication in Tim Travers, *The Killing Ground: The British Army, the Western Front and the Emergence of Modern Warfare, 1900–1918* (London: Allen and Unwin, 1987). Notwithstanding its general excellence, Travers's book should be used with caution. Specifically, the analysis is noticeably light in its treatment of the exceedingly important interallied context of British military effort; probably attaches undue significance to the cult of the offensive; is overly respectful of Michael Geyer's unduly bold theorizing about the alleged technocratic revolution

in the German army (see Michael Geyer, "German Strategy in the Age of Machine Warfare, 1914–1945," in Peter Paret, ed., *Makers of Modern Strategy: From Machiavelli to the Nuclear Age* [Princeton, N.J.: Princeton University Press, 1986], pp. 527–97); and signally fails to explain how a British army so flawed could have fought so well in the summer and fall of 1918. Travers is somewhat guilty of the familiar sin of forgetting that an army should not be judged according to some absolute standard of military effectiveness, but rather on the pragmatic issue of whether or not it was good enough to do the job asked of it.

On strategy see Sun Tzu, *The Art of War* (Samuel B. Griffith, trans.) (Oxford: Clarendon Press, 1963); Baron Antoine Henri de Jomini, *The Art of War* (Westport, Conn.: Greenwood Press, 1971; reprint of 1862 ed.); Basil Liddell Hart, *Strategy: The Indirect Approach* (London: Faber and Faber, 1967; first pub. 1941); J. C. Wylie, *Military Strategy: A General Theory of Power Control* (Westport, Conn.: Greenwood Press, 1980; first pub. 1967); Edward N. Luttwak, *Strategy: The Logic of War and Peace* (Cambridge, Mass.: Harvard University Press); and Gregory D. Foster, "A Conceptual Foundation for a Theory of Strategy," *The Washington Quarterly,* Vol. 13, No. 1 (Winter 1990), pp. 43–59.

CHAPTER 2: OF TIGERS AND SHARKS: GEOGRAPHY, CULTURE, AND STRATEGY

1. Jonathan R. Adelman, *Prelude to the Cold War: The Tsarist, Soviet, and U.S. Armies in the Two World Wars* (Boulder, Colo.: Lynne Rienner Publishers, 1988), p. 206.
2. Michael Vlahos, "The End of America's Postwar Ethos," *Foreign Affairs,* Vol. 66, No. 5 (Summer 1988), p. 1091.
3. Sun Tzu, *The Art of War,* p. 84.
4. Bozeman, *Politics and Culture in International History,* p. 324.
5. See John Keegan, *The Face of Battle* (New York: Viking Press, 1976).
6. Michael Howard, *The Causes of Wars and Other Essays* (London: Unwin Paperbacks, 1984; first pub. 1983), pp. 214–15.
7. Colin S. Gray, *Nuclear Strategy and National Style* (Lanham, Md.: University Press of America, 1986), and *The Geopolitics of Super Power* (Lexington, Ky.: University Press of Kentucky, 1988).
8. Ken Booth, *Strategy and Ethnocentrism* (London: Croom, Helm, 1979), p. 14.
9. For an interesting approach to national style which is quite different from that developed in this book, see Luttwak, *Strategy,* pp. 97–99, on "National Styles in Policy and War." Luttwak argues that "[i]n military policy, as in the conduct of war, there are thus definite national styles, marked by a particular position on the attrition-maneuver spectrum."

P. 98. He believes that "[n]ational styles do not arise from the permanent condition of nations" and "[b]ecause they reflect self-images of *relative* material strength or weakness, they depend on the specific enemy with which the comparison is made, and they can change over time as circumstances change, perhaps abruptly." P. 98, original emphasis. I find this to be unduly reductionist in that it tends to reduce *national* style merely to style, and to reduce choice of style simply to perceptions of relative material strength. Luttwak argues that attrition is the low-risk but expensive preference of the materially superior state, while maneuver is the high-risk but possibly relatively inexpensive choice of the materially inferior state. There is some obvious merit in this elementary formulation, but in my view it does not begin to cope with the richness of historical variety in the stylistic preferences, habits, and traditions of particular security communities.

10. Joseph Rothschild, "Culture and War," in Stephanie G. Neuman and Robert E. Harkavy, eds., *The Lessons of Recent Wars in the Third World,* Vol. 2: *Comparative Dimensions* (Lexington, Mass.: Lexington Books, 1987), p. 70. In this penetrating essay, Rothschild identifies four alternative ideas of culture: "ethnonational character," "civic commitment and social bonding," "a community's historically developed philosophical-anthropological values," and "the specific strategic, operational, and logistical cultures of specific armed forces that are the expressions of sustained institutional histories." P. 65.

11. *Ibid.,* p. 70.

12. *Ibid.,* p. 53.

13. Caspar W. Weinberger, *Annual Report to the Congress, Fiscal Year 1987* (Washington, D.C.: U.S. Government Printing Office, February 5, 1986), pp. 77–81.

14. Jomini, *The Art of War.* A powerful and persuasive critique is John Shy, "Jomini," in Paret, ed., *Makers of Modern Strategy,* pp. 143–85. As Shy observes, the reductionist and prescriptive spirit of Jomini reigns supreme in the U.S. defense community today. Shy's analysis may be supplemented with Azar Agat, *The Origins of Military Thought from the Enlightenment to Clausewitz* (Oxford: Clarendon Press, 1989), pp. 106–35. Agat judges acutely that "[t]he problem [with Jomini's theoretical work] was that he regarded his conceptions, which were a penetrating schematization of the Napoleonic form of operations, to be a universal military theory." P. 121. The debate over nuclear strategy and nuclear arms control long has been impoverished by rival ideologues who conduct defense analysis as though it were a craft that can be applied in the light of a few elementary general principles.

15. Reagan, *National Security Strategy of the United States (1987),* p. 21.

16. *Auftragstaktik* usually is understood to refer to the military method of the exercise of decentralized command, but—as John T. Nelsen II has

shown—it should really be comprehended as a pervasive philosophy for war-fighting. See Nelsen, *"Auftragstaktik:* A Case for Decentralized Battle," *Parameters,* Vol. 17, No. 3 (September 1987), pp. 21–34.

17. Bernard Brodie, *War and Politics* (New York: Macmillan, 1973), p. 332.

18. This is not to deny that Hannibal—though not the city of Carthage distantly behind him—sought total victory over Rome. Similarly, there is little doubt that in both the First and Second Punic Wars there were moments when Rome would have settled for a compromise peace.

19. J. Steinberg, "A German Plan for the Invasion of Holland and Belgium, 1897," in Paul M. Kennedy, ed., *The War Plans of the Great Powers, 1880–1914* (London: George Allen and Unwin, 1979), p. 160. Steinberg judges that "[t]he great Schlieffen never really took the Belgian army seriously." Pp. 159–60. Since the Belgian field army and Belgian fortresses stood astride the German lines of communication into France in the Schlieffen Plan, unexpectedly staunch resistance by the Belgians plainly had the potential for fatally disrupting the invasion timetable. Half a century later German racial stereotyping again was a potent source of error. Referring to the "technological surprise" achieved by the Russians in 1941 with their T-34 (medium) and KV-1 (heavy) tanks, Michael Handel speculates that "[p]erhaps because they felt far superior to their Slavic opponents, the Germans did not worry about Soviet tanks, which they assumed were largely obsolete." "Technological Surprise in War," *Intelligence and National Security,* Vol. 2, No. 1 (January 1987), p. 7.

20. Eric Larrabee, *Commander in Chief: Franklin Delano Roosevelt, His Lieutenants and Their War* (New York: Harper and Row, 1987), p. 336.

21. P. 33.

22. The Byzantine Empire was both a great continental and a maritime empire whose history illustrates most poignantly the interdependence of land power and sea power. The heartland of the empire was in Anatolia, the loss of most of which following the disastrous defeat at Manzikert in 1071 permanently precluded a stable recovery of imperial strength. However, it was the loss of sea power which, strictly, was the fatal element in the imperial decline. In however battered and reduced a form, the empire always could survive assault provided its navy could prevent a total landward and seaward siege of Constantinople. Over the course of a millennium the imperial capital fell only twice, in 1204 to the Fourth Crusade (with a Venetian fleet), and finally in 1453 to the Ottoman Turks, who had learned the lesson that Constantinople could not be taken solely by assault on the landward axis.

23. Halford J. Mackinder, *Democratic Ideals and Reality* (New York: W. W. Norton and Company, 1962; first pub. 1942), p. 11.

24. Alfred Thayer Mahan, *The Influence of Sea Power Upon History, 1660–1783* (London: Methuen, 1965; first pub. 1890), p. 25.

25. Mackinder, *Democratic Ideals and Reality,* p. 259.

26. Mackinder and Mahan have been very considerably misunderstood, both by people who were motivated to misunderstand them and by those who have not read sufficiently widely in their writings. There is no substitute for reading Mahan's founding work, *The Influence of Sea Power Upon History, 1660–1783* (1890), but there is probably more nutritious food for thought in his brilliant collection of essays, *The Problem of Asia and Its Effect Upon International Policies* (Boston: Little, Brown and Company, 1905; first pub. 1900), and in his analysis "Considerations Governing the Disposition of Navies," in *Retrospect and Prospect: Studies in International Relations, Naval and Political* (London: Sampson, Low, Marston and Company, 1902). As frequently is the case with Clausewitz's writings also, Mackinder's geopolitical theory—with its opposed land-power/sea-power centerpiece—can be misinterpreted all too easily if it is wrenched out of its historical and national-cultural context. Just as Clausewitz wrote as a Prussian of his time, knowing little and caring less about sea warfare and the kind of statecraft for deterrence and war which preponderance at sea encouraged, so Mackinder had the security of Britain and its scattered empire very much in mind in his theoretical writings.

27. Nicholas John Spykman, *The Geography of the Peace* (New York: Harcourt, Brace, 1944).

28. J. H. Parry, *The Discovery of the Sea* (Berkeley, Calif.: University of California Press, 1981; first pub. 1976), p. xi.

29. James Lucas, *War on the Eastern Front, 1941–1945: The German Soldier in Russia* (London: Jane's Publishing Company, 1979), p. 33.

30. Luttwak, *Strategy*, p. 92. Correctly, even brilliantly, Luttwak explains that operational art is not simply a description of what happens in a campaign or a theater of war (unhelpfully, in my opinion, he distinguishes theater from operational-level warfare). On the contrary, operational art is the use, by analogy, a conductor makes of the (tactical) performers in his orchestra.

31. Charles E. Callwell, *The Effects of Maritime Command on Land Campaigns Since Waterloo* (Edinburgh: William Blackwood and Sons, 1897), p. 29.

32. Mahan was very scornful of what he termed "a merely military navy," as contrasted with a navy which rested healthily upon a large maritime commerce. "It is the difference," he wrote, "between a natural and a forced growth." *Naval Strategy*, p. 163.

33. B. H. Liddell Hart, "Marines and Strategy," *Marine Corps Gazette*, Vol. 64, No. 1 (January 1980), p. 31. This article was first published in July 1960.

34. Quoted in Peter Gretton, *Maritime Strategy: A Study of Defense Problems* (New York: Praeger, 1965), p. 43. Emphasis added.

35. G. J. Marcus, *The Age of Nelson: The Royal Navy, 1793–1815* (New York: Viking Press, 1971), p. 213.

36. Quoted in J. Holland Rose, *Man and the Sea: Stages in Maritime and Human Progress* (Cambridge: W. Heffer and Sons, 1935), p. 219.
37. Gretton, *Maritime Strategy*, p. 3.
38. Paul M. Kennedy, *The Rise and Fall of British Naval Mastery* (New York: Charles Scribner's Sons, 1976), is the heaviest gun in the orthodox arsenal. The recent writings of Daniel A. Baugh make up a one-man revisionist movement that, while not wholly persuasive in its endeavor to provide a more "blue-water" view of British policy and strategy, still has value as a challenge to unduly settled opinions and judgments. See Baugh, "British Strategy during the First World War in the Context of Four Centuries: Blue-Water versus Continental Commitment," in Daniel M. Masterton, ed., *Naval History: The Sixth Symposium of the U.S. Naval Academy* (Wilmington, Del.: Scholarly Resources, 1987), pp. 85–110.
39. P. H. Colomb, *Naval Warfare: Its Ruling Principles and Practice Historically Treated* (London: W. H. Allen and Company, 1891), pp. 216–17.
40. Charles Burdick and Hans-Adolf Jacobsen, *The Halder War Diary, 1939–1942* (Novato, Calif.: Presidio Press, 1988), p. 227.
41. Halder told Hitler on April 21, 1942, that the army in the East was short of establishment strength by 625,000 (a figure that rose to 650,000 by June). The notes for Halder's presentation are reproduced in *ibid.*, pp. 613–14. See also Albert Seaton, *The Russo-German War, 1941–45* (New York: Praeger, 1970), p. 228, fn. 12. As with Napoleon in 1812, Hitler had gambled the life of his army (and country) on a quick victory in Russia, and failed. Unlike Napoleon, however, Hitler did not pursue single-mindedly a clear theory of victory over Russia. Clausewitz observed that Napoleon at least attempted what had to be attempted if Russia were to be demoralized into prompt collapse—which is to say he had to drive on Moscow, the center of gravity of the Russian state. *On War*, pp. 627–28. Hitler, determined not to repeat what he read as Napoleon's error in focusing narrowly upon Moscow, pursued operational objectives on diverging axes—Leningrad, Moscow, the Ukraine (and beyond that region, the Donets). The drive on Moscow (Operation *Typhoon)* was resumed on October 2 and proceeded fitfully with greatly weakened forces at the end of a fragile logistic trail in the face of an enemy who was accorded the time to recover his operational balance and fortify the capital in depth. The fall rains rendered rapid pursuit of the retreating Russians impossible; but when the asset of winter frosts by mid-November rendered the ground passable again, the German army no longer faced a lightly defended objective. The German advance on Moscow was halted definitively by December 5, but Clausewitz's "culminating point of victory" had been exceeded by several hundred miles and for at least two months.
42. Mackinder, *Democratic Ideals and Reality*, p. 70.

43. *Ibid.,* p. 39. Had Hitler taken the good advice proffered at different times by his Kriegsmarine and by Field Marshal Albert Kesselring and really secured the littoral of French North Africa, or had he seized Gibraltar or Malta when those options were feasible in 1940, 1941, and much of 1942, then he could have achieved the classical Roman strategic solution to the control of the Mediterranean. Hitler's theory of war, however, accommodated the sea environment only as a flank to be secured. As a German historian has noted, "Hitler's intention was to take the continental empire route to world power, and the key to this was the Soviet Union." Gerhard Schreiber, "The Mediterranean in Hitler's Strategy in 1940: 'Programme' and Military Planning," in Wilhelm Deist, ed., *The German Military in the Age of Total War* (Dover, N.H.: Berg Publishers, 1985), p. 258. Controversy still rages over whether Germany's Mediterranean commitment in World War II was a masterly distraction of Anglo-American military power, a painful dispersion of scarce German military assets in a theater whence even victory could lead nowhere, or a lost opportunity to assault Anglo-American global strategy.

44. Julian S. Corbett, *Some Principles of Maritime Strategy* (Annapolis, Md.: Naval Institute Press, 1972; first pub. 1911), pp. 235–63. The persisting attraction of invasion as a short cut to victory is well described in a book which examines no fewer than twenty-two invasion attempts (or serious designs) against Britain in modern times. Frank McLynn, *Invasion: From the Armada to Hitler, 1588–1945* (London: Routledge and Kegan Paul, 1987). The years in question were 1588, 1596, 1597, 1601, 1643, 1688, 1692, 1708, 1719, 1744, 1745–46, 1756, 1759, 1762, 1779, 1796, 1797, 1798, 1803, 1804, 1805, and 1940.

45. Mahan, *Retrospect and Prospect,* p. 169.

46. C. R. M. F. Cruttwell, *The Role of British Strategy in the Great War* (Cambridge: Cambridge University Press, 1936), p. 3.

47. Herbert Rosinski, *The Development of Naval Thought* (B. Mitchell Simpson III, ed.) (Newport, R.I.: Naval War College Press, 1977), p. 45.

48. Edward N. Luttwak, *The Pentagon and the Art of War: The Question of Military Reform* (New York: Simon and Schuster, 1984), p. 120. Emphasis added.

49. William V. Harris, *War and Imperialism in Republican Rome, 327–70 B.C.* (Oxford: Clarendon Press, 1985; first pub. 1979), p. 53.

Japan and maritime strategy are well handled in Clark G. Reynolds, "The Continental Strategy of Imperial Japan," U.S. Naval Institute *Proceedings* (henceforth *Proceedings*), Vol. 109, No. 8 (August 1983), pp. 65–70; and "The Maritime Strategy of World War II: Some Implications," *Naval War College Review,* Vol. 39, No. 3 (May/June 1986), pp. 43–50.

On the German theory of *Geopolitik,* see Jean Klein, "Reflections on

Geopolitics: From Pangermanism to the Doctrines of Living Space and Moving Frontiers," in Ciro E. Zoppo and Charles Zorgbibe, eds., *On Geopolitics: Classical and Nuclear* (Boston: Martinus Nijhoff Publishers, 1985), pp. 45–75. Also useful is Saul B. Cohen, *Geography and Politics in a Divided World* (London: Methuen, 1964).

On Republican and Imperial Rome, see F. E. Adcock, *The Roman Art of War Under the Republic* (Cambridge, Mass.: Harvard University Press, 1940); Edward N. Luttwak, *The Grand Strategy of the Roman Empire: From the First Century A.D. to the Third* (Baltimore: Johns Hopkins University Press, 1976); Brian Caven, *The Punic Wars* (London: Weidenfeld and Nicolson, 1980); Harris, *War and Imperialism in Republican Rome, 327–70 B.C.;* Arthur Ferrill, *The Fall of the Roman Empire: The Military Explanation* (London: Thames and Hudson, 1986); and Ramsay MacMullen, *Corruption and the Decline of Rome* (New Haven, Conn.: Yale University Press, 1988).

For the "life and times" of Carl von Clausewitz, see Peter Paret, *Clausewitz and the State* (New York: Oxford University Press, 1976).

The U.S. Navy's maritime strategy is explained in Admiral James D. Watkins et al., *The Maritime Strategy, Proceedings, Supplement* (January 1986); Linton F. Brooks, "Naval Power and National Security: The Case for the Maritime Strategy," *International Security,* Vol. 11, No. 2 (Fall 1986), pp. 58–88; and Colin S. Gray and Roger W. Barnett, eds., *Seapower and Strategy* (Annapolis, Md.: Naval Institute Press, 1989), Part 3.

On the utility of sea power, see J. R. Jones, "Limitations of British Sea Power in the French Wars, 1689–1815," in Jeremy Black and Philip Woodfine, eds., *The British Navy and the Use of Naval Power in the Eighteenth Century* (Leicester [U.K.]: Leicester University Press, 1988), pp. 3–49; and Charles E. Callwell, *Military Operations and Maritime Preponderance: Their Relations and Interdependence* (Edinburgh: William Blackwood and Sons, 1905).

CHAPTER 3: NATIONAL SECURITY POLICY AND MILITARY STRATEGY

1. Inis L. Claude, Jr., "The Common Defense and Great-Power Responsibilities," *Political Science Quarterly,* Vol. 101, No. 5 (1986), p. 732.
2. Michael Howard, "Men Against Fire: The Doctrine of the Offensive in 1914," in Paret, ed., *Makers of Modern Strategy,* p. 526.
3. See Colin S. Gray, "ICBM's and Deterrence: The Controversy Over Prompt Launch," *The Journal of Strategic Studies,* Vol. 10, No. 3 (September 1987), pp. 285–309. For some historical perspective see the essay "The Bolt from the Blue," in John Gooch, *The Prospect of War: Studies in British Defence Policy, 1847–1942* (London: Frank Cass, 1981), pp. 1–34. Correctly, Congressman Les Aspin, chairman of the House Armed Services Committee, argues that "the question is not whether we will have warning. The question is whether we will act on it." "What the Air Force Ought to Know About What the Congress Thinks About

ICBM Modernization," prepared text of speech at the Air University, Maxwell AFB, Ala., March 21, 1989, p. 7. It is sensible to worry about the possibility that U.S. National Command Authorities would not recognize strategic warning data for what it was. But it is also sensible to acknowledge that a would-be attacker could not be certain that strategic warning would, or would not, be received and correctly interpreted.

4. The grammatically dubious term *counter*deterrent is used to signify a military force intended to negate the coercive potential of an enemy's force. Therefore, viewed as a *counter*deterrent, U.S. strategic nuclear forces would be charged strictly with denying Soviet leaders any benefit, or expectation of benefit, from the use or threatened use of their strategic nuclear forces.

5. Winston S. Churchill, *The Second World War,* Vol. 1: *The Gathering Storm* (London: Penguin Books, 1985; first pub. 1948), pp. 186, 187.

6. The distinguished British military historian Cyril Falls, who was a participant-observer of his subject, began his important history by proclaiming: "Next [after explaining what the war meant to his generation] I wanted to do all I could to demolish a myth as preposterous as it is widely believed. For the first time in the known history of war, we are told, the military art stood still in the greatest war up to date." *The Great War, 1914–1918* (New York: Perigee Books, 1959), p. 10.

7. Correlli Barnett, *The Swordbearers: Studies in Supreme Command in the First World War* (London: Eyre and Spottiswoode, 1963), p. 195.

8. Richard Pipes, *Survival Is Not Enough: Soviet Realities and America's Future* (New York: Simon and Schuster, 1984), p. 273.

9. Understandably, scholar-critics of official practices and alleged malpractices prefer to confine their intellectual energy and ingenuity to the negative mission of finding *lacunae* in the efforts of others. For example, see Lawrence Freedman, *The Evolution of Nuclear Strategy* (London: Macmillan, 1981), particularly Chapters 25–26.

10. Raymond Price, "America's Foreign Policy Dilemma," *The Washington Times,* January 15, 1987, p. 1D.

11. Quoted in Michael Charlton, *The Star Wars History: From Deterrence to Defence: The American Strategic Debate* (London: BBC Publications, 1986), p. 35.

12. Carl H. Builder, *The Masks of War: American Military Styles in Strategy and Analysis* (Baltimore: Johns Hopkins University Press, 1989), p. 95.

13. Clausewitz, *On War,* p. 119.

14. Shy, "Jomini," p. 168. Jomini claimed that the "one great principle underlying all the operations of war" was "embraced in the following maxims:

1. To throw by strategic movements the mass of an army, successively, upon the decisive points of a theater of war, and also upon

the communications of the enemy as much as possible without compromising one's own.

2. To maneuver to engage fractions of the hostile army with the bulk of one's forces.

3. On the battle-field, to throw the mass of the forces upon the decisive point, or upon that portion of the hostile line which it is of the first importance to overthrow.

4. To so arrange that these masses shall not only be thrown upon the decisive point, but that they shall engage at the proper times and with energy. [Jomini, *The Art of War*, p. 70.]

15. Mahan, *The Influence of Sea Power Upon History, 1660–1783*, p. 88.

16. Jomini, *The Art of War*, p. 15.

17. *Ibid.*, pp. 36–38.

18. In his unfinished *magnum opus*, Clausewitz provided an extraordinarily perceptive treatment of the philosophy of war (and of statecraft), while Jomini most typically reduced the conduct of war in his theoretical writings to the military skills of the great commander. But the more enduring value of the nonprescriptive former should not blind contemporary readers to the sense that is to be found in Jomini. The reductionist method of Jomini virtually invites abuse, as even the recent history of U.S. defense debates illustrates all too amply. However, in order to make sense of a very complex world, and certainly for the exercise of policy and strategy, people do have to reduce a mass of data with the aid of some criteria for selection.

19. The rise of defense analysis in the Jominian spirit in the United States in the 1950s and 1960s is well traced in Fred Kaplan, *The Wizards of Armageddon* (New York: Simon and Schuster, 1983), particularly pp. 108–09.

20. Bruce Palmer, Jr., *The 25-Year War: America's Military Role in Vietnam* (Lexington, Ky.: University Press of Kentucky, 1984), p. 193. Emphasis in original.

21. As a realm of chance, war is permissive of great creativity on the part of individuals. Indeed, war provides scope for "genius"—not so much in the restricted sense of an extraordinary individual, but rather with reference to the capacity of many individuals to rise to an occasion and perform above the ordinary.

22. The Gallipoli venture was neither a forlorn hope nor need it have been a strategic dead end, though certainly it was launched with grave weaknesses in virtually all military departments. The position of the Central Powers probably could have been radically weakened as a direct and indirect consequence of allied success against Turkey in 1915. The Gallipoli adventure, like the expedition to close the Scheldt and destroy French naval assets at Antwerp in 1809, stands as a near-perfect example of how not to conduct combined operations. See Gordon C. Bond, *The*

Grand Expedition: The British Invasion of Holland in 1809 (Athens, Ga.: University of Georgia Press, 1979). This was the Walcheren fiasco. Fortunately, the World War II equivalent of Walcheren and Gallipoli was conceived only on a small scale as a pilot project, in part to demonstrate just how difficult it would be to secure a lodgement on the coast of France—this was the Dieppe raid of August 19, 1942. Understandably, Canadian judgments on British military leadership for and at Dieppe are roughly similar to Australian feelings about British leadership at Gallipoli and, in World War II, in Malaya and Singapore. The Canadians provided the bulk of the forces and hence the bulk of the casualties for the Dieppe adventure. It is arguable whether the Germans or the Allies learned more from Dieppe.

23. A classic case of genius in a strategy system, rather than in the ability of individuals, was the tradition of the British Royal Navy of the basic soundness of a concentration of force in the Western Approaches to the English Channel. From the mid-1740s until the end of the Napoleonic Wars, it was axiomatic that the safe course of action for a British admiral who had lost contact with a French fleet or squadron which succeeded in slipping past the blockade was to make for the mouth of the Channel. The stable geography (including the prevailing winds) of the Anglo-French wars meant that wherever a French fleet might be, and no matter how ingenious the French maritime campaign plan, command of the Channel by the Royal Navy's Western Squadron would frustrate any invasion design. The uncertainties of the weather, the imponderables of French plans, the wide variety in strategic competence on the part of British admirals, and the fragility of communications could all be offset reliably by a strategy system understood by all, practiced in war after war, and resting ultimately both upon a mastery of the relationship between geography and operations and upon a superior tactical fighting instrument at sea.

24. Frank C. Carlucci, *Annual Report to the Congress, Fiscal Year 1989* (Washington, D.C.: U.S. Government Printing Office, February 18, 1988), p. 17.

For the "strategy system" which tended to guide British statecraft and the practice of the Royal Navy in the eighteenth century, see Julian S. Corbett, *The Campaign of Trafalgar* (London: Longman, Green, 1910); G. J. Marcus, *Heart of Oak: A Survey of British Sea Power in the Georgian Era* (London: Oxford University Press, 1974), Chapter 2; Kennedy, *The Rise and Fall of British Naval Mastery;* and Daniel A. Baugh, "Great Britain's 'Blue-Water' Policy, 1689–1815," *The International History Review,* Vol. 10, No. 1 (February 1988), pp. 33–58.

The influence of Jomini on the U.S. military profession in the nineteenth century is discussed in Russell F. Weigley, *The American Way of War: A History of United States Strategy and Policy* (New York: Macmillan Publishing Company, 1973), pp. 82–84; Herman Hattaway and Archer Jones, *How the North Won: A Military History of the Civil War* (Urbana, Ill.: University of Illinois Press, 1983), pp. 12–14, 21–24 (n. 9); Richard E. Beringer *et al., Why the South Lost the Civil War* (Athens, Ga.: University of Georgia Press, 1986), Chapter 2; and Edward Hagerman, *The American Civil War and the Origins of Modern Warfare: Ideas, Organization, and Field Command* (Bloomington, Ind.: Indiana University Press, 1988), Chapter 1. It should be noted that, with minor exceptions, Jomini's writings were first translated into English only in 1854, while Clausewitz was not translated until 1873.

The Soviet liking for mathematical approaches to defense analysis is exemplified in V. V. Druzhinin and D. E. Kontorov, *Decision Making and Automation: Concept, Algorithm, Decision (A Soviet View).* Soviet Military Thought Series of the U.S. Air Force (Washington, D.C.: U.S. Government Printing Office, 1975; first pub. 1972). For a sympathetic Western commentary, see Donnelly, *Red Banner,* pp. 224–28.

The best study of Gallipoli is James, *Gallipoli,* though there is more to be said strategically in favor of the operation than James allows himself.

A superb analysis of the history of the U.S. government's efforts to design and redesign grand strategy since 1945 is Aaron L. Friedberg, "The Making of American National Strategy, 1948–1988," *The National Interest,* No. 11 (Spring 1988), pp. 65–75.

CHAPTER 4: THE FOG OF WAR, FRICTION, AND PLANS

1. Quoted in Jehuda L. Wallach, *The Dogma of the Battle of Annihilation: The Theories of Clausewitz and Schlieffen and Their Impact on the German Conduct of Two World Wars* (Westport, Conn.: Greenwood Press, 1986), p. 54.

2. Quoted in James, *Gallipoli,* p. 210. Hunter-Weston was engaged in writing letters while his troops were desperately engaged in combat. This attitude of Olympian detachment was not wholly without merit, given the contemporary problems of tactical communication, but Hunter-Weston—reflecting the British general staff culture of the period—took it way too far.

3. Clausewitz, *On War,* p. 178.

4. *Ibid.,* p. 120. In his *Naval Strategy,* Mahan refers to going "to school to War itself," and he calls war "that most excellent instructor." P. 5.

5. Clausewitz, *On War,* p. 119.

6. *Ibid.,* pp. 119, 120, 121.

7. *Ibid.,* p. 141.

8. See Paul S. Dull, *A Battle History of the Imperial Japanese Navy (1941–1945)* (Annapolis, Md.: Naval Institute Press, 1978), Chapters 9–11. H. P. Willmott has provided an admirably terse, yet accurate, summary of the U.S. advantages at Midway: "Against the enemy's superior tech-

nique and aircraft the Americans had a slight advantage of numbers [344 aircraft of all kinds on carriers and on Midway, to 234 carrier aircraft for the Japanese]. They had a more simple objective than the Japanese. They had radar and homing devices, and they had a knowledge of the enemy's order of battle, timetable and plans." *The Barrier and the Javelin: Japanese and Allied Pacific Strategies, February to June 1942* (Annapolis, Md.: Naval Institute Press, 1983), p. 343.

9. I have borrowed this pejorative term from Richard K. Betts. See the section "Strategic Romanticism" in his outstanding article "Conventional Strategy: New Critics, Old Choices," *International Security,* Vol. 7, No. 4 (Spring 1983), pp. 146–55.

10. Remarks by Representative Ike Skelton, *Congressional Record-House,* October 6, 1987, p. H 8234. Skelton was chairman of a House Armed Services Committee panel on military education.

11. See Beringer *et al., Why the South Lost the Civil War,* Chapter 17. The proposition that the defeat of the South was a political failure of Confederate nationhood is a contentious one which is not wholly persuasive. James M. McPherson points out the circularity in the low-morale theory of Confederate failure. Confederate political morale was related to Confederate military success or failure in the war. *Battle Cry of Freedom: The Civil War Era* (New York: Oxford University Press, 1988), pp. 853–58.

12. This is not to suggest that the German army was easily beaten in 1944–45. The German army was rarely tactically incompetent or seriously undermotivated. The German defense of Normandy and later of the frontiers of the Reich was conducted with a general tenacity, skill, and willingness to sacrifice which rendered its defeat a slow and bloody business.

13. See Luttwak, *Strategy,* pp. 92–96.

14. Donald Kagan, *The Fall of the Athenian Empire* (Ithaca, N.Y.: Cornell University Press, 1987), p. 423.

15. For understandable reasons, proponents of strategic defense choose to emphasize the merits of such defense for the deterrence of war, without spelling out the ways in which the defense of American society could lend credibility for deterrence to contingent U.S. threats to employ nuclear weapons. The value for deterrence from a mixed offense-defense posture has not been lost on the Soviet Union. See Genrikh Trofimenko, *The U.S. Military Doctrine* (Moscow: Progress Publishers, 1986), pp. 167–70; and the views of Marshal Sergei F. Akhromeyev as reported in Bill Keller, "Soviet Marshal Sees 'Star Wars' Giving U.S. Edge," *The New York Times,* October 30, 1987, p. 1.

16. Examples are legion, but consider the performance of the Luftwaffe's First Parachute Division in the defense of Cassino in 1943–44; or the withdrawal of the First U.S. Marine Division from the Chosin Reservoir in November–December 1950.

17. R. J. Overy, *The Air War, 1939–1945* (New York: Stein and Day, 1985; first pub. 1980), p. 310.
18. Clausewitz, *On War*, pp. 140–41. Emphasis in original.
19. SIOP: Single Integrated Operational Plan—the strategic nuclear war plan of the United States. RISOP: Russian (or Red) Integrated Strategic Operational Plan—the strategic nuclear war plan imputed to the Soviet Union on the basis of their capabilities and doctrine. The RISOP is designed to test the SIOP rather than to stand as a prediction of how the Soviet Union actually would choose to wage a central nuclear war.
20. Archibald Wavell, *Generals and Generalship* (New York: Macmillan Company, 1943; first pub. 1941), p. 10.
21. Jürgen E. Förster, "The Dynamics of *Volksgemeinschaft:* The Effectiveness of the German Military Establishment in the Second World War," in Millett and Murray, eds., *Military Effectiveness,* Vol. 3, particularly pp. 194–96. Förster records that the Army High Command (OKH) began planning a Russian campaign as early as mid-June 1940, before the receipt of any instructions from Hitler. P. 194.
22. Jonathan Schell, *The Abolition* (New York: Knopf, 1984).
23. Admiral Raeder persuaded Hitler on September 6, 1940, that as a hedge against the nonoccurrence of *Sea Lion* (the invasion of Britain), planning should proceed for the seizure of Gibraltar. Unfortunately for the Mediterranean strategy preferred by Hitler's admirals, the first British offensive in the Western Desert was launched against the Italians in Libya on December 6, 1940. That offensive had the effect of so frightening General Franco that on December 7 he withdrew the promise of cooperation with a German military move through Spain to attack Gibraltar on January 10, 1941. See F. H. Hinsley, *Hitler's Strategy* (Cambridge: Cambridge University Press, 1951), pp. 121–22. Students of the enduring implications of geography for strategic policy may be amused to learn that Hitler followed Napoleon in planning both to invade the south of Ireland and to position three divisions on the Spanish-Portuguese frontier in order to discourage British intervention in Portugal. Unlike Napoleon, Hitler did not translate these plans into action. *Ibid.,* pp. 104–105, 111.
24. Wylie, *Military Strategy.* p. 85. Emphasis in original.
25. The Luftwaffe lost the air war in 1944 because it had not been equipped and manned to conduct a long war of attrition. If German soldiers and sailors were to stand a reasonable chance of achieving victory in face of the burgeoning adverse balance of forces on land and at sea after 1942, they had to have a major advantage in the air. Because of his errors in grand strategy, it is probable that Hitler condemned the Wehrmacht to eventual defeat, regardless. Nonetheless, the price of the failures in defense-industrial planning for the Luftwaffe in the 1939–41 period of short-war optimism was paid in full after 1943 with an air force

too small in equipment and skilled operators to do what the country required of it.
26. Clausewitz, *On War*, p. 627.
27. Luttwak, *Strategy*, pp. 233, 234, 235.
28. Edward N. Luttwak, "Do We Need a New Grand Strategy?" *The National Interest*, No. 15 (Spring 1989), p. 14.
29. Michael Vlahos, "Wargaming, an Enforcer of Strategic Realism: 1919–1942," *Naval War College Review*, Vol. 39, No. 2 (March–April 1986), pp. 7–22.

The crucial subject of command is treated in Martin van Creveld, *Command in War* (Cambridge, Mass.: Harvard University Press, 1985), and John Keegan, *The Mask of Command* (New York: Viking, 1987). Bruce G. Blair, *Strategic Command and Control: Redefining the Nuclear Threat* (Washington, D.C.: Brookings Institution, 1985), and John Steinbruner, "Nuclear Decapitation," *Foreign Policy*, No. 45 (Winter 1981), pp. 16–28, address the problems of commanding nuclear forces.

Nuclear targeting questions are examined in Desmond Ball and Jeffrey Richelson, eds., *Strategic Nuclear Targeting* (Ithaca, N.Y.: Cornell University Press, 1986); Ashton B. Carter, John D. Steinbruner, and Charles A. Zraket, eds., *Managing Nuclear Operations* (Washington, D.C.: Brookings Institution, 1987); Scott D. Sagan, *Moving Targets: Nuclear Strategy and National Security* (Princeton, N.J.: Princeton University Press, 1989); and Janne Nolan, *Guardians of the Arsenal: The Politics of Nuclear Strategy* (New York: Basic Books, 1989).

For the uses of Ultra see F. H. Hinsley *et al.*, *History of the Second World War: British Intelligence in the Second World War, Its Influence on Strategy and Operations*, 4 vols. (to date) (London: H.M.S.O., 1979, 1982, 1984, and 1988); Ronald Lewin, *Ultra Goes to War* (New York: McGraw-Hill, 1978); Ralph Bennett, *Ultra in the West: The Normandy Campaign of 1944–45* (New York: Charles Scribner's Sons, 1979); *idem, Ultra and Mediterranean Strategy* (New York: William Morrow and Company, 1989); and John Winton, *Ultra at Sea* (London: Leo Cooper, 1988).

The principles of war are applied and assailed, respectively, in F. Maurice, *British Strategy: A Study of the Application of the Principles of War* (London: Constable and Company, 1929), and Bernard Brodie, *Strategy in the Missile Age* (Princeton, N.J.: Princeton University Press, 1959), pp. 21–27.

The superiority of Britain's Royal Navy as a fighting instrument in the days of sail is well examined in John Creswell, *British Admirals of the Eighteenth Century: Tactics in Battle* (Hamden, Conn.: Archon Books, 1972); and John Horsfield, *The Art of Leadership in War: The Royal Navy from the Age of Nelson to the End of World War II* (Westport, Conn.: Greenwood Press, 1980).

On arms control, it would be difficult to improve upon Patrick Glynn,

"The Sarajevo Fallacy: The Historical and Intellectual Origins of Arms Control Theology," *The National Interest,* No. 9 (Fall 1987), pp. 3–32. A useful endeavor to review the record is Albert Carnesale and Richard N. Haass, eds., *Superpower Arms Control: Setting the Record Straight* (Cambridge, Mass.: Ballinger Publishing Company, 1987).

The view that great war among great powers is going the way of the duel, into terminal disrepute, is advanced forcefully in John Mueller, *Retreat from Doomsday: The Obsolescence of Major War* (New York: Basic Books, 1989).

The Russian war effort from 1914 to 1917 is well handled in Winston S. Churchill, *The Unknown War: The Eastern Front* (New York: Charles Scribner's Sons, 1931), and Norman Stone, *The Eastern Front, 1914–1917* (London: Hodder and Stoughton, 1975).

CHAPTER 5: TECHNOLOGY AND THE ART OF WAR

1. Quoted in James, *Gallipoli,* p. 86.
2. Correlli Barnett, *Britain and Her Army, 1509–1970: A Military, Political and Social Survey* (London: Penguin Books, 1974; first pub. 1970), p. 426.
3. J. F. C. Fuller, *Armament and History: A Study of the Influence of Armament on History from the Dawn of Classical Warfare to the Second World War* (London: Eyre and Spottiswoode, 1946), p. 21.
4. The Hunnic bows were of quite extraordinary technological complexity, could be aimed accurately in all directions by their users (from the saddle) moving at speed, and offered assured penetration against armor. The weapon system was the Hunnic horse archer, not just the composite bow. Fighting power was a function of the mobility accorded by the horse, the tactical flexibility granted by the very expert horseman, and the accurate and penetrating firepower of a horse archer who could discharge his arrows *"tous azimuts."*
5. Greek fire, a secret weapon of the imperial Byzantine navy (probably invented by a Syrian architect, Callinicus), played a critical, and possibly even a literally decisive, role in the defeat of the two great Arab sieges of Constantinople in 673–77 and 717–18. The "fire" was a highly combustible mixture of phosphorus and saltpeter which could be discharged from bronze tubes on board ship or delivered by projectile. It could not be extinguished by water. Given the immense strength of Constantinople's landward defenses, the indifferent skills of the Arabs as siege engineers, and the geographical position of the city (roughly a triangle with a landward base and two sea-facing sides), the significance of a weapon like Greek fire which denied the besiegers the ability to enforce a maritime blockade or press an assault from the sea can hardly be exaggerated.
6. By way of contrast, the British army could have resolved its antitank problem by using its relatively plentiful supply of 3.7-inch antiaircraft

guns in the antitank role—as the Germans had come to use their 88-mm antiaircraft guns. Alas, the British military mind in 1941 was not a flexible and adaptable instrument. Antiaircraft artillery was deemed to be properly used only in the antiaircraft role. Also, the British army in 1941 and 1942 persisted, in the face of what should have been persuasive education by experience to the contrary, in believing that tank forces operating autonomously—though rarely in a concentrated fashion—were the most suitable tank killers. Time after time German tanks lured British tanks into lethal range of an 88-mm gun line. See Bidwell and Graham, *Fire-Power,* Chapters 13–14; and David Fraser, *And We Shall Shock Them: The British Army in the Second World War* (London: Hodder and Stoughton, 1983), pp. 147–80. Fraser judges that "[w]hat was lacking, too often, in British formations was not knowledge of the desert so much as understanding of the mechanics of war itself, and experience of working together as a team of all arms." P. 149. Unlike the British, the Germans who were dispatched to North Africa in great haste and employed immediately in defense of Mussolini's empire had no prior personal or institutional knowledge whatsoever of desert warfare. It should be recalled that Chapter 1 emphasized the importance of "doctrine of war" along with "theory of war." Mastery of a suitable doctrine of war for the orchestration of combat contributions by combined arms means that the fighting power of the whole military machine can be considerably greater than the sum of its parts. Through the two world wars, the German army persistently excelled in developing, training with, and applying in the field a true doctrine of war. That the German armed forces were not sufficiently militarily effective (i.e., Germany lost) in 1914–18 and 1939–45 highlights the critical distinction between "fighting power"—which the Germans developed very efficiently—and strategic effectiveness.

7. If NATO were to lose a continental campaign in short order, it is improbable that any small set of technical deficiencies in military equipment would be most responsible. Should such a campaign be waged and lost, it is entirely possible that the new—if probably distinctly temporary—ineffectiveness of most of NATO's antitank guided weapons (ATGW) against the reactive armor now widely carried by Soviet tanks would be of considerable tactical importance. But the decisiveness (or otherwise) of the factor of Soviet tank vulnerability would be critically dependent upon the total operational and strategic context. If NATO were undone in a short war on land it would be because the Alliance had failed to cohere politically, or to act militarily sufficiently in concert *in a timely manner,* in the face of a Soviet enemy employing deception at all levels to prosecute a "deep battle" operational doctrine truly with combined arms. In other words, viewed in technical and tactical isolation, Soviet reactive tank armor is not a war-winner. But, against a NATO Alliance which may well countermobilize too slowly, lacks the

ability flexibly to deploy and redeploy for effective forward defense and concentrated counterattack, and has a distinctly fragile logistics infrastructure, very hard-to-kill tanks must have an operational significance they would lack in a less permissive context. Reactive armor comprises boxed explosives which detonate to disperse the otherwise concentrated force of shaped-charge antitank projectiles designed to kill by their chemical energy. Reactive armor is effective only against HEAT (High Explosive Anti-Tank) ordnance, and not against the APFSDS (Armor Piercing Fin Stabilized Sabot) rounds which kill by kinetic energy. Unfortunately, the ammunition in NATO's antitank arsenal (particularly the infantry antitank guided weapons) is, by design, light in its kinetic-energy kill resources. The very rapid Soviet addition of the relatively low technology explosive reactive armor to their tank-heavy forces in Central Europe in the mid-1980s had the effect of depriving NATO's infantry of the benefit which should have accrued from the better part of a decade's worth of reequipment for antitank protection. Reactive armor does not render tanks invulnerable, but its effective negation of virtually all extant ATGW meant that the number of NATO's reasonably "sure kill" antitank weapons was drastically diminished for a while. Technical answers to reactive armor are not hard to find, but they cost a great deal of money and time to acquire. Meanwhile, the capital instrument of ground warfare—the main battle tank—benefits from additional years of major military effectiveness. For the view that reactive armor is evidence of technological inferiority—inability to produce satisfactory composite armor—and is unlikely to yield any notable advantage, see Malcolm Chalmers and Lutz Unterseher, "Is There a Tank Gap? Comparing NATO and Warsaw Pact Tank Fleets," *International Security,* Vol. 13, No. 1 (Summer 1988), particularly pp. 40–43. The authors point correctly to the weight problem posed by reactive armor for the relativly small tanks of the U.S.S.R.; to the availability of kinetic-energy and "tandem" antitank rounds for the defeat of reactive armor; and to the premature detonation problem posed by artillery fragments. However, overall, the article is as unbalanced in its determination to look on the bright side as are those writings which identify Soviet reactive armor with the crack of doom.

8. The relationship between economic deprivation and military defeat for Germany in 1918 was a synergistic one. Historians have not always been as careful as they should in tracing the intimate connections between a Germany failing in the field after four years of war and bereft of confidence in military victory and economic hardship. See C. Ernest Fayle, *History of the Great War, Seaborne Trade,* Vol. 3: *The Period of Unrestricted Submarine Warfare* (London: John Murray, 1924), p. 404. Provided it is read correctly, which is to say provided it is not read as a claim for the autonomous efficacy of economic warfare, there is everything to recommend the view of C. R. M. F. Cruttwell that "without

the blockade, it is at least doubtful whether the Allies could have forced Germany to a military defeat." *A History of the Great War, 1914–1918* (Oxford: Clarendon Press, 1934), p. 187. Functioning in malign synergism with the allied blockade was Imperial Germany's ultimate gamble in 1916 to convert virtually the whole of her industrial structure to the production of munitions and other tools of war. This was the so-called Hindenburg program. This program for total war succeeded in expanding vastly Germany's military war production, but only at the fatal cost of the collapse of the civilian economy in 1918—with the inevitable consequence of social and political collapse also.

9. Indeed, Cruttwell advises that "[a]n economic blockade had been no part of our pre-war strategy. It was not of course a novel idea, for it drew its precedent from the Napoleonic struggle. But no definite conclusion had been worked out as to whether it would be either technically or diplomatically possible a century later." *The Role of British Strategy in the Great War,* p. 98. In good part for fear of negative U.S. reactions, the allied economic blockade of the Central Powers was applied only slowly and tentatively in the first year of the war.

10. Stone, *The Eastern Front, 1914–1917,* p. 42. The German interest in waging a preventive war was well reported to St. Petersburg. See D. C. B. Lieven, *Russia and the Origins of the First World War* (London: Macmillan, 1983), p. 49. For reasons of political appearances, German officials desirous of justifying a "war now" option in the 1912–14 period had to be very careful how they handled a Russian threat perceived as maturing only by 1916–17.

11. Colonel Friedrich Hossbach, "Minutes of the Conference in the Reich Chancellery, Berlin, November 5, 1937, from 4:15 to 8:30 P.M.," in Louis L. Snyder, ed., *Hitler's Third Reich: A Documentary History* (Chicago: Nelson-Hall, 1981), pp. 268–69. This is known as the "Hossbach Memorandum."

12. In fact, to cite a generically familiar phenomenon, there were important differences of opinion in Washington over just how rigorous should be the economic pressure applied against Japan. It was not policy to embargo all oil exports to Japan, but—in practice—that is how the policy was administered. In 1941 the United States had the policy leitmotiv of postponing for as long as possible a final confrontation with Imperial Japan, but U.S. policy means, in the form of economic sanctions (particularly on oil), had the effect of accelerating Japan's decision to fight. The U.S. government in 1940–41 had little understanding of the consequences of its sanctions "policy"—to dignify the rather erratic, and even inconsistent, outcomes of official deliberations—upon Japan. Japan's internal divisions over foreign policy and military strategy made even Washington's hesitant and rather erratic course seem like a model of purposive order by comparison.

13. Bernard Brodie, "Technological Change, Strategic Doctrine, and Po-

litical Outcomes," in Klaus Knorr, ed., *Historical Dimensions of National Security Problems* (Lawrence, Kans.: University Press of Kansas, 1976), p. 299. Emphasis in original.

14. Travers, *The Killing Ground, passim.*

15. This controversial claim rests upon the following considerations: arms-control agreements focus political attention upon military rivalry; to be negotiable and more or less verifiable they have to constrain the more obvious, rather than the more important, features of arsenals; agreements can provide endless fuel for charges of noncompliance; they oblige states to worry about numerical balances which may be of small importance save with reference to political perceptions aggravated by legislated ceilings and the like; agreements serve to redirect, rather than remove, military competitive behavior; and, finally, they tend to wrench consideration of particular military "balances" out of their geostrategic and foreign policy contexts—at least in the reality of defense policy-making in democracies.

16. Bearing in mind the thesis of my text that "people matter most," it is interesting to note that a leading historian of maritime empire, Charles R. Boxer, has observed that "[t]he admitted superiority of the relatively well-armed Portuguese ships over the unarmed Muslim merchant vessels of the Indian Ocean was reinforced by a tenacity of purpose on the part of the European intruders which was largely lacking in their Asian opponents." *The Portuguese Seaborne Empire, 1415–1825* (New York: Alfred A. Knopf, 1969), pp. 50–51. The history of the Portuguese maritime empire in Asia also serves to illustrate a further persisting thread in this book: the proposition that empire founded upon a tenuous economic, and particularly a tenuous technological, base will not long endure in the face of challenge from better endowed countries. As early as the mid–sixteenth century, apparently, Portuguese ships were becoming a byword for poor construction, incompetent navigation, and underarmament.

17. The clearest statement and development of this point remains Samuel P. Huntington, "National Policy and the Transoceanic Navy," *Proceedings,* Vol. 80, No. 5 (May 1954), pp. 483–93. A recent example of such a service-oriented strategy is Watkins *et al., The Maritime Strategy.* The frustrations which attend the absence of conceptually plain, service-oriented strategy are well described in Carl H. Builder, *The Army in the Strategic Planning Process: Who Shall Bell the Cat?* R-3513-A (Santa Monica, Calif.: Rand Corporation, Arroyo Center, April 1987). Builder poses the right questions. For example: "If the Air Force has an air strategy, and the Navy has a maritime strategy, why doesn't the Army have a land or a ground-power strategy? Or a continental strategy." P. 71. No less significant is the fact that Builder provides a plausible answer. "In sum, the Army does not have a strategic theory like the

Air Force and Navy because its circumstances—its lack of control over terrain, engagement, and supporting resources—deny it the freedom to define war on its own terms." P. 73.

18. A classic, though overstated, development of this theme is B. H. Liddell Hart, *The British Way in Warfare* (London: Faber and Faber, 1932), Chapter 1, "The Historic Strategy of Britain." For a powerful critique, see Howard, *The Causes of Wars*, pp. 189–207. Theoretical inspiration for Liddell Hart may be located in Corbett, *Some Principles of Maritime Strategy*, Part I.

19. Albert Wohlstetter, "Bishops, Statesmen, and Other Strategists on the Bombing of Innocents," *Commentary*, Vol. 75, No. 6 (June 1983), pp. 15–35; "Between an Unfree World and None: Increasing Our Choices," *Foreign Affairs*, Vol. 63, No. 5 (Summer 1985), pp. 962–94; and (with Richard Brody) "Continuing Control as a Requirement for Deterring," in Carter, Steinbruner, and Zraket, eds., *Managing Nuclear Operations*, pp. 142–96.

20. Herbert Richmond, *Sea Power in the Modern World* (London: G. Bell and Sons, 1934), Chapter 1.

21. It is interesting to note that on January 6, 1915, in one of the most important documents in modern British history, the director of military operations at the War Office, Charles E. Callwell, predicted that time was on the Allies' side. Particularly because the Russians were estimated to have twenty million men of military age, it was calculated with confidence that Germany would face exhaustion before her enemies. The somewhat predetermined conclusions of this key paper ("A Comparison of the Belligerent Forces") were proved to be correct, though not on the time scale predicted, and with the United States playing the trump card role on land that the Secretary of State for War, Lord Kitchener, had anticipated for Britain's New Armies. Some members of the British government sought a more heroic role for the British army than merely cleaning up in the final stage of continental warfare. Also, there were hopes for the striking of "decisive" blows of an amphibious kind (Gallipoli, a Zeebrugge project [not actually attempted, and then only as a raid, until 1918]). British fears for the precipitate collapse of continental allies, with historical memories in mind of the repeated failure of coalition partners in the last Great War (1793–1815), further stimulated London to endorse near-term continental campaigning on a scale not readily reconcilable with the traditional British way in warfare—and certainly not reconcilable with the caricature of that "way" which British statesmen had comprehended in the summer of 1914.

22. Luttwak's *Strategy* is the most recent, if unusually ambitious, attempt to penetrate the eternal truths of conflict. In *Strategy* the author eschews doctrinal prescription—*how* to fight, wage crises, compete in statecraft—and instead endeavors to explain how conflict "works." Readers

should note, or be warned, that Luttwak elects to treat technical, tactical, operational, and theater-level interactions all as subsets of strategic behavior.

23. The rigidity of central control which characterized Jellicoe's handling of the Grand Fleet reflected his very expert judgment that only by fighting as a cohesive unit in line ahead (shades of the Fighting Instructions from the 1650s to the very early 1800s) could his ships compensate by weight of broadside for their many faults in matériel. In a memorandum written on July 14, 1914, Jellicoe (as Second Sea Lord) advised the First Lord of the Admiralty that "[t]he inferiority of the protection of the British ships of the 1909–1911 classes against guns and torpedoes is very striking. This is undoubtedly a weak point in the design of our ships." He proceeded to argue that "far from the British ships showing a superiority in displacement the exact opposite is usually the case and assuming equality in design it is highly dangerous to consider that our ships as a whole are superior or even equal [to the ships of the Germans as] fighting machines." Quoted in Barnett, *The Swordbearers*, p. 123. It is no longer very controversial to argue that Jellicoe behaved responsibly and demonstrated outstanding flair in fleet handling at Jutland—given what he, above all men, knew about the technical weaknesses of his fleet, and given his justified reservations about the battle sense of his subordinate admirals. Jellicoe assuredly lacked the "Nelson touch," but he won a critical strategic victory through the tactically indecisive engagement at Jutland. The general mêlée for a battle of annihilation which Nelson sought at Trafalgar was practicable only because the vice admiral had the utmost confidence in the fighting power of his tactical instrument. Nelson knew that in a "pell-mell battle" waged at the closest of quarters, the Royal Navy could not lose. Jellicoe knew no such thing. Jellicoe wanted to be another Nelson. But the German navy of May 31, 1916, was not, alas, the French navy of October 21, 1805, and the Royal Navy of the latter date did not bear very favorable comparison with the former.

24. Paddy Griffith, *Rally Once Again: Battle Tactics of the American Civil War* (Ramsburg [U.K.]: Crowood Press, 1987). As the title strongly implies, a different judgment pervades Hagerman, *The American Civil War and the Origins of Modern Warfare*.

25. Griffith, *Rally Once Again*, p. 133.

26. World War I was to show not only that the military profession as guardians of a science of war tended to take an unkindly view of "interference" by civilian politicians (i.e., amateurs in the conduct of war, dangerously ignorant of operational realities and inclined as a consequence to advocate "map strategy"—as with Prime Minister Lloyd George's assorted enthusiasms for Balkan and Middle Eastern adventures)—but also that a general staff culture could create an exceedingly dysfunctional distance between the staff and the fighting soldier. British front-line soldiers came

to distrust and even to hate the sedentary, château-bound staff with an intensity they did not feel for their German enemy. Much of the front-line hostility to the staff culture was as ill-founded as it was probably inevitable, given the absence or limitations of tactical radio in that period.

27. John Terraine, *The Western Front, 1914–1918* (London: Hutchinson, 1964), p. 158.

28. Truly, in Hegel's words, "the owl of Minerva spreads its wings only at the fall of dusk." The U.S. Army's belated enthusiasm for operational artistry is facing in the 1990s the strategic problem of a vanishing enemy in *the* prospective (European) theater of operations.

29. For a leading example, see Edward N. Luttwak, "The Operational Level of War," *International Security,* Vol. 5, No. 3 (Winter 1980–81), pp. 61–79; and *Strategy,* Chapter 7. Luttwak believes that his *International Security* article had a vital catalytic effect on U.S. Army doctrine. In *Strategy* he states as follows: "Since the publication of my article 'The Operational Level of War' in 1981, the phrase has received wide circulation in American military circles owing to its subsequent adoption in the basic doctrinal manual of the U.S. Army *(FM 100-5)*." P. 260, fn. 2. There is widespread agreement that a 1981 study on German army doctrine in the First World War had an important fueling role—even though its focus was on tactics rather than operational art. The study was Timothy T. Lupfer, *The Dynamics of Doctrine: The Changes in German Tactical Doctrine During the First World War,* Leavenworth Papers No. 4 (Fort Leavenworth, Kans.: Combat Studies Institute, U.S. Army Command and General Staff College, July 1981).

30. Eliot A. Cohen, "Toward Better Net Assessment: Rethinking the European Conventional Balance," *International Security,* Vol. 13, No. 1 (Summer 1988), p. 56. Emphasis in original.

31. Sébastien le Prestre de Vauban (1633–1707), marshal of France, was a military engineer and theorist of genius who revolutionized the science of fortress construction and siegecraft. He designed and supervised the construction or reconstruction of French frontier fortresses, both for the purpose of rendering France effectively secure against invasion and as bases for the conduct of forward operations. Vauban's fortresses could be taken by his own methods of scientific siegecraft, but only at the price of great—and calculable—expenditure in time, material, and men (should a final assault be necessary). The need for an invader to conduct lengthy sieges of frontier fortresses threatened the logistical integrity of his enterprise, provided time for a field army to assemble and maneuver to menace the besieger, and could promote political and strategic dissension in the ranks of the besieger should he comprise a multistate coalition of contingents.

32. Luttwak, *Strategy,* p. 92.

33. Nelson's "tactical memorandum" for his captains before Trafalgar ad-

dressed exactly the problem of how to ensure that his intentions would be obeyed in the confusion of battle and through the cannon smoke. He wrote, "In case signals can neither be seen or perfectly understood no captain can do very wrong if he places his ship alongside that of an enemy." Reproduced in Corbett, *The Campaign of Trafalgar,* pp. 448–49. Also see Julian S. Corbett, ed., *Fighting Instructions, 1530–1816* (London: Navy Records Society, 1905), pp. 280–320.
34. Robin Higham, quoted in Handel, "Technological Surprise in War," p. 1.
35. *Ibid.*

The arguable tactical, operational, and strategic significance of Soviet reactive tank armor is explored in Benjamin F. Schemmer, "Interview with Philip A. Karber," two parts, *Armed Forces Journal International,* Vol. 124, Nos. 10, 11 (May, June 1987), pp. 42–60 and 112–37 respectively. Debate is joined in the letters by Steven J. Zaloga, Malcolm Chalmers, and Lutz Unterseher, "Correspondence: The Tank Gap Data Flap," *International Security,* Vol. 13, No. 4 (Spring 1989), pp. 180–94.

On Japan's approach to war in 1941, see Nobutaka Ike, ed., *Japan's Decision for War: Records of the 1941 Policy Conferences* (Stanford, Calif.: Stanford University Press, 1967); Jonathan G. Utley, *Going to War with Japan, 1937–1941* (Knoxville, Tenn.: University of Tennessee Press, 1985); and Michael A. Barnhart, *Japan Prepares for Total War: The Search for Economic Security, 1919–1941* (Ithaca, N.Y.: Cornell University Press, 1987).

The complex relationship between technology and war is examined in Maurice Pearton, *Diplomacy, War and Technology Since 1830* (Lawrence, Kans.: University Press of Kansas, 1984; first pub. 1982); and Martin van Creveld, *Technology and War: From 2000 B.C. to the Present* (New York: Free Press, 1989).

On offense-defense relations, with specific reference to the SDI, see Colin S. Gray, "The Transition from Offense to Defense," *The Washington Quarterly,* Vol. 9, No. 3 (Summer 1986), pp. 59–72; Albert Wohlstetter, "Swords without Shields," *The National Interest,* No. 8 (Summer 1987), pp. 31–57; and Samuel F. Wells and Robert S. Litwak, eds., *Strategic Defenses and Soviet-American Relations* (Cambridge, Mass.: Ballinger Publishing Company, 1987).

The connection between empire building and technological advantage may be traced in G. V. Scammell, *The First Imperial Age: European Overseas Expansion, c. 1400–1715* (London: Unwin Hyman, 1989); and Daniel R. Headrick, *The Tools of Empire: Technology and European Imperialism in the Nineteenth Century* (New York: Oxford University Press, 1981).

Full, if not overfull, detail on the Battle of Jutland may be located in John Campbell, *Jutland: An Analysis of the Fighting* (London: Conway Maritime Press, 1986). Also see Arthur J. Marder, *From the Dreadnought to Scapa Flow, The Royal Navy in the Fisher Era, 1904–1919,* Vol. 3: *Jutland and After (May 1916–December 1916)* (London: Oxford University Press, 1966).

On American military reform and its connection to operational art, see Asa A. Clark IV *et al.,* eds., *The Defense Reform Debate: Issues and Analysis* (Baltimore: Johns Hopkins University Press, 1984). Also significant is William S. Lind, *Maneuver Warfare Handbook* (Boulder, Colo.: Westview Press, 1985). Lind's response to his critics should not be missed: "Misconceptions of Maneuver Warfare," *Marine Corps Gazette,* Vol. 72, No. 1 (January 1988), pp. 16–17.

CHAPTER 6: TECHNOLOGY AND THE EXPERIENCE OF WAR

1. Handel, "Technological Surprise in War," p. 28.
2. Quoted in Charles Webster and Noble Frankland, *Official History of the Second World War, The Strategic Air Offensive Against Germany,* Vol. 2 (London: H.M.S.O., 1961), p. 190.
3. Nelson's most critical tactical advantages at Trafalgar were the superior rate of fire of the gun crews in his ships; the high morale in his fleet and the low morale in the Franco-Spanish Combined Fleet; and the effectiveness of his system of decentralized command, resting as it did upon mutual confidence between the fleet commander and his subordinates. Luttwak's "paradoxical logic of war" *(Strategy, passim)* requires careful handling if it is to be held valid for the maritime dimension to the eight Anglo-French wars which studded the years from 1689 to 1815. Far from nothing failing like success, the British Royal Navy forged a tradition of victory which, by the time of Trafalgar in 1805, had strong elements of the self-fulfilling prophecy about it. The French expected to lose at sea.
4. Williamson Murray points out persuasively that as a radically new technology, the jet-powered Me 262 would have appeared too late, in too few numbers, and been piloted by too few veteran warriors, even had Hitler not compounded the difficulties of orderly production by insisting upon design changes for the fighter-bomber role. *Luftwaffe* (Baltimore: Nautical and Aviation Publishing Company of America, 1985, rev. ed.), pp. 238–39.
5. The Panzer Mk V *Panther*—along with the Mk VI *Tiger* and the *Ferdinand* SP gun—was rushed into production and was first employed in large numbers at Kursk in July 1943. In due course the modified *Panther* was to prove itself probably the most successful tank design of the war (in competition with the T-34). But, at the critical juncture in the Kursk salient, the *Panther* was technically highly unreliable and prone to catch fire. Moreover, the Germans tactically misemployed their new heavy tanks at Kursk, sending them forward as the break-in weapon against what must rank among the deepest and best prepared field defenses in

military history. The *Panther,* the *Tiger* (and *King Tiger*) and the *Ferdinand* essentially were designed not to wage mêlée encounter battles at point-blank range—as at Kursk—where their advantage in frontal armor protection and long-range gunnery were at a severe discount, but to conduct standoff firefights.

6. By way of sharp contrast to the military planning for the Polish campaign, Hitler intervened both with respect to the choice of axis of attack against the French and British in May 1940 (in favor of the Ardennes over a replay of the Schlieffen "right wheel"), and at crisis points in that campaign (generally on the side of caution). The victories of 1940 in Norway and France had an ultimately fatal effect in demoralizing the generals and devaluing the apparent worth of their professional military knowledge, generically promoting a "victory disease" on the German part, a faith in irresistible national prowess, and inflating Hitler's assessment of his competence as *Feldherr.* See Joachim C. Fest, *Hitler* (New York: Vintage Books, 1975; first pub. 1973), p. 634. In Fest's words: "[Hitler, in 1940] had conquered his own generals. In the light of his brilliant success over the feared enemy, France, even the reluctant generals acknowledged his 'genius' and admitted that he had analyzed the situation far better than they. . . . For Hitler himself the triumphant conclusion of the campaign in France brought a magnification of his already unbridled arrogance. It provided the maximum corroboration of his sense that he was a man of destiny." The professionals of the German army could not argue very persuasively with undeniable success. The euphoria of victory in May–June 1940 set the stage for Hitler's decision—announced to his generals on July 31 that year—to attack the Soviet Union in May 1941. The uninterrupted string of military victories from September 1939 to the late fall of 1941 (the [incomplete] Vyazma-Bryansk encirclement) set the stage for Hitler's increasing involvement in the details of military operations. His "stand fast" orders before Moscow (and Leningrad) in December, in the face of the Soviet winter offensive, precipitated the first great (wartime) crisis in his relations with the generals, led to the retirement of the commander in chief of the army, Field Marshal Walther von Brauchitsch, and on the same date—December 19, 1941—to the Fuehrer's announcement that henceforth he would be in charge, in active command, of the army in Russia. In Hitler's own inimitable words, reported by the army chief of staff, General Franz Halder, "This little affair of operational command [of army groups] was something that anybody could do." Quoted in Albert Seaton, *The German Army, 1944–45* (London: Sphere Books, 1983; first pub. 1982), p. 185, fn.

7. Very much to the point is the controversy between Edward N. Luttwak and Gregory D. Foster on the subject of whether the United States today could implement a grand strategy, should such a strategy be identified. Luttwak argues that "anybody can analyze the actions of the

United States at the *level of grand strategy,* but to prescribe a specific grand strategy for the United States at this time implies the existence of an authority which can issue commands to that effect—and there is no such authority, not even the President and Congress combined, or not at any rate beyond the next election." Emphasis in original. "Correspondence," *Strategic Review,* Vol. 15, No. 4 (Fall 1987), p. 101. Foster recognizes the mutual dependence of strategy and political consensus, but differs from Luttwak in arguing that "[w]here consensus does not exist, it is because a compelling strategic rationale has not been adequately articulated. Absent a coherent, understandable strategy, political and ideological forces will rush in to fill the void." *Ibid.,* p. 103.

8. Rothschild, "Culture and War," pp. 53–54.
9. Quoted in Paret, *Clausewitz and the State,* p. 157.
10. From the first clash at Mons (August 23) until November 30, the B.E.F.'s casualties totaled 89,864. J. E. Edmonds, *History of the Great War, Military Operations: France and Belgium, 1914,* Vol. 2 (London: Macmillan and Company, 1925), p. 467.
11. One has to beware of circularity of argument in "decisive-point" analysis. The proposition that victory rewards the side which applies superior forces at the "decisive point" can obscure uncertainty over whether the point in question was in some objective sense prospectively the narrow realm for decision, or whether that point was rendered decisive by the application there of superior forces.
12. "It is clear that after 410 the Roman army no longer had any special advantage, tactically, over barbarian armies—simply because they had been barbarized." Ferrill, *The Fall of the Roman Empire,* p. 168 (also see pp. 83–85, 129). The close-to-unbeatable prowess of the Roman army of earlier centuries rested upon its "training and discipline" which "gave it an unparalleled advantage in tactically effective, close-order formation." P. 169. Incorporation of barbarian levies in the Roman army meant a catastrophic loss in tactical discipline and tactical effectiveness. In the fifth century, more or less Romanized barbarian generals came to be the arbiters of the fate of the Western Empire: this dependence upon unreliable barbarian mercenaries was a cardinal error in statecraft which the empire in the East avoided in this period.
13. Luttwak, *Strategy,* Chapter 3.
14. Handel, "Technological Surprise in War," p. 13.
15. Alternative views of the competence of British generalship may be gleaned from the following three books, all excellent in different ways: John Terraine, *Douglas Haig: The Educated Soldier* (London: Hutchinson and Company, 1963); Norman F. Dixon, *On the Psychology of Military Incompetence* (London: Futura Publications, 1979; first pub. 1976); and Travers, *The Killing Ground.* Travers pursues his interesting thesis that the British army in 1916–18 was undercommanded by a detached, château-bound commander in chief who was unduly permis-

sive of the various methods preferred by his army and corps commanders for the execution of his strategic grand designs, in "A Particular Style of Command: Haig and GHQ, 1916–18," *The Journal of Strategic Studies,* Vol. 10, No. 3 (September 1987), pp. 363–76.

16. Dixon, *On the Psychology of Military Incompetence,* p. 80.

17. Russell F. Weigley has claimed that "Britain's quest for the total defeat of Germany undercut the effectiveness of the British armed forces by imposing upon them strategic, operational, and tactical demands beyond any they could afford to meet." "The Political and Strategic Dimensions of Military Effectiveness," in Millett and Murray, eds., *Military Effectiveness,* Vol. 3, p. 343. The problem with Weigley's claim is that although it points accurately to the fact that Britain really could not afford to defeat Germany in the manner, and at the price, that such a goal required, also Britain's security could not afford an alternative to the defeat of Germany (bearing in mind that a compromise peace was not really an offer). Each of the belligerents, including the United States, aspired to achieve political results of a character possible only through the agency of a dictated peace. In other words, a clear military victory in the field was a prerequisite for satisfactory war termination for each belligerent.

18. An insightful, argumentative and readable account of the great German adventure of 1918 is Joseph Gies, *Crisis 1918: The Leading Actors, Strategies, and Events in the German Gamble for Total Victory on the Western Front* (New York: W. W. Norton and Company, 1974). I find considerable merit in Gies's conclusion that "[t]he true and meaningful explanation of Ludendorff's defeat in 1918 is surely to be found in the extravagance of his ambitions rather than in errors of battlefield judgment." P. 268. It may be true to claim, as have many Anglo-American military historians, that Ludendorff—in the tradition of his country—was too much the tactical opportunist, too little the true operational artist, and was dangerously disdainful of strategy. But, as Gies recognizes, it does not follow that in the material and moral conditions of spring 1918 there was a correct operational-strategic course which Ludendorff could have pursued to victory.

19. Tirpitz's long-term fleet-building strategy possibly made some sense at the turn of the century, when Britain was diplomatically isolated and had its navy widely deployed in local support of British interests around the world. But the Anglo-Japanese Alliance of 1902, the *entente* with France in 1904 (which initially was not anti-German in focus), and the concentration of the Royal Navy in home waters fatally undermined whatever strategic rationale there might have been in 1898–1900 for creating a German fleet inferior to the British battle line (globally). A Britain fearful of the Franco-Russian and Japanese battle fleets, and with its capital ships widely scattered among the oceans of the world, indeed would have been very respectful of a growing German navy.

Tirpitz reasoned that Britain would not dare risk the losses that would have to be suffered in defeating the new High Seas Fleet, because such a Pyrrhic victory (from the British perspective) would leave her markedly inferior to third parties.

20. A noteworthy exception to this caution was the raid launched into the Heligoland Bight on August 28, 1914. The raid was conducted by a light cruiser (and destroyer) force, with battle cruiser support from the Grand Fleet. The Royal Navy won the tactical engagement, but the narrowness of the margin for success in those constricted waters so close to the German fleet base in the Jade estuary so impressed London that the experiment was not to be repeated. At a cost of one light cruiser (the *Arethusa*) severely damaged, the Royal Navy sank three German light cruisers (the *Köln, Mainz,* and *Ariadne*) and a destroyer. In fact, the Battle of the Heligoland Bight was indeed "no more than an ill-planned skirmish" (Richard Natkiel and Antony Preston, *The Weidenfeld Atlas of Maritime History* [London: Weidenfeld and Nicolson, 1986], p. 152), but it was the first real naval engagement of the war, and as such its outcome reinforced in German minds an unpleasant sense of inferiority *vis-à-vis* the Royal Navy. Immediately welcome though the outcome was to London, its strategic effect was less favorable. The battle helped dampen whatever enthusiasm there might have been in Germany to "roll the dice" in a search for maritime decision by force of arms in the North Sea. Understandably enough, the Germans interpreted the raid of August 28 as evidence of the continued British adherence to the offensive doctrine of the Nelsonian navy—and therefore as proof of the wisdom of waiting for the Royal Navy to venture to its own destruction in Germany's coastal waters.

21. Paul Kennedy, "Why Do We Always Prepare to Fight the Last War?" *New Society* (London), Vol. 55, No. 950 (January 29, 1981), p. 184. Emphasis in original.

22. J. F. C. Fuller, *A Military History of the Western World,* Vol. 3: *From the American Civil War to the End of World War II* (New York: Da Capo Press, 1987; first pub. 1956), p. 296.

23. J. F. C. Fuller, *The Conduct of War, 1789–1961: A Study of the Impact of the French, Industrial, and Russian Revolutions on War and Its Conduct* (London: Eyre and Spottiswoode, 1962), pp. 160–65.

24. John J. Mearsheimer, "A Strategic Misstep: The Maritime Strategy and Deterrence in Europe," *International Security,* Vol. 11, No. 2 (Fall 1986), pp. 33–34.

25. It should be recalled that this phase of the Peloponnesian War lasted a full ten years (431–421 B.C.), and that Pericles died very early on of the plague (429). My point is not that Athens actually made correct synergistic use of the maritime offense and landward defense, but rather that Pericles' strategy was the superior one.

26. John J. Mearsheimer, "A Strategic Misstep," pp. 27–28 (fn. 61), 34.

27. Congressman Les Aspin has expressed hopes for creation of a new condition of conventional stability in Europe. "Stability will create a new vision—the militarily unappealing prospects of a World War I scenario, where attacks on trenches extracted massive casualties with little gain." Quoted in Mark Thompson, "In the Senate, Concern over the Impact of the Arms Treaty," *The Philadelphia Inquirer,* December 20, 1987, p. 1E. Aspin's argument is heroically insensitive to the political realities of coalition strategy-making. A former British military representative to NATO has written of the "difficulty . . . about striking the correct balance between a conventional phase [of a war in Europe] which is unacceptably short to the United States because of the nuclear risk that follows it and a conventional phase which is unacceptably long to the European nations who are fielding the battle [hosting the event] and are therefore in the process of being destroyed." Thomas Morony, "Transatlantic Military Differences," in The Royal United Services Institute for Defence Studies, ed., *Defence Yearbook, 1988* (London: Brassey's Defence Publishers, 1988), p. 103.

28. On Nelson's initiative in preventing the van of the Spanish fleet from evading battle, see A. T. Mahan, *The Life of Nelson: The Embodiment of the Sea Power of Great Britain* (London: Sampson, Low, Marston and Company, 1899; first pub. 1897), pp. 225–41. On Nelson's decision to ignore (which is to say merely to acknowledge rather than to repeat Signal No. 39, "leave off action") his superior's order at Copenhagen, see pp. 478–84. Nelson's subordinate captains faced the classic dilemma of whether to obey the fleet commander's order to disengage, or to obey the order of their immediate superior (Nelson), whose ship was still flying Signal No. 16, "engage the enemy more closely."

29. A caveat is worth noting about enemies training each other through experience. As so often is the case, this point is not equally valid for war on land and at sea. Combatants initially less competent in naval warfare tend to become even less competent as a war proceeds. A navy beaten in battle generally is obliged to avoid further contact, pending a fleet rebuilding program, lest it invite annihilation. The maritime environment is not as conveniently separable into reasonably distinctive theaters of war as is the land. By way of illustration, the British army could learn its trade at the hands of Napoleon's marshals in the Peninsula from 1809 to 1813, but the French navy could not acquire *survivable* experience of fleet-scale war at sea. In World War II, the Western Allies were trained by the Wehrmacht in North Africa and Italy in how to fight tolerably well with combined arms (doctrine of war), to the point where the U.S., British, and Canadian armies were judged effective enough to be launched against Normandy in the summer of 1944.

30. The British official history, with a bluntness unusual for the genre, judged that "[t]he Battle of Berlin [waged by RAF Bomber Command in the winter of 1943–44] was more than a failure. It was a defeat."

Webster and Frankland, *The Strategic Air Offensive Against Germany, 1939–45,* Vol. 2, p. 193.

31. ASV/H$_2$S was a technical triumph, but quite as important was the fact that for many months it was also a tactical triumph—the two are not synonymous. Because the Germans did not realize that their surging U-boat loss rate was in important part the result of radar detection, they did not adopt suitable countermeasures until September 1943. R. V. Jones, in *Most Secret War: British Scientific Intelligence, 1939–1945* (London: Coronet Books, 1979; first pub. 1978), notes that even the eventual German recognition of the threat posed by 10-cm A.S.V. radar was not an unmixed blessing for them. Allied use of airborne radar provided so satisfactory an explanation of the U-boat losses of the spring and summer of 1943 that Grand Admiral Dönitz was not motivated to question the security of his technically superb communications system—which might have led him deductively to postulate Ultra. Pp. 411–12.

32. Quoted in Cajus Bekker (pseud.), *Hitler's Naval War* (New York: Zebra Books, 1985; first pub. 1971), p. 22.

33. *Ibid.,* p. 34.

34. Many people continue to be amazed that a democracy such as Britain could have been as successful in intelligence and deception matters as the historical record now shows unmistakably to have been the case. Michael Handel has gone a long way toward explaining why Britain performed so admirably. "There is nothing more stimulating for intelligence work than a feeling of weakness and vulnerability, from which comes the impetus to learn as much as possible about the enemy. Those in second place must indeed try harder." "Technological Surprise in War," p. 13. Elsewhere, Handel has argued plausibly that "[h]istory clearly demonstrates that an inverse correlation exists between strength and the resort to deception. When states assume that they will win easily regardless of what the enemy does, they feel little need to resort to stratagem and deception." "Introduction: Strategic and Operational Deception in Historical Perspective," in Handel, ed., *Strategic and Operational Deception in the Second World War* (London: Frank Cass, 1987), pp. 30–31.

35. Hinsley *et al.*, *British Intelligence in the Second World War,* Vol. 2, p. 169.

36. Winton, *Ultra at Sea,* p. 195. Winton is quoting an unspecified "British naval staff appreciation of the use of ULTRA over the whole course of the war."

37. Bekker, *Hitler's Naval War,* p. xiii.

38. For a familiar example, military brilliance was not required in 1965–66 in order to perceive how the United States could compete most effectively in the war with North Vietnam. The United States needed to mobilize on a significant scale, deny the North Vietnamese Army (NVA) its sanctuaries in Cambodia and in the Laotian panhandle, close the

port of Haiphong, damage military and economic targets in and around Hanoi, and pose a credible threat to invade North Vietnam (for some leading contenders). But the problem for the United States in 1965–66 was not that the U.S. military establishment failed to identify such obvious "competitive" options as the above; rather it was that President Johnson rejected options such as these and that U.S. military leaders then said, "Yes, sir!" However, although the Joint Chiefs of Staff could not overrule the president on the broad rules of engagement for the conduct of war, or compel him to pursue a strategy that he found distasteful, they could—and should—have told him that success was not likely on the approved course. On excellent authority (of General Harold Johnson, Army Chief of Staff, 1964–68), General Palmer has written as follows: "Not once during the war did the JCS advise the commander-in-chief or the secretary of defense that the strategy being pursued most probably would fail and that the United States would be unable to achieve its objectives. The only explanation of this failure is that the chiefs were imbued with the 'can do' spirit and could not bring themselves to make such a negative statement or to appear to be disloyal." *The 25-Year War*, p. 46.

39. For example, it has been asserted forcefully that the offensive doctrines which were so popular in 1914 were adopted at least in part because they served the institutional interests of armies ("organizational biases").

40. It is all too true that in 1914–18, as today, maritime command was Britain's (the United States' today) to lose. But it is not correct to claim either that an enemy "fleet-in-being" or a "fortress fleet" (Corbett, *Some Principles of Maritime Strategy*, pp. 211–28) is as strategically neutralized as if it has been sunk, *or that the difference may not be very important*. Much of the positive strategic value of superior naval power is surrendered if that power is obliged to expend its energies as a jailer on blockade duty.

41. Such important military technologies, weapons, and "devices" as, for example, the *corvi* on Roman galleys in 260 B.C. in the First Punic War, the carronades introduced into the British Royal Navy in the 1780s, and the (artificial) Mulberry Harbor of 1944 were all battle- and even war-winners only in the sense that they enabled their owners to play their military "long suits." Specifically, the *corvus* (Latin, "crow")—a spiked boarding gangway—enabled the Roman navy to wage hand-to-hand infantry combat at sea. The carronade was a short-barreled gun with great smashing power at very short range which enabled the superior discipline, seamanship, and fighting spirit of the Royal Navy to achieve tactical victory. It was among the first tangible benefits for the Royal Navy of Britain's industrial "take-off." This short-range weapon was the perfect complement—indeed it was virtually a prerequisite—to the trend in tactical opinion away from faith in the traditional line-of-battle

approach to fleet combat. The carronade was much shorter and lighter than the conventional long guns, could be fired by a very much smaller crew twice as rapidly as those long guns, and could provide a very large caliber hull-smashing, man-killing, or rigging-ruining (with chainshot or langridge) capability of value at the closest of ranges. Needless to say, a fleet relying heavily upon the short-range carronade to batter the enemy into submission was a fleet that had to have the utmost confidence in the morale and discipline of its men. The Mulberry Harbor enabled the Allies initially to avoid assaulting heavily defended ports and permitted them to exploit their basic competitive advantage in mass (of men and material) by winning the battle of the build-up (in and opposing the continental lodgement).

42. Creveld, *Technology and War,* p. 312. Rather more arguable is Creveld's interesting, if commonsense, proposition that "the simpler the environment the greater the military benefits technological superiority can confer. By contrast [to the sea and the air environments] the terrestrial environment is much more complex. . . . The net effect is to take away some of the benefits of superior technology." Pp. 228–29. Creveld *should* be correct; both tactical logic and commonsense wisdom are on his side. However, the historical record appears to show that his proposition is nowhere near as correct as it ought to be. For example, it has long been appreciated that the critical weaknesses in French naval power in the age of sail lay in personnel and doctrine rather than technology; it is much less well appreciated that the same point applied to the Imperial German Navy also. The most authoritative student of the Anglo-German naval rivalry concluded his five-volume history by stating that "[t]he personnel factor in the British naval triumph [of the Great War, 1914–18] needs to be stressed." Arthur J. Marder endorsed the view that, notwithstanding its long-enduring material problems, the British Royal Navy had a self-confidence resting upon a tradition of victory and an *esprit de corps* that the Germans could not match. Indeed, Marder argues that "[t]he German Navy collapsed in part because it overlooked the fundamental truth that the human factor is always the decisive one." *From the Dreadnought to Scapa Flow, The Royal Navy in the Fisher Era, 1904–1919,* Vol. 5: *Victory and Aftermath (January 1918–June 1919)* (London: Oxford University Press, 1970), pp. 330, 332–33.

For ship detail on the age of fighting sail, see Brian Lavery, *The Ship of the Line,* Vol. 1: *The Development of the Battlefleet, 1650–1850* (Annapolis, Md.: Naval Institute Press, 1983).

The better general histories of the First World War include: Cruttwell, *A History of the Great War;* B. H. Liddell Hart, *History of the Great War* (London: Pan Books, 1972; first pub. 1934); Falls, *The Great War, 1914–1918;* John Terraine, *The First World War, 1914–18* (London: Leo Cooper, 1983; first pub. 1965); Marc Ferro, *The Great War, 1914–1918* (London:

Routledge and Kegan Paul, 1973; first pub. 1969); and Trevor Wilson, *The Myriad Faces of War: Britain and the Great War, 1914–1918* (Cambridge: Polity Press, 1986). For Sir Douglas Haig's explanation of the duration of the war, the casualties suffered, and the military methods employed, see "The Final Dispatch," in J. H. Boraston, ed., *Sir Douglas Haig's Dispatches (December 1915–April 1919)* (London: J. M. Dent and Sons, 1979; first pub. 1919), especially pp. 319–33. An indispensable, if again necessarily self-serving, view from the other side of the hill is General Ludendorff, *My War Memories, 1914–1918,* 2 vols. (London: Hutchinson and Company, no date [but written in 1918–19]).

Particularly stimulating studies of the Imperial German Navy are Rosinski, *The Development of Naval Thought,* pp. 53–59, 69–91; Holger H. Herwig, *"Luxury Fleet": The Imperial German Navy, 1888–1918* (London: George Allen and Unwin, 1980); Paul Kennedy, *Strategy and Diplomacy, 1870–1945: Eight Studies* (London: George Allen and Unwin, 1983), pp. 129–60; and Ivo Nicolai Lambi, *The Navy and German Power Politics, 1862–1914* (Boston: Allen and Unwin, 1984).

The Royal Navy's response to the German challenge, a challenge perceived very clearly as early as 1901–02, is detailed admirably in Arthur J. Marder, *From the Dreadnought to Scapa Flow, the Royal Navy in the Fisher Era, 1904–1919,* Vol. 1: *The Road to War, 1904–1914* (London: Oxford University Press, 1961). See also E. L. Woodward, *Great Britain and the German Navy* (London: Frank Cass and Company, 1964; first pub. 1935); and Aaron L. Friedberg, *The Weary Titan: Britain and the Experience of Relative Decline, 1895–1905* (Princeton, N.J.: Princeton University Press, 1988), Chapter 4.

The Battle of the Heligoland Bight (August 28, 1914) is summarized and analyzed in Julian S. Corbett, *History of the Great War, Naval Operations,* Vol. 1: *To the Battle of the Falklands, December 1914* (London: Longmans, Green and Company, 1920), Chapter 7; and Geoffrey Bennett, *Naval Battles of the First World War* (London: B. T. Batsford, 1968), Chapter 7.

Technological and tactical innovations in World War I may be approached via Wilhelm Balck, *Development of Tactics—World War* (Ft. Leavenworth, Kans.: General Service Schools Press, 1922); Pascal M. H. Lucas (Lt. Col., French Army), *The Evolution of Tactical Ideas in France and Germany During the War of 1914–1918* (trans. P. V. Kieffer) (Fort Leavenworth, Kans.: U.S. Army Command and General Staff College, 1925; first pub. 1923); G. C. Wynne, *If Germany Attacks: The Battle in Depth in the West* (Westport, Conn.: Greenwood Press, 1976; first pub. 1940); John Terraine, *White Heat: The New Warfare, 1914–18* (London: Sidgwick and Jackson, 1982); and Guy Hartcup, *The War of Invention: Scientific Developments, 1914–18* (London: Brassey's Defence Publishers, 1988).

By way of introduction to the much, if not over-, debated subject of the war aims of the belligerents in the Great War, see Fritz Fischer, *Germany's Aims in the First World War* (New York: W. W. Norton and Company,

1967; first pub. 1961); V. H. Rothwell, *British War Aims and Peace Diplomacy, 1914–1918* (Oxford: Clarendon Press, 1971); Barry Hunt and Adrian Preston, eds., *War Aims and Strategic Policy in the Great War, 1914–1918* (London: Croom, Helm, 1977); D. Stevenson, *French War Aims Against Germany, 1914–1919* (Oxford: Clarendon Press, 1982). The war aims of Nazi Germany are discussed brilliantly in Norman Rich, *Hitler's War Aims,* Vol. 1: *Ideology, the Nazi State, and the Course of Expansion,* and Vol. 2: *The Establishment of the New Order* (New York: W. W. Norton and Company, 1973 and 1974).

The American air war from 1941 to 1945 is handled superbly in the seven-volume official history, Wesley Frank Caven and James L. Cate, eds., *The Army Air Forces in World War II* (Chicago: University of Chicago Press, 1948–55). Given their dates of publication, these volumes could not give intelligence assets their due recognition. On the British side (in addition to Webster and Frankland, note 2, this chapter) see Overy, *The Air War, 1939–1945;* Terraine, *A Time for Courage;* and Martin Middlebrook, *The Berlin Raids: R.A.F. Bomber Command, Winter 1943–44* (New York: Viking Penguin, 1988).

The battles of the Atlantic in both world wars are examined in Dan van der Vat, *The Atlantic Campaigns: The Great Struggle at Sea, 1939–1945* (London: Hodder and Stoughton, 1988); and John Terraine, *Business in Great Waters: The U-Boat Wars, 1916–1945* (London: Leo Cooper, 1989).

The Pacific war has been revealed in a plenitude of good readable battle and campaign histories (preeminently in no fewer than nine of the volumes in Samuel Eliot Morison's monumental *History of United States Naval Operations in World War II* [Boston: Little, Brown and Company, 1947–62]). But adequate strategic histories of that war remain in woefully short supply. In addition to the U.S. Army's splendid official campaign histories in *The War in the Pacific* series, readers are recommended strongly to consult Richard M. Leighton and Robert W. Coakley, *United States Army in World War II, The War Department: Global Logistics and Strategy,* 2 vols. (1940–43 and 1943–45) (Washington, D.C.: U.S. Government Printing Office, 1955 and 1968); and Matloff and Snell, *Strategic Planning for Coalition Warfare,* 2 vols. For a useful bibliographical essay, see Ronald H. Spector, *Eagle Against the Sun: The American War with Japan* (New York: Free Press, 1985), pp. 567–72. Also see Christopher Thorne, *Allies of a Kind: The United States, Britain and the War Against Japan, 1941–1945* (New York: Oxford University Press, 1978); and John Costello, *The Pacific War* (New York: Quill, 1982). There is much of value for strategic understanding in Jeter A. Isely and Philip A. Crowl, *The U.S. Marines and Amphibious War: Its Theory, and Its Practice in the Pacific* (Princeton, N.J.: Princeton University Press, 1952); Dull, *A Battle History of the Imperial Japanese Navy;* H. P. Willmott, *Empires in the Balance: Japanese and Allied Pacific Strategies to April 1942* (Annapolis, Md.: Naval Institute Press, 1982); and *idem, The Barrier and the Javelin.*

**CHAPTER 7: THE SOVIET UNION AND THE STRATEGY OF
CONTINENTAL EMPIRE**

1. James Sherr, *Soviet Power: The Continuing Challenge* (New York: St. Martin's Press, 1987), p. 111.
2. Soviet terminology is very formalistic, precise, and different from that current in the West. "Soviet military science *[voyennaya nauka]* is a unified system of knowledge about preparation for, and waging of, war in the interests of the defense of the Soviet Union." S. N. Kozlov, ed., *The Officer's Handbook (A Soviet View),* Soviet Military Thought Series of the U.S. Air Force (Washington, D.C.: U.S. Government Printing Office, 1977; Moscow, 1971), p. 47. Knowledge of war is subordinate to military doctrine *(voyennaya doktrina),* which is "an officially accepted system of views in a given state and in its armed forces on the nature of war and methods of conducting it and on preparations of the country and army for war." Marshal A. A. Grechko, quoted in Harriet Fast Scott and William F. Scott, eds., *The Soviet Art of War: Doctrine, Strategy, and Tactics* (Boulder, Colo.: Westview Press, 1982), p. 4. The Soviet military science, which is subordinate to, yet which influences, military doctrine, has as its most important element what Soviet authorities term military art. "The theory of military art . . . studies and elaborates actual methods and forms of armed combat." Kozlov, ed., *The Officer's Handbook,* p. 57. For an excellent brief treatment of the language of Soviet military theory see Scott and Scott, eds., *The Soviet Art of War,* pp. 4–9. For easily accessible Soviet texts, readers should consult the items in the Soviet "Officer's Library" series translated and published by the U.S. Government Printing Office under the auspices of the U.S. Air Force. A comprehensive listing of items in the series— those available and those not—may be located in Harriet Fast Scott and William F. Scott, *Soviet Military Doctrine: Continuity, Formulation, and Dissemination* (Boulder, Colo.: Westview Press, 1988), "Appendix D: Original Plan of the Officer's Library Series," pp. 275–77.
3. Adam B. Ulam, *The Bolsheviks: The Intellectual and Political History of the Triumph of Communism in Russia* (New York: Collier Books, 1968; first pub. 1965), p. 179.
4. In his article "Do We Need a New Grand Strategy?" Luttwak argues that "[w]hat matters to us is that Soviet conduct so far has *not* been the normal conduct of a normal Great Power; it has resembled, rather, that of a Great Power at war." P. 3. Emphasis in original.
5. See R. W. Seton-Watson, *Disraeli, Gladstone, and the Eastern Question: A Study in Diplomacy and Party Politics* (New York: W. W. Norton and Company, 1972; first pub. 1935). It was ironic, first, that Britain, having "bolstered up Turkey" throughout the nineteenth century against Russian designs on the Straits (the Dardanelles) and hence possibly on the Mediterranean lifeline of the British Empire in the East, should

have conceded promptly to St. Petersburg a free hand over Constantinople as a spoil of war in 1914. Second, it was ironic that many of those liberal-minded British "Serbophiles"—including R. W. Seton-Watson whose book has been cited above—who helped create the new Serbian empire of Yugoslavia in 1919 (not to mention the greater Rumania) were to find in the 1920s that their much-admired Serbs were every bit as tyrannical in the imperial role (over Croats, Slovenes, Montenegrins, Albanians, and others) as had been the Turks. It should be remembered that the much decayed but still massive Ottoman Empire of the nineteenth century bestrode the land bridge to the jewel in Queen Victoria's imperial crown—India. Many modern critics of Britain's "Eastern" ventures in the First World War (Gallipoli, Palestine, and Mesopotamia, preeminently) are disposed to forget or discount the fact that the very India-minded British governments of 1914–16 were extremely sensitive to the threat which Turkish-inspired religious discontent could pose to the domestic tranquillity of the British Empire beyond Suez. John Buchan's novel *Greenmantle* (London: Hodder and Stoughton, 1916) spoke accurately to British fears.

6. Robert C. Tucker argues that "[a] sustaining myth is a notion or concept of that society [any society] as a common enterprise. It represents what is distinctively valuable about the society from the standpoint of its members." *Political Culture and Leadership in Soviet Russia: From Lenin to Gorbachev* (New York: W. W. Norton and Company, 1987), p. 22.

7. The Byzantine influence, though pervasive, nonetheless should not be exaggerated. After all, from 1240 to 1480 *the* "Russian" diplomatic problem was the agile management of its subordinate status as a vassal of the Tatars. Charles J. Halperin notes rightly that "[g]iven the importance of Russia's relations with its oriental neighbors, it is natural that Muscovy drew upon Tatar diplomatic practices in establishing its own. Accordingly, Muscovite diplomatic protocol was essentially Asian." *Russia and the Golden Horde: The Mongol Impact on Medieval Russian History* (Bloomington, Ind.: Indiana University Press, 1987; first pub. 1985), p. 92. Errors in diplomatic protocol could prove personally fatal to Russian envoys.

8. Hence Clausewitz's incomplete treatment of the distinctions between "real war" and "absolute war" or "ideal war"—with the latter posed as a matter of philosophical truth or logic, rather than historical fact. Clausewitz, *On War*, p. 88. When Clausewitz wrote forcefully about the carnage of war and the need to shed blood to achieve decision, he was both pointing to the essential character of armed struggle (a philosophical argument) and passing on the firsthand experience of a professional soldier who was contemptuous of those theorists who designed schemes for victory without pain.

9. Trofimenko, *The U.S. Military Doctrine*, p. 33.

10. Kozlov, ed., *The Officer's Handbook,* p. 65.

11. Bozeman, *Politics and Culture in International History,* p. 338.

12. A fact endorsed by Gorbachev's campaign to assert Soviet legality. Mikhail Gorbachev's book, *Perestroika: New Thinking for Our Country and the World* (New York: Harper and Row, 1987), contains many collector's items in the realm of hypocrisy in the section "Observance of Law—An Indispensable Element in Democratization" (pp. 105–10). While Gorbachev justly upbraids the lawlessness of Stalin's rule (pp. 106–07), readers should be surprised to learn that "[f]rom the very beginning of Soviet rule Lenin and the Party attached paramount importance to the maintenance and consolidation of law."

13. Through better campaign direction in 1941, before the mud generated by the fall rains halted movement, the Germans might have dealt the U.S.S.R. a blow from which it could not have recovered. However, even with the confusion over operational objectives which actually obtained, the war in the East still might have been won had Nazi Germany been able, culturally and programmatically, to organize and exploit the newly conquered former Soviet territories as willing clients. For racial and pseudogeopolitical reasons, Nazi Germany was entirely incapable of functioning as a liberator. In 1941 Hitler told his intimates that his purpose in the East was "to Germanize this country by the immigration of Germans, and to look upon the natives as Redskins." Quoted in Rich, *Hitler's War Aims,* Vol. 2, p. 330. The indigenous Slavic population (apart from Jews, Communist Party officials, and the like—who were to be shot promptly) was to be used as a reservoir of slave labor for the gigantic tasks of physical construction which Hitler intended for the East. Hitler's geopolitical vision for Germany was that of Mackinder's Eurasian Heartland (*Democratic Ideals and Reality,* pp. 74, 110, 259–60, 262). In Rich's words: "[W]ith the conquest of Russia, the German people would have been given what it needed to assert its position in the world. The possession of Russian space would make Europe an impregnable fortress, safe from all threat of blockade." *Hitler's War Aims,* Vol. 2, p. 330.

14. For unmitigated gall, Gorbachev's performance at the signing ceremony for the INF treaty at the Washington Summit in December 1987 would be difficult to beat. The Soviet leader thanked the peace activists who had contributed so usefully to the political process which eventually gave birth to the treaty. In fact, the peace activists threatened the steadiness of NATO's deployment plans and hence imperiled the basis for any arms-control agreement.

15. Quoted in Rich, *Hitler's War Aims,* Vol. 2, p. 419. The geopolitical logic of Eurasian continental empire as a secure base from which eventually the Americas could be assailed is central to Nicholas John Spykman, *America's Strategy in World Politics: The United States and the*

Balance of Power (Hamden, Conn.: Archon Books, 1970; first pub. 1942).

16. In circumstances where resistance seems foredoomed to fail, it would be prudent for states who feel threatened to seek security by joining or "bandwagoning" with the threatening hegemon, rather than by striving to provide a balance of power.

17. V. I. Lenin's answer, in favor of the more activist course, was outlined in his 1902 pamphlet, *What Is to Be Done?* Reprinted in Robert C. Tucker, ed., *The Lenin Anthology* (New York: W. W. Norton and Company, 1975), pp. 12–114. Lenin wrote the logical complement to *What Is to Be Done?* in 1917, with *The State and Revolution*. In this latter tract Lenin supplied tendentious doctrinal justification for the revolutionary party actually to seize and exercise power on behalf of the proletariat. Reprinted *ibid.*, pp. 311–98.

18. The prospective adventurism lay not in the seizing of power in Petrograd, which was no great challenge, but in attempting to assume responsibility for the government of Russia—as a brief prelude to socialist revolution in the West—in the face of a victorious German army and domestic chaos, and with the executive instrument of an almost trivially small cadre of dedicated Bolsheviks.

19. Sherr, *Soviet Power*, p. 18.

20. Gorbachev, *Perestroika*, p. 203.

21. Makhmut Akhmetovich Gareev, *M. V. Frunze, Military Theorist* (Washington, D.C.: Pergamon Brassey's, 1988; first pub. 1984), p. 208.

22. I am grateful to Gerald Ellison, *The Perils of Amateur Strategy: As Exemplified by the Attack on the Dardanelles Fortress in 1915* (London: Longmans, Green, and Company, 1926). In an interesting article early in 1989 (January 28, "Soviet View of Future War After Arms Cuts"), *Jane's Defence Weekly* (p. 141) quoted a Soviet "political analyst," Colonel Vladimir Chernyshev, on the subject of "four views of future defence." The colonel: (1) claims "both sides would work to have means for immediate counteraction (strategic offensive operations) in case of war"; (2) says "each side would confine themselves to defensive operations at the initial stage of the conflict, relying on deep layered, well prepared fixed defences and on the possibility of counter-offensive operations [both tactical *and strategic*] . . . prepared in advance"; (3) examines the possibility of "the defeat of the intruder on the defender's territory without counterattacking or going beyond one's national territory"; (4) envisions strictly defensive military postures allowing neither side to stage offensive operations or even counterattacks. No prizes will be awarded for guessing that the Soviet General Staff would rank these four options one to four in sharply descending order of professional appeal, not to say practicality.

23. For the Teutonic allusion, see Gunther E. Rothenberg, "Moltke,

Schlieffen, and the Doctrine of Strategic Envelopment," in Paret, ed., *Makers of Modern Strategy*, pp. 296–325.

24. In this context, a classical strategy is a strategy which employs force offensively and defensively for the proximate purpose of winning an armed struggle. While properly respectful of nuclear weapons, a classical strategy does not as a matter of military doctrine simply concede the technical vulnerability of the homeland—regardless of how far current capabilities are judged to be from an ability to render practicable the concept of "fortress U.S.S.R." (for example).

25. Whatever Soviet spokesmen may have said about the certainty or strong likelihood that a nuclear war begun in a modest way would expand precipitately, the fact remains that over the years it has been Moscow, rather than Washington, which has invested heavily in the kind of survivable strategic command system which would lend itself to the conduct of a limited nuclear war. Nonetheless, although it would be unwise to stereotype Soviet strategy for the waging of central war, it is important that some caveats noted by Stephen Meyer should be accorded their admittedly uncertain due: "Once one moves to nuclear strikes on the homeland, Soviet abilities to discern the scale and purpose of the attack decrease rapidly [attack assessment in nuclear war would be both technically and politically very difficult, particularly given the technical deficiencies of Soviet equipment: C.S.G.]. *Thus the Soviets' strategic culture and history are likely to be the primary determinants of their immediate reaction.* Everything in the Soviet experience points to the assumption that the attack has a single strategic purpose: to destroy the Soviet state. Why else initiate nuclear exchanges?" "Soviet Nuclear Operations," in Carter, Steinbruner, and Zraket, eds., *Managing Nuclear Operations*, p. 528. Emphasis added.

26. Those other means include synergistic mixes of further fortification (hardening), mobility (deception), changes in firing doctrine (to some variant of launch under attack), and the proliferation of numbers (aim points).

27. ". . . nowadays one cannot strive for greater security at the expense of others, nor can one settle for lesser security." Soviet Summit Press Release, *The Defensive Doctrine of the Warsaw Treaty*, December 1987, p. 2. Or: ". . . security is indivisible. It is either equal security for all or none at all." Gorbachev, *Perestroika*, p. 142.

28. Vigor, *Soviet Blitzkrieg Theory*, pp. 88–89.

29. *Ibid.*, p. 2. Emphasis in original.

30. In principle and certainly for a conflict of brief duration, there is no comparison between the logistical problems of the Soviet Union and the United States in reaching a European theater of war. However, if a war in Europe were to last for months rather than for days or weeks, the United States might well find its North Atlantic sea lines of communication traversing a more secure zone of logistical passage than the Soviet Union would find in much of Eastern Europe.

31. Paul Kennedy, "What Gorbachev Is Up Against," *The Atlantic,* June 1987, p. 29.
32. Donnelly, *Red Banner,* p. 270.
33. A. P. Thornton, *Doctrines of Imperialism* (New York: John Wiley and Sons, 1965), p. 47.
34. Kennedy, *The Rise and Fall of the Great Powers,* p. 514. Emphasis in original.

Particularly useful histories of the U.S.S.R. and its Russian roots are Richard Pipes, *Russia Under the Old Regime* (New York: Charles Scribner's Sons, 1974); *idem, The Formation of the Soviet Union: Communism and Nationalism, 1917–1923* (New York: Atheneum, 1980; first pub. 1954); Robert V. Daniels, *Russia: The Roots of Confrontation* (Cambridge, Mass.: Harvard University Press, 1985); and Mikhail Heller and Alexandr M. Nekrich, *Utopia in Power: The History of the Soviet Union from 1917 to the Present* (New York: Summit Books, 1986; first pub. 1982). Also see Sergei Averintsev, "The Idea of Holy Russia," *History Today,* Vol. 39 (November 1989), pp. 37–44.

Soviet military doctrine and strategy are addressed in N. V. Ogarkov, *Always in Readiness to Defend the Homeland,* JPRS L/10412 (Washington, D.C.: Foreign Broadcast Information Service, March 25, 1982); Gareev, *M. V. Frunze.* For the fundamentals of Soviet military theory as they were taught to the best and the brightest of the rising generation of General Staff officers, in 1973–75, see Graham Hall Turbiville, ed., *The Voroshilov Lectures, Materials from the Soviet General Staff Academy,* Vol. 1: *Issues of Soviet Military Strategy* (compiled by Ghulam D. Wardak) (Washington, D.C.: National Defense University Press, 1989).

Claims for the "unequivocally defensive" character of Soviet military doctrine are advanced in Soviet Summit Press Release, "The Defensive Doctrine of the Warsaw Treaty"; Vitaly Zhurkin, Sergei Karaganov, and Andrei Kortunov, "Reasonable Sufficiency—Or How to Break the Vicious Circle," *New Times,* No. 40 (October 12, 1987), pp. 13–15; Makhmut Gareev, "The Revised Soviet Military Doctrine," *The Bulletin of the Atomic Scientists,* Vol. 44, No. 10 (December 1988), pp. 30–34; *idem,* "Soviet Military Doctrine: Current and Future Developments," *RUSI Journal,* Vol. 133, No. 4 (Winter 1988), pp. 5–10; and Army General D. T. Yazov, "On Soviet Military Doctrine," *RUSI Journal,* Vol. 134, No. 4 (Winter 1989), pp. 1–4. An insightful Western commentary is Mary C. Fitzgerald, "The Dilemma in Moscow's Defensive Posture," *Arms Control Today,* November 1989, pp. 15–20.

For historical perspective on a very important and longstanding theme in Soviet military thought and planning, see Bruce W. Menning, "The Deep Strike in Russian and Soviet Military History," *The Journal of Soviet Military Studies,* Vol. 1, No. 1 (April 1988), pp. 9–28.

The Soviet system for strategic command is analyzed in Meyer, "Soviet

Nuclear Operations"; and in David Holloway and Condoleezza Rice, "The Evolution of Soviet Forces, Strategy, and Command," in Kurt Gottfried and Bruce G. Blair, eds., *Crisis Stability and Nuclear War* (New York: Oxford University Press, 1988), pp. 126–58.

By far the best and most comprehensive discussion of *maskirovka* (camouflage, concealment, and deception) is Brian Dailey and Patrick J. Parker, eds., *Soviet Strategic Deception* (Lexington, Mass.: Lexington Books, 1987). The new journal *Intelligence and National Security* is highly recommended.

On the Soviet experience in World War II see Seweryn Bialer, ed., *Stalin and His Generals: Soviet Military Memoirs of World War II* (New York: Pegasus, 1969); Seaton, *The Russo-German War, 1941–45;* John Erickson, *The Road to Stalingrad: Stalin's War with Germany* (London: Weidenfeld and Nicolson, 1975); *idem, The Road to Berlin: Continuing the History of Stalin's War with Germany* (Boulder, Colo.: Westview Press, 1983). Also consult David M. Glantz, "American Perspectives on Eastern Front Operations in the Second World War with Soviet Commentary," *The Journal of Soviet Military Affairs,* Vol. 1, No. 1 (April 1988), pp. 108–32; and Jonathan R. Adelman and Christann Lea Gibson, eds., *Contemporary Soviet Military Affairs: The Legacy of World War II* (Boston: Unwin Hyman, 1989).

The perils of negotiating with the Soviet Union are outlined admirably in Joseph G. Whelan, *Soviet Diplomacy and Negotiating Behavior: The Emerging New Context for U.S. Diplomacy* (Boulder, Colo.: Westview Press, 1983); Leon Sloss and M. Scott Davis, eds., *A Game for High Stakes: Lessons Learned in Negotiating with the Soviet Union* (Cambridge, Mass.: Ballinger Publishing Company, 1986); and Raymond F. Smith, *Negotiating with the Soviets* (Bloomington, Ind.: Indiana University Press, 1989).

On the Soviet economy, see the minor classic by Abraham S. Becker, *The Burden of Soviet Defense: A Political-Economic Essay,* R-2752-AF (Santa Monica, Calif.: Rand Corporation, October 1981); and Ed A. Hewett, *Reforming the Soviet Economy: Equality versus Efficiency* (Washington, D.C.: Brookings Institution, 1988).

CHAPTER 8: THE PERILS AND PLEASURES OF COALITION

1. King George VI writing to his mother, Queen Mary, after the evacuation of the British army from Dunkirk. Quoted in Michael Howard, *The Continental Commitment: The Dilemma of British Defence Policy in the Era of the Two World Wars* (London: Temple Smith, 1972), p. 143.
2. R. B. Wernham, *The Making of Elizabethan Foreign Policy, 1558–1603* (Berkeley, Calif.: University of California Press, 1980), p. 95.
3. Jack Snyder, for example, argues that if Gorbachev succeeds with his domestic reforms he is very likely, as a consequence, to lay the basis for an enduring détente with the West. "The Gorbachev Revolution: A Waning of Soviet Expansionism?" *International Security,* Vol. 12, No. 3 (Winter 1987/88), pp. 93–131.

4. ". . . the Allies possessed *twice* the manufacturing strength (using the distorted 1939 figures, which downplay the U.S.' share), *three* times the 'war potential,' and *three* times the national income of the Axis powers, even when the French shares are added to Germany's total." Kennedy, *The Rise and Fall of the Great Powers,* p. 355. Emphasis in original.

5. Official historians Matloff and Snell wrote of unconditional surrender that "[n]o study of the meaning of this formula for the conduct of war was made at the time by the Army staff, or by the joint staff, either before or after the President's announcement." *Strategic Planning for Coalition Warfare, 1941–1942,* p. 380.

6. A "forlorn hope" was the ironic name given in the eighteenth century to the first wave of assault into a "practicable breach" battered in the walls of a fortress. The first person into the breach was eligible for a battlefield promotion. This reward was rarely claimed.

7. The Commission on Integrated Long-Term Strategy which then–Secretary of Defense Weinberger established in October 1986 estimated in its January 1988 report that by the year 2010 the Soviet Union as an economic power would rank behind the United States, Japan, Western Europe, and China. *Discriminate Deterrence* (Washington, D.C.: U.S. Government Printing Office, January 1988), pp. 6–7.

8. For example, French military planners were somewhat constrained in the late 1930s by the need to reassure Britain that France would not behave in a provocative manner toward Germany. Also, a defensive military doctrine had the great expected advantage for France that it looked to provide the capability to buy time relatively cheaply while her British ally mobilized. France was determined not to repeat the experience of the First World War, wherein she nearly bled to death before the British fielded a continental-scale army by late 1916.

9. Apart from the fact that Germany did not want the possibly constraining complication of having to reward Imperial Japan for its assistance in the defeat of the Soviet Union, the opportunism in Japanese grand strategy regarded the war in Europe as critically useful as an enabler for its pursuit of limited objectives in Asia. In 1941, Japan was not interested in joint action within a Eurasian Axis coalition in a global struggle. Germany's bid for Eurasian continental superpower initially was viewed from Tokyo as a vital stage-setter for the pursuit of national goals, not as a vastly risky enterprise whose failure would have fatal implications for Japan. A recent study of Japanese policy notes that in 1940 "[t]he Japanese leaders had been intoxicated by Germany's spring victories." Barnhart, *Japan Prepares for Total War,* p. 192. Japan joined the Axis by the Tripartite Pact of September 27, 1940. That intoxication reappeared briefly in July 1941, but was soon replaced by a more sober assessment of Germany's prospects, as the General Staff's Intelligence Division predicted in August that the U.S.S.R. would fight on into 1942. Given Japan's critical need for raw materials—a policy impulse pointing

her military effort to the south—renewed skepticism over the ability of the Kwantung army in Manchuria to make much headway against local Soviet forces (as yet not drawn down in large numbers by redeployment to the West) served to encourage a "wait-and-see" attitude toward continental war against the U.S.S.R. *Ibid.*, pp. 239–40. In retrospect, as usual, it is fairly obvious that Japan might have succeeded in its geostrategically modest endeavors only if Germany had won its war with Russia. Furthermore, it is at least arguable that a Japanese assault upon Russia in the summer or fall of 1941 would have made the vital difference for Hitler's prospects on the road to Moscow. It was ironic that Japan began her war with the Western powers just one day after the launching of the great Soviet counteroffensive on December 6, 1941. If the Axis powers could have defeated the Soviet Union in 1941, thereby establishing a strategic land bridge between their European and Asian enterprises, it is possible—perhaps even probable—that the United States would have been too massively distracted by the renewed danger to Britain in the Atlantic to settle accounts in the near term with Japan. However, so strategically undisciplined was Hitler's imperial statecraft and so far removed from a common coalition view of the world were Berlin and Tokyo, that it is difficult to resist the proposition that the bloated territorial empire even of a much greater Germany still would have wrought its own demise.

10. The most prominent example in recent times was the cumulatively very expensive German involvement in support of Italy in the Balkans and the Mediterranean in World War II. Italy's status as an active ally created a southern theater of war which German military power, and the Luftwaffe in particular, could ill afford—given the scale of demands of the war in the East. Furthermore, that southern theater of war served as a critically important training ground for Western enemies who otherwise would have been unable to prosecute the war on land in the years 1940–43.

11. W. H. Parker notes that by the summer of 1941 "Haushofer and Mackinder had become household names in the United States where geopolitics had become all the rage." *Mackinder: Geography as an Aid to Statecraft* (Oxford: Clarendon Press, 1982), p. 173. Also see Brian W. Blouet, *Halford Mackinder: A Biography* (College Station, Tex.: Texas A and M University Press, 1987), Chapter 11. The original *Makers of Modern Strategy: Military Thought from Machiavelli to Hitler*, edited by Edward Mead Earle (Princeton, N.J.: Princeton University Press, 1941), contained a chapter by Derwent Whittlesey on "Haushofer: The Geopoliticians" (pp. 388–411). The flavor of the period is captured in the title of a book by Derwent Whittlesey, *German Strategy of World Conquest* (London: Robinson, 1942).

12. In the late 1940s, the U.S. military establishment was under no illusion that in the extant atomic stockpile it had ready to hand "the absolute

weapon." A committee headed by Air Force Lieutenant General H. R. Harmon commented in May 1949 that the 133 atomic bombs envisaged for delivery against seventy Soviet cities in the Trojan war plan of December 1948 would not suffice to "bring about capitulation, destroy the roots of Communism, or critically weaken the power of Soviet leadership to dominate the people." Quoted in David Alan Rosenberg, "The Origins of Overkill: Nuclear Weapons and American Strategy, 1945–1960," *International Security,* Vol. 7, No. 4 (Spring 1983), p. 16. In July 1948, the U.S. atomic stockpile contained fifty bombs, none of which were assembled; had thirty-two aircraft rigged to carry atomic bombs; and had no more than twelve air crews fully trained for atomic missions.

13. A thesis I have developed in *Strategic Studies and Public Policy: The American Experience* (Lexington, Ky.: University Press of Kentucky, 1982), Chapter 4.

14. Rosenberg, "The Origins of Overkill," p. 28.

15. Tacitus, *The Agricola and the Germania* (H. Mattingly and S. A. Handford, trans.) (London: Penguin Books, 1970), p. 81.

16. Cyril Falls, Introduction, to Kent Roberts Greenfield, ed., *Command Decisions* (London: Methuen and Company, 1960; first pub. 1959), p. xiv.

17. The Harmel Report, "The Future Tasks of the Alliance," was commissioned late in 1966 in response both to the anxieties occasioned by the French defection from NATO's military structure and to the general sentiment that the security context had changed substantially since the Alliance-building days of the early 1950s. The report added to the traditional deterrence function of NATO a "second function, to pursue the search for progress towards a more stable relationship in which the underlying political issues can be solved." The report is reproduced in Stanley R. Sloan, *NATO's Future: Toward a New Transatlantic Bargain* (Washington, D.C.: National Defense University Press, 1985), pp. 219–22.

18. Because of the physical situation of their homeland *vis-à-vis* an unfolding European campaign, French officials long have argued that the possibility of France unilaterally effecting the early nuclearization of a war is a source of healthy uncertainty in the minds of Soviet leaders. With respect to the British, Lawrence Freedman is probably correct in his argument that "[t]he main benefit of the U.K. nuclear force for NATO might be, therefore, not so much in attacking certain targets for the alliance but in preserving the national territory as a sanctuary, in serving as the major American base close to the battle." "British Nuclear Targeting," in Ball and Richelson, eds., *Strategic Nuclear Targeting,* p. 126. The fact remains that Soviet early-warning and attack-assessment systems—possibly functioning in a degraded wartime condition—technically could not determine the national origins of British or French SLBM attacks.

19. Joseph Joffe, "Can Europe Live with Its Defence?" in Lawrence Freedman, ed., *The Troubled Alliance: Atlantic Relations in the 1980's* (London: Heinemann, 1983), p. 134.
20. Edward N. Luttwak, *On the Meaning of Victory: Essays on Strategy* (New York: Simon and Schuster, 1986), p. 260.
21. Extended deterrence should not be regarded merely as a special case for attention on the agenda of concerns about nuclear strategy. Rather, extended deterrence has been the central theme and focus in the long debate about that strategy. Freedman recognizes this point when he writes: "[I]f there is an underlying theme [to this book] it is the attempt to develop a convincing strategy for extended deterrence, to make the United States' nuclear guarantee to Europe intellectually credible rather than just an act of faith." *The Evolution of Nuclear Strategy*, p. xvi, and *passim*. The premier historian of U.S. nuclear war planning, David Alan Rosenberg, makes substantially the same point: ". . . American nuclear strategy, virtually since the beginning of the atomic age, has been shaped by a commitment to defend American allies in Western Europe. U.S. planners initially chose in the late 1940's to make nuclear weapons the centerpiece of U.S. defense policy, even before the Soviet Union acquired a nuclear capability, in order to meet the challenge of Soviet conventional superiority in Europe." "Reality and Responsibility: Power and Process in the Making of United States Nuclear Strategy, 1945–68," *The Journal of Strategic Studies*, Vol. 9, No. 1 (March 1986), p. 49.
22. Rosenberg, "The Origins of Overkill," p. 14; and Desmond Ball, "The Development of the SIOP, 1960–1983," in Ball and Richelson, eds., *Strategic Nuclear Targeting*, p. 57.
23. In the 1950s and early 1960s Soviet nuclear "charges" were stored apart from their delivery vehicles, presumably because Soviet leaders were fearful of a loss of political control. In theory at least, the Soviet Union could have been disarmed of its nuclear arsenal by a surprise U.S. first strike. Soviet assets for the acquisition of political, strategic, and tactical warning of attack were impressive but far short of infallible. Some contemporary analysis demonstrated beyond a reasonable doubt in the mid-1950s that, again in principle, even the nominally vastly superior nuclear striking power of SAC was vulnerable to a surprise attack. Albert Wohlstetter *et al.*, *Protecting U.S. Power to Strike Back in the 1950's and 1960's*, R-290 (Santa Monica, Calif.: Rand Corporation, April 1956). For a skeptical perspective upon R-290, see Kaplan, *The Wizards of Armageddon*, pp. 121 ff.
24. Richard K. Betts, *Nuclear Blackmail and Nuclear Balance* (Washington, D.C.: Brookings Institution, 1987), p. 159.
25. There is insight in Freedman's observation that extended nuclear deterrence "is one of those areas where a policy has worked far better in practice than an assessment of the theory might lead one to expect."

The Evolution of Nuclear Strategy, p. xvi. Either the theory is wrong—and thoroughly incredible threats can deter—or, perhaps more likely, the theory has never really been tested. If the latter is true, then the absence of war in Europe since the founding of NATO in 1949 may have had little to do with the credibility of U.S. nuclear threats, latent or overt.

26. Henry Kissinger, "Arms Control Fever," *The Washington Post,* January 19, 1988, p. A15. Nuclear strategy used to attract criticism for its resemblance to the Christological disputes of the (Eastern) Roman Empire in the fifth century, but debate in the late 1980s over the conventional defense of NATO's Central Front became more and more suitable for skeptical treatment by an Edward Gibbon. For example, see John J. Mearsheimer, "Assessing the Conventional Balance: The 3:1 Rule and Its Critics"; Joshua M. Epstein, "The 3:1 Rule, the Adaptive Dynamic Model, and the Future of Security Studies"; and John J. Mearsheimer, Barry R. Posen, and Eliot A. Cohen, "Correspondence: Reassessing Net Assessment," in *International Security,* Vol. 13, No. 4 (Spring 1989), pp. 54–89, 90–127, and 128–79. This cottage industry is harmless enough, provided policymakers are not persuaded to take the theologians of Central Front model making and testing as seriously as those theologians would appear to take themselves and one another. People impressed by the *(tactical)* so-called three-to-one rule might care to know that Adolf Hitler held the rule in such high regard that he fulminated against commanders who failed to hold their ground in the face of an enemy who enjoyed less than a three-to-one advantage. The prospective disappearance of a Central Front keyed initially to the former inner German border should promote a healthy crisis in "modeling" circles.

27. Fred C. Iklé, "Atlantic Alliance Is the Global Guardian of the Democratic Order," *ROA National Security Report,* Vol. 4, No. 9 (September 1986), p. 8. "Why . . . shouldn't we confront the invading enemy with the risks of counterinvasions by NATO forces? And why shouldn't we, in the event of war, enlist our natural allies behind the enemy's front line—the more than 100 million people in Eastern Europe." P. 9. As usual, Iklé was ahead of his time.

28. See the claim by the author of PD-59, Odom, "Soviet Military Doctrine," p. 122.

29. Everyone agrees that the Soviet Union would wage a central nuclear war only in a militarily purposive fashion; but that is the extent of agreement. There is no argument over the merit in the proposition that the Soviet Union would not knowingly execute a central nuclear strike plan judged likely to produce a character and weight of U.S. response that must imperil the very existence of the Soviet (or Russian) state. But, having made those commonsense points, how would they translate into operational style? This author is impressed by the number of Western theorists who, when looking at the always ambiguous Soviet

evidence, tend to resolve their uncertainties by selecting a distinctly American-style Soviet adversary. This phenomenon of people looking at the Soviet Union and finding themselves in its *inferred reasoning* or preferred style in the conduct of war permeates *Discriminate Deterrence* (see pp. 35–37, 65) and Wohlstetter and Brody, "Continuing Control as a Requirement for Deterring." My doubts about the validity of a Wohlstetter thesis which amounts to portrayal of a Soviet style in the conduct of central *(inter alia)* war that is quintessentially that favored in the Rand tradition of U.S. strategic studies, flow not from disagreement about its attractiveness in the abstract. Instead, I am deeply skeptical that Soviet style in strategic rationality, informed by Soviet strategic culture, would produce operational variants of discriminating attacks recognizable as such in the intellectual universe crafted by Wohlstetter.

30. For example: Stephen M. Meyer, *Soviet Theatre Nuclear Forces, Part 2: Capabilities and Intentions,* Adelphia Papers No. 188 (London: Liss, Winter 1983–84); *idem,* "Soviet Nuclear Operations"; and William T. Lee, "Soviet Nuclear Targeting Strategy," in Ball and Richelson, eds., *Strategic Nuclear Targeting,* pp. 84–108.

31. See Wohlstetter, "Swords Without Shields" and "Between an Unfree World and None."

32. The British guarantee of Poland's independence—issued on March 31, 1939—and the subsequent mutual assistance pact (April 6) were intended by Chamberlain to leave Britain some policy latitude. The British government leaked to the press the fact that it drew a sharp distinction between the independence and the territorial integrity of Poland. The former was guaranteed, the latter might be at least in modest part negotiable. Unlike the Poles, who were absurdly overconfident of their ability to repel a German invasion, the British recognized fully both the impossibility of Poland offering any prolonged resistance and the impracticability of Western military assistance. Incredible though it is, the evidence shows that Chamberlain failed to understand that "[t]he decision, war or peace, had been voluntarily surrendered . . . into the nervous hands of Colonel Beck [the Polish foreign minister] and his junta comrades-in-arms." Donald Cameron Watt, *How War Came: The Immediate Origins of the Second World War, 1938–1939* (New York: Pantheon Books, 1989), p. 186. The real object of British concern in the late summer of 1939 was not Poland, but Rumania (and specifically the need to deny Rumanian oil to Germany).

33. The outbreak scenario for the war in Tom Clancy's novel *Red Storm Rising* (New York: G. P. Putnam's, 1986) is not particularly convincing. However, Clancy performs a useful service in illustrating the enduring truth that circumstances could arise (in his scenario, a Soviet energy crisis) wherein a Soviet decision to attack in Europe would appear to make great policy sense.

34. But the U.S. (and certainly the Soviet) defense community is full of

people who believe otherwise. See Epstein, "The 3:1 Rule, the Adaptive Dynamic Model, and the Future of Security Studies." Epstein's final broadside in his testy counterattack on John Mearsheimer is to assert that "[t]he main issue before us here is not the 3:1 rule [favored by Mearsheimer] versus the Adaptive Dynamic Model [favored by Epstein]. The main issue is whether the field of security studies is going to move in the direction of science." P. 127. It has been my professional misfortune to be obliged to listen to many pseudoscientific briefings on the defense of NATO's Central Front.

35. Morony argues that "perceptions about war in Europe *must* differ markedly between the man of 30 or 40 summers who lives on the West Coast of the United States and the survivor of one (or even two) world wars who has his house in Cologne. Indeed, there is even a doubt in the mind of some Europeans about whether the Americans understand war itself. . . . Thus while Europeans have developed a horror of war—of any war—because they know what it does to them, Americans have reason really only to fear the consequences of specifically nuclear attack." "Transatlantic Military Differences," p. 100. Emphasis in original.

36. Kenneth Hunt, *The Alliance and Europe: Part 2, Defence with Fewer Men,* Adelphi Papers No. 98 (London: IISS, Summer 1973), p. 3.

37. Reagan, *National Security Strategy of the United States (1988),* p. 13. To be flexible and discriminating are probably desirable tactical traits. But in and of themselves they do not suggest a strategy, let alone a theory of war as it is defined in Chapter 1 of this book.

38. This general truth was never more poignantly applicable than as a factor in the deliberations over grand strategy which rumbled rancorously in Anglo-American relations in 1942 and 1943. The opening of a Second Front in France appeared to be highly desirable in order to draw German forces away from the East and help reduce any Soviet temptation to make a separate peace. But, unless the Soviet Union could first break the German land-power sword, such an amphibious venture would invite disaster. Describing an "appreciation of the situation" paper drafted for the British Chiefs of Staff in 1942, John Strawson writes: "[B]ut the joint planners' document went on [having specified the many continuing drains on allied resources] to make a statement which, however unpalatable it might have been to the Americans, rang true to the British. It said that only the Russian Army was capable of defeating, or even containing, the German Army, and that the British and American forces were simply not powerful enough [certainly not in 1942, and probably not in 1943] to take on 'the *bulk* of the Axis forces on land.' " *The Italian Campaign* (New York: Carroll and Graff Publishers, 1988; first pub. 1987), p. 77. Emphasis in original.

39. See John W. Dower, *War Without Mercy: Race and Power in the Pacific War* (New York: Pantheon Books, 1986), pp. 260–61.

Problems of coalition management are handled admirably in Gordon A. Craig, "Problems of Coalition Warfare: The Military Alliance Against Napoleon, 1813–14," in Craig, *War, Politics, and Diplomacy: Selected Essays* (London: Weidenfeld and Nicolson, 1966), pp. 22–45; and Paul W. Schroeder, "Alliances, 1815–1945: Weapons of Power and Tools of Management," in Knorr, ed., *Historical Dimensions of National Security Problems,* pp. 227–62.

For NATO's early years, see Timothy P. Ireland, *Creating the Entangling Alliance: The Origins of the North Atlantic Treaty Organization* (Westport, Conn.: Greenwood Press, 1981); and Robert Endicott Ongood's classic, *NATO: The Entangling Alliance* (Chicago: University of Chicago Press, 1962).

On U.S. policy toward security in Europe in the formative years, see John Lewis Gaddis: *The United States and the Origins of the Cold War, 1941–1947* (New York: Columbia University Press, 1972); *Strategies of Containment: A Critical Appraisal of Postwar American National Security Policy* (New York: Oxford University Press, 1982), Chapters 1-4; and *The Long Peace: Inquiries Into the History of the Cold War* (New York: Oxford University Press, 1987), Chapters 2-3.

The 1914 crisis may be approached via the essays by L. C. F. Turner ("The Significance of the Schlieffen Plan" and "The Russian Mobilization in 1914") and N. Stone ("Moltke and Conrad: Relations between the Austro-Hungarian and German General Staffs, 1909–1914") in Kennedy, ed., *The War Plans of the Great Powers,* pp. 199–221, 252–68, and 222–51, respectively; and the excellent essay by Samuel R. Williamson, Jr., "The Origins of World War I," in Robert I. Rotberg and Theodore K. Rabb, eds., *The Origin and Prevention of Major Wars* (Cambridge: Cambridge University Press, 1989), pp. 225–48. See also the powerful little essay by David Kaiser, "Deterrence or National Interest? Reflections on the Origins of War," *Orbis,* Vol. 30, No. 1 (Spring 1986), pp. 5–11.

The title tells all in David Day's sad tale of great power–small ally relations, *The Great Betrayal: Britain, Australia and the Onset of the Pacific War, 1939–42* (North Ryde [Aus.]: Angus and Robertson, 1988).

Few works stand out on the vastly overwritten subject of NATO and nuclear weapons, but see David N. Schwartz, *NATO's Nuclear Dilemmas* (Washington, D.C.: Brookings Institution, 1983); and J. Michael Legge, *Theater Nuclear Weapons and the NATO Strategy of Flexible Response,* R-2964-FF (Santa Monica, Calif.: Rand Corporation, April 1983). Transatlantic differences are outlined in my "Theater Nuclear Weapons: Doctrines and Postures," *World Politics,* Vol. 28, No. 2 (January 1976), pp. 300–14.

Extended (nuclear) deterrence is discussed usefully in Edward N. Luttwak, "The Problems of Extending Deterrence," in *The Future of Strategic Deterrence, Part I,* Adelphi Papers No. 160 (London: IISS, Autumn 1980), pp. 31–37; Walter B. Slocombe, "Extended Deterrence," *The Washington Quarterly,* Vol. 7, No. 4 (Fall 1984), pp. 93–103; Lawrence Freedman,

"The Evolution and Future of Extended Nuclear Deterrence," in *The Changing Strategic Landscape, Part 3,* Adelphi Papers No. 236 (London: IISS, Spring 1989), pp. 18–31; and Paul K. Huth, *Extended Deterrence and the Prevention of War* (New Haven, Conn.: Yale University Press, 1988). For the size of the superpowers' nuclear stockpiles, see "U.S., Soviet Nuclear Weapons Stockpile, 1945–1989: Numbers of Weapons," *The Bulletin of the Atomic Scientists,* Vol. 45, No. 9 (November 1989), p. 53.

The possible "rationality of irrationality" is outlined in Thomas C. Schelling, *The Strategy of Conflict* (Cambridge, Mass.: Harvard University Press, 1960), *passim;* and Herman Kahn, *On Thermonuclear War* (Princeton, N.J.: Princeton University Press, 1960), pp. 291–95, 306. But see Robert Jervis, Richard Ned Lebow, and Janice Gross Stein, *Psychology and Deterrence* (Baltimore: Johns Hopkins University Press, 1985); Edward Rhodes, *Power and Madness: The Logic of Nuclear Coercion* (New York: Columbia University Press, 1989), Chapters 2, 7; and Frank C. Zagare, "Rationality and Deterrence," *World Politics,* Vol. 42, No. 2 (January 1990), pp. 238–60.

American military prowess at the beginning of wars is examined in Charles E. Heller and William A. Stofft, eds., *America's First Battles, 1776–1965* (Lawrence, Kans.: University Press of Kansas, 1986). The relevant chapter (number 10) in McPherson, *Battle Cry of Freedom,* is entitled "Amateurs Go to War."

CHAPTER 9: NUCLEAR WEAPONS AND STRATEGY

1. Lawrence Freedman, "The First Two Generations of Nuclear Strategists," in Paret, ed., *Makers of Modern Strategy,* p. 735.
2. McGeorge Bundy, *Danger and Survival: Choices About the Bomb in the First Fifty Years* (New York: Random House, 1988), p. 597.
3. Freedman, *The Evolution of Nuclear Strategy,* p. 400.
4. *Ibid.,* p. 395. Emphasis added.
5. The proposition that even a nuclear war modest in scale relative to the size of the superpower arsenals could trigger climatic catastrophe was advanced in Carl Sagan, "Nuclear War and Climatic Catastrophe," *Foreign Affairs,* Vol. 62, No. 2 (Winter 1983/84), pp. 257–92. As a live policy issue suitable for political exploitation, the nuclear winter hypothesis (and the credibility of its principal devotee, Carl Sagan) never recovered from the savaging it received at the hands of Richard N. Perle, then assistant secretary of defense for International Security Policy, in U.S. House of Representatives, Committee on Science and Technology (Subcommittee on Natural Resources, Agricultural Research and Environment) and Committee on Interior and Insular Affairs (Subcommittee on Energy and the Environment), *Nuclear Winter, Joint Hearing,* 99th Cong., 1st sess. (Washington, D.C.: U.S. Government Printing Office, March 14, 1985). The nuclear winter hypothesis had very little effect upon public debate, probably both because of the major

scientific uncertainties pertaining to it and because it did not raise important new fears in people's minds. The nuclear winter argument provided a novel twist of a more general horror to the possible consequences of large-scale nuclear war. But people's horror threshold had long since been reached on that subject.

6. Other important reasons include the belief that nuclear threats create a more reliable deterrent than does the "threat" to defeat a conventional invasion with conventional means. Also, dependence upon nuclear threats, particularly when those threats are directed against a superpower homeland, should deny the strategy pilot of the Western coalition the parachute option of waging war strictly abroad. Unilateral Soviet force cuts and withdrawals and asymmetrical CFE regimes are hoped in the West to provide technical fixes to the military imbalance in Europe that has structured East-West strategic relations since the 1940s. If these technical fixes indeed occur, NATO should take them to the bank, but should not assume that their real and their face value will be synonymous. The problems with what loosely may be called the "conventional deterrence" school of thought include: its tendency to neglect the fact that the European members of NATO flatly reject its tenets; its proclivity for ignoring the advantages of surprise which accrue to the aggressor; its typical silence on the issue of Alliance cohesion for concerted military preparatory moves in times of acute crisis; and its fondness for an overly simple arithmetical approach to war.

7. A rare endeavor at interdisciplinary communication between philosophers and strategic thinkers is presented in the "special issue on ethics and nuclear deterrence" of *Ethics,* Vol. 95, No. 3 (April 1985). Other works in this genre are Nigel Blake and Kay Pole, eds., *Dangers of Deterrence: Philosophers on Nuclear Strategy* (London: Routledge and Kegan Paul, 1983), and Henry Shue, ed., *Nuclear Deterrence and Moral Restraint: Critical Choices for American Strategy* (Cambridge: Cambridge University Press, 1989). It was my personal experience, as a participant in the symposium which preceded the *Ethics* publication cited above, that the more important disagreements tend to be among strategic thinkers and among philosophers, rather than between these two groups. The groups lacked a sufficient common frame of reference to conduct a very meaningful dialogue, a difficulty which obviously does not obtain in intradisciplinary debate.

8. Fifty-five million is the estimate of M. Jacques Mordal, cited without dissent in a careful discussion in John Terraine, *The Smoke and the Fire: Myths and Anti-Myths of War, 1861–1945* (London: Sidgwick and Jackson, 1980), p. 38. A range of 41–49 million is offered in R. Ernest Dupuy and Trevor N. Dupuy, *The Encyclopedia of Military History from 3500 B.C. to the Present* (New York: Harper and Row, 1986, second revised edition), p. 1198. These authors, with suitable reservations, offer

14,663,413 as a plausible total for the fatalities of World War I. P. 990. Provided they are treated as "ball-park estimates," these numbers will not mislead (notwithstanding the spurious precision of the 1914–18 total).

9. In the absence of very detailed assumptions about targets, scale of attack, weapon yields, heights of burst, and the weather, estimates of casualties in nuclear war are simply undisciplined guesses. But the more precise the assumptions—and the more calculable the casualties—the more easily do they slip into irrelevance as real-world decisions cause significant variation from the values specified. There is no evading the paradox that estimates are more useful the more precise they are, while the more precise they are the less confidence can be placed in them. Since nuclear war could occur in many sizes, it is the analytically un-helpful truth—for anybody seeking scientific certainty—that such a war could produce fatalities on the range of several hundred thousand (or even much less, were nuclear use confined to the sea and perhaps to outer space) to several hundred million.

10. Reagan, *National Security Strategy of the United States (1988)*, p. 15.

11. "By contrast [to countermeasures], circumvention has been of excep-tional importance in the process of decline [in the strategic relevance of nuclear weapons]. Instead of reducing the consequences of attack by organizational maneuver, as in the World War II encounter between civil society and bombardment, nuclear-era circumvention has evaded attack outrightly by outmaneuvering its political preconditions at any one time." Edward N. Luttwak, "An Emerging Postnuclear Era?" *The Washington Quarterly,* Vol. II, No. 1 (Winter 1988), p. 8.

12. Robert Gilpin, *War and Change in World Politics* (Cambridge: Cam-bridge University Press, 1981), p. 217.

13. American experience in the Civil War and in World War I encouraged the erroneous notion that strategy and the hard fighting which won wars could be antithetical. Allan R. Millett has explained clearly just why it was that the U.S. Army in World War II was not, as a rule, capable of operational excellence on the offensive. The "hard fighting" tradition of the army in its approach to war was in fact somewhat contradicted by the important deficiencies in military equipment, tactical doctrine, numbers of combat units, and—above all else—quality of personnel that the Germans were to expose from 1942 even until 1945. "The United States Armed Forces in the Second World War." The combat arms of the U.S. Army were too slim in quantity and were manned unduly by the less capable draftees. The unflattering results in relative military effectiveness in the field were entirely predictable. This is not to deny that the U.S. Army was good enough to perform the mission it was given.

14. Remark made in the author's presence in the course of a presentation

at the Hudson Institute, Croton-on-Hudson, New York, in 1979. Since his retirement from military life, General Milshtein has been associated with the Institute for the U.S.A. and Canada.

15. Kahn, *On Thermonuclear War*, p. 126.
16. Luttwak, *Strategy*, p. 160. Emphasis in original.
17. *Discriminate Deterrence*, p. 7. Emphasis added.
18. Reagan, *National Security Strategy of the United States (1988)*, p. 15.
19. *Discriminate Deterrence*, p. 30.
20. Michael Howard, Karl Kaiser, and François de Rose, "Deterrence Policy: A European Response," *The International Herald Tribune*, February 4, 1988, p. 4.
21. Freedman, "The First Two Generations of Nuclear Strategists," p. 778.
22. Notwithstanding the fact that many Americans agree with Freedman's pessimistic characterization of the state of nuclear strategy, it is probably true that many, or even most, of Freedman's professional American peers—which is to say mainstream, defense-minded scholars—would dissent from the view which he expressed in the passage quoted. Whether the dissent would be attributable to a different intellectual understanding of how nuclear weapons could be employed responsibly, or whether such dissent would reflect more a different view of policy necessity, one cannot say for certain. My point is that an American strategist, unlike a British one, knows that his country is the last line of its own, as of its coalition's, defense. It may not be too strong to say that Freedman's argument—that the nuclear strategists have "failed to come up with any convincing method of employing nuclear weapons should deterrence fail that did not wholly offend common sense"— simply is unacceptable, not to say unhelpful, for a superpower guarantor of the security of other states.
23. Michael Howard, "The Forgotten Dimensions of Strategy," in Howard, *The Causes of War*, pp. 103, 109–115.
24. Brodie, *War and Politics*, Chapter 9.
25. This is a nontrivial weakness in the strategic reasoning in Blair, *Strategic Command and Control*. Also, Soviet risk should figure more prominently than it does in R. James Woolsey, "U.S. Strategic Force Decisions for the 1990's," *The Washington Quarterly*, Vol. 12, No. 1 (Winter 1989), pp. 69–83.
26. For example, Reagan, *National Security Strategy of the United States (1987)*, p. 22.
27. Caspar W. Weinberger, *Annual Report to the Congress, Fiscal Year 1988* (Washington, D.C.: U.S. Government Printing Office, January 12, 1987), p. 46.
28. Donald C. F. Daniel, "The Soviet Navy and Tactical Nuclear War at Sea," *Survival*, Vol. 29, No. 4 (July/August 1987), pp. 318–35. Brooks makes the same point in his article "Naval Power and National Security," when he argues that "a nation with a military dominated by

artillerymen, a strategy focused on land, and a doctrine that suggests nuclear war cannot be limited is not going to cross the nuclear threshold based on at-sea tactical considerations." P. 79.

29. Howard, Kaiser, and de Rose, "Deterrence Policy."
30. Michael Howard, "War and Technology," *RUSI Journal,* Vol. 132, No. 4 (December 1987), p. 22. Emphasis added.
31. Howard, Kaiser, and de Rose, "Deterrence Policy."

The collapse of the Soviet hegemonic empire in East-Central Europe in 1989 and the current revolution in Soviet military doctrine and posture more in favor of defense-offense renders sensible analysis of the misnomer, "conventional deterrence" unusually difficult. If it is not an oxymoron to describe any of the literature on this subject as enlightening, readers are recommended to try John J. Mearsheimer, *Conventional Deterrence* (Ithaca, N.Y.: Cornell University Press, 1983); and Stephen E. Miller and Sean M. Lynn-Jones, eds., *Conventional Forces and American Defense Policy: An "International Security" Reader* (Cambridge, Mass.: MIT Press, 1989, revised edition).

A good balanced discussion of the nuclear winter hypothesis is Starley L. Thompson and Stephen H. Schneider, "Nuclear Winter Reappraised," *Foreign Affairs,* Vol. 64, No. 5 (Summer 1986), pp. 981–1005. For arguable analyses of the effects of nuclear attacks, see William H. Daugherty, Barbara Levi, and Frank N. von Hippel, "The Consequences of 'Limited' Nuclear Attacks on the United States," *International Security,* Vol. 10, No. 4 (Spring 1986), pp. 3–45; and Barbara Levi, Frank N. von Hippel, and William H. Daugherty, "Civilian Casualties from 'Limited' Nuclear Attacks on the Soviet Union," *International Security,* Vol. 12, No. 3 (Winter 1987/88), pp. 168–89. Compare the strategic assumptions which drive those analyses with the worldview of Wohlstetter and Brody, "Continuing Control as a Requirement for Deterring," pp. 162–63.

The moral choices associated with nuclear weapons and nuclear strategy are treated in William V. O'Brien, *The Conduct of Just and Limited War* (New York: Praeger Publishers, 1981); James Turner Johnson, *Can Modern War Be Just?* (New Haven, Conn.: Yale University Press, 1984); Joseph S. Nye, Jr., *Nuclear Ethics* (New York: Free Press, 1986); Gregory S. Kavka, *Moral Paradoxes of Nuclear Deterrence* (Cambridge: Cambridge University Press, 1987); and Robert E. Osgood, *The Nuclear Dilemma in American Strategic Thought* (Boulder, Colo.: Westview Press, 1988), particularly Chapter 6 on the subject of "just deterrence." For the case that war, not just nuclear war, is morally impermissible, see Robert L. Holmes, *On War and Morality* (Princeton, N.J.: Princeton University Press, 1989).

On the range of choice available in the catalogue of nuclear strategies, see the critical analyses by Gray, *Nuclear Strategy and National Style,* Chapter 9; David C. Hendrickson, *The Future of American Strategy* (New York: Holmes and Meier, 1987), especially Chapter 4; Robert A. Levine, *The*

Strategic Nuclear Debate, R-2565-FF/CC/RC (Santa Monica, Calif.: Rand Corporation, November 1987); and Robert Jervis, *The Meaning of the Nuclear Revolution: Statecraft and the Prospect of Armageddon* (Ithaca, N.Y.: Cornell University Press, 1989).

Readers interested in the state of scholarship on deterrence theory could do worse than consult "The Rational Deterrence Debate: A Symposium" (comprising articles by Christopher H. Achen and Duncan Snidal; Alexander L. George and Richard Smoke; Robert Jervis, Richard Ned Lebow, and Janice Gross Stein; and George W. Downs), *World Politics,* Vol. 41, No. 2 (January 1989), pp. 143–237, inclusive. The appealing but imprudent notion of existential (nuclear) deterrence is roughly handled in Lawrence Freedman, "I Exist; Therefore I Deter," *International Security,* Vol. 13, No. 1 (Summer 1988), pp. 177–95.

That bogeyman of liberal opinion for nearly a century and a half, the *arms race,* is analyzed pitilessly in Charles H. Fairbanks, Jr., "Arms Races: The Metaphor and the Facts," *The National Interest,* No. 1 (Fall 1985), pp. 75–90. People of a numerate persuasion may find some guidance in Walter Isard, *Arms Races, Arms Control, and Conflict Analysis: Contributions from Peace Science and Peace Economics* (New York: Cambridge University Press, 1988), Chapter 2. A good recent survey of the state of understanding of "the arms dynamic" in strategic rivalry is Barry Buzan, *An Introduction to Strategic Studies: Military Technology and International Relations* (New York: St. Martin's Press, 1987), Part 2.

CHAPTER 10: SEEING THE PROBLEM WHOLE

1. Richard Pares, "American Versus Continental Warfare, 1739–63," in Pares, *The Historian's Business and Other Essays* (Oxford: Clarendon Press, 1961), p. 168. Emphasis added.
2. The thesis of Ferrill, *The Fall of the Roman Empire.* Ferrill concludes his book with the following sentence: "[A]s the western army became barbarized, it lost its tactical superiority, and Rome fell to the onrush of barbarism." P. 169. Compare that powerfully simple statement of cause and effect with the complicated judgment of M. I. Finley: "In the later Roman Empire manpower was part of an interrelated complex of social conditions, which, together with the barbarian invasions, brought an end to the empire in the west. The army could not stand further depletion of manpower; the situation on the land had deteriorated because taxes were too high; taxes were too high because military demands were increasing; and for that the German pressures were mainly responsible. A vicious circle of evils was in full swing. Break into it at any point: the final answer will be the same provided one keeps all the factors in sight all the time." *Aspects of Antiquity: Discoveries and Controversies* (New York: Viking Press, 1969), pp. 160–61.
3. Despite some uncertainties in the evidence over the scale of Byzantine

physical loss at Manzikert, the historical argument does not pertain so much to the military facts of the battle as to its strategic significance. Fundamentally strong polities can lose a great battle, yet, in time, recover fully—particularly when much of the army escapes and the enemy (who in this case was far more interested in further conquests in the Islamic world than in seizing territory in the Byzantine Empire) does not exploit his victory promptly.

4. Kennedy, *The Rise and Fall of the Great Powers, passim.* Of course, Kennedy is not arguing the tautology that great powers become less great when their greatness (the necessary basis of which is economic strength) declines. His text advances the thesis that the maintenance of great powerhood devours, or can devour, its own economic foundations.

5. Luttwak, *Strategy,* p. 4. Emphasis in original.

6. Walter Lippmann, *U.S. Foreign Policy: Shield of the Republic* (Boston: Little, Brown and Company, 1943), pp. 9–10; and Samuel P. Huntington, "Coping with the Lippmann Gap," *Foreign Affairs,* Vol. 66, No. 3 (1988), pp. 453–77.

7. This is not to claim that one cannot deter unless one can win a war in a definitive military manner. But it is to claim that an enemy in need of deterring has to be persuaded that his enemies believe they could use their arms with nonsuicidal consequences to resist him successfully.

8. Huntington, "Coping with the Lippmann Gap," p. 466.

9. The SACEur, General John Galvin, has stated very bluntly indeed that in the event of war he expects to be able to use nuclear weapons to change the terms of engagement in a campaign that NATO is losing. "NATO's strategy remains forward defense and flexible response. We are going to defend all our terrain, but we are prepared to give ground in order to gain time and to use nuclear weapons if it looks as if we are losing military cohesion. The nuclear weapon is the deterrent factor." "The book on Gorbachev's design: Conversation with NATO Commander John Galvin," *U.S. News and World Report,* March 7, 1988, p. 44.

10. Admiral Carl H. Trost, quoted in "In the News," *The Submarine Review,* January 1988, pp. 89–90. The quotation is from a speech, "ASW: The Challenge in Space," delivered at the ASW Committee Banquet on May 20, 1987.

11. Space control is a formal, explicit objective specified as U.S. policy. See U.S. Department of Defense, *Department of Defense Space Policy* (mimeo), March 10, 1987, p. 5. "Space control functions consist of operations that ensure freedom of action in space for friendly forces while limiting or denying enemy freedom of action when so directed by the National Command Authority. They include satellite negation [including the posing of anti-satellite threats] and satellite protection." Just as command, or control, of the air should not be confused with effective possession for exclusive use (as in land warfare), so the heavy borrowing

from naval theory for application to the space ocean should be examined with some care. The meaning and purpose of command, or control, of the sea (or the air) is not always quite as straightforward as some canonical precepts might mislead the unwary into believing. As John Terraine cautions: "[A]ir superiority is never absolute; as long as the enemy has any aircraft at all (and any fuel) he is able to make occasional surprise forays and sometimes score successes." *A Time for Courage,* p. 665. The same argument applies to the maritime environment. So, when General Robert T. Herres advises that "[s]pace control is analogous to sea control," it should be understood that such control is never absolute. "The Future of Military Space Forces," *Air University Review,* Vol. 38, No. 2 (January–March 1987), p. 45. For the classic naval theories which have been raided for potential space application, see Alfred Thayer Mahan, *The Influence of Sea Power Upon the French Revolution and Empire, 1793–1812,* Vol. 2: (Boston: Little, Brown and Company, 1898; first pub. 1892), Chapter 19; and Corbett, *Some Principles of Maritime Strategy,* Chapter 1. Corbett's language, in particular, lends itself to transposition to space matters. For example: "[T]he object of naval [space] warfare must always be directly or indirectly either to secure the command of the sea [space] or to prevent the enemy from securing it" (p. 87); and "[W]e arrive, therefore, at this general conclusion. The object of naval [space] warfare is to control maritime [space] communications" (p. 116). One must beware lest an erroneous reading of Corbett's analysis of maritime strategy encourage a like error in the analysis of military space operations. Specifically, the *operational* object of naval warfare is indeed the control of maritime communications, but the *strategic* object of naval warfare is to influence the course of events on land.

12. Even if Mahanian notions of how war at sea ought to be conducted (in pursuit of "command") had been *au courant* in the sixteenth century, which they were not, Elizabeth's England could not provide the key, interlocking elements which produce "sea power" in its much more modern (late nineteenth century) meaning. In the late sixteenth-century England had no overseas bases. What is more, even if bases could have been secured, as was suggested, on the coast of Spain itself, in the Azores, in the Caribbean, or—as was attempted in some halfhearted ventures—on the Atlantic littoral of North America, the English state of the period lacked the financial, administrative, and logistical assets to sustain them. Because sixteenth-century England could not afford to wage public war at sea on the scale and with the persistence which a coordinated maritime offensive designed to secure major strategic effect would have required, English sea power was very much a private venture, expressing private interests (often compatible with the public weal) in pursuit of plunder and profit.

13. In response to the growing problem of piracy (or privateering, if some

legal sanction was granted the pirate), Spain began to organize convoys for its shipping as early as the 1540s. The idea of going systematically after Spanish bullion fleets as a matter of state policy for the strategic enfeeblement of Spain (as contrasted with the simple, complementary purpose of personal enrichment) appears first to have received serious official attention in France in 1558. See D. B. Quinn and A. N. Ryan, *England's Sea Empire, 1550–1642* (London: George Allen and Unwin, 1983), pp. 79–80. The authors argue that "[t]he object of the proposed raid [twelve warships and 1,200 troops would attack Santo Domingo and Puerto Rico, and then proceed to the Isthmus of Panama where they would interdict the silver bullion shipped from Peru] was to divert a year's supply of treasure into the coffers of France and to create such lack of confidence in Spain's ability to police the Caribbean that Philip's revenue from the Indies would be cut off for two years." Similar schemes were proposed in London in the late 1570s, the 1580s, and the 1590s. However, Spain responded heroically to this burgeoning first Battle of the Atlantic. In the 1560s she radically improved her convoying practices, and by the last years of the century had built what amounted to an imperial oceangoing battle fleet more than capable of seeing off English, French, and Dutch privateers. Also, the Spanish Empire vastly improved the fortifications of its key colonial trading and bullion transshipment *entrepôts* in the Caribbean (most notably Havana, Puerto Rico, and on "the Main" itself at Cartagena and Panama). The measure of the Spanish achievement in the organization and defense of its sea lines of communication to the Americas may best be appreciated by considering that the annual treasure *Flota* was only lost once, to the Dutchman Piet Hein, in 1628 off the coast of Cuba.

14. The fortified airhead which General Henri-Eugène Navarre established in November 1953 in the seventy-five square miles of the valley of Dien Bien Phu was dominated by the two hundred–plus artillery pieces which General Vo Nguyen Giap had placed on the hills.

15. Terraine notes that "[t]he tendency . . . of the [Allied] armies [in Europe in World War II] to ask for the wrong thing, or quite simply, too much of the Air, was to remain a persisting (indeed, increasing) feature of Allied operations. On the American side, it reflected a national level of machine-mindedness, and a disposition to make machines do the work of men in all circumstances." *A Time for Courage*, p. 578.

16. With reference to Field Marshal Bernard L. Montgomery's insistence in September 1944 that he be directed to lead a single narrow thrust in the invasion of Germany (thereby resolving the logistic dilemmas which would—and did—slow the pace of a broad-fronted invasion), Terraine observes: "[L]eaving aside detailed pros and cons of Montgomery's proposal, it is to be remarked, however, that since his first bold, and excellent, plan for the Battle of Normandy had failed *because his army was not able to carry it out,* a serious question-mark hangs over this next

daring proposal for the same reason. Even if, by some miracle of self-abnegation, the American Government had sanctioned the plan, is there any evidence that the [British] 21st Army Group could have performed it?" *Ibid.*, pp. 667–68. Emphasis added.

17. Betts, "Conventional Strategy: New Critics, Old Choices," particularly pp. 146–55.

18. *Ibid.*, p. 146.

19. Quoted in Peter P. Witonski, ed., *Gibbon for Moderns: The History of the Decline and Fall of the Roman Empire, with Lessons for America Today* (New Rochelle, N.Y.: Arlington House Publishers, 1974), p. 15.

20. See Ross Hassig, *Aztec Warfare: Imperial Expansion and Political Control* (Norman, Okla.: University of Oklahoma Press, 1988), Chapter 8. Hassig notes that "[c]aptured enemies were enslaved and later sacrificed to the gods; as a general rule, they were neither freed nor ransomed." P. 115. In the Aztec worldview, the taking of prisoners for sacrifice was a purpose and benefit of war. It would not be true to claim that they went to war *exclusively* for the purpose of collecting victims for their religious practices.

21. The centralization of power certainly was facilitated, for a while, by the development of practical siege artillery trains using gunpowder. However, it is well to remember that the varieties of castle-based feudalism in Western Europe were in sharp decline long before siege cannon appeared on the scene; that relatively few medieval castles truly were impregnable even before the availability of cannon; and that there was a constant dialectic between the methods of fortification and siegecraft. Siege cannon ended the general utility of thin-walled fortification, not of fortification per se; they also priced (siege) warfare beyond the reach of private purses. Writing about the methods of war in the early and mid–sixteenth century, J. R. Hale has observed that "[b]ecause the military engineers' response to artillery was to design stronger fortifications which could shelter forces an enemy would be unwise to leave intact behind him as he pressed forward, guns led to longer sieges, and these extended the campaigner's active year beyond the old rhythm of summer fighting followed by disbandment or winter-quarters ease." *War and Society in Renaissance Europe, 1450–1620* (London: Fontana Press, 1985), p. 46. Nonetheless, the significance of the new artillery was profound indeed, notwithstanding that the art of fortification, *in due course,* restored the balance between besieger and besieged. See Michael Howard, *War in European History* (Oxford: Oxford University Press, 1976), pp. 14, 34–36. Howard notes that "[t]he castle had dominated medieval warfare, when the only resources available to the besieger were those of classical antiquity—catapults, battering-rams, escalade, and, most effective of all, hunger. The great gun brought this to an end" (pp. 34–35).

22. Richard K. Betts, *Heavenly Gains or Earthly Losses? Toward a Balance*

Sheet for Strategic Defense, Brookings General Series Reprint No. 428 (Washington, D.C.: Brookings Institution, 1988), p. 235. Emphasis added.

23. This is the persuasive thesis of Basil Greenhill and Ann Giffard, *The British Assault on Finland, 1854–1855: A Forgotten Naval War* (London: Conway Maritime Press, 1988). The authors observe wryly that "[t]he fall of Sebastopol (strictly the occupation of its southern part by French and British forces) did not end the war. There was no reason why it should have done. The allies had a toe hold on a tiny part of the coast of the remote part of the Russian Empire. To advance further would have required an effort and commitment of resources of colossal proportions, and where would the advance have gone?" P. 338.

24. *Ibid.,* p. 341. In a memorandum (probably written for the minister of war) entitled "The Dangers of Continuing the War in the Year 1856," Major General D. A. Miljutin of the Russian General Staff advised that Anglo-French forces could be transported by sea in three weeks to the Crimea, while the Russian troops required three months to reach the Crimea from the Moscow area. Paraphrased in Winfried Baumgart, *The Peace of Paris, 1856: Studies in War, Diplomacy, and Peacemaking* (Santa Barbara, Calif.: ABC-Clio, 1981; first pub. 1972), pp. 77–78.

25. "But the decline of Rome was the natural and inevitable effect of *immoderate greatness.* Prosperity ripened the principle of decay; the causes of destruction multiplied with the extent of conquest; and as soon as time or accident had removed the artificial supports, the stupendous fabric yielded to the pressure of its own weight." Gibbon, *The Decline and Fall of the Roman Empire,* Vol. 4, pp. 173–74. Emphasis added.

26. Clausewitz, *On War,* p. 75. Emphasis in original.

27. C. E. Callwell, *Small Wars* (Wakefield [U.K.]: EP Publishing, 1976; reprint of third edition, first pub. 1906), p. 90. In American vernacular, "the battle is the payoff."

28. Clausewitz, *On War,* p. 97.

29. *Ibid.,* p. 128. Emphasis in original.

30. Carl Builder is on target when he writes: "Strategies explain. To understand a strategy is to understand why—or at least to understand the reasons the military give for the actions they take, or want to take." *The Masks of War,* p. 47.

On military space problems and opportunities, see Colin S. Gray, *American Military Space Policy: Information Systems, Weapon Systems and Arms Control* (Cambridge, Mass.: Abt Books, 1983); Uri Ra'anan and Robert L. Pfaltzgraff, Jr., eds., *International Security Dimensions of Space* (Hamden, Conn.: Archon Books, 1984); *America Plans for Space* (Washington, D.C.: National Defense University Press, 1986); Paul B. Stares, *Space and National Security* (Washington, D.C.: Brookings Institution, 1987); and Kenneth N.

Luongo and W. Thomas Wander, eds., *The Search for Security in Space* (Ithaca, N.Y.: Cornell University Press, 1989).

Amid the plethora of technical studies of space systems and space operations, and of "committed" writings on the subject of the SDI, there is only a thin trickle of speculation which seeks to understand the military space environment with reference to potential combat. See Thomas Karas, *The New High Ground: Systems and Weapons of Space Age War* (New York: Simon and Schuster, 1983), Chapter 7; Ashton B. Carter, "Satellites and Anti-Satellites: The Limits of the Possible," *International Security*, Vol. 10, No. 4 (Spring 1986), pp. 46–98; David E. Lupton, *On Space Warfare: A Space Power Doctrine* (Maxwell AFB, Ala.: Air University Press, June 1988); and Simon P. Worden and Bruce P. Jackson, "Space, Power, and Strategy," *The National Interest*, No. 13 (Fall 1988), pp. 43–52.

The outstanding treatment of Soviet military space strategy is Nicholas L. Johnson, *Soviet Military Strategy in Space* (London: Jane's Publishing Company, 1987). Also see U.S. Department of Defense, *The Soviet Space Challenge* (Washington, D.C.: U.S. Government Printing Office, 1987); and John L. Piotrowski, "A Soviet Space Strategy," *Strategic Review*, Vol. 15, No. 4 (Fall 1987), pp. 55–62.

On the English maritime experience in early modern times, see Kenneth R. Andrews, *Trade, Plunder, and Settlement: Maritime Enterprise and the Genesis of the British Empire, 1480–1630* (Cambridge: Cambridge University Press, 1984), particularly Chapter 11. For the Spanish Empire in that period see John Lynch, *Spain under the Habsburg*, Vol. 1: *Empire and Absolutism*, and Vol. 2: *Spain and America, 1598–1700* (New York: New York University Press, 1984; first pub. 1964 and 1969). R. A. Stradling, *Europe and the Decline of Spain: A Study of the Spanish System, 1580–1720* (London: George Allen and Unwin, 1981), is also useful.

For medieval warfare, see Philippe Contamine, *War in the Middle Ages* (Oxford: Basil Blackwell, 1984; first pub. 1980).

Two excellent studies of the Crimean War in Russian perspective are Albert Seaton, *The Crimean War: A Russian Chronicle* (London: B. T. Batsford, 1977); and John Shelton Curtiss, *Russia's Crimean War* (Durham, N.C.: Duke University Press, 1979).

AFTERWORD: SHARING THE LOAD/SHEDDING THE LOAD: U.S. STRATEGY FOR THE TWENTY-FIRST CENTURY

1. Vlahos, "The End of America's Postwar Ethos," p. 1106.
2. Reagan, *National Security Strategy of the United States (1988),* p. 1.
3. D. W. Brogan, *The American Character* (New York: Alfred A. Knopf, 1944), p. 151.

Robert S. McNamara's style and preferred instruments of management are appraised in James M. Roherty, *Decisions of Robert S. McNamara: A*

Study in the Role of the Secretary of Defense (Coral Gables, Fla.: University of Miami Press, 1970); and Stephen Peter Rosen, "Systems Analysis and the Quest for Rational Defense," *The Public Interest,* No. 76 (Summer 1984), pp. 3–16. For friendlier assessments of the McNamara era, see Alain K. Enthoven and K. Wayne Smith, *How Much Is Enough? Shaping the Defense Program, 1961–1969* (New York: Harper and Row, 1971); and Thomas E. Anger, ed., *Analysis and National Security Policy* (Alexandria, Va.: Center for Naval Analyses, 1988).

Selected
Bibliography

The works listed below are recommended as useful for the understanding of strategy.

Adcock, F. E. *The Roman Art of War Under the Republic*. Cambridge, Mass.: Harvard University Press, 1940.

Ball, Desmond, and Jeffrey Richelson, eds. *Strategic Nuclear Targeting*. Ithaca, N.Y.: Cornell University Press, 1986.

Barnett, Correlli. *Britain and Her Army, 1509–1970: A Military, Political and Social Survey*. London: Penguin Books, 1974; first pub. 1970.

Betts, Richard K. *Nuclear Blackmail and Nuclear Balance*. Washington, D.C.: Brookings Institution, 1987.

———. "Conventional Strategy: New Critics, Old Choices," *International Security*, Vol. 7, No. 4 (Spring 1983), pp. 146–55.

———. *Surprise Attack: Lessons for Defense Planning*. Washington, D.C.: Brookings Institution, 1982.

Bidwell, Shelford, and Dominick Graham. *Fire-Power: British Army Weapons and Theories of War, 1904–1945*. London: George Allen and Unwin, 1982.

Bobbitt, Philip, Lawrence Freedman, and Gregory F. Treverton, eds. *U.S. Nuclear Strategy: A Reader*. New York: New York University Press, 1989.

Brodie, Bernard. *War and Politics*. New York: Macmillan, 1973.

———. *Strategy in the Missile Age*. Princeton, N.J.: Princeton University Press, 1959.

Builder, Carl H. *The Masks of War: American Military Styles in Strategy and Analysis*. Baltimore: Johns Hopkins University Press, 1989.

Buzan, Barry. *An Introduction to Strategic Studies: Military Technology and International Relations*. New York: St. Martin's Press, 1987.

Callwell, Charles E. *Military Operations and Maritime Preponderance: Their Relations and Interdependence*. Edinburgh: William Blackwood and Sons, 1905.

Carter, Ashton B., John D. Steinbruner, and Charles A. Zraket, eds. *Man-*

aging Nuclear Operations. Washington, D.C.: Brookings Institution, 1987.

Churchill, Winston S. *The Second World War,* 6 vols. London: Penguin Books, 1985; first pub. 1948–53.

Clausewitz, Carl von. *On War* (Michael Howard and Peter Paret, trans.). Princeton, N.J.: Princeton University Press, 1976; first pub. 1832.

Corbett, Julian S. *Some Principles of Maritime Strategy.* Annapolis, Md.: Naval Institute Press, 1972; first pub. 1911.

Creveld, Martin van. *Technology and War: From 2000 B.C. to the Present.* New York: Free Press, 1989.

———. *Command in War.* Cambridge, Mass.: Harvard University Press, 1985.

———. *Supplying War: Logistics from Wallenstein to Patton.* Cambridge: Cambridge University Press, 1977.

Cruttwell, C. R. M. F. *The Role of British Strategy in the Great War.* Cambridge: Cambridge University Press, 1936.

Donnelly, Christopher N. *Red Banner: The Soviet Military System in Peace and War.* Coulsdon [U.K.]: Jane's Information Group, 1988.

Fairbanks, Charles H. "Arms Races: The Metaphor and the Facts," *The National Interest,* No. 1 (Fall 1985), pp. 75–90.

Foster, Gregory D. "A Conceptual Foundation for a Theory of Strategy," *The Washington Quarterly,* Vol. 12, No. 1 (Winter 1990), pp. 43–59.

Freedman, Lawrence. *The Evolution of Nuclear Strategy.* London: Macmillan, 1981.

Gottfried, Kurt, and Bruce G. Blair, eds. *Crisis Stability and Nuclear War.* New York: Oxford University Press, 1988.

Gray, Colin S. *The Geopolitics of Super Power.* Lexington, Ky.: University Press of Kentucky, 1988.

———. *Nuclear Strategy and National Style.* Lanham, Md.: Hamilton Press, 1986.

Handel, Michael. "Clausewitz in the Age of Technology," *The Journal of Strategic Studies,* Vol. 9, Nos. 2–3 (June/September 1986), pp. 51–92.

Hinsley, F. H. *Hitler's Strategy.* Cambridge: Cambridge University Press, 1951.

Hoffman, Fred S., Albert Wohlstetter, and David S. Yost, eds. *Swords and Shields: NATO, the U.S.S.R., and New Choices for Long-Range Offense and Defense.* Lexington, Mass.: Lexington Books, 1987.

Howard, Michael. *The Causes of Wars and Other Essays.* London: Unwin Paperbacks, 1984; first pub. 1983.

Huntington, Samuel P. "Playing to Win," *The National Interest,* No. 3 (Spring 1986), pp. 8–16.

The International History Review, Vol. 10, No. 1 (February 1988), "On Sea Power."

Jenkins, Romilly. *Byzantium: The Imperial Centuries, A.D. 610–1071.* Toronto: University of Toronto Press, 1987; first pub. 1966.

Jervis, Robert. *The Meaning of the Nuclear Revolution: Statecraft and the Prospect of Armageddon.* Ithaca, N.Y.: Cornell University Press, 1989.

Jomini, Baron Antoine Henri de. *The Art of War.* Westport, Conn.: Greenwood Press, 1971; reprint of 1862 ed.

Kagan, Donald. *The Fall of the Athenian Empire* (final book in 4-volume history of the Peloponnesian War). Ithaca, N.Y.: Cornell University Press, 1987.

Kahn, Herman. *On Thermonuclear War.* Princeton, N.J.: Princeton University Press, 1960.

Kaplan, Fred. *Wizards of Armageddon.* New York: Simon and Schuster, 1983.

Kennedy, Paul. *The Rise and Fall of the Great Powers: Economic Change and Military Conflict from 1500 to 2000.* New York: Random House, 1987.

———. *The Rise and Fall of British Naval Mastery.* New York: Charles Scribner's Sons, 1976.

Knorr, Klaus, ed. *Historical Dimensions of National Security Problems.* Lawrence, Kans.: University Press of Kansas, 1976.

Lewin, Ronald. *Hitler's Mistakes.* London: Leo Cooper, 1984.

Liddell Hart, Basil. *Strategy: The Indirect Approach.* London: Faber and Faber, 1967; first pub. 1941.

Luttwak, Edward N. "An Emerging Postnuclear Era?" *The Washington Quarterly,* Vol. 11, No. 1 (Winter 1988), pp. 5–15.

———. *Strategy: The Logic of War and Peace.* Cambridge, Mass.: Harvard University Press, 1987.

Mackinder, Halford J. *Democratic Ideals and Reality.* New York: W. W. Norton and Company, 1962; first pub. 1942.

Mahan, Alfred Thayer. *Retrospect and Prospect: Studies in International Relations, Naval and Political.* London: Sampson, Low, Marston and Company, 1902.

———. *The Problem of Asia and Its Effect Upon International Policies.* Boston: Little, Brown and Company, 1905; first pub. 1900.

———. *The Influence of Sea Power Upon History, 1660–1783.* London: Methuen, 1965; first pub. 1890.

Marder, Arthur J. *From the Dreadnought to Scapa Flow, The Royal Navy in the Fisher Era,* 5 vols. London: Oxford University Press, 1961–70.

Millett, Allan R., and Williamson Murray, eds. *Military Effectiveness,* 3 vols. Boston: Allen and Unwin, 1988.

Murray, Williamson, and Alvin Bernstein, eds. *The Making of Strategy.* Boston: Allen and Unwin, forthcoming.

Overy, R. J. *The Air War, 1939–1945.* New York: Stein and Day, 1985; first pub. 1980.

Palmer, Bruce, Jr. *The 25-Year War: America's Role in Vietnam.* Lexington, Ky.: University of Kentucky, 1984.

Paret, Peter, ed. *Makers of Modern Strategy: From Machiavelli to the Nuclear Age.* Princeton, N.J.: Princeton University Press, 1986.

Rotberg, Robert I., and Theodore K. Rabb, eds. *The Origin and Prevention of Major Wars.* Cambridge, Mass.: Cambridge University Press, 1989.

Sagan, Scott D. *Moving Targets: Nuclear Strategy and National Security.* Princeton, N.J.: Princeton University Press, 1989.

————. "1914 Revisited: Allies, Offense, and Instability," *International Security,* Vol. 11, No. 2 (Fall 1986), pp. 151–75.

Schelling, Thomas C. *Arms and Influence.* New Haven, Conn.: Yale University Press, 1966.

Seaton, Albert. *The Russo-German War, 1941–45.* New York: Praeger, 1970.

Spykman, John. *America's Strategy in World Politics: The United States and the Balance of Power.* Hamden, Conn.: Archon Books, 1970; first pub. 1942.

Summers, Harry. *On Strategy: A Critical Analysis of the Vietnam War.* Novato, Calif.: Presidio Press, 1982.

Sun Tzu. *The Art of War* (Samuel B. Griffith, trans.). Oxford: Clarendon Press, 1963.

Terraine, John. *A Time for Courage: The Royal Air Force in the European War, 1939–1945.* New York: Macmillan Publishing Company, 1985.

Thucydides. *The Peloponnesian War* (Rex Warner, trans.). London: Cassell, 1962; reprint of 1954 ed.

Watts, Barry D. *The Foundations of U.S. Air Doctrine: The Problem of Friction in War.* Maxwell AFB, Ala.: Air University Press, December 1986.

Weigley, Russell F. *The American Way of War: A History of United States Strategy and Policy.* New York: Macmillan Publishing Company, 1973.

Wernham, R. B. "Elizabethan War Aims and Strategy," in S. T. Bindoff et al., eds., *Elizabethan Government and Society: Essays Presented to Sir John Neale.* London: Athlone Press, 1961, pp. 340–68.

Wylie, J. C. *Military Strategy: A General Theory of Power Control.* Westport, Conn.: Greenwood Press, 1980; first pub. 1967.

Index

About the Author

Colin Gray lives in northern Virginia, where he is chairman of a leading national security "think tank," the National Institute for Public Policy. He has been a government adviser for many years on such subjects as nuclear strategy, military space policy, naval issues, and arms control. He has a wife, Valerie, who is a novelist and reference librarian; a daughter, Antonia, who is an aspiring artist; and a golden retriever, Lady Penelope Honeybear, who is very good at digging.

In addition to writing reports on nuclear targeting and ICBM basing modes, Colin Gray reads medieval history, swims, and visits obscure battlefields.